BELTS AND ROADS
UNDER
BEIJING'S THUMB

*Economic Domination &
Debt-Trap Diplomacy*

Rachel A. Winston, Ph.D.

Copyright © 2021 by Lizard Publishing

All rights reserved. No part of this book may be reproduced, stored, or transmitted by any means. In accordance with U.S. Copyright law, the scanning, uploading, and electronic sharing of any part of this book without the permission of the publisher constitutes unlawful piracy and theft of the author's intellectual property. Prior written permission must be obtained. Inquiries concerning the reproduction of any material from this book must be submitted to Lizard Publishing.

Lizard Publishing ®

7700 Irvine Center Drive, Suite 800

Irvine, CA 92618-3047

www.lizard-publishing.com

Our mental process is fueled by three tenets:

• Ignite the hunger to learn and the passion for making a difference

• Illuminate the expanse of knowledge by sharing cutting edge thinking

• Innovate to create a world that may only exist in our dreams

Maps and Illustrations by graphic designer, Abiyy Suryowibisono

Book design by Michelle Tahan and Obinna Chinemerem Ozuo

Typeface: Garamond

Book Website: southchinaseabook.com

First Edition: July 2021

Rachel Winston is available for speaking events.

ISBN: 978-1946432124 (paperback), 978-1946432131 (hardback), 978-1946432117 (ebook)

LCCN: 2020917700

This book was published in the U.S.A. Lizard Publishing is a premium quality provider of educational reference, career guidance, and motivational publications/merchandise for global learners, educators, and stakeholders in education.

This book is dedicated to Dr. David A. Waugh and Robert A. Helmer whose ceaseless support and undying devotion have made this book possible.

Acknowledgments

"If I see so far, it is because I stand on the shoulders of giants."
– Isaac Newton

There is never enough room to acknowledge every person who contributed to an individual's perspective, assisted in the development of a person's knowledge base, or taught indelible lessons that last a lifetime. In this book, I gratefully acknowledge my family, friends, colleagues, and professors.

I would also like to thank my fellow students and scholars I have met along the way from whom I have learned from their perspective and wisdom.

Isaac Newton once said, "If I see so far, it is because I stand on the shoulders of giants." A few of those giants in my life whose shoulders have lifted me higher and helped teach me invaluable lessons include: James Borton, James Sullivan, John E. Mearsheimer, Peter F. Drucker, Volker Benkert, Robert Citino, Joseph A. Maciariello, Mihaly Csikszentmihalyi, Ei-ichi Negishi, Jill Board, Charlie Glaser, Deb Ferber, Loren O'Connor, Jeremy Korr, Helen Eckmann, Ned Camuso, Kat Ringenbach, Melanie Borrego, Glenn Worthington, Frank Weber, Michael McGuire, Lata Murti, Laura Galloway, William Gibson, Karin Storm, Ellen Derwin, David Long, Isa Ribadu, Melissa Meyer, Marnie Elam, Leigh Ann Wilson, John Freed, Karen Woodcock, Sheila Steinberg, Mike and Margaret Moodian, Massiel Perez-Calhoon, Michael Okaisabor, Abiyy Suryowibisono, and Jasmine Flores.

Meet the Author

Rachel A. Winston, Ph.D.

As a retired university professor, Full-Time Faculty Member of the Year, elected statewide leader, and winner of the McFarland Literary Achievement Award, Dr. Winston writes and publishes on key educational, societal, and international issues. She taught at UCLA, Brandman University, Chapman University, Embry Riddle Aeronautical University, Cal State Fullerton and holds graduate degrees from Harvard University, the University of Chicago, the University of Texas at Austin, George Washington University, Claremont Graduate University, Pepperdine University, and Cal State Fullerton.

Inspired by trips with U.N. officials in the 1960s to the Golan Heights, Crimea, Caucuses, and Ukraine during the Cold War, and East Germany when still behind the Iron Curtain, Dr. Winston later worked on Capitol Hill and with the White House. As a mathematician, chemist, and computer scientist, her life led her to more than fifty countries. Attending graduate school in Hong Kong, presenting at speaking events in China, and conducting research in Southeast Asia, Dr. Winston's research for her theses for Harvard University and the University of Chicago offered numerous insights as she built relationships with people throughout Asia.

Dr. Winston turned her research into the book *Raging Waters in the South China Sea* and continued to write *China's Power Grab and Expanding Claims*, followed by *Belts and Roads Under Beijing's Thumb*. Her graduate work in World War II Studies and visits to concentration camps in Germany, Poland, and the Czech Republic led her to research genocide and write the books in the *Awakened Now* series: *Awakened to Tomorrow's Future*, *Nazi Germany to Xinjiang Province*, and *Persecution of Uyghur Muslims*.

Foreword

This decade will be like no other as Winston points out in *Belts and Roads*. China's reach has planted seeds in every continent and well over half of the nations around the planet. Beijing has invested in its global initiative to advance its soft and hard power strategically in an ingenious, provocative plan to have other countries pay for infrastructure to increase access for its commercial ventures while adding military units at ports and railroad access areas to "protect" its investment – all paid by other countries through their opaque loans.

These changes are not all subtle. Beijing diplomats have inserted themselves strategically into many of the United Nations committees, including Human Rights, while placing its Muslim population in forced labor concentration camps to supply manufactured products around the world. At the same time, China ramped up advanced robotic technologies that can obliterate cities and target areas overtly using drone bombing technologies and covertly using broad, insidious surveillance methods that can control and subdue whole populations.

The CCP's Belt and Road Initiative is not an entirely new strategy. Following WW II, Kennan's 'long telegram' proposed a model for a U.S. containment strategy vis-à-vis the Soviet Union, which was implemented assiduously. Yet, today, neither the United States, European Union, nor the Russian Federation have limited China's growth and, rather, complicitly aided in its expansionist agenda. Political bodies – large and small - are significantly contributing to China's ballooning balance of payments in abundant surplus. China's economic and military growth is upon us now and world-domination grows near as most countries are subjugated through loans, strapping them to its territorial orbit.

Overwhelming debt, particularly in underdeveloped countries whose prospect of repayment is unlikely, has saddled states, doomed with economic woes that demand payment by surrendering territory and natural resources. This, too, is not new. During the 1970s and 1980s debt crisis, while oil-producing nations were awash with money, many South American and African countries desperately needed capital. Anxious to put their resources to work, international banks loaned huge sums, much later wiped clear via loan forgiveness to prevent widespread national financial insolvency. This time, though, the world has a new banker, one without moral restraint.

Winston lays out the plan, execution, and consequences of China's expansive economic choke-hold, threatening the sovereignty of these nations. Belts and Roads, a euphemism for widespread infrastructure investment, has the veneer of massive 'win-win' opportunities with friends, the Chinese, whose rhetoric belies the underbelly of a pervasive global threat on an order of magnitude unseen before. It is absolutely dissimilar to, though possibly inspired by, the paid-for Marshall Plan, now reframed to construct the world in its image of 'Socialism with Chinese Characteristics'. These loans are not designed to create free and equal trading partners.

Winston's refreshing and authoritative command of knowledge, combined with impressive credentials, gives voice to the overarching threat of our time. This is the 21st-century story of a rags-to-riches renegade nation, subordinating one nation after another, without the force of any serious external threat. Wielding its political power, while blatantly violating rule-of-law, Beijing no longer feels compelled to conform to international standards of morality codified by the United Nations, religious principles, or pleas for basic human rights.

Dr. David Waugh, United Nations (Retired)

Table of Contents

1. Planning, Acquisitions, and Promises Along the Belt and Road — 1

1. Belt and Road to Glory: Nearly Impossible to Refuse Money — 2
2. Five Primary BRI Goals: Finance, Connectivity, People, Policy Coordination, & Unimpeded Trade — 10
3. Paving the Way to Prosperity: How to Get Other Countries to Fund the Employment of a Billion People — 14
4. Global Land Grab: Seizing or Buying Up Land Around the World — 20
5. Cleansing Xinjiang Province of 'Terrorists': Re-Education Camps Clear the Way for China's BRI through East Turkistan — 28
6. Speeches, Promises, and Agreements: Delivering Skilled Diplomacy, Sharpened Rhetoric, Large Loans, and Infrastructure — 36

2. Corridors — 44

1. China and the Stans: Highways, Railroads, and Ports — 46
2. Iron Silk Road: Part of the China-Central Asia- West Asia Economic Corridor (CCAWEC) — 52
3. China-Pakistan Economic Corridor: China's Direct Access Port to the Persian Gulf — 60
4. Indochina Peninsula Corridor: Direct Route from China to Singapore — 70
5. BCIM Economic Corridor: Linking China to Bangladesh, Myanmar, and India — 76
6. New Eurasian Land Bridge: Railway through Xinjiang, Kazakhstan, Russia, Belarus, Poland, and Germany — 82
7. China-Mongolia-Russia Economic Corridor: The BRI's Project to the North — 90

    8. The Corridors of African Trade and Benevolence: Rare Earth Metals and Other Natural Resources   98

3. Maritime Silk Road   108

    1. China's Maritime Silk Road: From Ming and Qing to Today   110

    2. Importance of Maritime Traffic and Trade: Getting Massive Quantities of Products to the People   116

    3. Piracy on the High Seas: Alarming Increase in Global Pirate Attacks   122

    4. String of Pearls Port Strategy: What's Behind China's Grand Maritime Pursuit?   128

    5. South China Sea and the Strait of Malacca: China's First Priority is to Resolve its Navigation Dilemma   136

    6. China's Foreign Ports: Djibouti, Gwadar, Sri Lanka, and a Global String of Pearls   144

    7. Blockage at the Suez Canal: What Happens if Transport Shipping Passages Close?   154

4. Ice/Polar/Arctic Silk Road   162

    1. The Polar Silk Road: Cutting Through Sheets of Ice in the Arctic Ocean to Extend China's Trading Routes   166

    2. Strategic Transitway in the Arctic North: Providing an Alternate and Shorter Transport Route for Trade   174

    3. International Efforts and Agencies Responsible for the Arctic: Research, Collaboration, Advocacy, Laws, and Guidelines   182

    4. China's Strategic Interests in Transiting the Arctic: Motivated by Money, Energy, Trade, and Resources   192

    5. Cutting through Arctic Ice: Creating a Transitway by Cleaving and Thawing   200

    6. Fast Melting Ice: Environmentalists Analyze Arctic Destruction and Clarify Climate Change   208

    7. The Russian Connection: China's Geopolitical Relationship with Russia   216

    8. EEZs, Ports, and Competing Interests: Who's Competing for What and Why is the Arctic Heating Up?   226

5. Digital Silk Road   236

    1. Digital Silk Road: The Era of Global Political Influence and Social Control   238

2. The Spread of ZTE, Huawei, and Invasive Technologies: "Danger, Danger Will Robinson" — 244
   3. The Power of Digital Authoritarianism: Aggressive Ambitions of Chinese State Media — 256
   4. Digital Africa: Wiring Up a Continent for Connectivity and Surveillance — 262
   5. Digitizing the World: Global Social Control at the Switch of a Button — 272

6. Conclusion — 278

   6. Without Rule of Law Danger Sits on the Horizon: The Chinese Dream is Inconsistent with a World of Peace and Sovereignty — 282

7. Index — 290

Acronyms and Terms

	Acronyms and Terms
3 Buckets of Oil	China's 'Big Three' oil corporations or "Three Buckets of Oil" - PetroChina, Sinopec, and CNOOC
5G	5th generation mobile network
60/40 Rule	Under Philippine law, Philippine government must own at least 60% of capital used in contracts involving natural resources. Furthermore, 60% of the profit must remain with the Philippine government.
99-Year Lease	This was the length of time Great Britain leased Hong Kong after the Opium Wars and the time China leased Hambantota Port in Sri Lanka when Sri Lanka struggled to pay its debt.
AC	Arctic Council
ACAP	Arctic Contaminants Action Program
ACFTA	African Continental Free Trade Area
ADB	Asian Development Bank
ADF	Australian Defense Force
ADIZ	Air Defense Identification Zone
AECO	Association of Arctic Expedition Cruise Operators
AEI	American Enterprise Institute
AFP	Armed Forces of the Philippines
AIIB	Asian Infrastructure and Investment Bank
AIV	Advisory Council on International Affairs
AMAP	Arctic Monitoring and Assessment Program
AMM	ASEAN Foreign Ministers' Meeting
Anarchy	The idea that the world lacks any supreme authority or sovereign. In an anarchic state, there is no hierarchically superior, coercive power that can resolve disputes, enforce law, or order the international system.
APEC	Asia-Pacific Economic Cooperation
ARF	ASEAN Regional Forum
ARIA	Asia Reassurance Initiative Act

Acronyms and Terms

ASEAN	Association of Southeast Asian Nations - (One Vision, One Identity, One Community) - Regional, intergovernmental association of ten Southeast Asia countries. The 10 member nations include: Brunei, Cambodia, Indonesia, Laos, Malaysia, Myanmar (Burma), the Philippines, Singapore, Thailand, and Vietnam.
ASEAN Plus Three	This cooperative group includes the 10 ASEAN states plus China, Japan, and the Republic of Korea
ASEAN Plus Six	These sixteen countries (the 10 ASEAN states plus Australia, China, India, Japan, South Korea, and New Zealand) form the Regional Comprehensive Economic Partnership.
ASMA	Antarctic Specially Managed Area
ASPA	Antarctic Specially Protected Area
ATCM	Antarctic Treaty Consultative Meeting
AU	African Union
BBNJ	Biodiversity Beyond National Jurisdiction
BCIM	Bangladesh-China-India-Myanmar Economic Corridor
BEAC	Barents Euro-Arctic Council
BRI	Belt and Road Initiative
CADF	China-Africa Development Fund
CAFF	Conservation of Arctic Flora and Fauna
CBP	U.S. Customs and Border Protection
CCAMLR	Convention on the Conservation of Antarctic Marine Living Resources
CCAS	Convention for the Conservation of Antarctic Seals
CCFFA	Central Commission on Foreign Affairs
CCP	Chinese Communist Party
CCWRFA	Central Conference on Work Relating to Foreign Affairs
CDB	China Development Bank
CDIS	Coordinated Direct Investment Survey
Century of Humiliation	The approximately one hundred years from 1842, with the Treaty of Nanjing, to October 1, 1949 when the People's Republic of China was formally established.
CEP	Committee on Environmental Protection
CFR	Council on Foreign Relations
CGA	Coast Guard Administration
CGIT	China Global Investment Tracker
CHEXIM	Export-Import Bank of China
CHIIA	China Investment in Australia
CICA	Conference on Interaction and Confidence Building Measures in Asia
CICIR	China Institutes of Contemporary International Relations

Acronyms and Terms	
CIIS	China Institute of International Studies
CIS	Commonwealth of Independent States
CLCS	Commission on the Limits of the Continental Shelf
CLETC	China Light Industrial Corporation for Foreign Economic and Technical Cooperation
CMC	Central Military Commission
CMREC	China-Mongolia-Russia Economic Corridor
CNOOC	China National Offshore Oil Corporation (Chinese State-Owned Enterprise - SOE)
CNPC	China National Petroleum Corporation (Chinese State-Owned Enterprise - SOE)
CoC	Code of Conduct
COMNAP	Council of Managers of National Antarctic Programs
COMPLANT	China National Complete Plant Import and Export Corporation Group
COVID-19	The coronavirus COVID-19 pandemic that broke out in the fall of 2019 in Wuhan, China
CPEC	China-Pakistan Economic Corridor
CPI	Consumer Price Index
CSFAC	China State Farm Agribusiness Corporation
CSIC	China Shipbuilding Industry Corporation (Chinese State-Owned Enterprise - SOE)
DoC	Declaration of the Conduct of Parties in the South China Sea
DPJ	Democratic Party of Japan
DPP	Democratic Progressive Party
DRC	Democratic Republic of Congo
DSM-IV	Diagnostic and Statistical Manual of Mental Disorders
ECOSOC	Economic and Social Council
EDCA	Enhanced Defense Cooperation Agreement - An agreement signed in 2014 between the U.S. and the Philippines with the goal of supporting U.S. Philippine relations and military cooperation. The EDCA was declared constitutional in 2016.
EEAS	European External Action Service
EEU	Eurasian Economic Union
EEZ	Exclusive Economic Zone – The United Nations Convention on the Law of the Sea (UNCLOS) defines the region as the band extending 200 nautical miles off the shores of a coastal state in which that state has the jurisdiction over the exploration of natural resources and exploitation of marine resources in its adjacent continental shelf.
EIA	Environmental Impact Assessment
EPB	European Polar Brand

Acronyms and Terms

ETIM	East Turkestan Islamic Movement
EU	European Union
EXIM	Export-Import Bank of China
Facemask Diplomacy	This initiative was China's effort to sell facemasks to countries worldwide during COVID-19.
FAO	Food and Agriculture Organization
FDI	Foreign Direct Investment
First Island Chain	A string of islands from lower Philippines up to the top of Japan that are a near-in region. China hopes to push the U.S. presence outside of this area.
Five Eyes Alliance	An intelligence sharing alliance between Australia, Canada, New Zealand, United Kingdom, and the United States founded in 1941.
FOCAC	Forum on China-Africa Cooperation
FOIP	Free and Open Indo-Pacific Strategy
FONOPs	Freedom of Navigation Operations
FPA	Foreign Policy Analysis
FTA	Free Trade Agreements
GDP	Gross Domestic Product
GNP	Gross National Product
Gray Zone Operations	Intense political, economic, informational, and military competition that is just short of war. China uses 'Gray Zone' tactics to "win without fighting" to further its maritime claims and alter the status quo without going to war.
GPEA	Greenpeace East Asia
Great Power	The ability of a sovereign state to exert its influence on a global scale.
GRINGOs	Government-Run or Government-Initiated NGOs
Hedging	The management of risk relationships between two opposing parties to protect security and sovereignty by diversifying commitments and simultaneously balancing and engaging. The term 'hedging' is increasingly found in the U.S. strategic discourse, particularly regarding China. The White House 2006 National Security Strategy document stated that the U.S. strategy "seeks to encourage China to make the right strategic choices for its people, while we hedge against other possibilities."
Hegemon	A political state having dominant influence or authority over others. States can have global or regional hegemony.
HYSY	Hiayangshiyou "Ocean Oil" - CNOOC deepwater oil platforms
IAATO	International Association of Antarctic Tour Operators
IASC	International Arctic Science Committee
ICAO	International Civil Aviation Organization
ICC	International Criminal Court
ICE	U.S. Immigration and Customs Enforcement

Acronyms and Terms

ICJ	International Court of Justice
ICPR	International Covenant on Civil and Political Rights
ICRW	International Convention on the Regulation of Whaling
IDF	Indigenous Defense Fighter (Taiwanese Fighter Jet)
IFIs	International Financial Institutions
IISD	International Institute for Sustainable Development
ILO	International Labor Organization
IMF	International Monetary Fund
IMO	International Maritime Organization
IPCC	Intergovernmental Panel on Climate Change
IR	International Relations
IRCT	International Rehabilitation Council for Torture Victims
ISA	International Seabed Authority
ISAF	International Security Assistance Force
ITC	International Trade Center
IUU	Illegal, unreported, and unregulated fishing practices
IWC	International Whaling Commission
JADIZ	Japanese Air Defense Identification Zone
JASDF	Japan Air Self Defense Force
JMSU	Joint Marine Seismic Undertaking – a collaboration between China, the Philippines, and Vietnam to survey for hydrocarbon resources
KADIZ	(South) Korea Air Defense Identification Zone
KIG	Kalayaan Island Group
KMT	Kuomintang
Kowtow	Kneel and touch the ground with the forehead in worship or submission as part of Chinese custom
LAC	Line of Actual Control
LDP	Liberal Democratic Party (Japan)
LNG	Liquefied Natural Gas
Maglev	Magnetic Levitation - A train system that operates using magnets that allow the train to levitate off the track, reducing friction.
Malacanang	The Philippine presidential palace is a high governmental meeting location and residence of the Philippine president. It is incorporated into written text and speeches in the same way as the White House is in the U.S.
MERICS	Mercator Institute for China Studies
MFA (MoFA)	Ministry of Foreign Affairs
MFEZ	Multi Facility Economic Zone (Zambia)
MIC2025	Made in China 2025

Acronyms and Terms

MoC	China's Ministry of Commerce
MOFCOM	Ministry of Commerce
MOFTEC	Ministry of Foreign Trade and Economic Cooperation
MOU	Memorandum of Understanding
MPA	Marine Protected Area
MSR	Maritime Silk Road
NATO	North Atlantic Treaty Organization
NBA	National Basketball Association
ND	Northern Dimension
NDB	New Development Bank
NDRC	National Development and Reform Commission
NGO	Non-Governmental Organization
Nine-Dash Line	China bases its determination of rights to the South China Sea based upon a nine-dash line drawn on a map in 1947. At times, this demarcated map had ten and eleven dashes in a roughly U shape. The boundaries of what they term their 'historic claim' are vague, but roughly encompass about ninety percent of the South China Sea. The ICJ determination in Philippines v. China was that, based upon UNCLOS, China has 'no basis' for their claim.
NM	Nautical Miles
NOC	National Oil Companies
NSC	National Security Council
OBOR	One Belt, One Road
ODA	Official Development Assistance
ODI	Overseas Direct Investment
OECD	Organization for Economic Cooperation and Development
ONGC	Indian Oil and Natural Gas Corporation (Indian State-Owned Enterprise - SOE)
ONI	Office of Naval Intelligence
OPEC	Organization of Petroleum Exporting Countries
OSPAR	Convention for the Protection of the Marine Environnment of the North-East Atlantic
PAME	Protection of the Arctic Marine Environment
PAP	Singapore's People's Action Party
Paracel Islands	A disputed archipelago with 130 coral islands and reefs in the South China Sea that is occupied by China and claimed by Taiwan and Vietnam inhabiting a population of over 1,000. They are also called Xisha Islands and Hoang Sa Archipelago.
PCA	Permanent Court of Arbitration

Acronyms and Terms

PetroVietnam	Vietnam Oil and Gas Corporation (Vietnamese State-Owned Enterprise - SOE)
PH	The Philippines
PLA	People's Liberation Army (China)
PLAAF	People's Liberation Army Air Force (China)
PLAN	People's Liberation Army – Navy (China)
PLANAF	People's Liberation Army Navy Air Force (China)
PPE	Personal Protective Equipment
PPP	Purchasing Power Parity
PRC	People's Republic of China
PSSA	Particularly Sensitive Sea Area
R2P	Responsibility to Protect
RCEP	Regional Comprehensive Economic Partnership
RIMPAC	Rim of the Pacific
RMB	Renminbi – The official name for China's money introduced in 1949 is considered "the people's currency". A yuan is one unit of RMB.
ROC	The Republic of China (Taiwan)
SAFE	State Administration of Foreign Exchange
SAIS	School of Advanced International Studies
Salami Tactics (Salami Slicing)	A process of cutting away at the opposition by utilizing threats and alliances and politically dominating a landscape by slicing the opponent's power piece by piece.
SAR	Special Administrative Region
SASAC	State-owned Assets Supervision Administration Commission
SCAR	Scientific Committee on Antarctic Research
SCO	Shanghai Cooperation Organization
SCS	South China Sea
Second Island Chain	An extended region into the Pacific Ocean out to Guam from Asia.
Sinopec	China Petroleum & Chemical Corporation (Chinese State-Owned Enterprise - SOE)
SME	Small and Medium-sized Enterprises
SOE	State-Owned Enterprise
SONA	State of the Nation Address
Sorties	An air sortie is a military mission where aircraft are sent out on a combat mission.
SREB	Silk Road Economic Belt
SSA	Sub-Saharan Africa
THAAD	Theater High-Altitude Area Defense

Acronyms and Terms	
TIP	Turkestan Islamic Party
TPP	Trans-Pacific Partnership
Twitter Fingers	An individual who uses social media rapidly and rabidly, retweeting incessantly.
U.S.	United States
UDHR	Universal Declaration of Human Rights
UN	United Nations
UNCLOS	United Nations Convention on the Law of the Sea – This is an international treaty that was signed in 1982 and came into force in 1994 as an agreement that defines the rights and responsibilities of the world's oceans and seas. As of 2019, 168 parties have joined.
UNCTAD	United Nations Conference on Trade and Development
UNDP	United Nations Development Program
UNEA	United Nations Environment Assembly
UNEP	United Nations Environment Program
UNESCO	United Nations Educational, Scientific, and Cultural Organization
UNFCCC	United Nations Framework Convention on Climate Change
UNIDO	United Nations Industrial Development Organization
USAID	United States Agency for International Development
USD	United States Dollar
USSR	Union of Soviet Socialist Republics (14 countries; Founded on December 30, 1922; Dissolved on December 26, 1991)
VAT	Value-Added Tax
VPN	Virtual Private Network
WB	World Bank
WHO	World Health Organization
WIPO	World Intellectual Property Organization
Wolf Warrior Diplomacy	The newly introduced, aggressive method of diplomacy used by China in 2020 and named after Chinese blockbuster action films.
WPS	West Philippine Sea
WTO	World Trade Organization
WWF	World Wide Fund for Nature, previously known as World Wildlife Fund when founded in 1961.
XUAR	Xinjiang Uyghur Autonomous Region
Yuan	A unit of renminbi (RMB)
ZOPFAN	Zone of Peace, Freedom and Neutrality – Declaration signed in 1971 by the foreign ministers of the ASEAN member states.
ZTE	Zhong Xing Telecommunications – a Chinese communications and technology corporation.

Part 1

Planning, Acquisitions, and Promises Along the Belt and Road

Generosity and Debt with Soft and Hard Power

The Belt and Road Initiative is a sweeping project encompassing overland express routes, ports, digital connectivity, and both underground and undersea passages enabling China to

1. spread its soft power propaganda,
2. access the natural resources to sustain its economy,
3. sell more goods to Asia, Africa, Oceania, and the Americas, and
4. have a global say in world affairs.

In a masterful, integrated plan of thousands of stand-alone projects, designed to promote China worldwide, Beijing seeks to share its message of socialism with Chinese characteristics.

The Belt and Road Initiative has taken hold in more than a hundred countries where mostly insolvent projects leave countries seeking help from international funding agencies like the International Monetary Fund and the World Bank. Without the money to pay back the loans, each country will need to find alternative ways to pay off its debt, ways that suit Beijing's needs. With projects funded worldwide and pandemic-associated defaults, concerned leaders question the possibility that the Chinese Communist Party (CCP) could

1. control a country's physical assets,
2. demand a state's natural resources,
3. dictate domestic decision-making, and
4. influence votes in world bodies like the United Nations.

Chapter 1
Belt and Road to Glory
Nearly Impossible to Refuse Money

Introduction

Beijing's government-owned companies provided money flowing into ailing economies in return for valuable assets. Just like the United States borrowing trillions of dollars from China during the pandemic, at some point, the debt is due, and payment is required one way or another.

The United States' Gross Domestic Product (GDP), is a calculation of the total monetary value of all the finished goods and services produced within the U.S. borders over a specific period. At the present time, the U.S. spends more than a quarter more of its entire GDP than its output.

In May 2021, the U.S. debt to foreign countries was $7 trillion. The U.S. debt clock shows U.S. debt to GDP over time as,[1]

1960 – 52.95%

1980 – 34.57

2000 – 58.15%

2021 – 127.72%

and this is before trillions more proposed dollars are borrowed for a variety of 2021 initiatives. There is significant benefit in spending, but at some point, payment is demanded. There is no free money.

U.S Public Debt Compared to its GDP

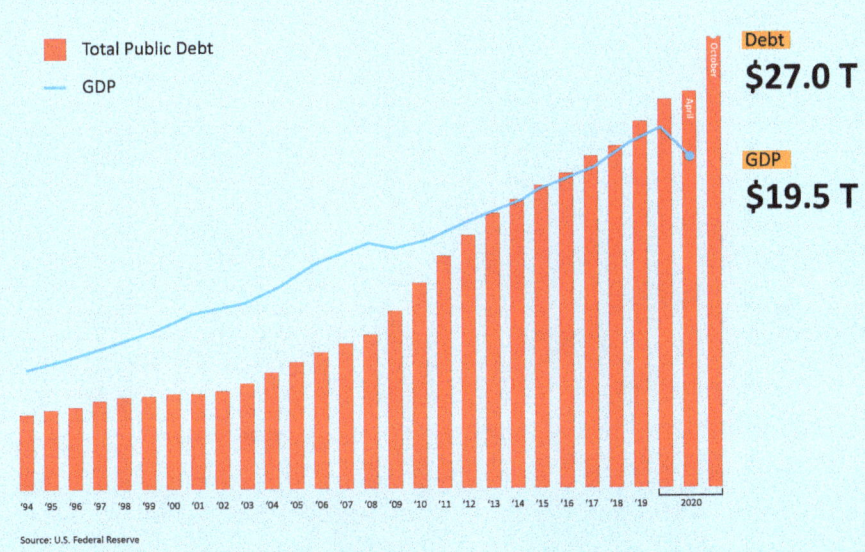

Source: U.S. Federal Reserve

---

1   USDebtClock.org, "US Debt Clock.org," *USDebtClock.org,* n.d., https://www.usdebtclock.org/

While the United States' situation is astonishing and America must reign in its spending, many other countries have also borrowed significant amounts with respect to their GDP. Djibouti has arguably taken more loan money than it can pay back. Djibouti owes 70-80% of its GDP to China. Djibouti's leaders appear undaunted, given the commitments that China has made to build the country into the next Singapore or Dubai of Africa.[2] Djibouti City, the capital city of Djibouti, is a small coastal centerpeice situated at the thoroughfare entrance from the Indian Ocean to the Mediterranean with immense strategic importance. Within this country, China has built roads, railroads, bridges, and ports to connect its freight to destinations across Africa.

Montenegro, a small country on the Adriatic Sea, borrowed approximately $1.56 billion (1.3 billion euros) from China to construct a highway that pushed its debt to almost 80 percent of it GDP.[3] Defaulting on the loan risks Montenegrin's forfeiture of land or infrastructure. Montenegro approached the European Union (EU), the International Monetary Fund (IMF), and the World Bank for help with little success. China's BRI expansion projects overwhelm countries economically with projects that are not viable.

Montenegro Owes China $1 Billion for a Road

---

2 Associated Press, "'The Singapore of Africa': Tiny Nation of Djibouti Finds Itself at Strategic Crossroads as Superpowers Vie for Influence," *South China Morning Post,* April 9, 2018, https://www.scmp.com/news/world/africa/article/2140936/singapore-africa-tiny-nation-djibouti-finds-itself-strategic

3 Financial Times, "Montenegro Fears China-Backed Highway will Put it on Road to Ruin," *Financial Times,* April 10, 2019, https://www.ft.com/content/d3d56d20-5a8d-11e9-9dde-7aedca0a081a

The Maldives, an island nation in the Indian Ocean and a snorkeler's paradise, is a group of 26 atolls and 1192 islands of which 185 are inhabited. China loaned money to build the China-Maldives Friendship Bridge. The Speaker of the Maldives's Parliament, Mohamed Nasheed said that the Maldives debt to China is $3.1 billion even though its GDP is $4.9 billion. The Maldives' president shut down his legislature and judiciary, demonstrating a growing concern that Beijing is creating seaports, airports, and land bases in the country for China's military as an alternative to the debt-trap payment strategy.[4]

Other countries are not only suffering from debt, but are left with poorly-constructed, Chinese built facilities as well. The shoddy work has resulted in significant problems that require repairs, long delays, and overcharges. In an *Australian.com* article, "Beijing Aid 'Doesn't Always Help'", the news source described a dangerous 55-seater aircraft and a $26.7 million courthouse in Apia, Samoa with cracked walls and flooded sewage systems. In Vanuatu, a Chinese construction group built a wharf requiring millions in repairs. In Fiji, quality control problems plagued a Chinese-built housing project.[5]

Nevertheless, Beijing's money has been too difficult to pass up. Worse, 140 countries are involved. People worldwide are concerned, though with the rollout of China's surveillance network, some are jailed if they point out fraud, graft, and deceit. Experts and researchers are concerned that China's integrated commerce and transportation system will eventually control the oceans through its 'String of Pearls' strategy, requiring customs, supervision,

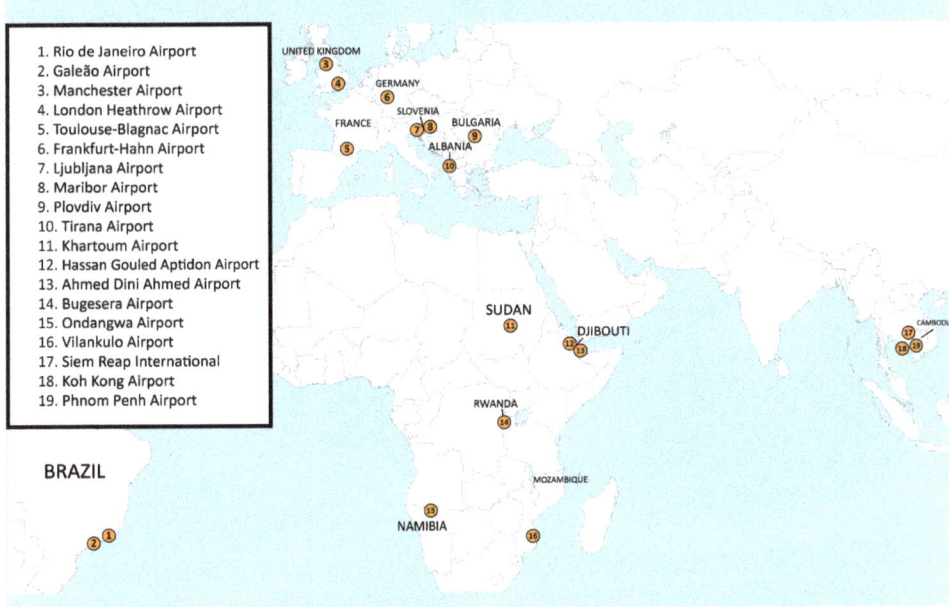

Partial List of Airports in which China Owns a Stake

1. Rio de Janeiro Airport
2. Galeão Airport
3. Manchester Airport
4. London Heathrow Airport
5. Toulouse-Blagnac Airport
6. Frankfurt-Hahn Airport
7. Ljubljana Airport
8. Maribor Airport
9. Plovdiv Airport
10. Tirana Airport
11. Khartoum Airport
12. Hassan Gouled Aptidon Airport
13. Ahmed Dini Ahmed Airport
14. Bugesera Airport
15. Ondangwa Airport
16. Vilankulo Airport
17. Siem Reap International
18. Koh Kong Airport
19. Phnom Penh Airport

---

4   David Brewster, "A 'Free and Open Indo-Pacific' and What it Means for Australia," *The Interpreter,* March 7, 2018, https://www.lowyinstitute.org/the-interpreter/free-and-open-indo-pacific-and-what-it-means-australia

5   Ben Bohane, "South Pacific Nation Shrugs Off Worries on China's Influence," *The New York Times,* June 13, 2018, https://www.nytimes.com/2018/06/13/world/asia/vanuatu-china-wharf.html

e-commerce, and legal oversight.[6] With back pocket payoffs to corrupt leaders and predatory lending projects that cannot be paid off, numerous countries will have to pay back these loans in one way or another.

Belt and Road Thoroughfare

The BRI identified six major Eurasian land passageways including,

- China-Central Asia-West Asia Economic Corridor (CCAWEC)
- China-Pakistan Economic Corridor (CPEC)
- Indochina Peninsula Corridor
- Bangladesh-China-India-Myanmar (BCIM) Economic Corridor
- New Eurasian Land Bridge (NELB)
- China-Mongolia-Russia Economic Corridor (CMREC)

China's Belt and Road Initiative
Trains, Roads, Planes, Ports, and Tunnels

---

6   Dipanjan Roy Chaudhury, "China's 'Own Courts' for BRI Rows Raise Eyebrows," *The Economic Times*, Updated February 14, 2018, https://economictimes.indiatimes.com/news/defence/chinas-own-courts-for-bri-rows-raise-eyebrows/articleshow/62909654.cms

Beijing's efforts are a work in progress. Not all of these corridors are completed. Some of them are fraught with challenges, particularly since two go through Myanmar and the country's military coup is throwing the country into a struggle with little end in sight. Foreign countries that might have ordinarily intervened are mired in their own internal problems or are unwilling to enter the fray.

Conclusion

A group of researchers have unearthed data to create a comprehensive source of China's loans to 140 countries, showing systematic underreporting and "hidden debt".[7] In a 77-page report by AidData, China has surpassed all other lenders as the world's largest creditor, surpassing the World Bank, IMF, and all other governments.[8] Confidentiality clauses prevent disclosure of loan details and collateral sources, though China is allowed to cancel loans or accelerate repayment on China's terms.

Despite the knowledge of these risks (or lack of due diligence), countries worldwide continue to sign onto the BRI. Meanwhile, during the pandemic, Beijing continues to offer financial support, development, and infrastructure in the form of loans. Before the pandemic, China painted a picture for each country of a glorious future with visions of magnificent cities, state-of-the-art train networks, improved roads, digital access, and maritime trade. In 2021, offers to support countries with new loans continued.

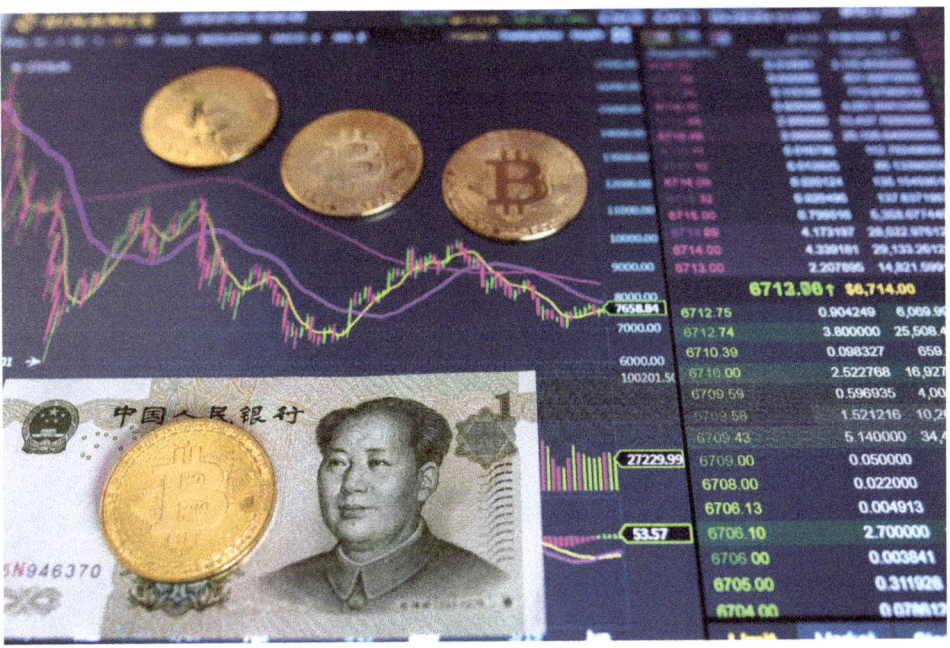

---

7   Sebastian Horn, Carmen M. Reinhart, and Christoph Trebesch, "How Much Money Does the World Owe China?," *Harvard Business Review*, February 26, 2020, https://hbr.org/2020/02/how-much-money-does-the-world-owe-china

8   Reuters Staff, "Database Reveals Secrets of China's Loans to Developing Nations, Says Study," *Reuters*, March 31, 2021, https://www.reuters.com/article/uk-china-emerging-debt/database-reveals-secrets-of-chinas-loans-to-developing-nations-says-study-idUSKBN2BN14H

With the desire to achieve their country's potential and build economic value, it is unsurprising why a leader may want a few billion or trillion from a government handing out money. Most people would take a free check or free education or free business grants or debt cancelation from a government handing out money without considering the long-term costs. Especially during the pandemic, the need from countries was great, and Beijing was there to loan 'free' money.

The BRI spotlights China's construction of smooth, secure, and enhanced overland and oversea routes. There is no doubt that underdeveloped countries could use state-of-the-art technologies, improved transportation corridors, and access to cutting edge communications. Many residents in poor countries still travel on dirt roads, do not have access to clean water, and lack educational resources like computers. The need is great.

Xi Jinping reminds countries that China was once a poor country that could not feed its people. Millions died from lack of food and clean water as the nation attempted to lift itself out of poverty. Disease was rampant and medical supplies and medicines were severely limited. Most of China's citizens lived in the countryside, attempting to live off the land. Now look at China, President Xi proudly remarks, reminding state leaders that their countries can also lift themselves out of poverty.

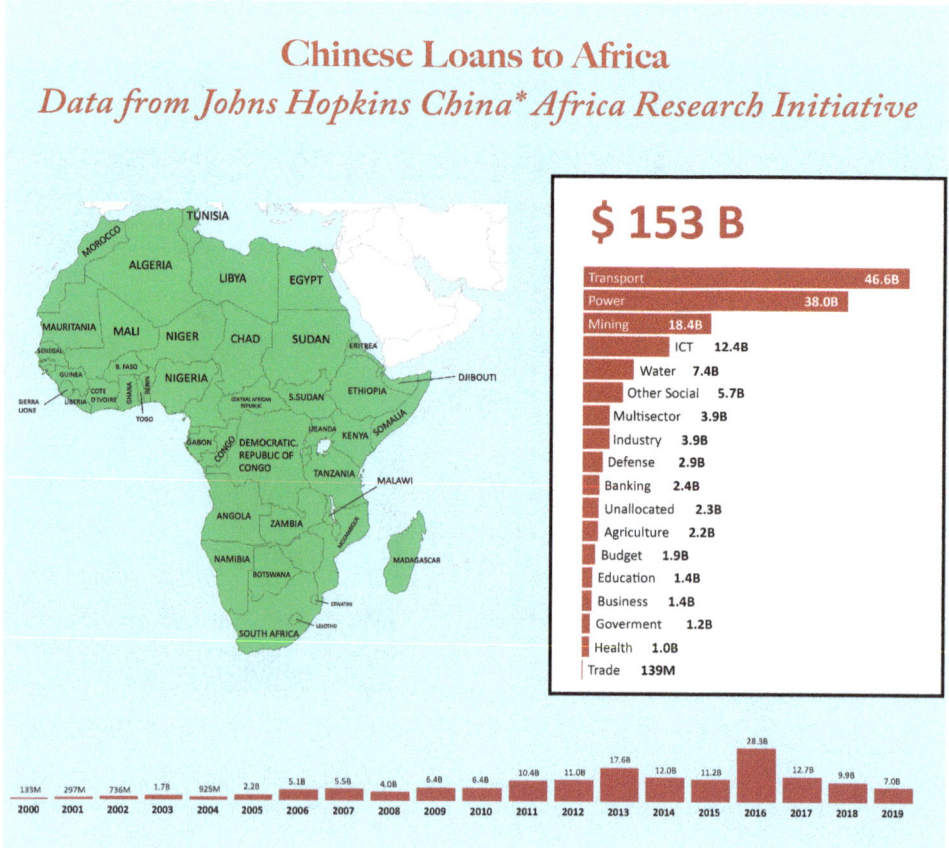

China's loans offer hope and promise for leaders who are keenly aware of the possibility that their countries too could dramatically improve their future prospects. Many leaders also know the risks, but the reward is too enticing.

What's at Stake?

First, an increasing number of countries are indebted to China well beyond their ability to pay. Beijing is likely to tolerate indebtedness throughout the pandemic, including debt restructuring, or else face a global backlash. However, at some point, China will make countries pay in one form or another. This wave of defaults is likely to foretell China's grip on societies with increasing social control, limits on freedom, and totalitarian measures to quell groups unwilling to let the CCP take over their countries.

Second, free money is rarely without costs. Not only do China's loans accrue interest, Beijing's banking institutions will require payment at some point in the same way credit card companies eventually demand payment of the principal and interest.

Third, in essence, what is at stake is the freedom and social control of future generations. While the next decade may force a race to stave off China's military aggression in the South and East China Seas and manage defaults on loans across the globe, 2050 will not look like 1980, 1990, or 2000. The looming question is what society will do today. In June 2021, the G7 issued a joint statement condemning China, but without enforcement, communique is a just words. Will countries continue to take China's seductively offered 'free' money or will they see the black clouds on the horizon soon enough to allow a strong wind to blow and push the threat away?

Chapter 2
Five Primary BRI Goals

Finance, Connectivity, People, Policy Coordination, & Unimpeded Trade

Introduction

The Belt and Road Initiative (BRI) has grown each year with enhanced loans, capabilities, coordination, integration, connectivity, and diplomacy. These mirror China's five primary BRI goals:

1. financial integration
2. digital connectivity
3. people-to-people relationship building
4. policy coordination
5. unimpeded trade

To accomplish these goals, China seeks to incorporate its banking system into the world market and replace the U.S. dollar with the Chinese yuan as the global currency. Through contracts and agreements, plus bilateral and multilateral policies between governments, it offers greater integration of rules, processes, and financial cooperation. Robust trade is promised between BRI partners, and any political and subversive elements within countries will be watched, punished, or eliminated.

In 2021, 140 countries have signed on to China's Belt and Road Initiative. Two new countries, Botswana & the Democratic Republic of Congo, signed on in January 2021.[1] Loan signatories include countries in all continents except Antarctica, though China is taking a greater stake in Antarctica as well. The breadth of countries includes 40 countries in Sub-Saharan Africa, 34 in Europe and Central Asia, 25 in East Asia and the Pacific, 17 in the Middle East and North Africa, 18 in Latin America and the Caribbean, and 6 in Southeast Asia.[2]

Integrating Goals with Operational Processes

China's multifaceted BRI goals seek to integrate loans, banking, and financial transition to the RMB, while also improving states' economic development through digital connectivity, transportation systems, and robust trade. However, China's focus on relationship building is an essential component of the BRI goals as Beijing brings countries under its wing to shape the international geopolitical system.

By incorporating Chinese television networks, Chinese language newspapers, and education in Mandarin in schools globally, China's long-term ambition is to change the world's lingua franca. While this language acquisition process and the transition to the RMB may take many decades, China plays the long game in its goal development process. The first step is working with people to build trust and to demonstrate the contrast between Marxist socialism's efficiency and democracy's inability to act quickly to resolve challenges.

---

1 Belt and Road Portal, "Homepage," *Belt and Road Portal,* n.d., www.yidaiyilu.gov.cn
2 Belt & Road News, "List of Belt & Road Member Countries," *Belt & Road News,* n.d., https://www.beltandroad.news/list-of-belt-road-member-countries/

Through win-win rhetoric and friendmaking, China has brought nations on board, distinguishing between no-strings-attached development and the sluggish requirements of permits, environmental surveys, viability studies, and legal hoops. China's loans untether states from these requirements and create efficient policy coordination between Beijing and each state. Leaders are offered quick funding solutions to infrastructure challenges.

Team Membership for All Who Sign On

Everyone wants to be part of the winning team. Winners play together and celebrate successes together. Losers are left out of the final rounds. Unless they reformulate their strategy fast, losing teams may be relegated to follow the leader status, wishing they were a global leader again. Thus, China is building its winning team, comparable to preparing for a major competition with the West. Possibly later, Beijing may create a completely new league where those who sign on to play are invited to participate in a completely new "United Nations" of Belt and Road Initiative partner countries.

China has integrated itself into all aspects of the current U.N. and is on every one of its international bodies. Beijing even has a seat on the Human Rights Commission while it tortures and imprisons its people in forced labor camps. China also holds membership in international legal bodies, while it violates international law on a grand scale.

China is creating this new league with 140 nations, making up its collective partnership. The lure is tantalizing with Chinese loans in the billions. In offering vast sums of money, transportation opportunities, connectivity, and trade, Beijing's diplomats span the planet in an unprecedented number of meetings and presentations, promising that China's new partners will be on the winning side of history.

A Chinese saying goes, "more friends make the journey easier".

China's money provided welcome relief to countries at a time when each needed to emerge from their pandemic-induced coma. Loans were offered in exchange for energy and mineral resources that China needed to remain the world's leading manufacturer. China embraced the goal of extending a hand in friendship by opening up diplomatic channels and promoting trade. At the Second Belt and Road Forum in April 2019, Xi Jinping described China's commitment to cooperation, emphasizing its creation of a diversified financial system, all-around connectivity, infrastructure development, economic growth, and people-to-people cultural exchanges.[3]

Internally and externally, China promotes its goals with only peaceful intentions, vowing to help countries succeed in a new world order and in a positive global environment. Beijing promotes the BRI by expressing its generosity as pioneering, collaborative, and supportive through video clips, explainers, and even Silk Road bedtime

---

3   The Second Belt and Road Forum for International Cooperation, "Xi Jinping Chairs and Addresses the Leaders' Roundtable of the Second Belt and Road Forum for International Cooperation (BRF)," *The Second Belt and Road Forum for International Cooperation,* April 28, 2019, http://www.beltandroadforum.org/english/n100/2019/0429/c22-1392.html

stories for children.[4] The more friends that join, the more success every partner can achieve.

Leaders See China's Money as a Path to Overall Improvement

It would be difficult to name even one president who would not want the most current technology, connectivity, media, education, bridges, roads, railroads, airports, and cargo ports. Further, there is no country that does not want to improve its trade balance, use its resources to make a better home for its people, lift its population out of poverty, improve transportation so that workers can better access jobs, and offer better digital connection speeds to ramp up to the potential of tomorrow. After all, as one advertisement put it, everyone in Nigeria could be the next Elon Musk if they had the tools to do so.

Conclusion

China's BRI goals are financial integration, digital connectivity, relationship building, policy coordination, and unimpeded trade. These BRI elements offer countries access to the world's biggest market for their goods and an avenue to get cheap products delivered quickly and efficiently. The Belt and Road Initiative is Beijing's core mechanism for China's bilateral trade relations. By integrating the world under its umbrella, Beijing can provide improved coordination among partners, strengthen domestic political stability, and deliver goods worldwide.

Everyone who joins must adhere to the One China principle. Thus, supporting Hong Kong, Tibet, or Taiwan independence is strictly prohibited. Violations of this order result in tensions and threats, like when the Solomon Islands thanked Taiwan for assisting them during the pandemic, and China's spokesperson vehemently protested the inference that Taiwan was a country. Getting a lesson in Chinese diplomacy, leaders in the Solomon Islands learned that to be a BRI 'partner', China demands political obedience and unwavering loyalty to its diplomatic protocols.[5]

What's At Stake?

First, Beijing's goals are noble. In many areas of the world, development is sorely needed. However, China's lack of transparency sows distrust.

Second, China's BRI goals allow partners to work together and coordinate finances, connectivity, policies, and trade. The current social order is slowly accepting a world governed by the rules of Marxist socialism.

Third, China's benevolence, complemented with strict assertiveness, creates anxiety and a feeling of being controlled, even if that is not Beijing's intent.

---

4 Angela Stanzel, "China's Belt and Road – New Name, Same Doubts?," *European Council on Foreign Relations*, May 19, 2017, https://ecfr.eu/article/commentary_chinas_belt_and_road_new_name_same_doubts/

5 Joseph D. Foukona, "Solomon Islands Gets a Lesson in Chinese Diplomacy," *The Interpreter*, June 29, 2020, https://www.lowyinstitute.org/the-interpreter/solomon-islands-gets-lesson-chinese-diplomacy

Chapter 3
Paving the Way to Prosperity
How to Get Other Countries to Fund the Employment of a Billion People

Introduction

One of China's big picture challenges is how to employ 1.4 billion people and both bring them out and keep them out of poverty. To this end, Beijing coordinates a massive effort to manufacture products for global markets to distribute them through a network of roads, railroads, ports, and airports through its Belt and Road Initiative (BRI). China has secured jobs for millions of its citizens sent to countries to work on BRI projects. Millions of others are taught discipline in a "work sets you free" mentality. One result is the existence of Chinese towns dotted around the planet in a form of neo-colonialism.

As angst grows surrounding the CCP's excessive reliance on employing its own people for projects, citizens in host countries complain that they are deprived of jobs. Meanwhile, Chinese workers' passports are seized so they cannot escape, made to work without pay, beaten for protesting conditions, and forced to labor, day in and day out, some while infected with the coronavirus.[1] When the Chinese laborers working on BRI projects are able to escape, knocking out the bars that enclose their housing, the defectors describe their experience as if they were escaping from hell.[2]

Human Capital

Belt and Road Initiative projects rely on imported Chinese labor, which displaces families in host countries. These workers construct their own living spaces, thus denying local workers opportunities for employment. Educated locals seeking work remain unemployed. Chinese contractors require knowledge of Mandarin, and training opportunities are unavailable for the human capital available in host countries. Chinese project developers cite the lack of qualifications, language skills, work ethic, and training.

Poor treatment on jobs has increased dissatisfaction. Locals actually employed are exploited and paid low wages. Dangerous conditions are commonly found on the construction sites of tunnels, bridges, and dams. Labor conditions are unsafe with few protections for workers and no grievance process in situations of injury to employees, local or Chinese. Exceedingly long hours and incidents of abuse are widespread.

The Rise in Anti-Chinese Sentiment

Chinese workers have been sent to construction sites worldwide. In dozens of countries, whole villages have been created to house and feed the thousands of workers deployed. In some areas, an entire cadre of Chinese residents have pushed out locals. Immediate and apparent differences in culture have created a backlash in some countries. The rapid influx of Chinese workers leaves little time for the area's residents to become accustomed to the new ways of life, and language barriers cause translation challenges. In these circumstances, not all of the Chinese newcomers are warmly embraced.

---

1   China Labor Watch, "CLW Reports," *China Labor Watch*, n.d., https://chinalaborwatch.org/reports/

2   Lily Kuo and Alicia Chen, "Chinese Workers Allege Forced Labor, Abuses in Xi's 'Belt and Road' Program," *The Washington Post*, April 30, 2021, https://www.washingtonpost.com/world/asia_pacific/china-labor-belt-road-covid/2021/04/30/f110e8de-9cd4-11eb-b2f5-7d2f0182750d_story.html

Anti-Chinese sentiments grow out of frustration. Culture, language, and customs are noticeably different. Friction is frequent due to the changes taking place. Wages are often paid with local country monies going to the Chinese. Resentment also rises as locals are frustrated by the conditions left behind by the Chinese enclaves. Criticisms regarding social integration have emerged from different directions, creating challenges for leaders.

Local leaders and citizens object to the lack of employment and dire working conditions for those who are employed.[3] "Zambian citizens complain about the abuse of labor norms as they faced discrimination by the Chinese," often being unable to return to their homes. They are threatened by the Chinese who they describe as becoming involved in every sphere of business.[4] In Zambia, where China owns over forty percent of the national debt, there is growing anxiety in the wake of the influx of 80,000 Chinese nationals who have moved in and set up warehouses and infrastructure projects.[5]

Some BRI projects were initiated without citizen input. Often, local communities were 'resettled' and forced to move without prior notice. They were often offered compensation which never materialized. Protests ensued when whole areas of Cambodian land that

---

3 David Hutt, "Are Southeast Asia's Anti-China Nationalists Democrats?," *The Diplomat*, November 3, 2020, https://thediplomat.com/2020/11/are-southeast-asias-anti-china-nationalists-democrats/

4 Mahua Venkatesh, "Anti-China Sentiment Spreads in Africa, Flares Up in Zambia," *India Narrative*, January 17, 2021, https://www.indianarrative.com/world-news/anti-china-sentiments-spread-in-africa-flare-up-in-zambia-2968.html

5 Ibid.

residents farmed were flooded for a Chinese dam.⁶ Parit Chiwarak, a 22-year-old political science student leader with the protest movement Milk Tea Alliance (#MilkTeaAlliance), explained, "Everyone is the victim of China and its authoritarianism."⁷

Clamping Down - Zero Tolerance for Unrest

Strict rules are placed on employees who are expected to work selflessly. The socialist mentality of employment for the good of the state is viewed differently outside of China and occasionally within China as well. China's state-owned broadcaster, *CGTN*, commented about the anti-Chinese sentiment in Myanmar, saying "China won't allow its interests to be exposed to further aggression. If the authorities cannot deliver and the chaos continues to spread, China might be forced into taking more drastic actions to protect its interests."⁸

For example, Southeast and Central Asia are deeply important for China's ambitious efforts to expand their markets through the Belt and Road Initiative. Kazakhstan, which Kazakh authorities consider the buckle in China's BRI projects, is flush with anti-China protests in a backlash against China's investments. Unrest in Kazakhstan increased when President Xi Jinping called for a "great wall of iron" to clamp down on Muslims in

---

6   Sun Narin, "'Our Ancestors' Graves Have Been Drowned': Cambodian Dam Wipes Out Hill Tribe Way of Life," *VOA Cambodia*, December 7, 2018, https://www.voacambodia.com/a/our-ancestors-graves-have-been-drowned-cambodian-dam-wipes-out-hill-tribe-way-of-life/4689817.html

7   Timothy McLaughlin, "How Milk Tea Became an Anti-China Symbol," *The Atlantic*, October 13, 2020, https://www.theatlantic.com/international/archive/2020/10/milk-tea-alliance-anti-china/616658/?utm_source=twitter&utm_medium=social&utm_campaign=share

8   Elaine Kurtenbach, "Myanmar Factory Attacks Put Focus on Chinese Influence," *Associated Press,* March 18, 2021, https://apnews.com/article/beijing-china-martial-law-myanmar-df4e07d2903350b4fc119189deaac492

Xinjiang Province, detaining up to 2 million Uyghurs, Kazakhs, and Kyrgyz.[9]

Concerns about Environmental Damage

In Thailand, when China assessed marine areas to destroy in order to improve Beijing's Belt and Road shipping lane navigation, locals protested the proposed blasting complaining that the demolition would kill fish, disrupt migrating birds, and erode farmland.[10] In another situation involving dams along the Mekong, representatives of forty NGOs issued a Declaration of Solidarity to stop the construction of the Xayaburi dam "in support of the 60 million Cambodians, Laotians, Thais, and Vietnamese whose lives and livelihoods are threatened by it fearing that the dam would cause irreversible ecological and hydrological impacts on the entire lower Mekong River basin system."[11]

While the environmental problems caused by Chinese firms are damaging, locals have complained loudest about the workers and the work environment. Beijing replicates its state-owned enterprises in each country. As Robin Hu, Singaporean wealth fund leader explained, "A common lament of recipient nations is that despite all the investments from huge infrastructure projects, there's a lack of local employment opportunities…[These enterprises] tend to air drop the entire ecosystem, from their engineers to the construction workers to the chefs, into the countries to do the project."[12]

Conclusion

The Belt and Road Initiative employs millions of Chinese people, lifting many out of poverty and giving them job skills to advance in their careers to lead future projects. Meanwhile, few people in host countries are offered employment on these projects, and when they are, they are low-skill, low-wage positions. Abuse is rampant, and payment is often delayed or not forthcoming. By insisting on bringing in thousands of Chinese workers to these projects and displacing communities for construction efforts without consultation, frustration builds.

With each BRI project, Chinese employees are required to do the work. They, as opposed to locals, can be more easily disciplined and kept under control utilizing force and intimidation. Chinese citizens' passports are taken, and they cannot escape. A regimented work ethic is demanded. This type of control is more difficult with local employees. Thus, when host countries sign on to the BRI, they pay Chinese employees to live and work wherever that may be. China is resolving its workforce issue by having other countries fund the employment of its people, but at what costs?

---

9 Bradley Jardine, "Why are there Anti-China Protests in Central Asia?," *The Washington Post*, October 16, 2019, https://www.washingtonpost.com/politics/2019/10/16/why-are-there-anti-china-protests-central-asia/

10 Oliver Ward, "Anti-Chinese Feeling: Strong Sentiment Turns into Strong Actions," *ASEAN Today*, June 27, 2017, https://www.aseantoday.com/2017/06/anti-chinese-feeling-strong-sentiment-turns-into-strong-actions/

11 Kraisak Choonhavan, "Vietnam Demands Halt to Mekong Dams," *Earth Journalism Network*, June 10, 2014, https://earthjournalism.net/stories/vietnam-demands-halt-to-mekong-dams

12 Nyshka Chandran, "China Can Make its Belt and Road Project More Successful if it Taps Locals, Experts Say," *CNBC*, September 14, 2018, https://www.cnbc.com/2018/09/14/china-must-do-more-to-tap-locals-in-belt-and-road-initiative-panel.html

What's at Stake?

First, China's trillion-dollar investment in the world's infrastructure offers countries the opportunity to grow faster and access resources unavailable before. Yet, by importing its workers, tensions have risen.

Second, dissension among locals is rampant, with Chinese workers constructing whole towns and importing a vastly different culture. Additionally, when locals are hired, they are inculcated into a pressure-cooker environment of abuse and discrimination. Thus, for the BRI to succeed in other countries, Beijing must work collaboratively with partner countries and its citizens.

Third, without safe working conditions and standards regarding employment both for Chinese workers and those employed in host countries, animosity and anti-Chinese sentiment are likely to grow. Belt and Road Initiative projects have the very real possibility of success with internationally recognized safety and employment practices along with transparency and communication with local officials. This openness and safety practice has not transpired.

Chapter 4

Global Land Grab

Seizing or Buying Up Land Around the World

Introduction

Unsure of Beijing's future intentions, some analysts believe China's goal is global domination, while others believe that its actions are merely in response to the U.S.-led geopolitical environment. However, claiming the South China Sea just because at one time, long ago, its ships sailed there is a stretch of the imagination. China's claim was not in response to the United States, nor was the illegal confiscation of the Paracel Islands from Vietnam. Furthermore, the militarization of the South China Sea by the People's Republic of China is unprecedented. No other country has taken islands from another country's Exclusive Economic Zone and planted military bases on them with such alacrity.

Revisionism and Claims

The technical term for rewriting history so that it suits a current narrative is called revisionism. China is quickly rewriting history books, pointing to a newly invented past as evidence of China's claim to land on its borders. Meanwhile, the CCP is buying up land to redefine its broader claims to East Asia, Southeast Asia, South Asia, and its northern and western borders. China's story does not end there as it claims the Arctic as a 'near-Arctic' state and the Antarctic by developing the Three Poles Project while claiming the leadership position in the poles and Himalayas.

China claims territory from most of its neighbors, calling the areas' disputed'. However, by international law, these are not disputed, they are land grabs in small salami slices so that the world does not become anxious about a few feet or a few miles, nibbling away at its edges. Thus, China's revisionism has redefined China's borders, incrementally causing disputes over areas that belong to other sovereign states.

Tibet

The world did not act when China took Tibet in the 1950s, though many protested. As thousands took to the airwaves and journalists wrote about the Tibetan cause for years, the only change was China's authoritarian control. Later, the architect of the Tibetan social control processes was led by ruthless Chen Quanguo, who took his surveillance, repression, and torture to the next level. Chen was promoted to build and oversee hundreds of concentration camps in Xinjiang Province, complemented by a dense network of 'convenience stations' for police surveillance, and the employment of ethnic minorities to clamp down on the local people.[1]

Some fought to free Tibet for decades. Many Tibetans have either self-immolated, committed suicide, or have been killed in the fight for Tibet's freedom. The Dalai Lama has traveled worldwide many times over to audiences large and small attempting to gain the attention of the world. Nevertheless, Tibet is still occupied by China and to solidify its claim, Beijing has moved tens of thousands of ethnic Chinese into Tibet to ensure the country looks and feels like a Chinese entity.

---

1   Sophie Richardson, "China Poised to Repeat Tibet Mistakes," *Human Rights Watch*, January 20, 2017, https://www.hrw.org/news/2017/01/20/china-poised-repeat-tibet-mistakes

Pakistan

Pakistan is China's close friend. As *Xinhua*, Beijing's media news source, explained, "The special friendship between China and Pakistan is a historical choice, and is deeply rooted in the hearts of the two peoples, who have always extended a helping hand to each other in times of need."[2] The China-Pakistan friendship is championed as China offers money and Pakistan pays China back with natural resources and land. Pakistan gave China mining rights to take gold and uranium from land disputed by India. The IMF fined Pakistan $5.95 billion in 2019 for offering these resources to China.[3] In another instance of generosity, Pakistan gave China 1,942 km² of land claimed by India in the Kashmir and Ladakh region.[4]

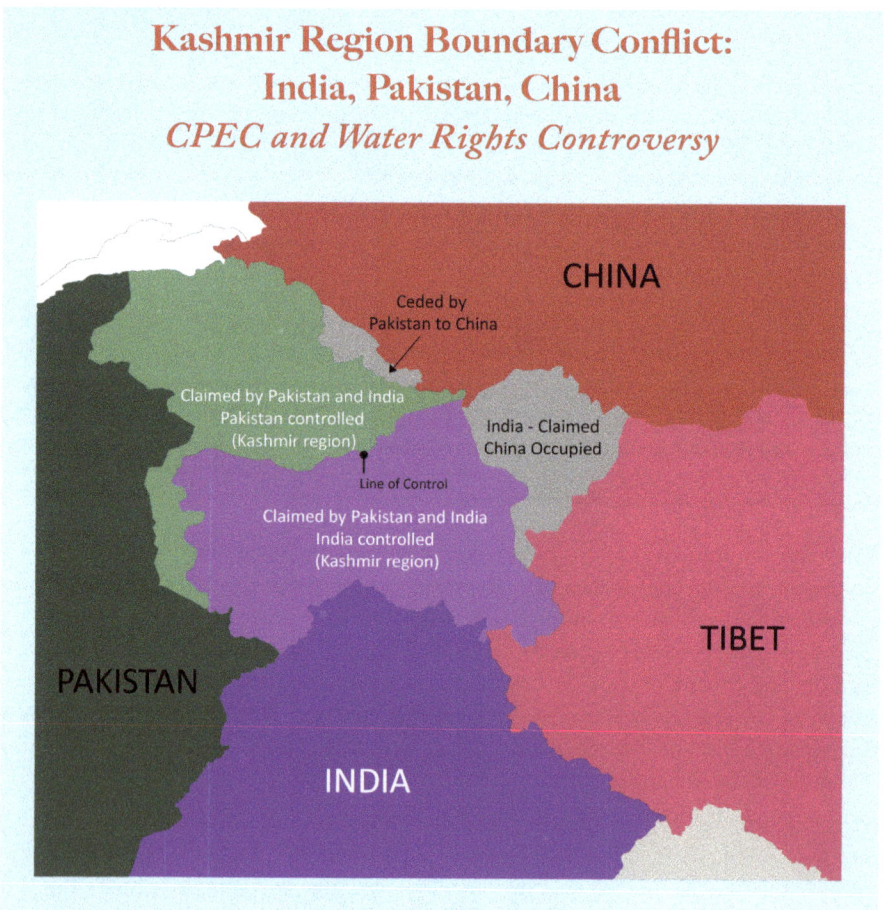

---

2   Xinhua, "6 Years On, Xi's Pakistan Visit Booms Development, Friendship with Shared Future," *Xinhua Net*, April 19, 2021, http://www.xinhuanet.com/english/2021-04/19/c_139891385.htm

3   Adnan Aamir, "China Rescue Option Emerges as Pakistan Slapped with $5.9bn Fine," *NIKKEI Asia*, July 19, 2019, https://asia.nikkei.com/Politics/International-relations/China-rescue-option-emerges-as-Pakistan-slapped-with-5.9bn-fine

4   Olwapps.net, "Sino-Pakistan Agreement," *Olwapps.net*, n.d., http://www.owlapps.net/owlapps_apps/articles?id=21819349&lang=en

In 2020, Pakistan began the process of handing China its islands in Sindh, in Southern Pakistan.[5] As Pakistan spirals into a debt trap, owing China about $100 billion, Beijing looks for more assets to acquire.[6] With China owning Pakistani mines, ports, and land, there is a real concern about how much Pakistan will cede to its iron clad brother, China, especially given India's claims on the land it gives away in the north.

India

In June 2020, China captured 60 km² (23 mi²) of Indian-patrolled territory.[7] In the follow-up, in September 2020, India's Defense Minister Rajnath Singh presented to Parliament a report that China has illegally occupied 38,000 km² of Indian land and also claims another 90,000 km² that belongs to India.[8] These land grabs have worsened as China encroached into the Himalayan territories of India, Nepal, and Bhutan. These borders are difficult to pinpoint due to their high elevations, snow-capped peaks, river changes, and rocky terrain. They stretch all along India's 3,379 km (2,100 mi) border called the Line of Actual Control (LAC).

On June 16, 2020, after China crossed into India and constructed structures on Indian territory, its People's Liberation Army killed 20 Indian troops. Tensions are high in India's Sikkim state, situated approximately 14,000 ft above sea level. The June 2020 skirmish occurred after Indians took down a Chinese tent on Indian territory. Pangong Tso Lake, spans from the Indian Ladakh to the Autonomous Region of Tibet China controls this region, as well as Pakistani land.[9] China continues to encroach on Indian land, testing India to make inroads.

Bhutan

Beijing's May 2021 land grab of Bhutan territory is part of China's continued salami slicing of Bhutanese land on the Tibet border.[10] However, unless China takes over the influence of the Bhutanese government, like it has in other countries, there could be a serious conflict. China is clandestinely seizing land from its small Himalayan neighbor, Bhutan, using its favored tactic, altering the international order without war. According

---

5   IANS, "Is Pakistan Planning to Gift Sindh Islands to China through the PIDA Ordinance?," *The Economic Times*, Updated October 15, 2020, https://economictimes.indiatimes.com/news/defence/is-pakistan-planning-to-gift-sindh-islands-to-china-through-the-pida-ordinance/articleshow/78679914.cms?from=mdr

6   Saikiran Kannan, "CPEC Crisis: China Plays Hard as Pakistan Spirals Deeper into Debt Trap | Deep Dive," *India Today*, Updated November 23, 2020, https://www.indiatoday.in/news-analysis/story/cpec-crisis-china-plays-hard-pakistan-in-debt-trap-1742696-2020-11-20

7   Joe Wallen, Sophia Yan, and Ben Farmer, "China Annexes 60 Square KM of India in Ladakh as Simmering Tensions Erupt between Two Superpowers," *The Telegraph,* June 12, 2020, https://www.telegraph.co.uk/news/2020/06/12/china-annexes-60-square-km-india-ladakh-simmering-tensions-erupt/

8   IANS, "China in Illegal Occupation of 38,000 Sq Km of Indian Land, Effort to Alter Status Quo Not Acceptable: Rajnath," *National Herald*, September 15, 2020, https://www.nationalheraldindia.com/national/china-in-illegal-occupation-of-38000-sq-km-of-indian-land-effort-to-alter-status-quo-not-acceptable-rajnath

9   Nectar Gan, "4 Chinese Soldiers Died in Bloody India Border Clash Last Year, China Reveals," *CNN*, Updated February 20, 2021, https://www.cnn.com/2021/02/19/asia/china-indian-border-casualty-intl-hnk/index.html

10 Hal Brands, "China's Land Grab in Bhutan is the New Face of War," *Bloomberg*, May 16, 2021, https://www.bloomberg.com/opinion/articles/2021-05-16/china-s-land-grab-in-bhutan-is-the-new-face-of-war

to *Foreign Policy*, announced in May 2021, China is fortifying its Tibetan border to gain leverage on India by stealthily constructing villages with roads and security installations on land that belongs to Bhutan.[11]

In 2020, China claimed Bhutan's Sakteng Wildlife Sanctuary as its own, in an example of salami-slicing new territory it had not claimed before.[12] Bhutan was surprised when China announced its new claim on Bhutan's eastern territory. In a meeting on wildlife conservation, Bhutan was offered international funds to develop its sanctuary.[13]

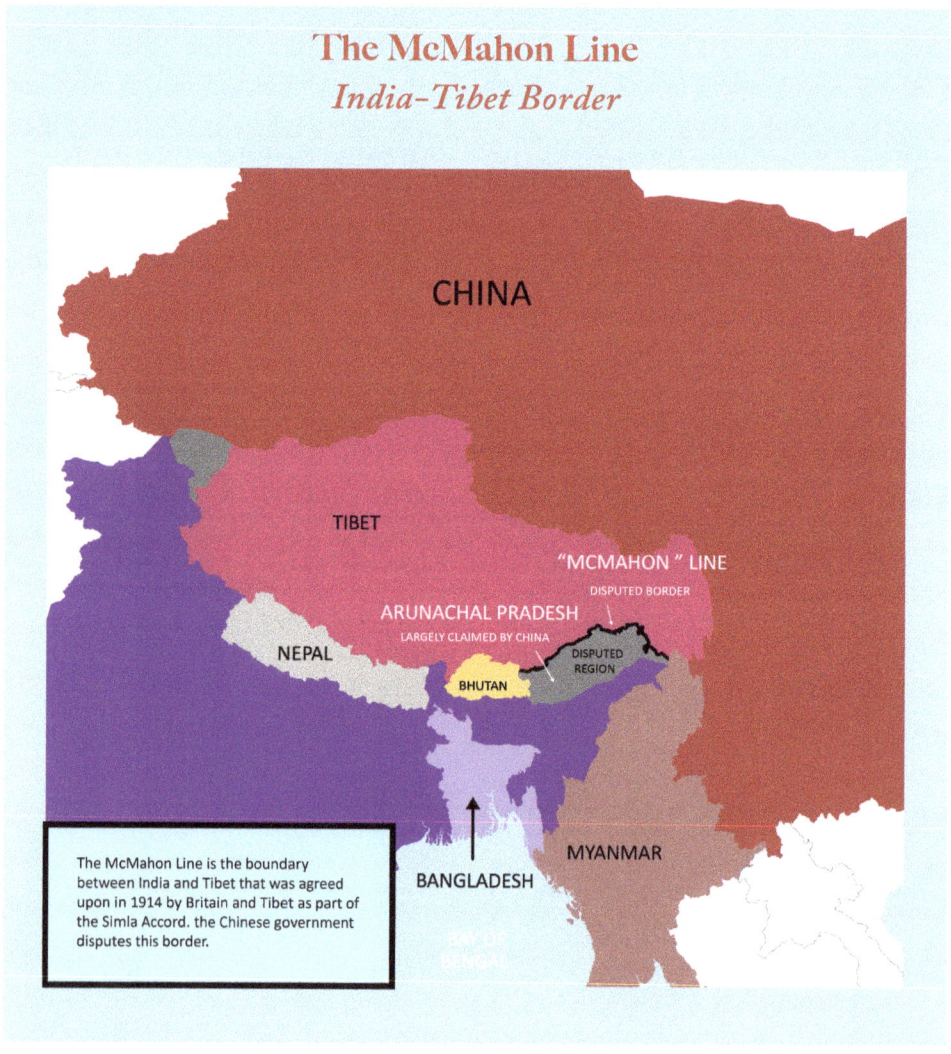

---

11 Robert Barnett, "China is Building Entire Villages in Another Country's Territory," *Foreign Policy*, May 7, 2021, https://foreignpolicy.com/2021/05/07/china-bhutan-border-villages-security-forces/

12 Anbarasan Ethirajan, "Why Bhutan's Sakteng Wildlife Sanctuary is Disputed by China," *BBC News*, November 25, 2020, https://www.bbc.com/news/world-asia-55004196

13 Ibid.

Nepal

A Nepalese government report cited China's encroachment at eleven locations, taking over land belonging to Nepal while building up border infrastructure and diverting rivers that previously acted as its natural boundary.[14] Meanwhile, China offers foreign direct investment (FDI) while influencing Nepalese decision-making. This meddling included a recent December 2020 change in the Nepalese leaders where the Chinese Communist Party (CCP) acted as the 'mediator' to ensure and secure its interests with a compatible government.[15]

In November 2020, China took more of Nepal's land.[16] "The land grab in the Humla district appears to be motivated by the strategic view the district's mountain peaks offer over the Himalayas."[17] In this grab, China annexed 150 hectares of Nepalese land, and in May 2020, China border guards in remote villages were busy annexing more land to the Chinese state.[18]

Cambodia

In 2020, Chinese developers seized and demolished Cambodian's land to construct one of Beijing's BRI projects called Dara Sakor for an airport, deep water seaport, and casino. The Cambodian government handed over a protected area under authorization by royal decree to the Chinese-owned Union Development Group (UDG). China falsely registered it as Cambodian-owned. The land, leased for 99 years to the Tianjin Wanlong Group, includes 90,000 acres or 20% of Cambodia's coastline that extends into the Botum Sakor National Park, more than three times the size allowed by Cambodian law.[19]

According to the U.S. office of the Treasury,[20]

> The PRC has used UDG's projects in Cambodia to advance ambitions to project power globally. UDG-funded activities have forced Cambodians from their land and devastated the environment, hurting the livelihoods of local communities, all under the guise of converting Cambodia into a regional logistics hub and tourist destination. As is too often the case with Beijing's One Belt One Road initiative, these activities have disproportionately benefitted the PRC, at the expense of the Cambodian people.

---

14 ANI, "Nepal Fears China Encroachment," *The Times of India,* June 24, 2020, https://timesofindia.indiatimes.com/india/nepal-fears-china-encroachment/articleshow/76542042.cms

15 Dhanwati Yadav, "Is the Growth of Sino-Nepal Relations Reducing Nepal's Autonomy?," *China Brief* 21, no. 5 (2021), https://jamestown.org/program/is-the-growth-of-sino-nepal-relations-reducing-nepals-autonomy/

16 ANI, "China Has Annexed 150 Hectares of Nepal: Report," *The Economic Times*, Updated November 3, 2020, https://economictimes.indiatimes.com/news/defence/china-has-annexed-150-hectares-of-nepal-report/articleshow/79017299.cms

17 Ibid.

18 Ibid.

19 GlobalSecurity.org, "U.S. Treasury Sanctions Chinese Developer for Land Seizure, Graft in Cambodia Project," *GlobalSecurity.org*, September 15, 2020, https://www.globalsecurity.org/wmd/library/news/china/2020/china-200915-rfa02.htm

20 U.S. Department of the Treasury, "Treasury Sanctions Chinese Entity in Cambodia Under Global Magnitsky Authority," *U.S. Department of the Treasury,* September 15, 2020, https://home.treasury.gov/news/press-releases/sm1121

Of additional concern are media reports by Cambodian government spokesperson, Phay Siphan. He suggested that Dara Sakor could be converted to host Chinese military assets. A permanent PRC military presence in Cambodia could threaten regional stability and undermine the prospects for the peaceful settlement of disputes, the promotion of maritime safety and security, and the freedom of navigation and overflight.

According to a 2020 *Wall Street Journal* article, the UDG was involved in building a Chinese military base with Chinese military equipment in Sihanoukville under terms of a secret 30-year deal with Beijing with automatic renewals every ten years to host Chinese

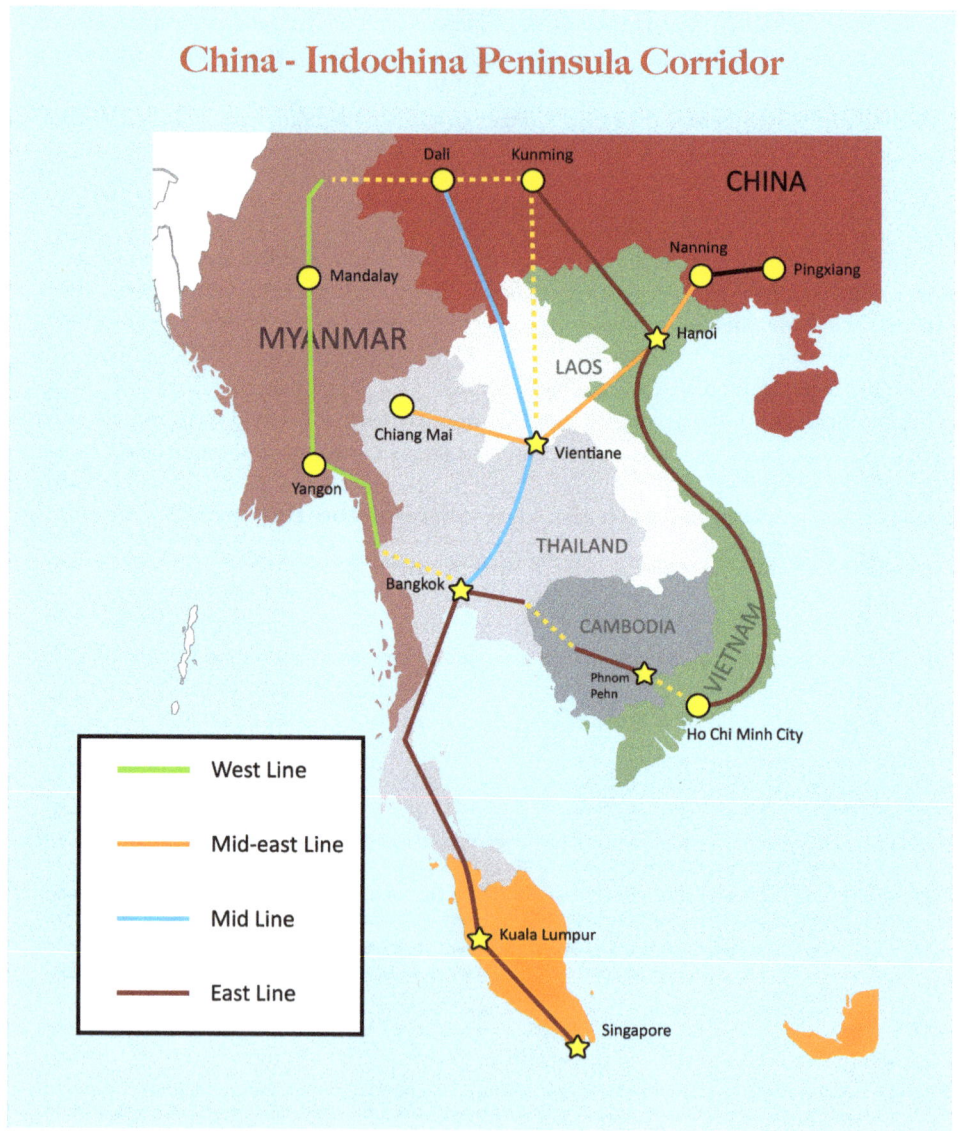

military personnel and warships.[21] According to *Reuters*, Cambodia destroyed the U.S.-funded tactical headquarters on its largest naval base as China is helping with an expansion, which raised increased speculation of plans to host China's military.[22]

Conclusion

This chapter could be an entire book on China's land grab expansionism throughout the world. Only a few places were highlighted. However, in many cities worldwide, China has bought up ports, airports, train routes, and land. Furthermore, nestled in China's BRI contracts are clauses that 'protect' Chinese interests, including taking or leasing land and infrastructure if the country or entity cannot pay. This process is being replicated globally, particularly in the 2020s as individuals and governments are strapped for cash and are willing to give up their sovereignty and land for much-needed money.

The South China Sea is one of the most prominent places where China has over-reached, taking Philippine and Vietnamese islands. However, Beijing also claims water areas belonging to Brunei, Indonesia, and Malaysia. To add to the list, China also claims the Japanese Senkaku Islands and land on its northern and western border. This chapter will not go into China's land acquisitions in Africa, though other chapters will.

What's at Stake?

First, media sources report that China's land grab are the result of land disputes. Consequently, as long as China can get away with taking twenty to a hundred square miles of land at a time in every country, calling their land grab 'a dispute', China will, before long, extend down to Singapore and across to Iran.

Second, no country wants to bite the hand that feeds it and China knows that it can use its economic might as a weapon over every country, but particularly countries that owe them money.

Third, China pressures countries to keep their negotiations private while coercing them to do what Beijing asks both domestically and internationally. The internal pressure on domestic issues is resolved by taking over governments and controlling its leaders. External pressure is happening in the United Nations and other international governing bodies where heavily indebted, borrowing countries pledge to vote with China in order to keep China's money flowing.

---

21 Gordon Lubold and Ian Talley, "U.S. Sanctions Chinese Firm Helping Build Military Base in Cambodia," *The Wall Street Journal*, Updated September 15, 2020, https://www.wsj.com/articles/u-s-sanctions-chinese-firm-helping-build-military-base-in-cambodia-11600181357

22 Prak Chan Thul, "Cambodia Says it Razes U.S.-Built Naval Facility to Move It," *Reuters*, October 4, 2020, https://www.reuters.com/article/us-usa-cambodia-military/cambodia-says-it-razes-u-s-built-naval-facility-to-move-it-idUSKBN26P0JA

Chapter 5

Cleansing Xinjiang Province of 'Terrorists'

Re-Education Camps Clear the Way for China's BRI through East Turkistan

Introduction

For the Belt and Road Initiative to be successful across the Asian BRI corridors, Beijing needed to ensure absolute control over Xinjiang Province, once known as East Turkistan. One look at a map shows the critical geopolitical significance of this "Autonomous Region". Xinjiang Province stands in the way of Beijing's railroad transportation plans for manufactured products headed for Central Asia and Europe. Concerns about a "9/11" in China and angst in Tibet sowed a mix of frustration and fear.

After an incident in 2009, Beijing felt the CCP needed to act quickly before the spark turned into flames. The massacre of Uyghur Muslims was the precipitating incident that led to China's overwhelming repression and widespread incarceration. As the Belt and Road Initiative took form in 2013 with Xi Jinping's election, a ramped up effort fostered the growth of slave labor camps in the name of 're-education' to remove the adult citizenry, take away children for reprogramming, and lay down the tracks to Beijing's golden future.

Introduction of Forced Labor Camps

As Tibetans were persecuted, taken from their land, and put into forced labor camps, signs of religious persecution in China also increased. The Chinese Communist Party (CCP) worried about Islamist extremism in their far west Xinjiang Province (East Turkistan). Thus, in the 1990s the Han Chinese crackdown on the Uyghurs began. One major incident was the Ghulja Massacre on February 5, 1997. The CCP murdered or imprisoned Uyghurs after the Chinese military opened fire on the unarmed peaceful protesters.[1] More intense suppression was instituted after 9/11. The CCP was determined to prevent a similar occurrence in China. Stricter security measures were put in place and surveillance over the population began to restrict freedom.[2]

The Uyghurs resented Han Chinese rule, but frustration erupted in 2009 with riots and chaos between the Muslim Uyghurs and the Han Chinese in Ürümqi, near the China-Kazakh border. In July 2009, a Han Chinese woman accused a Uyghur factory worker of sexual assault. Following those allegations, Chinese workers cornered and beat two Uyghurs to death, and many were injured.[3] Footage of the killings spread through Xinjiang, prompting large-scale protests with approximately 1,000 rioters.[4] On July 5, 2009, known as the 'Uyghur Massacre', mobs of Uyghur residents took to the streets and a brawl between Han Chinese citizens, CCP police, and Uyghurs ensued using sticks and metal bars. Chinese state media reported that 197, mostly Han Chinese, were killed and

---

1 Hong Kong Free Press, "The Ghulja Massacre: Remembering China's Brutal Crackdown on a Peaceful Xinjiang Protest," *Hong Kong Free Press*, February 7, 2020, https://hongkongfp.com/2020/02/07/ghulja-massacre-remembering-chinas-brutal-crackdown-peaceful-xinjiang-protest/

2 Edward Wong, "Riots in Western China Amid Ethnic Tension", *The New York Times*, July 5, 2009, https://www.nytimes.com/2009/07/06/world/asia/06china.html

3 Tania Branigan, "Ethnic Violence in China Leaves 140 Dead," *The Guardian*, July 6, 2009, https://www.theguardian.com/world/2009/jul/06/china-riots-uighur-xinjiang

4 Erin Handley, "How China's Mass Detention of Uyghur Muslims Stemmed from the 2009 Urumqi Riots," *Australia Broadcasting Corporation (ABC) News*, July 4, 2019, https://www.abc.net.au/news/2019-07-05/china-xinjiang-urumqi-riots-10th-anniversary-uyghur-muslims/11270320

roughly 1,700 were injured.⁵ The Uyghur casualty rate and death toll in China-controlled media sources was not published, though Chinese armored vehicles ran over people and law enforcement sprayed crowds of Uyghurs with firepower.

The Beginning of the End for the Uyghurs

The CCP believed the population of Xinjiang Province needed to speak Chinese and live culturally like the Han Chinese people. Meanwhile, the Uyghurs had maintained their own culture for centuries. Their food was different; their practices were different; they spoke their own language. To fully integrate the Uyghurs, waves of Han Chinese were incentivized to move to Xinjiang with government subsidies and housing.

Many were initially housed in Uyghur homes. This served a triple purpose: (1) teach the Uyghurs to be 'Chinese' and (2) supervise the actions of residents, (3) and teach the families Mandarin. Those who did not adapt were taken to camps for a more formal re-education. Cameras were installed in homes. All cell phones were implanted with a chip to monitor activities. QR codes were put outside of homes.⁶ Also, the Chinese government closed Uyghur stores, disallowed group gatherings, and removed Muslim places of worship.

5   Erin Handley, "How China's Mass Detention of Uyghur Muslims Stemmed from the 2009 Urumqi Riots," *Australia Broadcasting Corporation (ABC) News*, July 4, 2019, https://www.abc.net.au/news/2019-07-05/china-xinjiang-urumqi-riots-10th-anniversary-uyghur-muslims/11270320

6   Sigal Samuel, "China's Crackdown on Muslims is Being Felt Beyond Its Borders," *Vox*, March 30, 2019, https://www.vox.com/future-perfect/2019/3/30/18287532/china-uighur-muslims-internment-camps-turkey

Uyghurs have been rounded up and sent to forced labor camps to be 're-educated' and trained to pick cotton, manufacture goods, and perform hard labor for multinational corporations. Their hair is removed for the worldwide wig and hair extension market. While learning Chinese language and laws, they are forced to renounce Islam and Uyghur cultural and religious practices. When they do not perform fourteen hours a day in backbreaking work, they are tortured or their organs are surgically extracted, called 'organ harvesting' for the global organ 'donation' market. The CCP stripped the Uyghurs of their rights as they transported them to locked, guarded, and isolated concentration camps.

Concentration Camps

Four hundred pages of leaked files expose China's plan to "show no mercy" on the eleven million Uyghurs living in Xinjiang province where up to two million Uyghur, Kazakh, and Uzbek Muslims are imprisoned in camps that satellite images show are expanding.[7] According to the Council on Foreign Relations, detainees are interrogated, tortured, and raped in prison-like conditions. They are compelled to pledge loyalty to the CCP, renounce Islam, sing praises for communism, and study Mandarin.[8]

According to a May 19, 2021 *Forbes* article, the Muslims held in forced labor camps produce most of the world's solar panels, taking over the market with their 'efficient', low-cost labor in conditions described as 'genocide' and 'slavery'.[9] Manufacturers outside of China have been pushed out of the market with China's cheap coal, government subsidies, and 'surplus labor'. *AP* reports that "much of the world's polysilicon, used in photovoltaic cells for solar panels, comes through China's Xinjiang province, where China is waging a sustained campaign against Chinese Muslims and ethnic minorities."[10] China has flooded the solar panel market at less than the price to manufacture them, called dumping, with manual laborers at Xinjiang's facility paid 42 Chinese yuan (around $6.50) per ton to crush silicon manually.[11]

Americans who purchase hair extensions may be wearing the head of hair shaved off and dyed from the hair of imprisoned and tortured detainees in concentration camps. In a July 2020 *CNN* report, a 13-ton shipment of human hair that arrived in the Port of New York from Xinjiang. China is thought to have been taken the hair from the heads of Uyghur

---

7   Austin Ramzy and Chris Buckley, "'Absolutely No Mercy': Leaked Files Expose How China Organized Mass Detentions of Muslims," *The New York Times*, November 16, 2019, https://www.nytimes.com/interactive/2019/11/16/world/asia/china-xinjiang-documents.html

8   Lindsay Maizland, "China's Repression of Uyghurs in Xinjiang," *Council on Foreign Relations*, Updated March 1, 2021, https://www.cfr.org/backgrounder/chinas-repression-uyghurs-xinjiang

9   Michael Shellenberger, "China Helped Make Solar Power Cheap through Subsidies, Coal and Allegedly, Forced Labor," *Forbes*, May 19, 2021, https://www.forbes.com/sites/michaelshellenberger/2021/05/19/china-made-solar-cheap-through-coal-subsidies--forced-labor-not-efficiency/?sh=6547d8fd71ec

10 Ellen Knickmeyer, "Kerry: US Weighs Sanctions on China Solar over Forced Labor," *Associated Press*, May 12, 2021, https://apnews.com/article/china-middle-east-race-and-ethnicity-religion-forced-labor-7aed002b2719c5a530f104022b14b53e

11 Michael Shellenberger, "China Helped Make Solar Power Cheap through Subsidies, Coal and Allegedly, Forced Labor," *Forbes*, May 19, 2021, https://www.forbes.com/sites/michaelshellenberger/2021/05/19/china-made-solar-cheap-through-coal-subsidies--forced-labor-not-efficiency/?sh=6547d8fd71ec

Muslims enslaved in hundreds of forced labor concentration camps where torture and genocide is believed to occur.[12]

Growing Clamor of Concern

On May 18, 2021, after outcries over China's genocide, U.S. Speaker of the House, Nancy Pelosi called for a diplomatic boycott of the 2022 Beijing Olympic saying, "Let's not honor the Chinese government by having heads of state go to China…For heads of state to go to China in light of a genocide that is ongoing - while you're sitting there in your seat - really begs the question, what moral authority do you have to speak again about human rights any place in the world?"[13]

In March 2021, Mitt Romney called for a similar boycott in a *New York Times* op-ed,[14]

> China deserves our condemnation. The Chinese Communist Party has reneged on its agreement to allow Hong Kong self rule; it has brutally suppressed peaceful demonstrators and incarcerated respected journalists. It is exacting genocide against Uighurs and other ethnic minorities; Uighur women are forcefully sterilized or impregnated by Han Chinese men. Adults, ripped from their families, are sentenced

---

12 Allison Gordon, "13-Ton Shipment of Human Hair, Likely from Chinese Prisoners, Seized," *CNN*, Updated July 2, 2020, https://www.cnn.com/2020/07/02/us/china-hair-uyghur-cpb-trnd/index.html

13 David Brunnstrom and Michael Martina, "Pelosi Calls for U.S. and World Leaders to Boycott China's 2022 Olympics," *Reuters*, May 19, 2021, https://www.reuters.com/lifestyle/sports/pelosi-says-us-should-diplomatically-boycott-2022-olympics-china-2021-05-18/

14 Mitt Romney, "The Right Way to Boycott the Beijing Olympics," *The New York Times*, March 15, 2021, https://www.nytimes.com/2021/03/15/opinion/politics/beijing-olympics-mitt-romney.html

into forced labor and concentration camps. Among ethnic Chinese, access to uncensored broadcast news and social media is prohibited. Citizens are surveilled, spied upon and penalized for attending religious services or expressing dissent.

Prohibiting our athletes from competing in China is the easy, but wrong, answer. Our athletes have trained their entire lives for this competition and have primed their abilities to peak in 2022. When I helped organize the Salt Lake City Games in 2002, I gained an understanding of the enormous sacrifice made by our Olympic hopefuls and their families. It would be unfair to ask a few hundred young American athletes to shoulder the burden of our disapproval.

A March 2021 commentary in *USA Today* stated, "The spotlight on the International Olympic Committee is going to be mighty uncomfortable these next 11 months, and president Thomas Bach and his buddies have no one to blame but themselves."[15] After the drumbeat for a boycott of the 2022 Beijing Olympic Games began in 2020 with 180 human rights groups speeding up the tempo, an increasing number of countries issued statements questioning China's concentration camps, forced labor, and genocide.

These actions are not new, but they are becoming increasingly visible. In December 2020, the Guardian reported on the half million slave laborers forced to pick cotton after being rounded up, put on trains, and incarcerated to produce Western goods.[16] In February 2021, the United States signed a ban on Xinjiang cotton, which created a supply chain nightmare for American companies using forced labor in camps tied to genocide and unwitting shoppers who purchase many of their clothing items from Uyghur slaves.[17] According to Beijing's media outlet, *China Daily*, 84.9% of the cotton produced in China comes from Xinjiang Province,[18] where Uyghurs are forced into hard labor for long hours.

The paramilitary group linked to China's slave labor camps, Xinjiang Production and Construction Corps (XPCC), oversees the production of millions of garments from as many as 1,000 brands from companies like Amazon, H&M, Target, and Zara.[19] The U.S. Customs and Border Protection (CBP) seized millions of dollars in shipments tied to XPCC from textiles and shoes to tomato sauce and solar panels,[20] as well as more than $4 million USD in fake jewelry from brands such as Tiffany, Pandora, Cartier, Bvlgari, Dior,

---

15 Nancy Armour, "Opinion: Mitt Romney Onto Something in His Call for a Targeted Boycott of 2022 Beijing Olympics," *USA Today*, March 15, 2021, https://www.usatoday.com/story/sports/columnist/nancy-armour/2021/03/15/mitt-romney-calls-targeted-boycotts-2022-beijing-olympics-push-ioc/4708174001/

16 Helen Davidson, "Xinjiang: More than Half a Million Forced to Pick Cotton, Report Suggests," *The Guardian*, December 15, 2020, https://www.theguardian.com/world/2020/dec/15/xinjiang-china-more-than-half-a-million-forced-to-pick-cotton-report-finds

17 Marc Bain, "The US is Intensifying its Crackdown on Forced Labor in China's Xinjiang Region," *Quartz*, January 13, 2021, https://qz.com/1956856/the-us-has-issued-a-sweeping-ban-on-cotton-from-chinas-xinjiang/

18 Mao Weihua and Zheng Caixiong, "Xinjiang Still China's Largest Cotton Producer in 2019," *China Daily*, Updated January 8, 2020, https://www.chinadaily.com.cn/a/202001/08/WS5e156c70a310cf3e3558336b.html

19 Marc Bain, "The US is Intensifying its Crackdown on Forced Labor in China's Xinjiang Region," *Quartz*, January 13, 2021, https://qz.com/1956856/the-us-has-issued-a-sweeping-ban-on-cotton-from-chinas-xinjiang/

20 Owen Churchill, "US Bans all Imports of Cotton and Tomato Products from Xinjiang, Citing Allegations of Forced Labour," *South China Morning Post*, January 14, 2021, https://www.scmp.com/news/china/article/3117641/us-bans-all-imports-cotton-and-tomato-products-xinjiang-citing

Gucci, Chanel, Rolex, Versace, and Tous.[21]

The Chinese Communist Party's Perspective

According to the *Global Times*, the Xinjiang cotton association urged foreign brands and institutions to stop their 'wrong behaviors'.[22] "Pure, white cotton shouldn't be tainted," the *Global Times* exclaimed as angry Chinese citizens clamored to announce their support for Xinjiang cotton.[23] With calls for boycotts from netizens and the CCP's call to cut off the foreign supply chains, Chinese citizens voiced their outrage, suggesting that Chinese companies raise the stakes in the production and distribution of manufactured goods.

The pushback in China intensified, infuriated about the 'erroneous' worldwide smear that ignored the progress of human rights in Xinjiang and undermined the legitimate rights and interests of cotton growers, garment workers, and regional ethnic groups who are being re-educated so they can improve their living standards through work. The paper explained that Western "lies of the century" engage in hypocritical behaviors with fake concerns and

---

21 U.S. Customs and Border Protection, "CBP Officers in Cincinnati Seize $4.26 Million in Fake Jewelry," U.S. *Customs and Border Protection*, April 27, 2021, https://www.cbp.gov/newsroom/local-media-release/cbp-officers-cincinnati-seize-426-million-fake-jewelry

22 Global Times, "'Xinjiang's White Cotton Will Not Be Stained': Industry Associations Condemn Western Boycott," *Global Times*, March 29, 2021, https://www.globaltimes.cn/page/202103/1219733.shtml

23 GT Staff Reporters, "'Pure, White cotton Shouldn't be Tainted!' Chinese Voice Support for Xinjiang," *Global Times*, March 25, 2021, https://www.globaltimes.cn/page/202103/1219499.shtml

disgusting interference.²⁴ Also, the CCP's state-run tabloid *Global Times* explained that no matter how much anti-China forces smear Xinjiang, they will not hinder China's prosperity and development.²⁵

Conclusion

Since 2009, the Chinese Communist Party has been cleansing Xinjiang Province of 'terrorists' by taking people out of their homes, putting them on trains, and sending them to concentration camps. Ostensibly to 're-educate' the Uyghur Muslims, CCP leaders teach Mandarin, wipe away Muslim culture, and 'retrain' their prisoners to be good Marxist socialists. Xinjiang Muslims are relocated to forced labor camps where they work day-and-night to pick cotton, manufacture clothing, and produce solar panels.

The mass incarceration, forced labor, and re-education of millions of Uyghurs in Xinjiang Province offers China a new path forward to ensure the success of the Belt and Road Initiative's corridors through the autonomous region. The CCP suggests that the millions who are imprisoned are dangerous terrorists who threaten China and need to be reprogrammed with Chinese language, culture, values, and ideologies. With the region secured and millions of suspected 'terrorists' taken from their homes, the way is cleared for China's Belt and Road Initiative through East Turkistan (Uyghur name for Xinjiang Province) and onward to Europe.

What's at Stake?

First, the genocide against the Uyghurs, Kazakhs, and Uzbek Muslims is not getting significant public attention due to the large numbers of American firms using slavery to produce their products and the blacklisting of all who speak out against China. Beijing's 'Wolf Warriors' destroy the reputations of actors, musicians, and athletes who speak against China. However, nearing the 2022 Beijing Olympics, the sound is likely to amplify even without the voices of stars who would ordinarily unleash social media in support of more than a million enslaved people imprisoned in concentration camps.

Second, after World War II, the world said, "Never Again". However, China has constructed more concentration camps than Nazi Germany. The CCP kidnaps, tortures, and imposes its beliefs in gross violation of human rights that society vowed in the last century would never again happen.

Third, China controls the dialogues in Muslim nations with large outlays of capital investment as Beijing labels millions of Muslims terrorists and silences dissent. This quiet is especially alarming since concentration camps for 'Muslim terrorists' could be replicated in any other country.

---

24 Global Times, "'Xinjiang's White Cotton Will Not Be Stained': Industry Associations Condemn Western Boycott," *Global Times*, March 29, 2021, https://www.globaltimes.cn/page/202103/1219733.shtml

25 Ibid.

Chapter 6

Speeches, Promises, and Agreements

Delivering Skilled Diplomacy, Sharpened Rhetoric, Large Loans, and Infrastructure

Introduction

Xi Jinping's exemplary oratory skills are remarkable in the devious crafting of his words and in his warm delivery. He presents himself with eloquence and benevolence, appealing to his audience's cultural, economic, and political needs. Xi expresses the breadth of a state's context with historical and sociocultural sophistication. His calm but targeted pronouncements create a distinction between the generosity of China's support for a better world and the United States' offensive weaponry and reactionism. With grace and gratitude, Xi Jinping is the good leader who has a plan to help countries succeed when the United States merely wants to maintain its domineering imperialistic drive for power.

President Xi's impressive ability to use poetic language and cultural context to draw in listeners while distorting the truth is so exemplary that George Orwell would be proud. Hypocrisy is rampant. His navy "protected" islands in the South China Sea while taking them away from their U.N.-decreed owner. He set up a location on an island to help his fishermen and then installed a military base. He sheltered 200 paramilitary boats outside of a Philippine island, tying them together to be safe from a storm when there was no storm. His coast guards rammed fishermen's boats, capsizing them, and left the scene. Xi said they were violating laws that the CCP instituted that no other country agreed to obey. He declared periods where countries were banned from fishing except those fishermen from China who continued to fish. The numbers of doublespeak actions and words are too numerous to list.

Masterful Orator

Xi Jinping is masterful at telling each world leader that they are the focal point of the new world order led by China and that their country will be the source of some of the greatest benefits in history. In 2019, after declaring his "deep personal relationship" with Putin, Xi unveiled two Chinese pandas as a gift, explaining, "Russia is the country that I have visited the most times, and President Putin is my best friend and colleague."[1] Putin responded by declaring that he was "pleased to say that Russian-Chinese relations have reached an unprecedented level."[2]

In Peru, Xi announced to the people, "Peru and China are 'neighbors' connected by the Pacific Ocean," explaining that "The family-like friendship between our two nations has also taken root and sprouted in the heart of our two peoples."[3] Chile is, likewise, a brother to China. Xi said, "The Chinese people like to refer to a good relationship as 'a bond of gold and jade.' The gold medals for 2008 Olympic Games in Beijing were made of gold from Chile and jade from China. These medals are symbols of the brotherly relations

---

1 BBC, "China's Xi Praises 'Best Friend' Putin During Russia Visit," *BBC*, June 6, 2019, https://www.bbc.com/news/world-europe-48537663

2 Ibid.

3 Xi Jinping, "Sailing Forward to Build A Bright Future of China–Latin America Relation," *Speech at the Peruvian Congress*, November 21, 2016.

between the Chinese and Chilean peoples."⁴

On a state visit to Myanmar for its 70th anniversary of China-Myanmar diplomatic relations, Xi noted, "Our people have lived alongside each other for thousands of years. In Myanmar language, pauk-phaw means siblings from the same mother. It is an apt description of the fraternal sentiments between our two peoples, whose close ties date back to ancient times."⁵ In Cambodia, Xi presented the Queen Mother Monineath a "Friendship Medal" for forging "an unbreakable iron-clad friendship," reflecting the shared community and partnership and the brotherhood Cambodia has with the Chinese people.⁶

In Kazakhstan, Xi heralded their relationship together, saying, "China and Kazakhstan are neighbors as close as lips to teeth."⁷ At the Pakistani Parliament in Islamabad, Xi noted, "The Pakistani people say that China-Pakistan friendship is higher than the mountain, deeper than the sea and sweeter than honey. And we Chinese fondly refer to the Pakistani people as our good friends, good neighbors, good partners, and good brothers…As an old Chinese saying goes, 'Meeting a good friend for the first time is like having a reunion with an old friend.' This is exactly how I feel during my visit to Pakistan."⁸

President Xi's Speeches Announcing Friendship with Pakistan

The reality: Pakistan's debt to China is so high, it may not escape. Since Pakistan agreed to a $60 billion China-Pakistan-Economic-Corridor, the country has turned over land, mines, and other resources to China in a debt it may never be able to repay.⁹ Furthermore, the International Monetary Fund rejected Pakistan's request for aid, possibly leading to a more severe debt trap than Sri Lanka.¹⁰

Meanwhile, the rhetoric back and forth between China and Pakistan is of their close cooperation, friendship, and long-term, all-weather alliance. President Xi commented, "By all-weather, we mean that our two countries will always move ahead together, rain or shine. This description of China-Pakistan partnership is a most appropriate one, as it aptly defines

---

4   Xinhua, "Full Text of Chinese President's Signed Article in Chilean Newspaper," *Global Times*, November 22, 2016, https://www.globaltimes.cn/content/1019584.shtml

5   Ministry of Foreign Affairs of the People's Republic of China, "Full Text of Xi's Signed Article on Myanmese Newspapers," *Ministry of Foreign Affairs of the People's Republic of China*, January 16, 2020, https://www.fmprc.gov.cn/mfa_eng/wjdt_665385/zyjh_665391/t1733312.shtml

6   Consulate-General of the People's Republic of China in Los Angeles, "Xi Jinping Holds an Awarding Ceremony 'Friendship Medal' of the People's Republic of China for Cambodian Queen Mother Norodom Monineath Sihanouk," *Consulate-General of the People's Republic of China in Los Angeles*, November 6, 2020, http://losangeles.china-consulate.org/eng/topnews/t1830868.htm

7   Xi Jinping, "Promote Friendship Between Our People and Work Together to Build a Bright Future," *Speech at Nazarbayev University*, September 7, 2013.

8   Xi Jinping, "Building a China-Pakistan Community of Shared Destiny to Pursue Closer Win-Win Cooperation," *Ministry of Foreign Affairs of the People's Republic of China*, April 21, 2015, https://www.fmprc.gov.cn/mfa_eng/wjdt_665385/zyjh_665391/t1257158.shtml

9   Saim Saeed, "Pakistan Learns the Cost of an Alliance with China," *Politico*, March 3, 2021, https://www.politico.eu/article/pakistan-learns-cost-of-economic-alliance-with-china/

10 Panos Mourdoukoutas, "IMF Won't Stop China From Turning Pakistan into the Next Sri Lanka," *Forbes*, July 4, 2019, https://www.forbes.com/sites/panosmourdoukoutas/2019/07/04/imf-wont-stop-china-from-turning-pakistan-into-the-next-sri-lanka/?sh=684aa64a4cc7

the all-weather friendship and all-round cooperation between China and Pakistan."[11] Since Pakistan has no way out, there is no doubt that their alliance will not be broken without Pakistan giving up some of its sovereignty.

Xi Jinping quoted an Urdu poem to describe his affinity for Pakistan, "My friend's lovely image dwells in the mirror of my heart; I tilt my head slightly, and here it comes into my sight."[12] Xi reminded the Pakistanis that his special friendship is a historical choice, deeply rooted in the hearts of the two peoples, who have always extended a helping hand to each other in times of need.

---

11 Xi Jinping, "Building a China-Pakistan Community of Shared Destiny to Pursue Closer Win-Win Cooperation," *Ministry of Foreign Affairs of the People's Republic of China*, April 21, 2015, https://www.fmprc.gov.cn/mfa_eng/wjdt_665385/zyjh_665391/t1257158.shtml

12 Xinhua, "6 Years On, Xi's Pakistan Visit Booms Development, Friendship with Shared Future," *Xinhua Net*, April 19, 2021, http://www.xinhuanet.com/english/2021-04/19/c_139891385.htm

Xi describes how Pakistanis will learn Mandarin and cooperate in education and media, explaining that the friendship is a "pacesetter for amicable relations between countries".[13]

Over the years, thanks to the nurturing of generations of leaders and people from all sectors of both countries, China-Pakistan friendship has flourished like a tree growing tall and strong," Now younger generations have taken over the relay baton of exchanges. The Chinese education sector has welcomed an increasing number of Pakistani students, while more and more people in Pakistan are learning Chinese. Besides, there have also been closer cooperation between sister cities, media outlets and think tanks from both countries. During the state visit six years ago, Xi noted that the friendship between China and Pakistan is based on trust and mutual support.

President Xi's Speech at the 2021 World Economic Forum[14]

President Xi's speech to the World Economic Forum is quintessential Chinese Communist Party (CCP) rhetoric. Xi stated, "We should stay committed to keeping up with the times instead of rejecting change. Now is the time for major development and major transformation."[15] The country that benefitted the most from the virus that came from China is China. There is no question as to why China might want this 'success' to continue.

Xi commented, "We should stay committed to international law and international rules, instead of seeking one's own supremacy."[16] This statement comes from the country that violates the United Nations Convention on the Law of the Sea every day in the South China Sea and elsewhere. This statement comes from the country that violates the U.N. Convention against Torture and Other Cruel, Inhuman or Degrading Treatment or Punishment[17] with its concentration camps in Xinjiang Province, including abductions, torture, rapes, and killings. China's persecution of the Uyghur Muslims raised the alarm in the UNCHR, a body that China requested to join for greater influence.[18]

Xi continued, "We need to deliver on the Paris Agreement on climate change and promote green development."[19] In 2020, China increased its coal power capacity more than three times all other countries in the world combined or "the equivalent of more than one large coal plant per week. In addition, over 73 gigawatts (G.W.) of new coal power projects

---

13 Xinhua, "6 Years On, Xi's Pakistan Visit Booms Development, Friendship with Shared Future," *Xinhua Net*, April 19, 2021, http://www.xinhuanet.com/english/2021-04/19/c_139891385.htm

14 Xi Jinping, "Let the Torch of Multilateralism Light Up Humanity's Way Forward," *World Economic Forum*, January 25, 2021, https://weforum.ent.box.com/s/7p4cs71tyy60yjbkbelomf02j83cgwor

15 Ibid.

16 Ibid.

17 United Nations Human Rights Office of the High Commissioner, "Convention Against Torture and Other Cruel, Inhuman or Degrading Treatment or Punishment," *United Nations Human Rights Office of the High Commissioner*, December 10, 1984, https://www.ohchr.org/en/professionalinterest/pages/cat.aspx

18 United Nations Human Rights Council, "Human Rights Council Concludes its General Debate on Human Rights Situations that Require the Council's Attention," *United Nations Human Rights Council,* March 13, 2019, https://www.ohchr.org/EN/HRBodies/HRC/Pages/NewsDetail.aspx?NewsID=24322&LangID=EE

19 Xi Jinping, "Let the Torch of Multilateralism Light Up Humanity's Way Forward," *World Economic Forum*, January 25, 2021, https://weforum.ent.box.com/s/7p4cs71tyy60yjbkbelomf02j83cgwor

were initiated in China, five times as much as in all other countries, while construction permits for new coal projects accelerated."[20] Xi explained in the same breath, "The earth is our one and only home. To scale up efforts to address climate change and promote sustainable development, bears on the future of humanity."

Proceeding to share in the global community's cooperative efforts, Xi said, we must "adhere to mutual respect and accommodation, and enhance political trust through strategic communication. It is important that we stick to the cooperation concept based on mutual benefit, say no to narrow-minded, selfish beggar-thy-neighbor policies, and stop unilateral practice of keeping advantages in development all to oneself."[21] During 2020, China violated its agreement with Britain regarding Hong Kong, invaded India and killed Indian soldiers, built a Chinese village inside Bhutan, and claimed or took territory from more than a dozen other countries without dialogue.

President Xi stated in his speech that countries sought "stronger representation and voice in global economic governance. We should recognize that with the growth of developing countries, global prosperity and stability will be put on a more solid footing, and developed countries will stand to benefit from such growth."[22] This statement is on the backdrop of China blocking India's bid for permanent representation on the U.N. Security

---

20 Centre for Research on Energy and Clean Air, "China Dominates 2020 Coal Plant Development," *Centre for Research on Energy and Clean Air,* February, 2021, https://globalenergymonitor.org/wp-content/uploads/2021/02/China-Dominates-2020-Coal-Development.pdf

21 Xi Jinping, "Let the Torch of Multilateralism Light Up Humanity's Way Forward," *World Economic Forum,* January 25, 2021, https://weforum.ent.box.com/s/7p4cs71tyy60yjbkbelomf02j83cgwor

22 Ibid.

Council.[23] With the second largest country in population, this representation should be reasonable.

Conclusion

President Xi states there should be no exceptionalism on the international stage while declaring his country's exceptionalism. He says that laws should not be distorted while militarizing islands in other states' Exclusive Economic Zones. China violates World Trade Organization rules by manipulating its currency and subsidizing its products, sometimes below its own production cost.

During President Xi's 2021 World Economic Forum speech, he said, "The strong should not bully the weak. Decision should not be made by simply showing off strong muscles or waving a big fist."[24] By putting one state after another in debt to it and coercing states to act upon Beijing's will, he is the bully in the room.

What's at Stake?

First, "Xi Jinping warned that one civilization forcing itself on another would be 'stupid' and 'disastrous'."[25] The irony is that China travels to all ends of the planet to foist its Belt and Road Initiative on 140 countries that have signed on to take loans. The 'force' President Xi referred to is that of the United States, though Beijing's actions speak louder than words.

Second, misrepresentations of BRI contracts hype valuable property, sound infrastructure, and investments that will turn a significant profit for countries are the most notable examples of doublespeak, exemplified in dozens of examples in this book.

Third, President Xi's sales pitches are exemplary, combined with the fact that state leaders continue to take China's money while putting their country in perilous debt. It is hard to comprehend.

---

23 Shishir Gupta, "China is Biggest Stumbling Block in India's UNSC Permanent Membership," *Hindustan Times*, Updated November 19, 2020, https://www.hindustantimes.com/india-news/china-is-biggest-stumbling-block-in-india-s-unsc-permanent-membership/story-yTpTstOwjEY7vYz5t2NiNN.html

24 Xi Jinping, "Let the Torch of Multilateralism Light Up Humanity's Way Forward," *World Economic Forum*, January 25, 2021, https://weforum.ent.box.com/s/7p4cs71tyy60yjbkbelomf02j83cgwor

25 Liu Zhen and Teddy Ng, "Chinese President Xi Jinping Warns of Disaster if One Civilisation Imposes its Will on Another," *South China Morning Post*, May 15, 2019, https://www.scmp.com/news/china/diplomacy/article/3010287/cultural-superiority-stupid-and-disastrous-chinese-president

Part 2
Corridors

The Corridors of the Belt and Road Initiative

China's Belt and Road Initiative spans the globe. Its specially tailored corridors traverse all of Eurasia with a vast network of roads, trains, energy pipelines, economic zones, and infrastructure development. It aims to connect the continent for access along its New Silk Road. Furthermore, with China at the helm, its products can quickly reach large markets. Beijing's plan is to replace the dollar with the RMB, keeping all countries on board with strict control through loans the countries cannot pay back, with terms containing severe penalties for noncompliance.

The China-Pakistan-Economic-Corridor is China's flagship transportation link, a more than $60 billion dollar project connecting China's Xinjiang Province with China's port city of Gwadar. Combined with highways, railways, digital communications, pipelines, and mining projects, Chinese inspired, designed, and constructed Pakistan industrial zones create economic opportunity areas and energy plants connected to its cities. Further, China stands to benefit substantially by carving out a route to the Arabian Sea and the Indian Ocean, that bypasses the Strait of Malacca to transport oil and natural gas going to China and manufactured products coming from China heading to the Middle East, Africa, and Europe.

Seeking alternative routes to Southeast Asia, South Asia, and Europe, China also created northern, southern, and central corridors across Eurasia as well as those to India and Singapore. Bottlenecks, like the Strait of Malacca and Suez Canal, thwart China's progress, which has pushed China's landlocked provinces to find new and more efficient routes. For example, Myanmar offers routes to the Indian Ocean transporting Chinese goods from Kunming to Mandalay and then on to either Yangoon or Kyaukphyu. However, like other dangers in BRI projects, these transit routes are fraught with turmoil, for example Myanmar's 2021 military coup.

China seeks to protect its trillion-dollar investment through security operations and military relationships in each country, many threatened by terrorism and disturbances. In a massive effort in Xinjiang Province, the CCP has taken Uyghur Muslims from their homes, put them on train cars, and imprisoned them in re-education, factory, concentration camps. Additionally, with terrorist activities in some countries, China has forced BRI signatories to provide police security details as well, like Pakistan's 'Special Security Division'.

There is no doubt that these regions needed reliable roads, bridges, and trains. The question is at what cost to the country and to China.

Chapter 1
China and the Stans
Highways, Railroads, and Ports

Introduction

The suffix, "-stan" means "land of", "place of", or "where one stands" in Persian and Urdu. Each of The 'Stans' is a collection of societies of historic groups. One of 'The Stans', not included at this time, is East Turkestan. In 1884, the Manchu Empire annexed East Turkestan in a bloody, grueling war, calling the territory Xinjiang, meaning "New Frontier." Seven countries now make up 'The Stans' - Afghanistan, Kazakhstan, Kyrgyzstan, Pakistan, Tajikistan, Turkmenistan, and Uzbekistan.

Central Asia's Former Soviet States

Kazakhstan, Kyrgyzstan, Tajikistan, Turkmenistan, and Uzbekistan were former republics of the Soviet Union. As neighbors, they have a shared history, communist background, and Turkish language foundation (though there are variations). These countries have intra-regional trade relations, though the regimes are often incompatible with partially closed borders and political tensions with Afghanistan.[1] Central Asia, as these five countries are often called, is considered a single region, though the countries differ in cultural and ethnic composition. Their infrastructures vary with often incompatible roadways and railways to airways, seaways, waterways, and pipelines carrying oil, gas, and water.[2]

Although Kazakhstan and Turkmenistan are upper middle-income economies and Kyrgyzstan, Tajikistan, and Uzbekistan are lower middle income economies, their economic systems are challenged in that they have not transitioned to market economies, resulting in commodity-based economics rocked by fluctuations in prices. Furthermore, since these landlocked countries (except for the Caspian Sea) were Soviet republics, their infrastructure connections were to and through Russia, which means that they continue to lack connectivity to major markets to the east, south, and west. Thus, China's Belt and Road Initiative (BRI) offered an intriguing opportunity to get no-questions-asked infrastructure loans so that these countries could connect to the rest of the world.

'Stan' Railway Infrastructure

Turkmenistan's transportation infrastructure is the fastest developing sector of its national economy, including roadways, railways, airways, seaways, waterways, oil, gas and water pipelines. In sharp contrast, the government of Kyrgyzstan's railway network, "Kyrgyz Railways"[3] has been neglected, due to a focus on more pressing issues such as road infrastructure.

---

1   Uuriintuya Batsaikhan and Marek Dabrowski, "Central Asia – Twenty-Five Years After the Breakup of the USSR," *Russian Journal of Economics 3*, no. 3 (2017): 296-320, https://www.sciencedirect.com/science/article/pii/S2405473917300429

2   Manoj Sharma, "5 Commonly Used Transport Modes," *Your Article Library*, n.d., https://www.yourarticlelibrary.com/geography/transportation/5-commonly-used-transport-modes/49185

3   Emil Avdaliani, "China Pushes on with Central Asia Trade Ambitions Despite Missing Kyrgyz Rail Link," *Intellinews,* August 15, 2020, https://www.intellinews.com/china-pushes-on-with-central-asia-trade-ambitions-despite-missing-kyrgyz-rail-link-189743/?source=azerbaijan

In Kazakhstan, the largest country in Central Asia, rail is the major means of transportation of both people and goods. The Kazakh economy is more dependent on railways than anywhere else globally.[4] In 2013, Kazakhstan constructed another railway to provide China with a new 'silk road'. This route access transports goods from China's Xinjiang Province where intensive development is underway, to European destinations. In return, Kazakh oil is piped to China.[5]

Kazakhstan's railway dependence creates the need for the Kazakh government to ensure that the country's railway systems are efficient and productive. To further improve its rail

---

4   Bolat Nurgaliyev, "China's Belt and Road Initiative: Kazakhstan and Geopolitics," *The Astana Times*, June 3, 2020, https://astanatimes.com/2020/06/chinas-belt-and-road-initiative-kazakhstan-and-geopolitics/

5   Raushan Nurhsayeva, "Kazakhs Launch 'Silk Road' China-Europe Rail Route," *Reuters*, June 10, 2013, https://www.reuters.com/article/us-kazakhstan-railway/kazakhs-launch-silk-road-china-europe-rail-route-idUSBRE9590GH20130610

system, the country integrated the three distinct rail networks, which it inherited when it gained its independence from Russia in 1991. In the Kazakh president's 2020 State of the Nation Address, Kassym-Jomart Tokayev introduced reforms to encourage private-sector investment and to increase Kazakhstan's dependence on cheap goods produced elsewhere.[6]

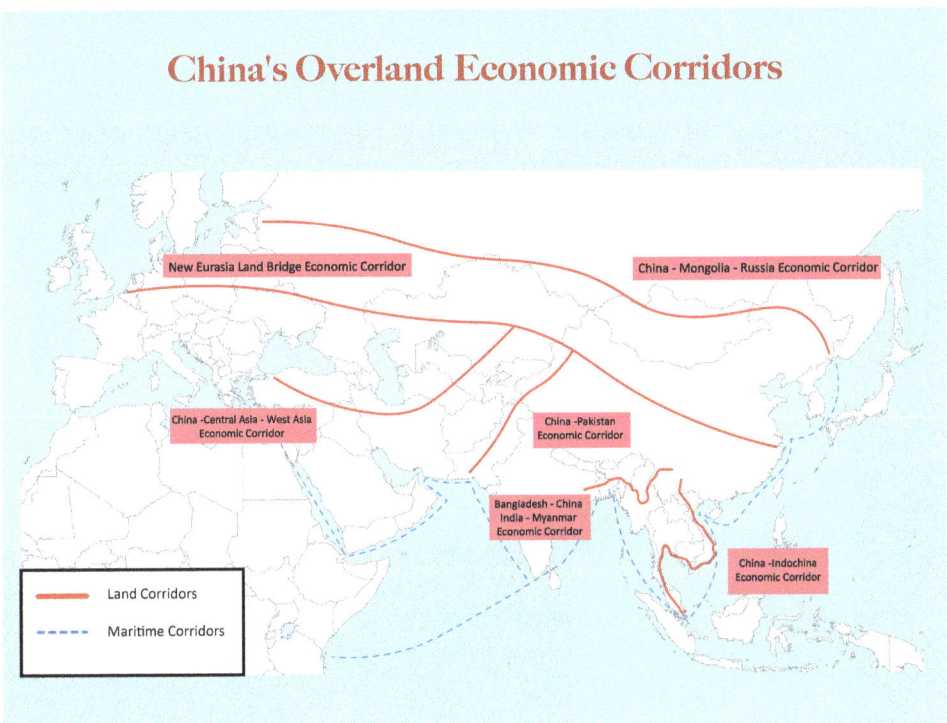

Juxtaposing railway use to a decade ago, or even a year ago, highlights the tremendous growth and development taking place. Transit cargo volume through Kazakhstan increased up to 54 percent from January to June 2020, compared to the previous year, remarked Kazakhstan's Temir Zholy (KTZ) with the national railway company press service. The rail line has a capacity of more than 450,200 twenty-foot containers.[7] Part of this capacity is on the 'silk road' to the Aktau/Aqtau Port on the Caspian Sea. This route through Baku, Azerbaijan supplies the greater Belt and Road supply chain with efficiency and readiness as China's alternative to the Trans-Siberian railway to Central Asian and European markets.[8]

---

6 State of the Nation, "Kazakhstan In A New Reality: Time For Action," *The Astana Times,* September 3, 2020, https://astanatimes.com/2020/09/kazakhstan-in-a-new-reality-time-for-action/

7 Aidana Yergaliyeva, "Cargo Transit Through Kazakhstan Increases 54 Percent Over First Half Year," *The Astana Times*, July 13, 2020, https://astanatimes.com/2020/07/cargo-transit-through-kazakhstan-increases-54-percent-over-first-half-year/

8 Chirs Devonshire-Ellis, "Caspian Developing as Maritime, Haulage, & Rail Hub Between Europe & Asia," *Silk Road Briefing*, August 7, 2020, https://www.silkroadbriefing.com/news/2020/08/06/caspian-developing-as-maritime-haulage-rail-hub-between-europe-asia/

Afghanistan has three railroad lines, each in the northern part of the country, serving as links to neighboring countries. A new rail link along China's Belt and Road connects the city of Herat to the city of Khaf in Iran for both cargo and passengers, the first passenger rail line in Afghanistan.[9] Completed in December 2020, the Khaf-Herat East-West corridor provides China access through Afghanistan to Iran for transport to the Caucasus, Turkey, and Europe.[10]

As a result of the China-Pakistan Economic Corridor (CPEC) projects, Pakistan's railway systems have significantly improved. Before the CPEC projects began, Pakistan's railway system was dilapidated at best. The welcome change has allowed Pakistanis to see their railway systems completely transformed although the impact of the COVID-19 pandemic budget cuts on CPEC projects slowed progress enough for doubts to arise.[11]

Until 2012, there were no railways in Tajikistan. In 2012, the presidents of Tajikistan, Afghanistan, and Iran signed an agreement to construct roads and railways as well as oil, gas, and water pipelines to connect the three countries.[12] The railroad system spans 680 kilometers (420 miles), providing an international freight traffic link to countries outside of Tajikistan's borders.[13]

Uzbekistan heavily depends on rail transport for freight and passenger movement.[14] According to Uzbekistan's Ministry of Investments and Foreign Trade, the new road-rail line offers states a less expensive alternative route that is 295 km shorter than the alternative transport route through Kazakhstan's Horgos and Dostyk border crossing points, reducing delivery times and making the new route more attractive and competitive for businesses.[15]

After more than twenty years of unsuccessful negotiations on the construction of the China–Kyrgyzstan–Uzbekistan railway, Chinese and Uzbekistani officials agreed on a combined road-rail line. Negotiations over the railroad are still ongoing.[16] However, a few

---

9   MENAFN, "Iran, Afghanistan to Complete Border Railway Station Soon," *MENAFN*, October 2, 2020, https://menafn.com/1100894034/Iran-Afghanistan-to-Complete-Border-Railway-Station-Soon

10 Railway Pro, "Iran-Afghanistan Railway Connection Opened," *Railway Pro*, December 16, 2020, https://www.railwaypro.com/wp/iran-afghanistan-railway-connection-opened/

11 Syed Fazl-e Haider, "The Impact of the COVID-19 Pandemic on the China-Pakistan Economic Corridor," *China Brief 20*, no. 13 (2020), https://jamestown.org/program/The-Impact-of-the-COVID-19-Pandemic-on-the-China-Pakistan-Economic-Corridor

12 Tehran Times, "Iran, Afghanistan, Tajikistan Sign Agreement on Road, Railway Construction," *Tehran Times*, March 25, 2012, https://www.tehrantimes.com/news/397760/Iran-Afghanistan-Tajikistan-sign-agreement-on-road-railway

13 Maria Smotrytska, "Belt and Road in Central and East Europe: Roads of Opportunities," *Modern Diplomacy*, October 1, 2020, https://moderndiplomacy.eu/2020/10/01/belt-and-road-in-central-and-east-europe-roads-of-opportunities

14 Asian Development Bank, "Sector Assessment (Summary): Railway Transport," *Asian Development Bank*, n.d., https://www.adb.org/sites/default/files/linked-documents/48025-003-ssa.pdf

15 Ministry of Investments and Foreign Trade of the Republic of Uzbekistan, "The First Block Train Along the China-Kyrgyzstan-Uzbekistan Multimodal Transport Corridor," *Ministry of Investments and Foreign Trade of the Republic of Uzbekistan*, June 9, 2020, https://mift.uz/en/news/the-first-block-train-along-the-china-kyrgyzstan-uzbekistan-multimodal-transport-corridor

16 Podrobno, "China has Proposed Several Options for the Route of the New Uzbekistan-Kyrgyzstan-China Railway," *Podrobno translated into English*, October 14, 2019, https://podrobno.uz/cat/uzbekistan-i-kitay-klyuchi-ot-budushchego/kitay-predlozhil-neskolko-variantov-marshruta-novoy/

days before announcing the launch of the new road-rail transport line, fresh border disputes erupted between Kyrgyzstan and Tajikistan and between Kyrgyzstan and Uzbekistan.[17]

Conclusion

Railway lines serve as a critical transportation opportunity for China to deliver its goods across Eurasia, especially if other countries are paying for the construction equipment, man power, and trains. Along the 'Silk Road' to Europe, particularly after the Suez Canal blockage in March 2021, railways through 'The Stans' offered an important avenue for China's manufactured products.

Violent border clashes between Kyrgyzstan and Uzbekistan on the one hand and border skirmishes with Tajikistan on the other threaten to affect the future of strategically important transport connections along with the promise of bringing prosperity and development to countries within this landlocked region.[18] Any detriment to the development of these railroads will also directly influence the construction of additionally necessary infrastructures in these countries.

What's at Stake?

First, China can claim that having other countries pay for its new thoroughfare is a win-win since the countries also benefit from having new and upgraded lines. However, for China, what is at stake is that violence between countries creates an environment that is not stable or reliable. For other countries who are also footing the bill, they must ensure that they are able to benefit from the high costs of infrastructure development.

Second, 'The Stans' are extremely important on the road to Europe. For China to go across the land route, they need to cross Afghanistan, Kazakhstan, Kyrgyzstan, Pakistan, Tajikistan, Turkmenistan, and Uzbekistan or go through Russia. One way or the other Beijing must work to keep political lines of communications open. However, not all of the citizenry in these countries are in favor of spending billions of dollars on infrastructure projects when they have other pressing needs.

Third, in order to keep friendly relations with each of these countries, there is a constant threat that the Chinese Communist Party (CCP), social media trolls, or Chinese instigators of trouble will involve themselves in the political affairs of 'the Stans'. The CCP aims to ensure that regimes are friendly to China. Involving themselves in foreign countries, advocating the advancement of one power group over another, Beijing seeks to gain political advantage.

---

17 Fozil Mashrab, "China-Kyrgyzstan-Uzbekistan Road-Rail Connection Launched Amid Violent Border Clashes," *Eurasia Daily Monitor 17*, no. 97 (2020), https://jamestown.org/program/china-kyrgyzstan-uzbekistan-road-rail-connection-launched-amid-violent-border-clashes/

18 Ibid.

Chapter 2
Iron Silk Road
Part of the China-Central Asia-West Asia Economic Corridor (CCAWEC)

Introduction

The China-Central Asia-West Asia Economic Corridor (CCAWEC) is a link in China's Belt and Road Initiative (BRI) and its worldwide infrastructure development, manufacturing, and network loan program. CCAWEC is one of the six land routes hallmarking the 2015 BRI announcement. The CCAWEC crosses five Central Asian Countries (Kazakhstan, Kyrgyzstan, Tajikistan, Uzbekistan, and Turkmenistan) as well as the Caucasus, Middle East, and the Balkans, including countries in the Central Corridor, Albania, Armenia, Azerbaijan, Bosnia, Bulgaria, Georgia, Iran, Iraq, Israel, Jordan, Lebanon, Macedonia, Moldova, Montenegro, the Palestinian Authority, Romania, Serbia, Syria, and Turkey.[1][2] In 2019, China Railways Express (CR Express) took its cargo across Eurasia from China (Xian) to Europe (Prague) in eighteen days.[3] Transit ventured out from China through Kazakhstan, Azerbaijan, Georgia, Turkey (through Istanbul's Marmaray Tunnel under the Bosphorus) before arriving in Central Europe.

Joining China with the Arabian Peninsula, the CCAWEC follows the "Silk Road Economic Belt" (SREB). It connects to the "21st Century Maritime Silk Road" (MSR) from China's Xinjiang Uyghur Autonomous Region (XUAR), crossing Central Asia before arriving at the Persian Gulf, the Mediterranean Sea, and the Arabian Peninsula.[4] Though containing valuable resources, economic opportunities, and trade cooperation,[5] numerous social, economic, political, and military variables exist.[6]

China's 'Iron Silk Road'

The 'Iron Silk Road' connects Eurasia in a vast network of rail lines, joining dozens of countries, shortening transport, and providing passenger rail service. Improved travel enhances businesses and facilitates the distribution of products.

The three major corridors are the Northern Corridor, Central Corridor, and Southern Corridor. The Northern Corridor roughly aligns with the Trans-Siberian Railway through Russia. The Central Corridor goes through 'The Stans', around the Caspian and Black Seas, and up into Europe. The Southern Corridor goes around the Himalayas into India, and Pakistan, down to the Arabian Sea, up to Tehran, Iran and across Turkey to Istanbul before connecting to lines bound for Europe. Thus, Iran and Turkey are essential participants with

---

1   PTI, "China Denies Abandoning BCIM Corridor," *India Times*, Updated June 10, 2019, https://timesofindia.indiatimes.com/world/china/china-denies-abandoning-bcim-corridor/articleshow/69728533.cms

2   Ministry of Foreign Affairs of the People's Republic of China, "Joint Communique of the Leaders' Roundtable of the 2nd Belt and Road Forum for International Cooperation," *Ministry of Foreign Affairs of the People's Republic of China*, April 27, 2019, https://www.fmprc.gov.cn/mfa_eng/zxxx_662805/t1658766.shtml

3   OECD, "Chapter 2. The Belt and Road Initiative in the Global Trade, Investment and Finance Landscape," *OEC Business and Finance Outlook* 2018, September 3, 2018, https://www.oecd-ilibrary.org/sites/bus_fin_out-2018-6-en/index.html?itemId=/content/component/bus_fin_out-2018-6-en

4   Current Affairs Correspondent West Asia, "China-Central Asia-West Asia Economic Corridor under Belt & Road," *Belt & Road News*, May 8, 2020, https://www.beltandroad.news/2020/05/08/china-central-asia-west-asia-economic-corridor-under-belt-road/

5   Ibid.

6   Ibid.

significant power in the 'Iron Silk Road'. These two countries are likely to feel emboldened on the international scene and they control the transport of goods across the continents.

This strategic relationship with Iran and Turkey is one reason why China is likely to work closely with Tehran and Ankara, giving them a bigger voice on the world stage while controlling what they say and with whom they partner. This relationship is also why China is likely to ensure that these governments remain in firm control and are loyal to Beijing. As such, Erdogan is unlikely to speak out again about the concentration camps in Xinjiang Province, even though he previously called China's persecution of the Uyghur Muslims 'acts of genocide'. Note, the people being tortured and persecuted are of Turkish descent.

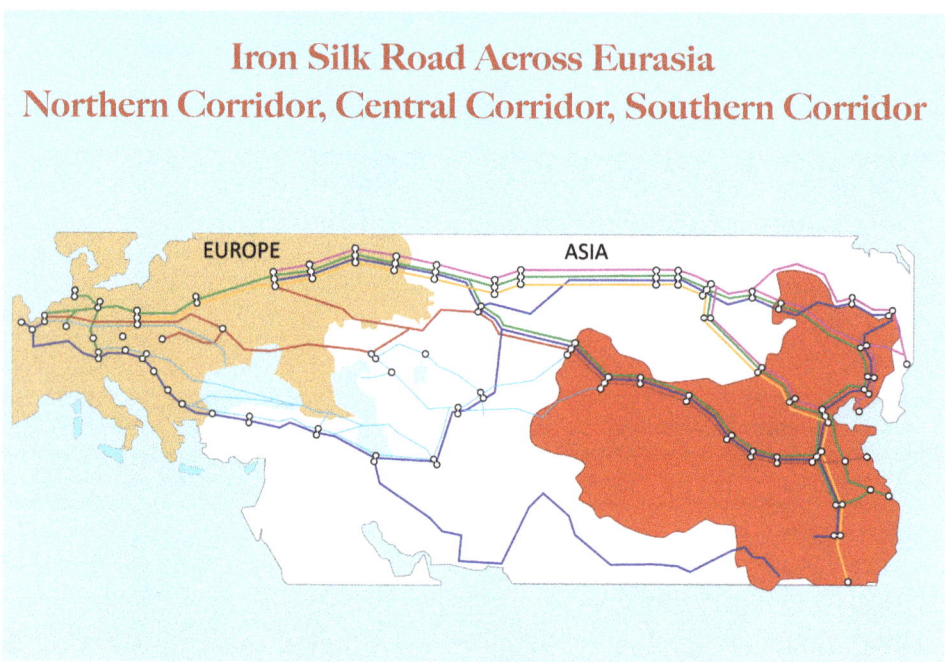

Baku-Tbilisi-Kars (BTK)

Part of the 'Iron Silk Road' is the Baku–Tbilisi–Kars (BTK) railroad connecting Azerbaijan, Georgia, and Turkey.[7] The Port of Baku, Azerbaijan, on the Caspian Sea, serves as a railroad head for this project. A feature writer for the Turkish paper, *Hurriyet*, explained that the railroad line consolidates the BRI while testing Russia along this essential passageway from China to Europe.[8] The China Railways Express (CR Express) offers

---

7   Daily Sabah, "First Train from China to Europe makes 'Silk Railway' Dream Come True in Turkey," *Daily Sabah*, November 7, 2019, https://www.dailysabah.com/business/2019/11/06/first-train-from-china-to-europe-makes-silk-railway-dream-come-true-in-turkey

8   Mustafa Aydin, "The 'Iron Silk Road'," *Hurriyet Daily News,* November 9, 2017, http://www.hurriyetdailynews.com/opinion/mustafa-aydin/the-iron-silk-road-122150

significant economic opportunity, though its benefits have not been realized. While the project was slated to be completed by 2010, year-after-year delays extended the date for the first operational freight train to 2017 and passenger service from Baku to Kars to 2021.

The promise of economic gains has enticed countries to join in on the BRI project. National leaders appreciate that infrastructure advancement can have a long-term benefit, although the political and financial risks are equally significant. However, for China, the CR Express offers numerous benefits, ensuring safe passage for its goods while leaving the railway costs to the borrowing countries.

Emboldening Turkey's Leadership: A Key Link

Turkey is one of approximately 140 nations included in the mix of China's BRI's financial, business, and political arrangements. China, meanwhile, is expanding its businesses, connecting people, and resuscitating the antiquated Silk Road. Initially, Turkey vacillated in its acceptance of loan guarantees while speaking out against China's concentration camps, calling what Erdogan saw in Xinjiang Province "genocide".[9] However, Xi Jinping was ultimately able to find a price point for Turkish President Recep Tayyip Erdogan's silence.[10] China could even offer Erdogan enough money in projects, power, and infrastructure to extradite Uyghur people of Turkish heritage back to China to be imprisoned, persecuted, and tortured.[11]

China's money and power expedited development activities like the Trans-Caspian East-West-Middle Corridor (Central Corridor), starting from China, going through Central Asia (Kazakhstan or Kyrgyzstan-Uzbekistan-Turkmenistan), crossing the Caspian Sea, and proceeding through Azerbaijan and Georgia toward Turkey. The Central Corridor covers the China-Central Asia-West Asia (CCAWEC) street and rail transportation network, intersecting with the Caspian Sea. Central Asian nations stand to profit by the China-Europe exchange by getting their products to markets in a way that was never before possible. The only caveat is that they must pay for the infrastructure using borrowed money.

To this end, Turkey signed a Memorandum of Understanding (MOU) with China in November 2015, connecting Turkey to the Central Corridor of the BRI. In July 2017, President Erdogan visited China to gain ground in coordinating the BRI through his country, marking a Common Cooperation Protocol and setting up a Coordination Council with Azerbaijan and the Central Asian Republics. The Lapis Lazuli - Transport Corridor Agreement - was inked by Turkey, Georgia, Azerbaijan, Turkmenistan, and Afghanistan as a provincial collaboration.[12]

Presented as a project that would offer immense possibilities, the Baku-Tbilisi-Kars (BTK) railroad was initiated to convey travelers and payloads. Likewise, Turkey petitioned China for large capital finance undertakings - $1 billion for port construction, $2.1 billion for a coal-fired power plant, a 51% interest in a third Bosphorus bridge, and $5 billion in insurance.[13] All this was promised along with a third nuclear power plant, Chinese military and missiles, communications and surveillance infrastructure, Eurasian Tunnel, and a "China-friendly" Istanbul Airport.[14]

Turkey's railway network plan included the development of the 2000 km Edirne-Kars High-Speed Rail Turkey and three ports, specifically Filyos on the Black Sea, Çandarlı on the Aegean, and Mersin container port on the Eastern Mediterranean, though progress has

---

9   Kuzzat Altay, "Why Erdogan Has Abandoned the Uyghurs," *Foreign Policy*, March 2, 2021, https://foreignpolicy.com/2021/03/02/why-erdogan-has-abandoned-the-uyghurs/

10 Aykan Erdemir and Philip Kowalski, "China Buys Turkey's Silence on Uyghur Oppression," *The Diplomat*, August 21, 2020, https://thediplomat.com/2020/08/china-buys-turkeys-silence-on-uyghur-oppression/

11 Palki Sharma, "Why Erdogan Has Decided to Extradite Uighurs to China," *WION*, July 27, 2020, https://www.wionews.com/world/why-erdogan-has-decided-to-extradite-uighurs-to-china-316326

12 Shoaib Ahmad Rahim, "The Geopolitics of the Lapis Lazuli Corridor," *The Diplomat*, December 22, 2017, https://thediplomat.com/2017/12/the-geopolitics-of-the-lapis-lazuli-corridor/

13 Sinan Tavsan, "Turkish Sovereign Wealth Fund Courts China's Belt and Road," *NIKKEI Asia*, August 12, 2020, https://asia.nikkei.com/Editor-s-Picks/Interview/Turkish-sovereign-wealth-fund-courts-China-s-Belt-and-Road

14 Ayca Alemdaroglu and Sultan Tepe, "Erdogan is Turning Turkey into a Chinese Client State," *Foreign Policy*, September 16, 2020, https://foreignpolicy.com/2020/09/16/erdogan-is-turning-turkey-into-a-chinese-client-state/

been slow.[15] After the pandemic caused a precipitous drop in the Turkish lira's value and a currency shortage, Beijing offered more loans and the use of the Chinese yuan to make payments to aid in facilitating China-Turkey financial cooperation.[16]

Turkey's support for the Central Corridor is essential for China. For Turkey, this additional money puts Erdogan under Beijing's thumb while opening Ankara to the East, including the Caucasus, Central Asia, and China, and boosting exchange. The Corridor puts Turkey at a strategic intersection between Europe and Asia to outcompete the

Iron Silk Road
Beauty, Opportunity, and Danger Along China's Eurasian Railroad

---

15 M. Sait Akman, "Turkey's Middle Corridor and Belt and Road Initiative: Coherent or Conflicting?," *Italian Institute for International Political Studies,* November 28, 2019, https://www.ispionline.it/en/publication/turkeys-middle-corridor-and-belt-and-road-initiative-coherent-or-conflicting-24526

16 Ayca Alemdaroglu and Sultan Tepe, "Erdogan is Turning Turkey into a Chinese Client State," *Foreign Policy,* September 16, 2020, https://foreignpolicy.com/2020/09/16/erdogan-is-turning-turkey-into-a-chinese-client-state/

Northern Passage through Russia and Southern Passage through Iran. At long last, Turkey can diminish Russia's impact on its security.[17]

CCAWEC Central Corridor

The Central Corridor relies on coordination with China's BRI states' local activity and is not yet as strong as the Northern Corridor.[18] Central Corridor products are moved through land and sea without stable national control systems, frequent in-fighting, and limited public conventions. The Caspian Sea crossing also requires collaboration among neighboring nations.

The China-Central Asia-West Asia Economic Corridor (CCAWEC) is pivotal in China's plan to build infrastructure and dominate markets throughout Eurasia. Along this route, countries like Kazakhstan, Azerbaijan, Iran, and Turkey play prominent roles. Additionally, the Caspian Sea is central to the BRI's CCAWEC plan, with the Kazakh port of Aktau and the Azerbaijani port of Baku. China's additional infrastructure investment in the Azerbaijani port of Baku supports the alternative route from Turkmenistan's Turkmenbashi seaport to Baku's transportation hub.[19] China's investment and the Baku-Tbilisi-Kars (BTK) railway make Azerbaijan a vital component of Beijing's plan to transport Chinese goods.[20]

Numerous countries along the CCAWEC corridor have prospered from the loans offered by Beijing emissaries. Though these loans will have to be repaid, and the debt may stranglehold these nations, significant infrastructure improvements have transformed these countries from decades behind to cutting-edge partnerships in the global supply chain.

Conclusion

The CCAWEC is integral to Beijing's merchandise and resource transport to Europe. This undertaking will significantly increase Beijing's income and ability to loan more money and build its income, assets, and military. Though in 2021, the predominant transport mechanism is conveyed via ocean, and will probably remain that way through 2025, land choices could widely reduce transportation expenses. Meanwhile, China uses Chinese language studies in schools, Chinese television programming, and anti-Western shows to increase its popularity in Central Asia.

Maintaining a smart, strong, and supportive persona is essential to China's Central

---

17 M. Sait Akman, "Turkey's Middle Corridor and Belt and Road Initiative: Coherent or Conflicting?," *Italian Institute for International Political Studies,* November 28, 2019, https://www.ispionline.it/en/publication/turkeys-middle-corridor-and-belt-and-road-initiative-coherent-or-conflicting-24526

18 Ibid.

19 Bai Lianlei, "Azerbaijan in the Silk Road Economic Belt: A Chinese Perspective," *Caucasus International* 6, no. 1 (2016), jrn2016_541.pdf (elibrary.az)

20 Reza Yeganehshakib, "The Baku-Tbilisi-Kars Railroad: Peace & Prosperity Through the Revival of the Silk Roads," *Silk Road Briefing*, April 15, 2019, https://www.silkroadbriefing.com/news/2019/04/15/baku-tbilisi-kars-railroad-peace-prosperity-revival-silk-roads/

BRI Corridor, which relies heavily on local conditions and international events.[21] However, China does not depend on one avenue for its success; rather it relies on differentiated arrangements to achieve its objectives. Mining and energy ventures and port projects in Haifa, Israel; Piraeus, Greece; Trieste, Italy; and the Kumkapi Port in Istanbul, Turkey; have made this corridor a regional center point.

Additional ports are slated in Filyos, Çandarli, and Mersin. The Russian impact in the Northern Corridor is another major political obstacle. Turkey's local and international strategies particularly towards China will be significant variables for its fate.[22]

Dramatic political changes can and do take place. President Erdogan was once an anathema to China, pointing out China's persecution and genocide of the Uyghur Muslims of Turkic heritage. While Turkey called on boycotts of Chinese goods and accepting Uyghur exiles in 2009, Erdogan said, "The incidents in China are, simply put, a genocide. There is no point in interpreting this otherwise."[23] In 2016, Erdogan began arresting Uyghurs in the hundreds and deporting them back to be tortured in Chinese concentration camps.

China has used this BRI investment opportunity to incorporate its surveillance systems and telecommunications monitoring into these countries with Huawei and ZTE technologies. These systems allow governments to suppress any dissension by providing strict controls over digitized media, military, transport, and national health data. Furthermore, by accessing China's cash, Erdogan does not need to present Turkey's borrowing proposals to the International Monetary Fund (IMF), World Bank, European Union (EU), or other Western institutions that may ask him to be more prudent with its loans.

What's at Stake?

First, the CCAWEC offers China greater access to transport its cheap goods to European markets along with opportunities to increase its income. The more money China can make from its forced labor in its hundreds of concentration camps, the more Beijing can impose its will on its people while also investing in its military.

Second, countries that are unable to pay back China's massive loans are undeniably indebted to China. If repayment terms are not met, these countries will live under Beijing's thumb, kowtowing to the CCP's demands.

Third, by installing Huawei and ZTE software and technologies, China can impose more pressure, deeper surveillance, and social control. Authoritarian leaders and Beijing will therefore be able to tighten control on citizens throughout Central Asia.

---

21 M. Sait Akman, "Turkey's Middle Corridor and Belt and Road Initiative: Coherent or Conflicting?," *Italian Institute for International Political Studies*, November 28, 2019, https://www.ispionline.it/en/publication/turkeys-middle-corridor-and-belt-and-road-initiative-coherent-or-conflicting-24526

22 Ibid.

23 Reuters, "Turkish Leader Calls Xinjiang Killings 'Genocide,'" *Reuters*, July 10, 2009, https://www.reuters.com/article/us-turkey-china-sb/turkish-leader-calls-xinjiang-killings-genocide-idUSTRE56957D20090710

Chapter 3
China-Pakistan Economic Corridor

China's Direct Access Port to the Persian Gulf

Introduction

In 1950, when Pakistan officially ended its relations with the Republic of China (ROC - Taiwan), the People's Republic of China (PRC) on Mainland China prioritized the maintenance of a close and steady relationship.[1] China and Pakistan established official relations on May 21, 1951, and celebrated its 50th anniversary in 2001 with colorful celebrations in the two countries.[2] On March 21, 2002, China and Pakistan met for a groundbreaking ceremony to develop the Gwadar deep-sea port project presided over by President Pervez Musharraf.

Pakistan serves as China's primary link to the Islamic world. In 1972, Pakistan played a significant role in crossing over the communication deficit between the PRC and the West by encouraging U.S. President Richard Nixon's noteworthy 1972 visit to China.[3] Over time, Pakistan's relationship grew closer to China. In 2011, the Pakistani Prime Minister called China his country's 'best friend'.[4] The PRC has given financial, military, and specialized help to Pakistan, and each nation considers the other a nearby vital ally.[5,6]

Close Ties and Friendship

The relations between Pakistan and China have been portrayed by Pakistan's diplomat to China as "higher than the mountains, more profound than the seas, more grounded than steel, dearer than visual perception, better than nectar."[7]

According to Stockholm International Peace Research Institute, Pakistan is China's largest arms purchaser. Almost 47% of Chinese arms exports go to Pakistan.[8] According to a 2014 *BBC World* Service Poll, 75% of Pakistanis see China's impact as a welcome event, with only 15% communicating a negative viewpoint. In the Asia-Pacific region, Chinese individuals hold the third-best assessments of Pakistan's impact on the planet, behind Indonesia and China itself.[9] Pakistan has been one of China's significant exchange partners.

---

1 Salman Masood, "Pakistan President to Visit China, a Valued Ally," *The New York Times,* October 13, 2008, https://www.nytimes.com/2008/10/13/world/asia/13pstan.html

2 China Daily, "China-Pakistan Relations," *China Daily,* Updated November 14, 2006, http://www.chinadaily.com.cn/china/2006-11/14/content_732562.htm

3 Yoav J. Tenembaum, "Kissinger's Visit, 40 Years On," *The Diplomat,* July 8, 2011, https://thediplomat.com/2011/07/kissingers-visit-40-years-on/

4 BBC News, "Pakistani PM Hails China as his Country's 'Best Friend'," *BBC News,* May 17, 2011, https://www.bbc.co.uk/news/world-south-asia-13418957

5 Steven Jiang, "Pakistan Cements China Ties Amid Tension with U.S.," *CNN,* May 17, 2011, http://edition.cnn.com/2011/WORLD/asiapcf/05/17/china.pakistan.friend/

6 People's Daily Online, "China, Pakistan Joined in Bonds of Brotherhood," *People's Daily Online,* May 18, 2011, http://english.peopledaily.com.cn/90001/90776/90883/7384378.html

7 The Economist, "Pakistan and China, Sweet As Can Be?," *The Economist,* May 14, 2011, http://www.economist.com/node/18682839

8 Siemon T. Wezeman and Pieter D. Wezeman, "Trends in International Arms Transfers, 2013," *Stockholm International Peace Research Institute,* 2013, https://web.archive.org/web/20140317170940/http://books.sipri.org/product_info?c_product_id=475

9 BBC World Service POLL, "Negative Views of Russia on the Rise: Global Poll," *GlobeScan,* June 3, 2014, http://www.globescan.com/images/images/pressreleases/bbc2014_country_ratings/2014_country_rating_poll_bbc_globescan.pdf

With the China-Pakistan Economic Corridor, Xinjiang Province is the most affected. This vital project links Kashgar city (free economic zone) in landlocked Xinjiang Province with the Pakistan port of Gwadar, a deep-water port used for commercial and military purposes.

Pakistan is involved regionally with the Economic Co-operation Organization (ECO): Afghanistan, Azerbaijan, Iran, Kazakhstan, Kyrgyzstan, Pakistan, Tajikistan, Turkey, Turkmenistan, and Uzbekistan and the South Asian Association of Regional Co-operation (SAARC): Bangladesh, India, Pakistan, Maldives, Nepal and Sri Lanka.

Challenges for China and Pakistan to Overcome

Of the 122 announced CPEC projects, 32 were completed by May 2021. That development is part of the 15-year infrastructure plan costing $87 billion,[10] (one-fourth of Pakistan's entire GDP) which in total is estimated at 284 billion in 2021.[11] With 15,000 Chinese workers, a 1,200-mile rail line, ports, airport, roads, coal, solar, and wind, the transportation network stretches from China's forced labor camps in Xinjiang to the port city Gwadar.[12] Originally, the entire CPEC project was estimated at $46 billion.

In March 2021, the Council on Foreign Relations described stalled projects, corruption, terrorist attacks, and Chinese contractors overcharging Islamabad by $3 billion, and large kickbacks to Chinese investors.[13] Meanwhile, the returns China originally estimated never materialized. Pakistan's expected riches mirrored the failed promises China made about returns on Sri Lanka's port investment that never appeared. The Gwadar commercial shipping and Lahore metro investments are not viable. Mired by losses, Pakistan is deeply in debt and sought bailout support from the International Monetary Fund (IMF). Shockingly, the IMF has bailed out Pakistan twenty-two times, the last time in 2020.

China's Assertion of Pakistani Military Control on CPEC Projects

China took strict control over CPEC and Pakistan by acquiring a retired Pakistani general to militarily oversee the project. In 2021, he engaged the Pakistani army, silenced critics of China's genocide of the Xinjiang Muslims, quieted anger over the economic downturn, and dispeled criticism of the accumulating, overwhelming debt. Furthermore, with China's surveillance apparatus and fiber-optic communications equipment, China can better manage and crackdown on critics, sever civil liberties, and institute Chinese socialist

---

10 Jonathan E. Hillman, "The China-Pakistan Economic Corridor at Five," *CSIS*, April 2, 2020, https://www.csis.org/analysis/china-pakistan-economic-corridor-five

11 International Monetary Fund, "World Economic Outlook Database October 2020," *International Monetary Fund*, October 2020, https://www.imf.org/en/Publications/WEO/weo-database/2020/October/weo-report

12 Rafiq Dossani and Niels Erich, "China's Field of Dreams in Pakistan," *The RAND Blog*, October 16, 2017, https://www.rand.org/blog/2017/10/chinas-field-of-dreams-in-pakistan.html

13 David Sacks, "The China-Pakistan Economic Corridor – Hard Reality Greets BRI's Signature Initiative," *Council on Foreign Relations*, March 30, 2021, https://www.cfr.org/blog/china-pakistan-economic-corridor-hard-reality-greets-bris-signature-initiative

government and internet social control.¹⁴ With a Pakistani general in command of CPEC, China intends to make sure no voices are heard regarding Beijing's genocide of the Uyghur Muslims. Additionally, China is attempting to surround India with its military bases in Sri Lanka, Pakistan, Bangladesh, and possibly with support from the leaders of the military coup in Myanmar.

Military and mechanical exchanges foreshadow the financial link between the two countries. China has promised to expand its interest in Pakistan's economy and infrastructure.¹⁵ Opening the China-Pakistan Economic Corridor (CPEC) increases China's access to ports in a shortened access route to the Arabian Sea and onward to the Suez Canal.

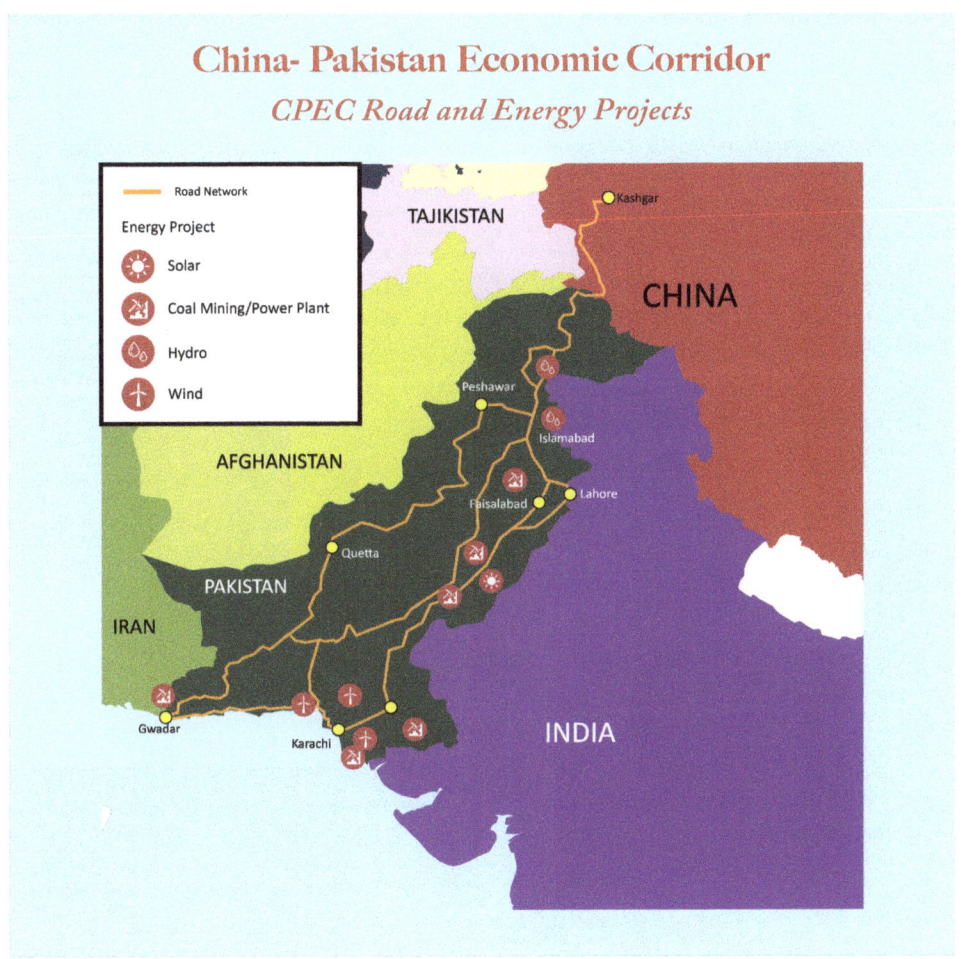

---

14 David Sacks, "The China-Pakistan Economic Corridor – Hard Reality Greets BRI's Signature Initiative," *Council on Foreign Relations*, March 30, 2021, https://www.cfr.org/blog/china-pakistan-economic-corridor-hard-reality-greets-bris-signature-initiative

15 Inpaper Magazine, "Top Ten Trading Partners," *Dawn*, January 15, 2012, http://www.dawn.com/news/688389/top-ten-trading-partners

The China-Pakistan Economic Corridor's network. has the potential to impact Iran, Afghanistan, India, and the Central Asian Republics with improved road, rail, and air transportation infrastructure. Free trade development and enhanced communication through academic, cultural, and organizational upgrades promise a win-win model for a shared fate, congruity, and advancement. Furthermore, in Pakistan, China plans to integrate its digital monetary system for Beijing's ascendance in the globalized world.

CPEC Investment Compared to Post-WWII Marshall Plan

CPEC was projected to quickly update Pakistan's infrastructure and fortify its economy by developing present-day transportation, communication, and financial zones. On November 13, 2016, China transported a load overland through CPEC to Gwadar Port on its oceanic shipment to Africa and West Asia. China's shortened transportation network was enhanced, and Pakistan paid the bill in loans and guarantees.

CPEC has been contrasted with that of the Marshall Plan implemented by the United States in post-war Europe.[16] Pakistani authorities hoped that CPEC would bring about the formation of as many as 2.3 million jobs and add 2 percent to the nation's yearly monetary growth rate. However, Pakistan's actual growth has declined, and only a tiny fraction of those positions have been realized.

ChinaMobile and Huawei have infused Pakistan with China's media communications and surveillance systems, and China Metallurgical Group Corporation (MCC) has taken advantage of Pakistan's mining and mineral resources. Calls for infrastructure development are needed in materials, cloth, concrete, building materials, and horticultural innovations to encourage new markets.

Gwadar Port, Airport, and City Investment

Gwadar is essential in China's Belt and Road Initiative and in its 21st Century Maritime Silk Road.[17] By 2018, more than $1 billion worth of projects were created around Gwadar Port alone. Additionally, China loaned Pakistan $230 million to build another global air terminal in Gwadar. After five years, Gwadar became fully operational in May 2021.

Improvement of Gwadar also includes a loan for a hospital. Additionally, China's venture into Gwadar provides loan money for clinical training, nursing and paramedical establishments, and other unified machinery and offices.[18]

In 2018, Beijing's Communist Party news source, *Xinhua*, announced that China loaned Pakistan additional money for 'sustainable, sweet desalted water'. A "seawater desalination plant was built and inaugurated by the China Overseas Ports Holding

---

16 Tareq Haddad, "Pakistan Builds State-of-the-Art Warships to Defend New Trade Routes with China," *International Business Times*, Updated January 6, 2017, http://www.ibtimes.co.uk/pakistan-builds-state-art-warships-defend-new-trade-routes-china-1599579

17 Shyam Saran, "What China's One Belt and One Road Strategy Means for India, Asia and the World," *The Wire*, September 10, 2015, https://web.archive.org/web/20151118041734/http://thewire.in/2015/10/09/what-chinas-one-belt-and-one-road-strategy-means-for-india-asia-and-the-world-12532/

18 Shahbaz Rana, "Eastern CPEC Route Unfeasible: Report," *The Tribune*, July 25, 2015, http://tribune.com.pk/story/926582/economic-corridor-eastern-cpec-route-unfeasible/

Company (COPHC), the operator of Gwadar port under the China-Pakistan Economic Corridor (CPEC) agreement."[19] The desalination plant at Gwadar will provide millions of gallons of water a day.[20]

Conclusion

China and Pakistan celebrated 70 years of its economic ties in May 2021. While there have been some successes, in January 2021, China attempted to wall off its China-only colony in Gwadar where hundreds of thousands of Chinese people live by creating 12.5 miles of barbed wire fence to keep the Pakistanis out in China's "sealed city".[21] Local Pakistanis became angered by China taking over its city and attempting to wall off the area. It is not only land Pakistan may need to give up.

Saindak Mines
Pakistan's 20-Year Lease to China Metallurgical Group Corporation

---

19 Jamil Bhatti, "Feature: Thirsty Gwadar Enjoys Sustainable, Sweet Desalted Seawater," *Xinhua*, July 13, 2018, http://www.xinhuanet.com/english/2018-07/13/c_137321878.htm

20 Rina Saeed Khan, "Thirsty to Thriving? Parched Pakistani Port Aims to Become a New Dubai," *Reuters*, April 23, 2018, https://www.reuters.com/article/us-pakistan-port-water/thirsty-to-thriving-parched-pakistani-port-aims-to-become-a-new-dubai-idUSKBN1HV07K

21 Keegan Elmer, "China-Pakistan Relations: Security Fence at Gwadar Port Creates New Tensions," *South China Morning Post*, January 2, 2021, https://www.scmp.com/news/china/diplomacy/article/3116180/china-pakistan-relations-security-fence-gwadar-port-creates

Beijing is planning to transfer energy from Pakistan to China through the Karot Hydropower Company as part of the CPEC in a large-scale project on a build-own-operate-transfer basis.[22] The project, estimated to cost USD $2 billion, is being developed by the China Three Gorges South Asia Investment Limited, an investment arm of China Three Gorges Corporation (CTG). Though this power facility will one day be owned by Pakistan, and Pakistan will be able to use the power it generates, that will not happen until Pakistan can pay the money back. Until then, this infrastructure project will be another facility owned by China but inside Pakistan and China will take the energy generated.

Ultimately, Pakistan will have to pay via one way or another. Hiring a Pakistani general and using the Pakistan army to protect Chinese laborers and assets is one way. If Pakistan cannot pay in money, it will pay in some other method. However, it is unlikely that China will leave Pakistan no matter how much the citizens dislike the arrangement or attempt incidents to thwart the projects. Beijing has too much of vested interest.

What's at Stake?

First, in the 1970's when a Chinese engineering firm worked with Pakistan to discover gold, silver, and copper at Saindak mines, China's appetite for metals awakened Beijing to its need to invest. Pakistan leased its mines for twenty years to Metallurgical Corporation of China, a China Metallurgical Group Corporation subsidiary that operates three mines.[23] China's opportunity to take the metals from regional mines helps to fuel its growing desire to build its future on Pakistan's precious metals.

Second, the 2015 launch of the China-Pakistan Economic Corridor led to marriages between young Pakistani women and Chinese businessmen. It was not all happily ever after. After discovering cases of human trafficking of Pakistani teens and Chinese men paying substantial sums to the girls' families, Father Morris Jalal, a Capuchin priest in Lahore, started a social media campaign against such phony marriages. In one case, Pakistani authorities charged 21 Chinese men for a scheme involving prostitution, reeled into the net with fake marriages, and the removal of Pakistani girls' organs for big money organ transplants.[24]

Third, Pakistan owes more money than it can pay. With the pandemic, Pakistan's economy declined. Without cash on hand, it is likely to pay China back by giving up its land, mines, energy, or other concessions. In short, Pakistan is likely to give up its sovereignty.

---

22 OECD Business and Finance Outlook 2018, "China's Belt and Road Initiative in the Global Trade, Investment and Finance Landscape," *OECD Business and Finance Outlook 2018*, 2018, https://www.oecd.org/finance/Chinas-Belt-and-Road-Initiative-in-the-global-trade-investment-and-finance-landscape.pdf

23 Kaleeq Kiani, "Chinese Firm to Retain Control of Saindak Until 2022," *Dawn*, October 27, 2017, https://www.dawn.com/news/1366479

24 Kathy Gannon, "AP Exclusive: 629 Pakistani Girls Sold as Brides to China," *AP*, December 6, 2019, https://apnews.com/article/c586d0f73fe249718ec06f6867b0244e

Project	Category	Location	Dollar Value (US)
2×660MW Coal-fired Power Plants at Port Qasim Karachi	Coal Mining / Power Plant	Port Qasim, Sindh	$1.9B
300MW Imported Coal Based Power Project at Gwadar, Pakistan	Coal Mining / Power Plant	Gwadar	$540M
Allama Iqbal Industrial City, Faisalabad Construction of Breakwaters &	Economic Zone	Faisalabad, Punjab	Unknown
Gwadar Smart Port City Master Plan	Port	Gwadar	$120M
Development of Free Zone	Economic Zone	Gwadar	$32M
Engro 2x330MW Thar Coal Power Project	Coal Mining / Power Plant	Thar-Block-II, Sindh	$1.0B
Gwadar East-Bay Expressway	Highway	Gwadar	$170M
Gwadar Fresh Water Treatment Facility	Fresh Water Treatment Facility	Gwadar	$130M
Gwadar – Turbat – Hoshab (M-8)	Highway	Gwadar to Turbat to Hoshab	$180M
Hakla D.I Khan Motorway	Highway	Hakla to Dera Ghazi Khan, Punjab	$1.7B
Havelian Dry port (450 M. Twenty-Foot Equivalent Units)	Port	Havellian, KPK	$65M
HUBCO Coal Power Project, Hub Balochistan	Coal Mining / Power Plant	Hub	$1.9B
HUBCO Thar Coal Power Project (Thar Energy)	Coal Mining / Power Plant	Thar-Block-II, Sindh	$500M
Hydro China Dawood Wind Farm(Gharo, Thatta)	Wind	Bhanbore, Sindh	$110M
Karachi-Peshawar (ML-1) railroad	Railway	Karachi to Peshawar	$6.8M
Karot Hydropower Station	Hydropower	River Jhelum, dual boundary of Rawalpindi, Punjab and Kotli, AJK	$1.7B
Khuzdar-Basima Road N-30 (110 km)	Highway	Basima to Khudzar	$260M

Project	Category	Location	Dollar Value (US)
KKH Phase II (Thakot-Havelian Section)	Highway	Thakot to Havelan, KPK	$1.3B
Kohala Hydropower Project	Hydropower	Kohala	$2.4B
Matiari to Lahore ±660kV HVDC Transmission Line Project	Power Transmission Line	Matiari, Sindh to Lahore, Punjab	$1.7B
New Gwadar International Airport	Airport	Gwadar	$230M
Orange Line - Lahore	Urban Public Transport	Lahore, Punjab	$1.6B
Pak China Friendship Hospital	Hospital	Gwadar	$100M
Pak-China Technical and Vocational Institute at Gwadar	Vocational and Technical Training Institute	Gwadar	$10M
Pakistan-China Optical Fiber Cable Project	Fiber Optics Cable	Rawalpindi, Punjab to Khunjerab, Gilgit-Baltisan	$44M
Peshawar-Karachi Motorway (Multan-Sukkur Section)	Highway	Karachi to Peshawar, Sindh	$2.9B
Quaid-e-Azam 1000MW Solar Park (Bahawalpur) Quaid-e-Azam	Solar	Bahawalpur, Pubjab	$780M
Rashakai Economic Zone, M-1, Nowshera	Economic Zone	Rashakai, KPK	Unknown
Sachal Wind Farm (Jhimpir, Thatta)	Wind	Jhimpir, District Thatta	$130M
Sahiwal 2x660MW Coal-fired Power Plant, Punjab	Coal Mining / Power Plant	Sahiwal, Punjab	$1.9B
SSRL Thar Coal Block-I 6.8 mtpa & Power Plant(2×660MW) (Shanghai Electric)	Coal Mining / Power Plant	Thar-Block-I, Sindh	$1.9B
Suki Kinari Hydropower Station, Naran, Khyber Pukhtunkhwa	Hydropower	River Kunhar, KPK	$1.7B
Surab-Hoshab (N-85)	Highway	Surab to Hoshab	$240M

Project	Category	Location	Dollar Value (US)
Surface mine in block II of Thar Coal field, 3.8 million tons/year	Coal Mining / Power Plant	Thar-Block-II, Sindh	$630M
ThalNova Thar Coal Power Project	Coal Mining / Power Plant	Thar-Block-II, Sindh	$500M
Three Gorges Second and Third Wind Power Project	Wind	Jhimpir, Sindh	$150M
UEP Wind Farm (Jhimpir, Thatta)	Wind	Jhimpir, Sindh	$250M
Upgradation of D.I.Khan (Yarik) - Zhob, N-50 Phase-I (210 km)	Highway	Yarik, KPK to Zhob	$1.0B
Zhob Quetta (N-50)	Motorway	Zhob to Quetta	$910M

Headlights in the Iron Silk Road Tunnel

Chapter 4
Indochina Peninsula Corridor

Direct Route from China to Singapore

Introduction

China-inspired projects along the China-Indochina Peninsula Economic Corridor (CICPEC) have allowed China to gain a foothold in many Southeast Asian countries. These loans started in 2010 and fused later into the larger Belt and Road Initiative when it was announced in 2013. One of China's rail transport opportunities was formerly referred to as the Nanning-Singapore Economic Corridor. The project, at first, had the potential to connect people between the countries along the coast but with recent events in Southeast Asia, the efforts have slowed. Other projects followed.

Engaging ASEAN in a Free Trade Corridor

The Association of Southeast Asian Nations (ASEAN) is a body of ten countries (Brunei, Cambodia, Indonesia, Laos, Malaysia, Myanmar, the Philippines, Singapore, Thailand, and Vietnam) that meet to consider how they can collaborate and cooperate on issues and projects that impact one another. The proposed thoroughfare was intended to connect neighboring economies and energize improvement over the ASEAN–China Free Trade Area.

Beijing wanted the Southeast Asian states to pay for its transportation and development corridor so that China had high speed access to the south. The countries bought into large BRI loans that they could not pay for and which trapped them into enormous debt. Beijing sought project terms allowing it to hire Chinese labor and to develop corresponding enterprises to connect the Chinese cities of Pingxiang, with Nanning, and Kunming, to Southern cities to the south through three different corridors.

One of the initial steps was the Nanning–Pingxiang fast line, which would frame the northern end of the corridor.[1] A 5000 km Nanning-Singapore rail route was in plans in 2010,[2] but has not yet been completed due to numerous problems along the way.

The China–Indochina Peninsula Economic Corridor, with Pingxiang, Nanning, and Kunming, as the rail head and Singapore as the end, goes through the Indochina Peninsula, transiting six ASEAN partners—Cambodia, Laos, Malaysia, Singapore, Thailand, and Vietnam. The Indochina peninsula, situated in the Southeast Asia subcontinent, and between the Indian Ocean and the Pacific Ocean, has one-of-a-kind points of interest and geologically favorable circumstances. This region has generally been considered the center point connecting the land-based, "Silk Road Economic Belt", ocean-route, "Maritime Silk Road", and sea-based, "Sea Silk Road" together.[3]

China has been working to develop three routes to Singapore. The eastern route is through Hanoi and Ho Chi Minh City, though this thoroughfare is not progressing well due to China's aggressive military acts against Vietnam in the South China Sea. China's

---

1   Railways Africa, "China-Singapore HS," *Railways Africa*, February 7, 2011, http://www.railwaysafrica.com/blog/2011/02/china-singapore-hs/

2   Lan Xinzhen, "Nanning-Singapore Economic Corridor," *Beijing Review*, Updated August 26, 2010, https://web.archive.org/web/20110707014054/http://www.bjreview.com.cn/quotes/txt/2010-08/24/content_293425_2.htm

3   Wang Jinbo, "The China-Indochina Peninsula Economic Corridor," *Routledge Handbooks Online*, May, 2019, https://www.routledgehandbooks.com/doi/10.4324/9780429203039-39

second alternative is through Laos, which made progress until the loan amount was unsustainable and the people of the country rebelled. The third route is the western route through Myanmar. This avenue is shorter. However, events happening in Myanmar in 2021 with China tacitly supporting the military coup has put this avenue in question.

The three alternatives offer choices for China, though they are all fraught with challenges. With China insisting that these countries pay without employing local residents and with its accompanying destruction of the environment, these projects are unlikely to move forward unless China can overthrow all government opposition and provide social control and monitoring to prevent all citizens from having a say in Beijing's plans.

Dams, Industrial Centers, and Other Projects

The Lancang–Mekong International Waterway, with its now devastatingly polluted and often dry river bed has killed animal and marine life in and around the river with blocked nutrients from Chinese built dams upstream. Though the rivers offer a mechanism for oil and gas to travel, environmental damage has wreaked havoc. Parts of the Mekong River are practically depleted of water due to upstream dams. A report shows that Chinese dams, not lower rain levels, were the biggest factor in the depletion of water for the people in Vietnam.[4]

BRI loan projects proposed in Malaysia have caused political stirs with investments in the billions of dollars without similar returns. Loans to Malaysia include the East Coast Rail Link (ECRL), and the land-based Malaysia China Kuantan Industrial Park (MCKIP), the China–Malaysia Qinzhou Industrial Park, and the Malaysia–China Guandan Industrial Park. One of the growing concerns with many BRI loans is that they do not allow in-country manpower to be used for employment opportunities. Chinese labor is used primarily on these projects while negating the opportunity for people within the countries to have an income. Additionally, politicians, like in Malaysia, are being accused of "selling off" their countries to China, saddling them with significant debt and cancelation fees in the multibillions.[5]

The Chinese-owned Sihanoukville Special Economic Zone (SSEZ) is a financial agreement between China and Cambodia that has drawn little backlash within the country ever since the autocratic government banned the country's opposition groups, convicted members, an imposed decades of imprisonment for opposing its authoritarian control.[6] Additionally, the United States has accused Cambodia of changing origination location designations for manufactured goods from China to Cambodia so that China can avoid

---

4 Alan Basist and Claude Williams, "Monitoring the Quantity of Water Flowing Through the Upper Mekong Basin Under Natural (Unimpeded) Conditions," *Sustainable Infrastructure Partnership, Bangkok,* 2020, https://558353b6-da87-4596-a181-b1f20782dd18.filesusr.com/ugd/bae95b_0e0f87104dc8482b99ec91601d853122.pdf?index=true

5 Asia Pacific Foundation of Canada, "Malaysia on the Verge of Cancelling Signature BRI Rail Project," *Asia Pacific Foundation of Canada*, n.d., https://www.asiapacific.ca/asia-watch/malaysia-verge-cancelling-signature-bri-rail-project

6 Radio Free Asia, "Conviction of Cambodia's Opposition Leadership Prompts International Backlash," *Radio Free Asia*, March 2, 2021, https://www.rfa.org/english/news/cambodia/backlash-03022021174915.html

tariffs imposed on Chinese goods.[7]

Why Singapore?

Singapore is at the southernmost tip of the landmass at the entrance to the Strait of Malacca. Its economy is thriving and has good regional connections. China and Singapore have close economic relations, and Singapore is also very popular with Chinese tourists. More than 5,200 Chinese organizations have money in Singapore.

Many Chinese firms are financially involved with Singapore, firms like Sinochem, COSCO, Huawei, and Wanke. Internet business pioneers like Alibaba and Jingdong would like to utilize Singapore's financial center point as a springboard to infiltrate the bigger Southeast Asian market.[8] In 2013, the Singapore branch of China's Industrial and Commercial Bank was assigned to be the clearinghouse and primary bank for Chinese currency outside of China.

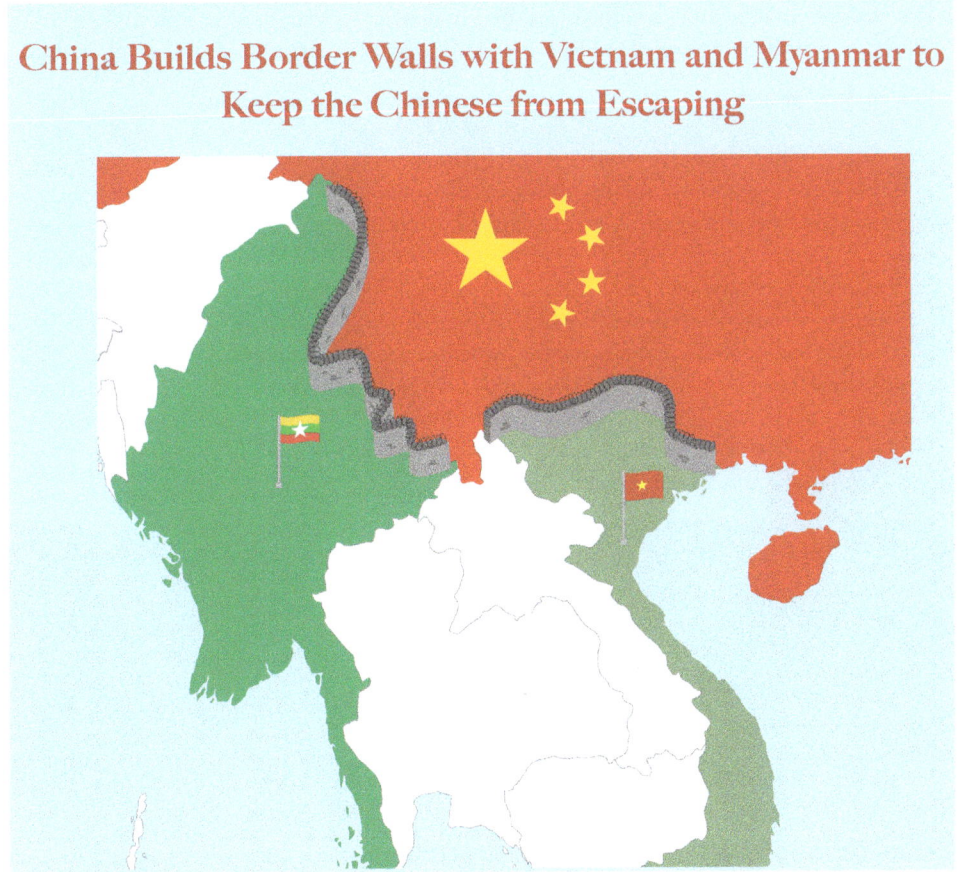

China Builds Border Walls with Vietnam and Myanmar to Keep the Chinese from Escaping

---

7   Prak Chan Thul, "U.S. Urges Cambodia to Probe China-Owned Economic Zone on Tariff Dodging," *Reuters*, June 27, 2019, https://www.reuters.com/article/us-usa-trade-china-cambodia/u-s-urges-cambodia-to-probe-china-owned-economic-zone-on-tariff-dodging-idUSKCN1TT0F3

8   Xinhua, "Xinhua Insight: New Momentum over China-Singapore Economic Corridor," *Shanghai Daily,* September 17, 2014, https://archive.shine.cn/article/article_xinhua.aspx?id=241473

Conclusion

The construction of the China-Indochina Peninsula Economic Corridor (CICPEC) involves seven countries, with each representing different functions and interests. A major concern is whether the corridor can bring economic benefits and social stability, while alleviating state and citizen concerns regarding the development of the corridor.[9]

Should the Nanning-Singapore Economic Corridor be completed, product transport for Beijing state corporations will help China grow, Chinese tourists will be able to travel more easily to vacation destinations. Vietnam, in particular, has numerous travel industry assets, with six areas recorded on the United Nations Educational, Scientific and Cultural Organization's (UNESCO) World Heritage List.

With cutting edge enterprises, Singapore, Malaysia, and Thailand have consistently been mainstream vacation locations in East Asia,[10] though the COVID-19 pandemic has devastated the travel industry including hotels, airlines, and cruise ships to restaurants, cultural centers, and craftsmen. The Indochina Peninsular Corridor has potential, but trust is lacking and words of benevolence and win-win only go so far when one is drowning in debt.

What's at Stake?

First, one of the many stumbling blocks is that China is building a "great wall" blocking Vietnam and Myanmar so that Chinese citizens who want to escape cannot leave. The wall on the Myanmar border is 1,200-1,300 miles of 6-9 ft tall, barbed wire sealed barriers.[11] The first phase has been completed. "On Dec. 12, [2020] an ethnic group in China tweeted two photos of a 410-mile wired fence with surveillance cameras and infrared alarm systems. The second and third phases will be completed by the end of 2021 and Oct 2022, respectively. High voltage fencing will be added where illegal crossings are most common."[12] In October, 2020, China began construction of two-meter (6.56-feet) high walls on the 796-mile Sino-Vietnamese border.[13] These walls have not generated much goodwill toward what Beijing calls win-win cooperation.

Second, China's aggressive tactics against Vietnam in the South China Sea have not won many friends in Hanoi. China has forcibly used its military apparatus to demand that Vietnam give up its islands, oil, and fish by sinking its ships and swarming its islands and rigs. Thus, the rail line China wants Vietnam to pay for in Vietnam has not been

---

9 Lan Xinzhen, "Nanning-Singapore Economic Corridor," *Beijing Review*, Updated August 26, 2010, https://web.archive.org/web/20110707014054/http://www.bjreview.com.cn/quotes/txt/2010-08/24/content_293425_2.htm

10 Ibid.

11 John Feng, "China Building 1,200-Mile Southern Great Wall Along Myanmar Border: Reports," *Newsweek*, December 15, 2020, https://www.newsweek.com/china-building-1200-mile-southern-great-wall-along-myanmar-border-reports-1554793

12 Vision Times Staff, "Communist China Builds Walls to Stop Citizens From Fleeing," *Vision Times*, December 31, 2020, https://www.visiontimes.com/2020/12/31/communist-china-builds-walls-to-stop-citizens-from-fleeing.html

13 Radio Free Asia, "中越邊境防中國人偷渡打工　中共修建數百公里長圍牆," Youtube video, 0:12, October 28, 2020, https://www.youtube.com/watch?v=ILL_gnkSx5U

completed. As long as China continues to use aggression against Vietnam, little progress will be made.

Third, Indochina is drowning in debt as a result of Beijing's loans, which is helping China coerce the Southeast Asia governments into voting with Beijing in international forums, change product origination designations to avoid tariffs, and place a growing mass of Chinese surveillance measures within the regional countries.

Dark Clouds at the End of the Tunnel

Chapter 5
BCIM Economic Corridor

Linking China to Bangladesh, Myanmar, and India

Introduction

The Bangladesh, China, India, and Myanmar Economic Corridor (BCIM) project intends to connect Kunming, China, to Kolkata, India, through Myanmar and Bangladesh.[1] The BCIM Forum for Regional Cooperation seeks to integrate trade, promote greater market access, and remove obstacles to investment between the four countries. Crossing 1.65 million km^2 and directly serving hundreds of millions of people with road, rail, and air transportation linkages, the BCIM will facilitate cross-border flow of people and goods.

Although this project made sense in 2013 when it was approved, it became fraught with complications.[2] With events like the People's Liberation Army (PLA) killing Indian troops as they entered Indian territory in 2020 and the 2021 Myanmar military coup with thousands of citizens killed or imprisoned, rumblings of trouble have threatened to jeopardize the BCIM.

In the Beginning

When Rheman Sobhan wrote about *Transforming Eastern South Asia: Building Growth Zones for Economic Cooperation* in 1999[3] and *Rediscovering the Southern Silk Route* in 2000, he described how Bangladesh could connect geographically contiguous zones through spatial planning, transportation networks, and market access through the BBIMN region that included Bangladesh, Bhutan, India, Myanmar, and Nepal.[4]

China's "Kunming Initiative" was born with the similar idea of offering numerous benefits to each of the countries involved. First, the BCIM would provide an industrial region where poor economies could be lifted up by investment, infrastructure, and additional markets. Second, industries in each of the countries would improve in their efficiency, transport, and logistics. Third, labor in the more impoverished areas of these countries would benefit from development of their manufacturing sectors as alternatives to Chinese production. Finally, greater connectedness offered the possibility of seamless communication and delivery.

With the goals of economic integration and regional development of infrastructure, BCIM prioritized three Ts, trade, transport, and tourism, though this evolved into TTE, trade, transport, and energy.[5]

---

1   Saibal Dasgupta, "Plan for Economic Corridor Linking India to China Approved," *Times of India*, December 20, 2013, https://timesofindia.indiatimes.com/world/china/Plan-for-economic-corridor-linking-India-to-China-approved/articleshow/27669821.cms

2   K. Yhome, "The BCIM Economic Corridor: Prospects and Challenges," *Observer Research Foundation*, February 10, 2017, https://www.orfonline.org/research/the-bcim-economic-corridor-prospects-and-challenges/

3   Shatadru Chattopadhayay, "Book Reviews: Rehman Sobhan, Transforming South Asia: Building Growth Zones for Economic Cooperation," *South Asia Economic Journal 2*, no. 1 (2001), https://journals.sagepub.com/doi/abs/10.1177/139156140100200108?journalCode=saea

4   Rehman Sobhan, *Rediscovering the Southern Silk Route: Integrating Asia's Transport Infrastructure* (University Press, 2000), https://www.amazon.com/Rediscovering-Southern-Silk-Route-Infrastructure/dp/9840515195

5   Mohd Aminul Karim and Faria Islam, "Bangladesh-China-India-Myanmar (BCIM) Economic Corridor: Challenges and Prospects," *The Korean Journal of Defense Analysis 30*, no. (2) (2018): 283-302, http://pubs.iclarm.net/resource_centre/4258.pdf

Evolution into the Belt and Road Initiative

The One Belt, One Road (OBOR), which morphed into the Belt and Road Initiative (BRI) was born in 2013. On December 18, 2013, the four BCIM countries drew up an arrangement, during two days of talks in Kunming, China, underscoring the need to rapidly improve their physical conditions.[6] The discussions delineated the route from Kunming to Kolkata, connecting Mandalay in Myanmar to Dhaka and Chittagong in Bangladesh.[7]

Alongside the ASEAN Free Trade Area, the passage would comprise one of the largest deregulation zones, consolidating regional street, rail, water, and air linkages.[8] This corridor would likewise improve exchanges between the BCIM nations and enable reciprocal trading.[9] Opportunities for BCIM included reducing the distrust between China and India and collaboration between Myanmar and Bangladesh. This relationship would move closer to generating a solution to the Rohingya refugee crisis.

After initially agreeing, India later boycotted the BCIM. By May 2019, the BCIM was no longer referenced as one of the BRI's thirty-five projects in the BRI's joint report at the second Belt and Road Forum. The BCIM agreement included extensive financial focal points, most strikingly: admittance to various business sectors in Southeast Asia, improved transportation framework, and production within industrial zones.[10]

The development of mechanical zones boosted ventures through business-to-business coordination. Furthermore, as China's labor costs increased, less expensive labor in the other countries could improve endeavors in manufacturing and agricultural areas. Chinese organizations could potentially provide improved cooperation and simplicity of access.[11] India's disengaged eastern and northeastern states would likewise improve through enhanced market interchange with China and the remainder of Asia.[12]

The 2013 Kolkata to Kunming (K2K) Car Rally

The birth of the BRI in 2013 provided an urgently needed escalation of activity. For the BCIM to succeed, a ramp up was required along with a publicity campaign. In February 2013, a vehicle rally from Kunming to Kolkata (K2K) proved to be an incredible

---

6   Ananth Krishnan, "BCIM Corridor Gets Push after First Official-Level Talks in China," *The Hindu Times*, Updated June 7, 2016, http://www.thehindu.com/news/international/world/bcim-corridor-gets-push-after-first-officiallevel-talks-in-china/article5483848.ece

7   Ibid.

8   Nathan Barlow, "The Bangladesh-China-India-Myanmar Trade Corridor," *Asia Briefing*, June 7, 2013, http://www.asiabriefing.com/news/2013/06/the-bangladesh-china-india-myanmar-trade-corridor/

9   Neeta Lal, "India and China Seek Economic Integration via Burma, Bangladesh," *The Irrawaddy*, November 6, 2013, http://www.irrawaddy.org/china/india-china-seek-economic-integration-via-burma-bangladesh.html

10 Ibid.

11 Asia Briefing, "The Bangladesh-China-India-Myanmar Trade Corridor," *Asia Briefing*, June 7, 2013, http://www.asiabriefing.com/news/2013/06/the-bangladesh-china-india-myanmar-trade-corridor/

12 Neeta Lal, "India and China Seek Economic Integration via Burma, Bangladesh," *The Irrawaddy*, November 6, 2013, http://www.irrawaddy.org/china/india-china-seek-economic-integration-via-burma-bangladesh.html

public relations success.[13] This show of progress took six years, but the K2K offered another occasion to demonstrate vitality and viability, particularly with countries whose relationships were often rocky.

In this instance, the four governments actively encouraged, supported, and promoted the first-ever BCIM vehicle rally from Kolkata and Kunming through Dhaka thus running through the four countries.[14] This 3,000 km route with eighty participants in twenty vehicles, each playing a symbolic role was intended to show that all four governments could work together. A grand reception was organized by the Bangladesh Center for Policy Dialogue with the other states' support.

The media championed the event as an essential milestone in fostering communication and cooperation between the BCIM countries. The route also presented a clear picture of the layout of the transportation and economic corridor. Areas that needed infrastructure and investment capital were also highlighted. The K2K car rally proved to be a key moment in the development of the BCIM.

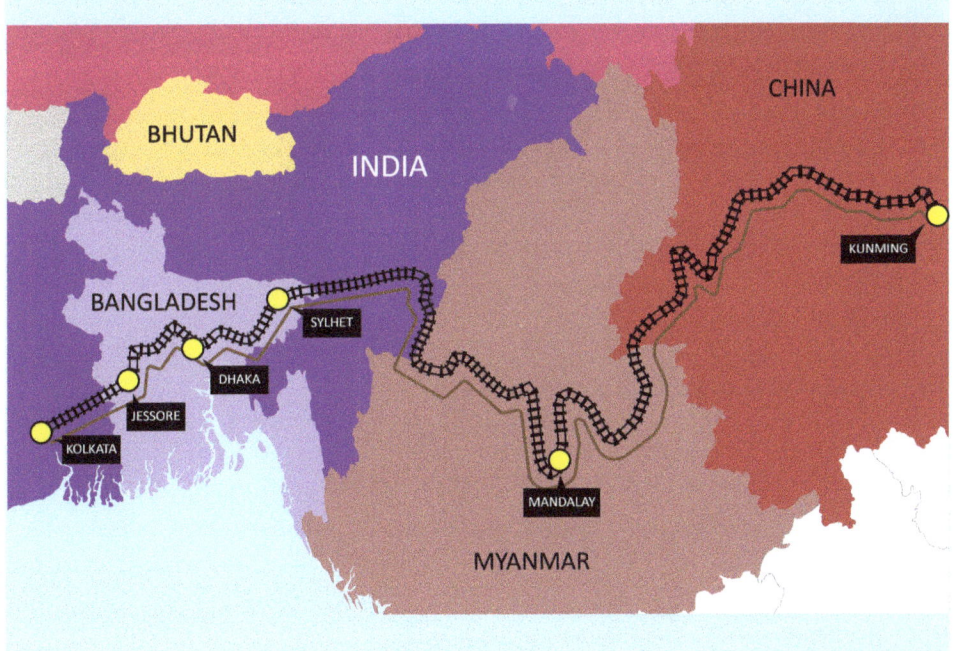

---

13   Sudha Mahalingam, "Kolkata-Kunming Rally Begins", *The Hindu,* February 23, 2013, http://www.thehindu.com/news/international/kolkatakunming-rally-begins/article4446805.ece

14   Nickeled and Dimed, "From Kunming to Kolkata Through the BCIM Route," *Nickeled and Dimed*, January 9, 2015, https://nickledanddimed.com/2015/01/09/from-kunming-to-kolkata-through-bcim-route-catageory-foreign-policy/

The most significant sign was reflected during Chinese Premier Li Keqiang's visit to India a few months after the vehicle rally. Unexpectedly, the BCIM was offered significant underwriting. Premier Li's India visit resulted in a joint articulation of consent to "building up a Joint Study Group on fortifying availability in the BCIM locale for closer monetary, exchange and individual-to-individual linkages and starting the improvement of a BCIM Economic Corridor."[15]

Challenges and Complexities

Bangladesh, China, India, and Myanmar are all exporters of manufactured goods, though the region also has abundant energy resources. Assessing these porducts and resource assets would significantly help these economies. Yet, a surprisingly low amount of trade passes between these countries due to geopolitical strife, disagreements, and distrust. In 2021, Myanmar military's action sounded the alarm around the world about the threats of possible authoritarian takeover and Chinese influence.

India's reluctance to commit to the BCIM was another significant factor, exacerbated by China's assertiveness in promoting its agenda. While China announced the effort as unifying and win-win, India saw China's overwhelming show of economic strength as a power play. India perceived that the BCIM was an avenue to access the Bay of Bengal. India's suspicions included China's efforts to become more involved in India's northern territories. In 2020, those suspicions were realized when China built villages on its border and killed twenty Indian soldiers.

Conclusion

China pushed to create trans-local corridors to integrate economies, which was helpful particularly for the nearby landlocked and underdeveloped countries. Under these circumstances, the potential for success was irresistible. Furthermore, these initiatives would give jobs to millions of poor, unemployed citizens.[16] Other possibilities were considered, like multi-modular transportation networks including inland water transportation and seaside shipping.[17]

Although India did agree to the BCIM at first, continued Sino-Indian conflicts like the Chinese soldier buildup on their border signaled China's growing dominance over south and southeastern countries. Economic cooperation appeared increasingly problematic. Flanked on its western border with its geopolitical rival, Pakistan, with whom China has heavily invested, India has not seen improved conditions.

With the COVID-19 pandemic, continued distrust, and heightened states of alert, the BCIM was dead on arrival. Although China continues to express an interest in reviving its

---

15 Ministry of External Affairs, "Joint Statement on the State Visit of Chinese Premier Li Keqiang to India", *Ministry of External Affairs, Government of India,* May 20, 2013 http://mea.gov.in/bilateral-documents.htm?dtl/21723/Joint+Statement+on+the+State+Visit+of+Chinese++Li+Keqiang+to+India

16 Patricia Uberoi, "The BCIM Forum: Retrospect and Prospect", *Working Paper, Paper, Institute of Chinese Studies,* November 1, 2013, 14.

17 Ibid.

comatose plan, the events of 2021 make this possibility unlikely to happen soon.[18]

What's at Stake?

First, citizens' lives are at stake with Myanmar's military coup in 2021 and, the People's Liberation Army's aggressive acts against India in the Himalayas. Furthermore, China's tacit support for Myanmar's coup had repercussions as Chinese businesses built in Myanmar were set on fire by angry protestors. Hundreds of citizens were killed as freedoms were taken away. Beijing was careful in its rhetoric since the CCP did not want its businesses or assets destroyed. Thus, while the peoples' freedom is at stake and Indian soldiers are threatened, China's businesses in Myanmar are also in danger.

Second, with armed insurgencies, cross-border disputes, and terrorism, what is at stake is the future of the BCIM and the wisdom of investing in countries where there is government instability.

Third, besides India's lack of trust in the Chinese, the multi-year Rohingya refugee crisis created a stumbling block for progress given the region's uncertain political and socioeconomic climate. In March 2021, 45,000 Rohingya were displaced after a fire ripped through one of the refugee camps, and a thousand people were killed, injured, or missing.[19]

Fourth, China claims that it owns Bhutan too. As such, the CCP fought and lost its first international battle to take Bhutan's Sakteng Wildlife Sanctuary in 2020. However, China has constructed a network of roads, buildings, and military outposts in Bhutan, establishing Chinese villages.[20] Thus, nearby countries have been threatened.

---

18 Dipanjan Roy Chaudhury, "Kunming Meet Revives BCIM Link Plan," *The Economic Times,* Updated June 24, 2019, https://economictimes.indiatimes.com/news/politics-and-nation/kunming-meet-revives-bcim-link-plan/articleshow/69921135.cms

19 Sebastian Strangio, "Fire Devastates Large Swathe of Rohingya Refugee Camp," *The Diplomat,* March 24, 2021, https://thediplomat.com/2021/03/fire-devastates-large-swathe-of-rohingya-refugee-camp/

20 Robert Barnett, "China is Building Entire Villages in Another Country's Territory," *Foreign Policy,* May 7, 2021, https://foreignpolicy.com/2021/05/07/china-bhutan-border-villages-security-forces/

Chapter 6
New Eurasian Land Bridge

Railway through Xinjiang, Kazakhstan, Russia, Belarus, Poland, and Germany

Introduction

The New Eurasian Land Bridge (NELB) is a global path connecting the Pacific and Atlantic oceans. Unlike the Siberian Land Bridge, which goes from Russia's eastern port of Vladivostok through Siberia to Moscow and continuing to the European nations, this "second" link goes from China's waterfront urban communities of Lianyungang and Rizhao to Holland's Rotterdam and Belgium's Antwerp ports. The 10,800-km-long rail connection passes through Kazakhstan, Russia, Belarus, Poland, and Germany and serves in excess of thirty nations and areas.[1]

Opened in the mid-1990s, the NELB developed new avenues of opportunity for the Belt and Road Initiative. The transportation route encourages freight exchange of manufactured items and energy (eventually people) between the nations of Asia and Europe. This effort was a milestone since few intercontinental rail courses existed, therefore highlighting the Belt and Road Initiative's potential.

Belt and Road Railway Projects in Europe
$13.4 Billion Given to China to Provide Transit for its Goods

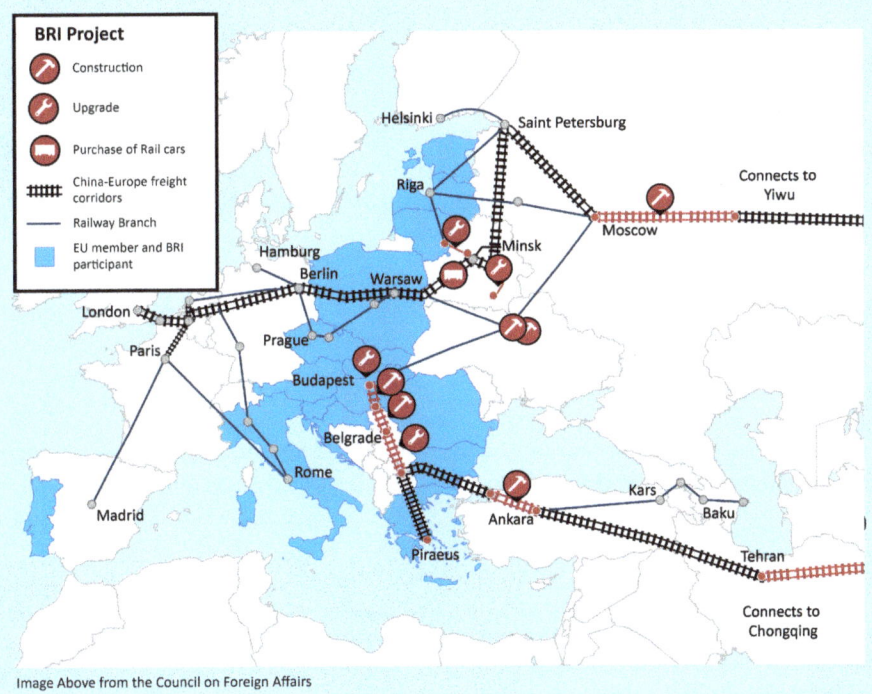

Image Above from the Council on Foreign Affairs

---

1. China Keywords, "New Eurasian Land Bridge," *China Keywords,* Updated April 19, 2017, http://www.china.org.cn/english/china_key_words/2017-04/19/content_40651850.htm

Chinese Railways Across Asia and into Europe

These railways include the Chongqing-Xinjiang-Europe Railway (arriving at Germany's Duisburg through Poland), the Chengdu-Xinjiang-Europe Railway, and the Yiwu-Xinjiang-Europe Railway (arriving at Madrid or London). Duisburg, Germany, a center for iron, steel, and chemicals, has the largest inland port. The development of related throughways, power transmission lines, and ports provided the added benefit of improved rail transport reducing shipping costs.[2]

The New Eurasian Land Bridge, alternatively called the Second or New Eurasian Continental Bridge, is the southern part of the Eurasian Land-Bridge rail line going through China. The Eurasian Land-Bridge is the overland rail link between Asia and Europe. More than 12,000 intercontinental trips were made during the pandemic, an increase of fifty percent more than the previous year with massive quantities of cargo.[3] According to China's *Xinhua* news source, the cost of this freight rail travel is one-fifth of air transport, taking 0ne-third of the time as compared to sea transport.[4]

The length of the Yiwu-Xinjiang-Europe Railway to Madrid, Spain is 13,000 km (8,100 mi), the longest in the world, surpassing the Trans-Siberian Railway. The second-longest is the Yiwu-Xinjiang-Europe Railway to London, England, which is 12,000 km (7,500 mi).

Rail Gauge Challenges

Due to the dissimilarities between standard rail gauges in China and Russia, shipping containers must be moved from Chinese to Kazakh railroad vehicles at Dostyk on the Chinese-Kazakh border and again at the Belarus-Poland fringe where European standard gauge begins. This repositioning is done with truck-mounted cranes.[5] Chinese media regularly reminds viewers that the New Eurasian Land/Continental Bridge reaches out from Lianyungang to Rotterdam through Kazakhstan.

Rail cargo from China over the Eurasian Land-Bridge passes north of the Caspian Sea through Russia. New intercontinental rail lines have been proposed, including one through Turkey and Bulgaria.[6] However, any course south of the Caspian Sea must go through Iran.[7] Thus, Iran's strategic position has drawn China closer and reframed their relationship.

The northern route offers advantages to the Kazakh economy. As acknowledgment of this reality, Kazakhstan's President Nursultan Nazarbayev encouraged Eurasian and Chinese

---

2   China Keywords, "New Eurasian Land Bridge," *China Keywords,* Updated April 19, 2017, http://www.china.org.cn/english/china_key_words/2017-04/19/content_40651850.htm.

3   Xinhua, "Xinhua Headlines: Cross-Border E-Commerce Gains Traction Aboard China-Europe Freight Trains," *Xinhua,* February 16, 2021, http://www.xinhuanet.com/english/2021-02/16/c_139746499.htm

4   Xinhua, "China-Europe Freight Trains Serve as Lifeline for Int'l Trade Amid Pandemic," *Xinhua,* March 19, 2021, http://www.xinhuanet.com/english/2021-03/19/c_139822181.htm

5   Business, "China Invites Bulgaria to Join High-Speed Asia-Europe Rail with Turkey," *Novinite*, October 28, 2010, http://www.novinite.com/view_news.php?id=121602

6   Ibid.

7   Keith Bradsher, "Hauling New Treasure Along the Silk Road," *The New York Times,* July 21, 2013, https://www.nytimes.com/2013/07/21/business/global/hauling-new-treasure-along-the-silk-road.html

pioneers at the eighteenth session of the Shanghai Cooperation Organization to develop the Eurasian rapid railroad (EHSRW), Beijing-Astana-Moscow-Berlin.[8] This transport corridor puts Kazakhstan in a leading role along this corridor.

In 2019, principal Chinese cargo trains passed through Turkey's Marmaray rail tunnel under the Bosphorus Strait to Europe. This trip ran from Xi'an with the China-to-Turkey transportation time decreased from a month to twelve days, providing an essential connection along the Iron Silk Road.[9]

The Belt and Road Initiative's Routes in Central Asia

---

8   Dmitry Babich, "President Tokayev Addresses the SCO Summit: Emphasizes Collective Responses to Common Threats," *The Astana Times*, November 13, 2020, https://astanatimes.com/2020/11/president-tokayev-addresses-the-sco-summit-emphasizes-collective-responses-to-common-threats/

9   Mustafa Hatipoglu and Emrah Gokmen, "First China Railway Express Line Train Reaches Turkey," *AA.com.tr*, July 11, 2019, https://www.aa.com.tr/en/turkey/first-china-railway-express-line-train-reaches-turkey/1637811

Early China-Europe Transportation Links

An overland exchange between China and Europe dates back centuries. What is new is the means of transport. Historically, the Silk Roads conveying exotic goods were essential to the Chinese economy. Desert springs along the course, supplying water at Merv, Bukhara, and Samarkand, surrounded central urban areas. The overland passageway was rife with disturbances as smugglers and bandits assaulted camel parades and struck urban communities. Yet, traders, eager to receive goods, aided in ensuring the brokers' security.

Under the terms of the Pax Mongolica (Mongol Peace) or Pax Tatarica (Tatar Peace), Genghis Khan's (1206-1227) Mongol Empire offered exchange protocols between traders over significant distances across the world's most extensive land-based domain. The decimation of overland exchanges followed around 1500 after Portuguese sailors commenced traveling ocean and sea routes from Europe to Asia around the Cape of Good Hope.

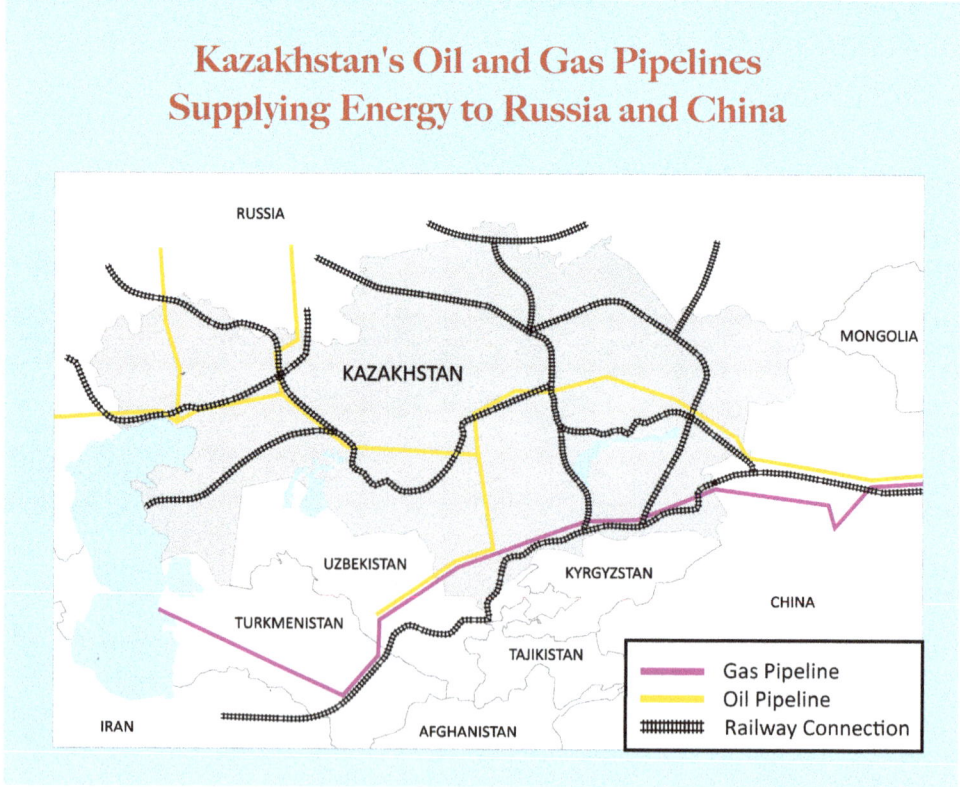

For the following 500 years, the sea was the predominant method of transport between Europe and East Asia. Camels took an extraordinary amount of time to walk across countries. The decreased oceanic vehicle costs strengthened this mode of transportation. By 2015, the biggest boats could hold 20,000 twenty-foot-proportional (TEU) shipping containers as they passed through the Suez Canal.

A few rail links traversing Asia and Europe were built in the twentieth century. However, none were significant transporters of Chinese cargo. The most notable was Russia's Trans-Siberian railroad, constructed between 1891 and 1905. The principal use was military, connecting the Russian Far East with the significant urban communities of western Russia. Linkages were built through Mongolia and onward to Beijing through Northeast China to the Pacific coast. Though thwarted by political interruptions like World War II and the 1960 Sino–Soviet split, these routes offered reciprocal exchanges. While the Russia–Korea augmentation of the Trans-Siberian railroad provided freight traffic between Russia and North Korea, this connection was never part of key Europe–Korea linkages.

Before 2011, railroads connecting China and Europe were not a serious contender to ocean cargo. Secondary trains were run along the Trans-Siberian Railroad on an impromptu basis for German vehicle organizations like VW/Audi in Changchun and BMW in Shenyang. Rail transport provided parts for their joint-venture manufacturing plants in upper east China.[10] Similar trains conveyed Korean vehicle parts from the port of Lianyungang to the Daewoo joint-venture plant in Andijan, Uzbekistan. However, following Daewoo's financial issues during the 1998 Asian Crisis, General Motors took over its vehicle division.

The former Daewoo plant is currently GM Uzbekistan, yet the principal nation of origin is still the Republic of Korea. Excursions through China indicated to Beijing that worldwide rail administrations, even over significant distances, like those serving GM were practical. Notwithstanding, utilization charges were required on an impromptu basis and often did not benefit other likely customers. Thus, substantial potential existed, which shined the path forward toward the horizon.

Freight Rail Development After 2010

The impetus behind the newly-developed rail administrations was the 'Go West' movement. International organizations offered China numerous privileges and with financial advantages as an 'underdeveloped country', China grew powerful with excess capital from balance of payment surpluses.

China entered the World Trade Organization in 2001.[11] At the same time, new railways motivated firms to produce and deliver Chinese goods from inland areas that had fallen behind China's upwardly mobile seaside regions. The effect on production was minor at first but soon mushroomed. This development also coincided with Beijing's decision to mass incarcerate millions of Uyghur Muslims. Calling all Muslims potential terrorists, China constructed hundreds of concentration camps to prevent them from creating a problem while providing Beijing with millions of workers in forced labor camps. Thus, the central and western regions became more viable production and manufacturing areas with fewer threats as it constructed railways across Xinjiang Province toward Europe.

---

10   Economic Research Institute for ASEAN and East Asia, "The Eurasian Land Bridge," *ERIA*, 2018, https://www.eria.org/research/the-eurasian-land-bridge-the-role-of-service-providers-in-linking-the-regional-value-chains-in-east-asia-and-the-european-union/

11   Ibid.

In 2010, a reinforced train link provided connections between Shenzhen terminals in Yantian and Chongqing. This link empowered Foxconn, Hewlett–Packard, and others to construct facilities in Chongqing, which became known as the "Land of Laptops".[12] The fortified railway created regional and local lines from Southeast Asia to the processing plant in Chongqing without issues for the Apple PC and HP printer supply chains.[13]

Conclusion

Given the enormous pressures on transportation systems, financial specialists sought to optimize routes.[14] However, with growth came expanded transportation overload along the Yangtze. The development of new alternative corridors prompted clogs, particularly at the Three Gorges Dam, with its five locks framework. Consequently, China's 'Go West' approach resulted in placing production resources into joint activities in Chongqing. This effort was a superior route than the one through the clogged Yangtze River. In the interim, VW opened another joint-venture plant in Chengdu, only 300 km west of Chongqing.[15]

The railroad organizations of Germany, Poland, Belarus, Russia, Kazakhstan, and China provided an answer. The proposed solution was a Chongqing-Duisburg train. Coordination was required between the legislatures of these six nations to guarantee smooth access across the frontiers. Since the trains were not designed to stop along the way, this effort seemed straightforward with the exception of internal and external strife, terrorism, and travel consent for reinforced containers.[16] A complete understanding among rail organizations was necessary since questions arose regarding travel expenses, thoroughfare use, and border checks at places like the China-Kazakhstan and Belarus–Poland fringes. China attempted to co-opt the heads of each state to offer them incentives, secure shipments, and maintain consistency. End-organizations, Deutsche Bundesbahn and China Railway Corporation, clarified customer requirements and sorted out stacking and emptying at the terminals.

Firms looking to decrease their costs provided momentum for the Land Bridge rail administrations.[17] Accelerating the efforts with train technology, German segment providers and automobile manufacturers like VW, Audi, and BMW sought efficient avenues to transport their goods made in China. Apple, HP, and Acer assisted since their components were also made in China. Transport was seen as a way to facilitate the purchase of hardware for Chinese and European markets. Auto parts and PCs fit into a middle-class market of

---

12   China Daily, "Chongqing: Land of Laptops," *China.org.cn*, June 16, 2014, http://www.china.org.cn/business/2014-06/16/content_32674371.htm

13   Chen Yingqun, "China-Europe Rail Links Boost Recovery," *China Daily*, Updated September 10, 2020, http://epaper.chinadaily.com.cn/a/202009/10/WS5f596938a310d95bf733f109.html

14   Economic Research Institute for ASEAN and East Asia, "The Eurasian Land Bridge," *ERIA*, 2018, https://www.eria.org/research/the-eurasian-land-bridge-the-role-of-service-providers-in-linking-the-regional-value-chains-in-east-asia-and-the-european-union/

15   Rui Hu, "Chengdu-Chongqing High-Speed Railway Expected to be Increased to 350 km/h," *ChongQing*, June 16, 2020, https://www.ichongqing.info/2020/06/16/chengdu-chongqing-high-speed-railway-expected-to-be-increased-to-350-km-h/

16   Economic Research Institute for ASEAN and East Asia, "The Eurasian Land Bridge," *ERIA*, 2018, https://www.eria.org/research/the-eurasian-land-bridge-the-role-of-service-providers-in-linking-the-regional-value-chains-in-east-asia-and-the-european-union/

17   Richard Pomfret, "The Eurasian Landbridge and China's Belt and Road Initiative," *Vox EU*, May 2, 2018, https://voxeu.org/article/eurasian-landbridge-and-chinas-belt-and-road-initiative

merchandise purchases for which airfreight and sea passage were deemed excessively costly as opposed to the much cheaper rail transport.[18]

Kazakhstan's Domestic and BRI Railway System

What's at Stake?

First, with rail corridors passing through Xinjiang Province, China has stepped up its effort to imprison more than a million Uyghur Muslims. Under the guise of re-education and protection against "terrorist" Muslim beliefs, they removed children from their homes and placed them into indoctrination camps to be molded into workers for the Chinese state. Parents have no access to their children as they are stripped from their homes.

Second, countries along each corridor are incentivized with loans to provide access and so they can reap financial rewards and transport mechanisms for their manufactured goods. Thus, it is unsurprising that the predominantly Muslim countries of Kazakhstan, Pakistan, Iran, and Turkey have said little about the hundreds of concentration camps incarcerating and torturing the Uyghurs.

Third, China's economy is growing at an extraordinary rate as other countries pay for infrastructure to build Beijing's empire. With more cheap manufactured goods demanded by China, its influence on the world will continue to grow.

---

18 Australian Government Productivity Commission, "Road and Rail Friehgt Infrastructure Pricing," *Productivity Commission Inquiry Report, no.* 41 (2006), https://www.pc.gov.au/inquiries/completed/freight/report/freight.pdf

Chapter 7
China-Mongolia-Russia Economic Corridor
The BRI's Project to the North

Introduction

The China-Mongolia-Russia Economic Corridor (CMREC) is one of the six significant corridors of China's Belt and Road Initiative (BRI). The project aims to reduce freight shipping times and limit bureaucratic barriers at the border and, in so doing, improve the infrastructure links between the three countries. The corridor also seeks to create new land and sea export routes for natural resources in Mongolia to shorten the route for Russian freight.[1]

Along with CMREC, there are other well-known projects which include the Northern Railway Corridor and the China-Mongolia Cross-border Economic Cooperation Zone from Zamiin Uud to Erenhot. The Northern Railway Corridor plays a key role in connecting Mongolia with China and Russia through its rail network.[2]

Mongolia's Landlocked, but Strategic Location Between China and Russia

Landlocked but situated in a strategic location, Mongolia has 3.3 million people on land that is more than 3.5 times as large as California. Also, for comparison, California has more than 45 times more people per square mile. Most of Mongolia is rural and undeveloped, with rugged land areas in the world's least densely populated country. A primarily Buddhist country, the national language is Mongolian, and society stems from a nomadic culture.

Mongolia's largest city is the capital, Ulaanbaatar (meaning red hero), with a population that is nearly half of the country's entire population. The city center is Genghis Khan Square and the 1830 Gandantegchinlen Monastery. Ulaanbaatar, often referred to as Ulan Bator or UB for short connects the Trans-Siberian Railway and the Chinese Railway.

Mongolia is rich in minerals and energy resources, but its location makes transportation difficult. The China-Mongolia-Russia-Economic-Corridor (CMREC) offers promising alternatives for delivering its valuable resources to new markets, like the intercontinental routes to Europe and transit onward from the Pacific Ocean to North and South America. While CMREC is necessary for broader routes for trade, China and Russia are well aware that they are Mongolia's nearest neighbors and stand to reap the rewards. Thus, loans are likely to require financial guarantees in the form of mineral and other resource repayments.

Historically, Mongolia was dependent on animal husbandry for its revenue. There are more than twenty times more livestock than humans, with about 70 million animals cared for by ranchers, including 32,300,000 sheep, 29,300,000 goats, 4,700,000 cattle, 4,200,000 horses, and 500,000 camels.[3] Crop production includes wheat, barley, oat, rye,

---

1 Geopolitical Monitor, "Belt and Road: China-Mongolia-Russia Corridor," *Geopolitical Monitor*, September 3, 2020, https://www.geopoliticalmonitor.com/fact-sheet-china-mongolia-russia-corridor/

2 Russia Business Today, "China, Mongolia, Russia Push for 'Economic Corridor'," *Russia Business Today*, September 18, 2018, https://russiabusinesstoday.com/economy/china-mongolia-russia-push-for-economic-corridor/

3 Food and Agriculture Organization of the United Nations, "*Mongolia at a Glance*," *Food and Agriculture Organization of the UN*, n.d., http://www.fao.org/mongolia/fao-in-mongolia/mongolia-at-a-glance/en/

buckwheat, oil plants, potatoes, and vegetables with vast forests of timber, hunting, and trapping fur-bearing animals. At the same time, nearly 70% of the grassland is threatened by desertification due to climate change along with anthropogenic factors, including overgrazing of livestock, erosion of farmland soils, burning, and climate change.[4]

However, by 2014, more than half of Mongolia's GDP came from exports. Some of these exports included apparel, copper, cashmere, wool, livestock, animal products, fluorspar, hides, coal, and crude oil. China purchased 84% of Mongolia's export products. Due to Mongolia's heavy reliance on commodities exports and China as its primary export market, its economy directly depends on the performance of the Chinese economy.[5]

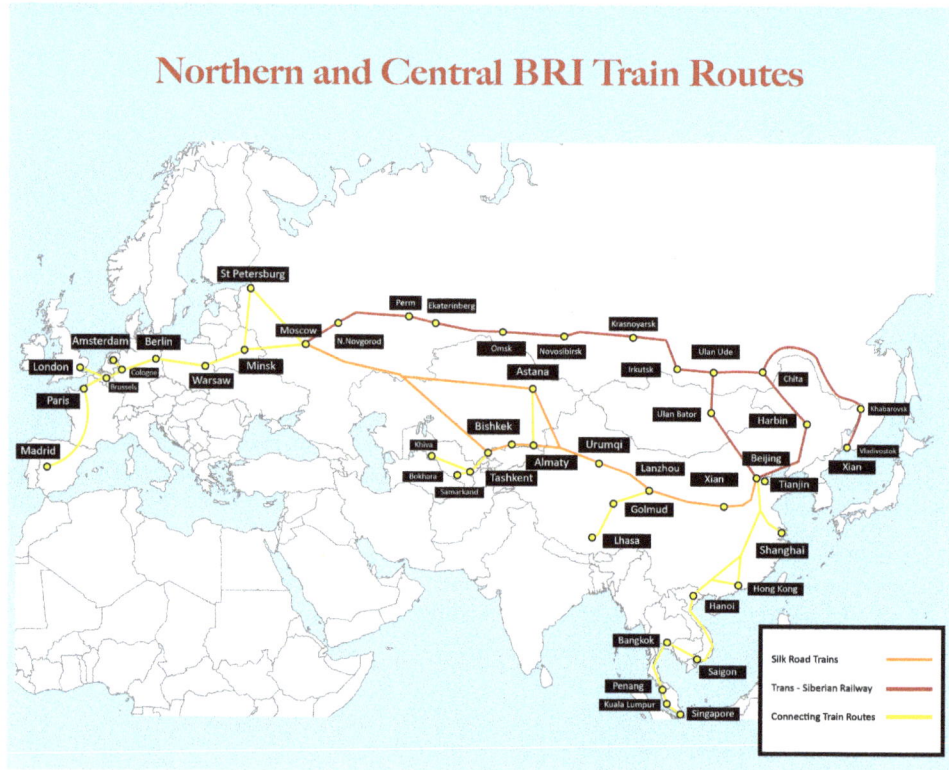

CMREC Progress

The China-Mongolia-Russia Economic Corridor (CMREC) was implemented as part of the Belt and Road Initiative by Chinese President Xi Jinping. The project strengthened China's plans to develop infrastructure projects and set up both economic cooperation

---

4   Food and Agriculture Organization of the United Nations, "*Mongolia at a Glance,*" *Food and Agriculture Organization of the UN,* n.d., http://www.fao.org/mongolia/fao-in-mongolia/mongolia-at-a-glance/en/

5   Antonio Graceffo, "Mongolia and the Belt and Road Initiative: The Prospects for the China-Mongolia-Russia Economic Corridor," *China Brief 20, no. 12* (2020), https://jamestown.org/program/mongolia-and-the-belt-and-road-initiative-the-prospects-for-the-china-mongolia-russia-economic-corridor/

zones and free trade zones in cities sharing borders.[6] The program proposes incorporating new models of international relations with new and existing resources, infrastructure, and production projects.[7] However, the primary purpose of the corridor is to facilitate the extraction and development of mineral deposits in Mongolia and Eastern Siberia.[8]

China's Relations with Mongolia

Diplomatic relations between Mongolia and China have existed for over 70 years. Both countries are committed to setting mutually beneficial standards for future cooperation.[9]

The CMREC program covers the following fields of cooperation:[10]

- Transportation infrastructure
- Cooperation in the industrial sector
- Development of border-crossing points
- Facilitation of trade and inspection procedures
- Cooperation in the energy sector
- Environment and ecology
- Education, science, and technology cooperation
- Humanitarian efforts
- Agricultural development

However, faced with the challenge of being landlocked, the Mongolian government has prioritized rail and road infrastructure, recognizing these as keys to its sustained growth and economic development. As a result, the Mongolian government presses for the full program realization, since, if implemented well, CMREC could be a huge turning point for its economy.

Meanwhile, Mongolian officials are wary of economic over-dependence on China. Already, China accounts for almost 80% of its export trade. As such, Mongolia is on the lookout for other international political allies and investment partners. This desire is evident in how the Mongolian government leases its mining industry, the South Gobi Oyu Tolgoi mine, to multinational Rio Tinto and Canadian Ivanhoe Mines despite China's interest.

---

6   Antonio Graceffo, "Mongolia and the Belt and Road Initiative: The Prospects for the China-Mongolia-Russia Economic Corridor," *China Brief 20, no. 12* (2020), https://jamestown.org/program/mongolia-and-the-belt-and-road-initiative-the-prospects-for-the-china-mongolia-russia-economic-corridor/

7   The China-Mongolia-Russia Economic Corridor Program, "Program – Establishing an Economic Corridor, China-Mongolia-Russia," *translated from Russian*, n.d., http://minpromtorg.govrb.ru/rus-ch-mn.pdf

8   Investing News Network, "New Trade Policies Unlock Foreign Investment in Mongolia," *Investing News*, December 9, 2020, https://investingnews.com/innspired/new-trade-policies-unlock-foreign-investment-in-mongolia/

9   Connor Judge, "What does the China-Mongolia-Russia Economic Corridor mean for Mongolia?," *Belt and Road Advisory*, 2019, https://beltandroad.ventures/beltandroadblog/china-mongolia-russia-economic-corridor

10 Ministry of Foreign Affairs of Mongolia, "Mongolia-Russia-China 'Economic Corridor'," *Ministry of Foreign Affairs of Mongolia*, November 28, 2017, https://www.unescap.org/sites/default/files/4.3%20Mongolia.pdf

Nevertheless, the economic engagement between Mongolia and China remains positive. Mongolia appears invested in CMREC, and there is a safe assumption among stakeholders that this attitude will persist. CMREC represents the hopes for sustainable regional development and collaboration in Mongolia.[11]

Due to the depreciation of commodity prices that has impacted exports, Mongolia's economy has taken a nosedive. Additionally, the Mongolian government's decision to renegotiate a deal with the mining company 'Rio Tinto' over the terms of its gold-mining site and the You Tolgoi decreased investor confidence. However, several developments, like a new agreement with Rio Tinto, have placed the country in the limelight.

Mongolia and China share a longstanding relationship, though largely contentious. Until the 1900s, when Mongolia transitioned to a market economy, the country had been under strong Soviet influence, and its distrust of the Chinese government was widespread. Today, China's global economic impact is felt strongly in Mongolia. China is Mongolia's largest import and export market, followed closely by Russia, its second-largest.

Owing to economic restructuring, demand for Mongolian exports by the Chinese has slowed. The Mongolian economy fell, especially in 2015 and 2016. The financial repercussion of China's fluctuating export trade has been of significant concern to the Mongolian government. As a result, Mongolian officials worry about its over-reliance on China.

More than once, Mongolia has endeavored to lessen China's influence on its economy. One of its most significant moves was to consider a "third-person" policy, gesturing to the United States for support. Regardless, Mongolia will require China's approval and support to grow sustainably. China is happy to render its help. CMREC is a crucial effort to improve logistics and trade between the countries.

China's Relations with Russia

CMREC published a list of priority projects, including the following policies with special emphasis on Sino-Russian relations:

- Modernization of the central railway network connecting Naushki and Ulan-Ude in Russia with Ulaanbaatar, Sükhbaatar, and Zamyn-Üüd in Mongolia and Erenhot, Beijing, Zhangjiakou, and Tianjin in China.
- Construction of the Western railway network linking the Russian city of Kuragino with Ürümqi through Mongolian territory.
- Construction of the Eastern railway network between Chifeng and Jinzhou in China, Borzya in Russia, and Choibalsan in Mongolia.
- Modernization of the Zarubino-Choibalsan-Ulanhot motorway passage.
- Establishment of an economic zone in Chinese and Russian regions.

---

11 Connor Judge, "What does the China-Mongolia-Russia Economic Corridor mean for Mongolia?," *Belt and Road Advisory*, 2019, https://beltandroad.ventures/beltandroadblog/china-mongolia-russia-economic-corridor

These projects are being financed through public-private partnerships (PPP) or by the state with assistance from the AIIB, SCO Interbank Consortium, New Development Bank (BRICS), Silk Road Fund, and other multilateral and national financial institutions.[12] Based on the projects described, CMREC favors China-Russia exchanges.

---

12 Connor Judge and Sanchir Jargalsaikhan, "Guest Post: China's Belt and Road Initiative – Mongolia Focus," *Mongolia Focus*, March 12, 2019, http://blogs.ubc.ca/mongolia/2019/obor-bri-mongolia-sco-neasia/

Conclusion

The CMREC was expected to improve commerce and customs clearance between China, Mongolia, and Russia while ushering in trade activity into Mongolia. These advantages have not proven to exist.[13]

There are also other projects under the BRI umbrella which are being implemented in Mongolia. However, the criteria for what makes up a BRI project is vague. In the broadest sense, these projects involve wind power, hydroelectric dams, solar power, port infrastructure, free-trade zones, Confucius Institutes, and other diplomatic exchanges.[14]

Mongolia continues to battle domestic challenges with its road network. With it's harsh climate, the corridor is difficult to maintain. Heavy freight, already using the route from Ulan Ude to Ulan Bator, damages the tarmac and creates potholes. However, new transportation opportunities exist for foreign investors familiar with shipping commodities along distant motorways.[15]

At the 2018 Mongolia-Russia Economic Forum, Mongolian President Khaltmaagiin Battulga questioned CMREC, explaining that the project is not advancing quickly. He said, "We wish to accelerate the implementation of the Trilateral Economic Corridor program, which is no more than a dialogue today. Mongolia, for its part, is ready to put all

---

13   Zolzaya Erdenebileg, "China-Mongolia Relations: Challenges and Opportunities," *China Briefing*, January 6, 2017, https://www.china-briefing.com/news/china-mongolia-relations/

14   Connor Judge and Sanchir Jargalsaikhan, "Guest Post: China's Belt and Road Initiative – Mongolia Focus," *Mongolia Focus*, March 12, 2019, http://blogs.ubc.ca/mongolia/2019/obor-bri-mongolia-sco-neasia/

15   Silk Road Briefing, "Russia-Mongolia-China Road Corridor to be Ready in 2018," *Silk Road Briefing*, September 13, 2017, https://www.silkroadbriefing.com/news/2017/09/08/russia-mongolia-china-road-corridor-ready-2018/

necessary efforts into this development." There seems to be solid support for CMREC.[16] Although efforts exist to transfer resources from the West to East-Asia, the BRI project is predominantly orientated towards the East West region. If this trend persists, the current CMREC program may be insufficient.[17]

What's at Stake?

First, Mongolia has enough resources to fuel its economy, but they are not being realized due to fluctuations in commodity prices. Mongolia is not the beneficiary of its wealth.

Second, while there are benefits to China's investment through CMREC, there are numerous costs. Mongolia's dependence on exports to China results in its economic instability. To better manage and stabilize inflows, Mongolia needs to look elsewhere to sell its products and develop its infrastructure.

Third, CMREC transportation corridors present a challenge and a threat to Mongolia's sovereignty. Mongolia is still required to invest significant amounts of capital when it already holds enormous debt. Concerns abound as to whether Mongolia will fall into the same debt trap with China as other countries have when they are unable to pay.

---

16 Connor Judge and Sanchir Jargalsaikhan, "Guest Post: China's Belt and Road Initiative – Mongolia Focus," *Mongolia Focus*, March 12, 2019, http://blogs.ubc.ca/mongolia/2019/obor-bri-mongolia-sco-neasia/

17 Ladislav Zemánek, "Belt & Road Initiative and Russia: From Mistrust Towards Cooperation," *De Gruyter*, 2020, https://www.degruyter.com/view/journals/humaff/30/2/article-p199.xml

Chapter 8

The Corridors of African Trade and Benevolence

Rare Earth Metals and Other Natural Resources

Introduction

China's involvement in Africa has stretched for decades, back to the days of Mao's leadership, when China began foreign investment, operation, and construction of infrastructure. Subsequent Chinese paramount leaders continued to invest in foreign countries, including those in Africa. However, when Xi Jinping announced the Belt and Road Initiative in 2013, Chinese investments in Africa and Asia under the Belt and Road Initiative grew. The idea behind the initiative formed around a network of Silk Road trade routes during the Han Dynasty, 2,000 years ago, connecting China to Africa, India, and the Mediterranean.[1]

China – Africa Loans

The African Union and 39 sovereign countries in Africa have signed a memorandum of understanding with China on developing the BRI together.[2] In 2014, the Brookings Institute questioned whether China's aid to Africa was a monster or a messiah as Chinese investment in Africa grew from $210 million in 2000 to $3.17 billion in 2011.[3] Africa's one-year debt to China in 2021 was $25 billion.[4]

According to Forbes, "The reason Chinese corporations are in Africa is simple, to exploit the people and take their resources. It's the same thing European colonists did during mercantile times, except worse. The Chinese corporations are trying to turn Africa into another Chinese continent. They are squeezing Africa for everything it is worth."[5] Michael Sata, Zambia's President from 2011-2014, said, "European colonial exploitation in comparison to Chinese exploitation appears benign, because even though the commercial exploitation was just as bad, the colonial agents also invested in social and economic infrastructure services whereas Chinese investment, on the other hand, is focused on taking out of Africa as much as can be taken out, without any regard to the welfare of the local people."[6]

A few of China's Belt and Road Initiative Projects include:

Mombasa-Nairobi & Nairobi to Naivasha Railway

Kenya has a new 301-mile railway line for cargo and passenger transportation,

---

1 European Bank for Reconstruction and Development, "Belt and Road Initiative," *European Bank for Reconstruction and Development*, n.d., https://www.ebrd.com/what-we-do/belt-and-road/overview.html

2 Pearl Risberg, "The Give-and-Take of BRI in Africa," *CSIS*, n.d., https://www.csis.org/give-and-take-bri-africa

3 Yun Sun, "China's Aid to Africa: Monster or Messiah?," *Brookings Institute*, February 7, 2014, https://www.brookings.edu/opinions/chinas-aid-to-africa-monster-or-messiah/

4 Kevin Acker, Deborah Brautigam, and Yufan Huang, "The Pandemic has Worsened Africa's Debt Crisis. China and Other Countries are Stepping In," *The Washington Post,* February 26, 2021, https://www.washingtonpost.com/politics/2021/02/26/pandemic-has-worsened-africas-debt-crisis-china-other-countries-are-stepping/

5 Panos Mourdoukoutas, "What is China Doing in Africa?," *Forbes*, August 4, 2018, https://www.forbes.com/sites/panosmourdoukoutas/2018/08/04/china-is-treating-africa-the-same-way-european-colonists-did/?sh=51e6ca6298ba

6 Scott D. Taylor, "The Nature of Chinese Capital in Africa," *Current History 117*, no. 799 (2018): 197-199, https://doi.org/10.1525/curh.2018.117.799.197

connecting Mombasa, its main Indian Ocean coastal city, with Kenya's capital and largest city, Nairobi. The project's construction started in 2013 and was completed in 2017.[7] The Mombasa-Nairobi Standard Gauge Railway project is Kenya's largest infrastructure project since its independence and a flagship project for its 2030 development agenda. The railway's main aim is to provide a fast, reliable, safe, and efficient mode of transportation. The journey from Mombasa to Nairobi was reduced from 10-15 hours to 7 hours, with corresponding transportation costs dropping from $12-$17 to $7.

The Chinese government funded 90% of the project, with the total expenses amounting to US$3.6 billion with a second loan of $1.5 billion for the extension from Nairobi to Naivasha.[8] The remaining 10% was funded by the Kenyan government. Meanwhile, Kenyans think the country got a bad deal compared to Ethiopia and Tanzania, countries that were offered a significantly lower cost. Additionally, the railway has lost $200 million

---

[7] Nancy Muthoni Githaiga and Wang Bing, "Belt and Road Initiative in Africa: The Impact of standard Gauge Railway in Kenya," *China Report 55*, no. 3 (2019), doi:10.1177/0009445519853697

[8] Mohammed Yusuf, "Cost of China-Built Railway Haunts Kenya," *VOA News*, February 26, 2020, https://www.voanews.com/africa/cost-china-built-railway-haunts-kenya

so far and cannot pay its debt.[9] The railroad followed the Chinese standard railway design; the project contractors were China Road and Bridge Corporation(CRBC) and China Communications Construction Company Ltd.[10]

Karuma Hydroelectric Power Station in Uganda

The Karuma Hydroelectric Power Station is a 600 MW run-of-the-river plant located on the Nile River, downstream of Lake Kyoga, and 270 km from Kampala, the capital of Uganda. Opened in 2021, the expected annual energy output is 4.4 billion kWh with six turbines operating in the underground powerhouse.[11] The Chinese state-owned enterprise, Sinhydro, completed construction. Funding for the USD $1,435 billion project was provided by Exim Bank of China.[12] The power station is the largest power generating facility in Uganda; its dam is the biggest in East Africa.

Adama II Wind Farm in Ethiopia

The Adama II Wind Farm is located in Ethiopia, 95 km away from the capital, Addis Ababa. The energy network links the capital with the port of Djibouti. The Adama II Wind Farm has a designed capacity of 153 MW, tripling the previous Adama wind farm, which had a capacity of 51MW. The wind farm took 18 months to construct and was inaugurated in 2015.[13] The project is the second-largest wind power project in Africa, and the largest wind power project contracted by China. It is also the first overseas project that adopts Chinese wind power standards and technologies.

Abuja-Kaduna Rail Line

Nigeria's Abuja-Kaduna Rail Line connects the capital city, Abuja, with Kaduna. With the estimated cost of $874 million, China's Exim Bank provided $500 million in the form of a concessionary loan for the project while the Nigerian federal government provided the rest of the money.[14] China Civil Engineering Construction Corporation (CCECC) began work on the project in 2011, though due to shortfalls and theft, the railway opened only in July 2016.[15]

---

9   Carlos Mureithi, "Kenya's Expensive Chinese-Built Railway is Racking Up Losses Even as Loans Come Due," *Quartz Africa,* October 8, 2020, https://qz.com/africa/1915399/kenyas-chinese-built-sgr-railway-racks-up-losses-as-loans-due/

10 Nancy Muthoni Githaiga and Wang Bing, "Belt and Road Initiative in Africa: The Impact of Standard Gauge Railway in Kenya," *China Report 55,* no. 3 (2019), doi:10.1177/0009445519853697

11 NS Energy, "Karuma Hydropower Project," *NS Energy,* n.d., https://www.nsenergybusiness.com/projects/karuma-hydropower-project-uganda/

12 Alchetron, "Karuma Hydroelectric Power Station," *Alchetron,* Updated May 28, 2018, https://alchetron.com/Karuma-Hydroelectric-Power-Station

13 Yanning Chen, "Comparing North-South Technology Transfer and South-South Technology Transfer: The Technology Transfer Impact of Ethiopian Wind Farms," *Energy Policy* 116, (2018), 1-9.

14 Railway Technology, "Abuja -Kaduna Rail Line," *Railway Technology,* n.d., https://www.railway-technology.com/projects/abuja-kaduna-rail-line/

15 Railway Gazette, "President Inaugurates Abuja-Kaduna Railway," *Railway Gazette,* July 26, 2016, https://www.railwaygazette.com/infrastructure/president-inaugurates-abuja-kaduna-railway/42876.article

Nigerian Railway Map
Lagos-Ibadan, Lagos-Kano, Warri-Abuja, Ibadan-Kano, and the Abuja-Kaduna Rail Lines

Lagos-Ibadan, Lagos-Kano, Warri-Abuja, Ibadan-Kano Rail Lines

Nigeria contracted the China Civil Engineering Construction Corporation (CCECC) for the Lagos-Ibadan Rail Line for $1.53 billion in 2012 but did not begin operations until December 2020 due to delays, including COVID-19. Nigeria borrowed an additional sum in 2018 for a $6.68 billion contract with CCECC to construct the Lagos-Kano Rail Line. In October 2019, the Nigerian government signed a $3.9 billion contract with CCECC for the Warri-Abuja Rail Line. In 2021, Nigeria asked Exim Bank of China for an additional loan of $5.3 billion to construct another railway, the Ibadan-Kano Rail Line.

Kampala Entebbe Expressway

Uganda borrowed $350 million from the Chinese government's Exim Bank of China to construct a four-lane toll highway to improve transportation and quality of life. The Uganda government also invested $126 million in the project, making the total cost of the expressway amount to $467 million with 40-year repayment terms. Before China Communication Construction Company (CCCC) constructed the road, travel times between Entebbe and Kampala took two hours, it now takes 40 minutes at 50 km/hr.[16]

Maputo – Katembe Bridge, Mozambique

The Maputo – Katembe Bridge, inaugurated in 2018, is the longest suspension bridge in Africa. The connection from Mozambican capital, Maputo, and Katembe, is the most expensive, costing $785 million, employing 450 Chinese workers, and putting Mozambique in an expected debt of 130.7 percent of its 2022 GDP according to the International Monetary Fund.[17] Mozambique financed the loan through Exim Bank of China, and construction was carried out by China Road and Bridge Corporation (CRBC).[18]

Ethiopia-Djibouti Railway Line

The Addis Ababa-Djibouti Railway is the first electrified railway line in East Africa. Started in 2011, construction of the 756km railway was completed in 2015 with passenger services beginning in October 2016 and commercial operations in January 2018. The project was constructed and operated by China's state-owned companies, China Civil Engineering Construction Corporation (CCECC) and China Railway Engineering Corporation (CREC), costing $4 billion, and is jointly owned by the governments of Ethiopia and Djibouti.[19] The two countries financed 30 percent and borrowed $3.3 billion from the Chinese government through China's Exim Bank.[20]

African Continental Free Trade Area (AfCFTA)

Seeking to boost its ability to create a single, more robust market, enhance competitiveness, and facilitate investment, 54 of the 55 African nations agreed to create a free trade area. Eritrea was not part of the agreement due to ongoing conflict, although

---

16 Elias Biryabarema, "Chinese-Built Expressway Divides Uganda as Debts Mount," *Reuters*, January 31, 2018, https://www.reuters.com/article/us-uganda-road/chinese-built-expressway-divides-uganda-as-debts-mount-idUSKBN1FK0V1

17 Agencia Efe, "Mozambique Inaugurates the Longest Suspension Bridge in Africa," *Efe.com*, November 10, 2018, https://www.efe.com/efe/english/life/mozambique-inaugurates-the-longest-suspension-bridge-in-africa/50000263-3809175

18 Club of Mozambique, "Mozambique: Is Maputo-Katembe Bridge Also to be Paid for With Gas Revenues?," *Club of Mozqmbique*, November 13, 2018, https://clubofmozambique.com/news/mozambique-is-maputo-katembe-bridge-also-to-be-paid-for-with-gas-revenues/

19 Railway Technology, "Ethiopia-Djibouti Railway Line Modernisation," *Railway Technology*, n.d., https://www.railway-technology.com/projects/ethiopia-djibouti-railway-line-modernisation/

20 Global Infrastructure Hub, "Addis Ababa – Djibouti Railway," *Global Infrastructure Hub*, November 30, 2020, https://www.gihub.org/resources/showcase-projects/addis-ababa-djibouti-railway/

in 2018, Ethiopia and Eritrea signed a peace agreement. However, the country defends its decision as of 2021 not to join.[21]

Of the 55 nations in the African Union, the United Nations recognizes all but Western Sahara (Sahrawi Arab Democratic Republic). Thus, the U.N. acknowledges 54 countries. Algeria, Angola, Benin, Botswana, Burkina Faso, Burundi, Cameroon, Cabo Verde, Central African Republic, Chad, Comoros, Congo, the Democratic Republic of Congo, Cote d'Ivoire, Djibouti, Equatorial Guinea, Egypt, Eritrea, Ethiopia, Gabon, Gambia, Ghana, Guinea, Guinea-Bissau. Kenya, the Kingdom of Lesotho, Liberia, Libya, Madagascar, Malawi, Mali, Mauritania, Mauritius, Morocco, Mozambique, Namibia, Niger, Nigeria, Rwanda, Saharawi Arab Democratic Republic, Sao Tome, and Principe, Senegal, Seychelles, Sierra Leone, Somalia, South Africa, South Sudan, Sudan, Kingdom of Swaziland, Tanzania, Togo, Tunisia, Uganda, Zambia, and Zimbabwe.

---

21 Abdur Rahman Alfa Shaban, "Eritrea Defends Decision to Sit Out Africa Free Trade Pact – For Now," *Africa News*, Updated July 29, 2020, https://www.africanews.com/2020/07/29/eritrea-defends-decision-to-sit-out-africa-free-trade-pact-for-now/

Delaying commencement until January 2021 due to COVID-19, AfCFTA is the largest free trade area agreeing to remove tariffs from 90% of goods and allow free access to goods and services across the African Union. According to a U.N. article, the AfCFTA's unified market with 1.2 billion people and a combined GDP of $3 trillion is hoping to increase its intra-African exports from 17% in order to create jobs and increase the standard of living across the continent.[22]

While some propose a "Buy Africa" mentality, China serves as 'the world's factory' and has undercut prices of African goods and commodities, explains Dennis Juru, stating, "The Buy-Africa-only mindset of AfCFTA doesn't work. As cross-border traders, we know China moves our goods more cheaply than anyone else."[23]

Conclusion

Africa struggled long before COVID-19, though its problems only increased with the pandemic. Eager to build their economies, and with China willing to loan the money in return for significant rewards and to employ its citizens, African nations reached out for loans to develop their infrastructure. China agreed to projects in some countries that were, frankly, somewhat volatile. Looting and vandalism threatened some projects, weather and disease threatened others. Wars made others challenging.

China is Africa's largest creditor, and Angola owes approximately one-third of this amount.[24]

China empowers its state-owned enterprises to take contracts, employ Chinese workers, and infuse soft power into countries. Indebted, countries face pressure to accept propaganda through their television, radio, and education systems while exerting influence in other ways as well. In 2018, Mike Pence remarked.

> China uses so-called "debt diplomacy" to expand its influence. Today, that country is offering hundreds of billions of dollars in infrastructure loans to governments from Asia to Africa to Europe and even Latin America. Yet the terms of those loans are opaque at best, and the benefits invariably flow overwhelmingly to Beijing. Just ask Sri Lanka, which took on massive debt to let Chinese state companies build a port of questionable commercial value. Two years ago, that country could no longer afford its payments, so Beijing pressured Sri Lanka to deliver the new port directly into Chinese hands.[25]

In Africa, the costs of China's Belt and Road infrastructure projects have costs that have ballooned, revenues have not met expectations, and governments cannot pay back the

---

22 Kingsley Ighobor, "AfCFTA: 100 Days Since Start of Free Trading, Prospects Seem Bright," *Africa Renewal,* April 7, 2021, https://www.un.org/africarenewal/magazine/april-2021/afcfta-100-days-start-free-trading-prospects-seem-bright

23 Ray Mwareya and Nyasha Bhobo, "Will China Help or Hurt the AfCFTA?," *The Africa Report,* February 2, 2021, https://www.theafricareport.com/61451/will-china-help-or-hurt-the-afcfta/

24 Kevin Acker, Deborah Brautigam, and Yufan Huang, "The Pandemic has Worsened Africa's Debt Crisis. China and Other Countries are Stepping In," *The Washington Post,* February 26, 2021, https://www.washingtonpost.com/politics/2021/02/26/pandemic-has-worsened-africas-debt-crisis-china-other-countries-are-stepping/

25 Trump White House Archives, "Remarks by Vice President Pence on the Administration's Policy Toward China," *Trump White House Archives,* October 4, 2018, https://trumpwhitehouse.archives.gov/briefings-statements/remarks-vice-president-pence-administrations-policy-toward-china/

loans. In addition to corruption and money going directly to leaders, African governments are unable to recoup the capital invested. African nations may face a 'debt trap', and they will be required to pay one way or another. China will find another way for them to pay, if not in cash, then oil, rare earth minerals, land, ports, Chinese military base, or a takeover of infrastructure. Any option will be beneficial for China's long-term goals of global dominance. If analysts do not want to call this situation a 'debt trap', they can use the term debt transfer, alternative resource handover, or what African researchers call the China-Africa Swap.[26]

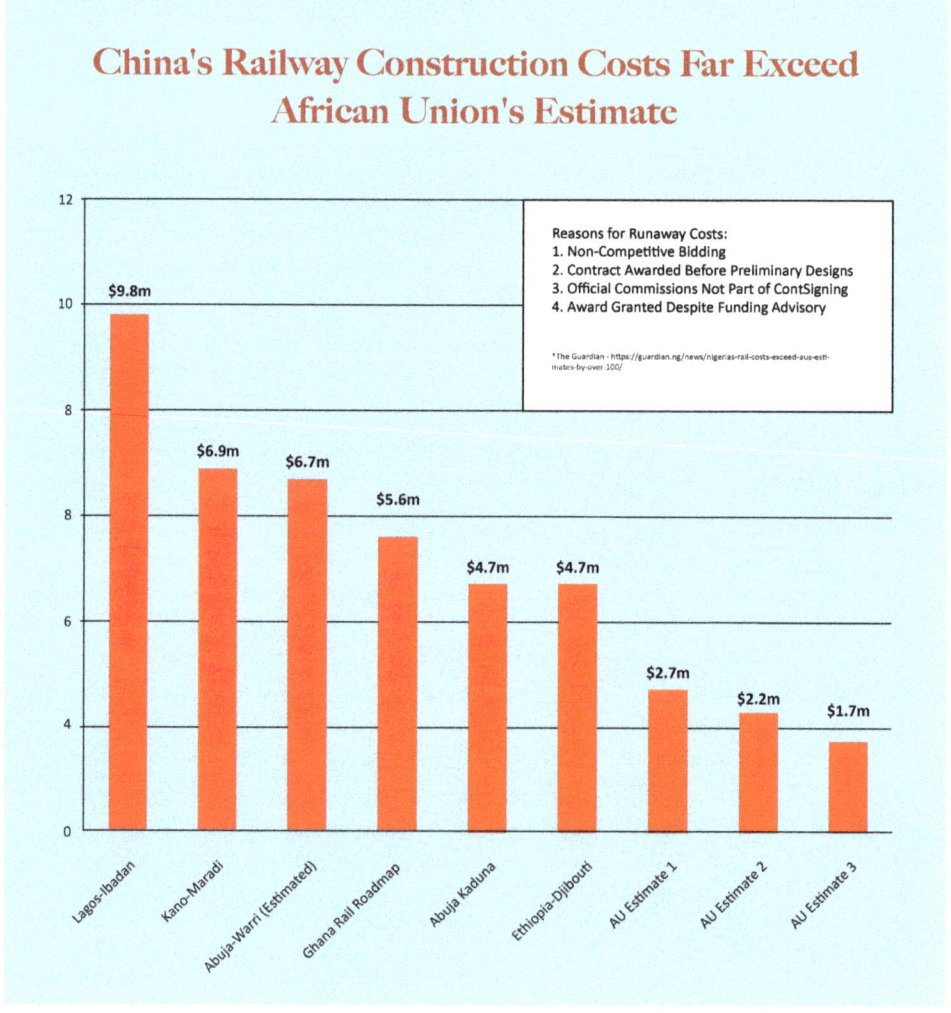

---

26   Eric Olander, "China's Infrastructure Finance Model is Changing. Here's How," *The Africa Report,* January 14, 2020, https://www.theafricareport.com/22133/chinas-infrastructure-finance-model-is-changing-heres-how/

What's at Stake?

First, trust is hard to recoup when it is broken. China built a beautiful African Union building and bugged it in a massive cyberespionage operation lasting for years.[27] Not wanting to jeopardize their loans with China, they did not announce the eavesdropping and surveillance for a year after discovering the surveillance mechanisms that delivered tapes and reports to China each day. China has the upper hand because it holds these country's purse strings.

Second, China has provided hundreds of loan deals to African nations. With no ability to pay what is at stake is the possibility that China will militarize ports for the People's Liberation Army Navy around Africa, which they have started, take the country's resources, deplete their fish, and provide surveillance mechanisms to ensure leaders remain loyal to the Chinese Communist Party (CCP).

Third, despite the 'Buy Africa' push for intra-African resources, goods, and services, China will continue to undercut other countries by supplying 'free' labor and subsidized goods and materials. The further China becomes embedded into the African economy, the less control countries will have on the import-export balance of trade with China, possibly to the detriment to African nations.

---

27 Mailyn Fidler, "African Union Bugged by China: Cyber Espionage as Evidence of Strategic Shifts," *Council on Foreign Relations*, March 7, 2018, https://www.cfr.org/blog/african-union-bugged-china-cyber-espionage-evidence-strategic-shifts

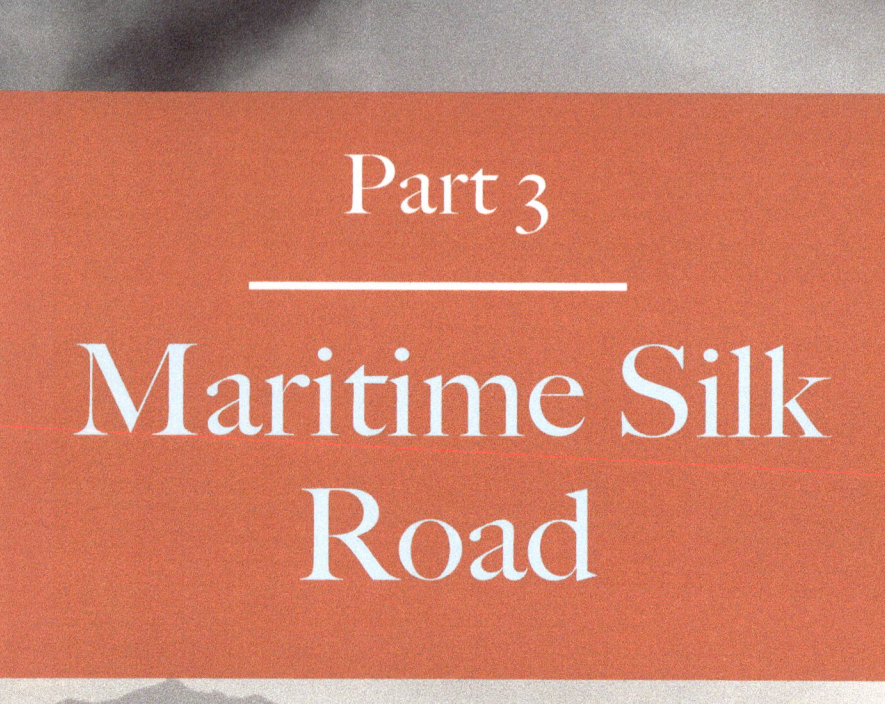

Part 3
Maritime Silk Road

China's Ports & Pearls Delivery Mechanism

Maritime trade offers significant potential for delivering goods. With the increase in sea traffic and with container ships the length of skyscrapers, maritime routes are increasingly important. To this end, China has constructed ports dotted around Eurasia and Africa that it either owns or controls in more than a dozen countries through its 'String of Pearls' strategy, including Gwadar, Hambantota, Djibouti, Sudan, Oman, Seychelles, Maldives, Bangladesh, Myanmar, Thailand, Cambodia, and Hong Kong, just to name a few.

One striking port stands out and it is in a country indebted to China. A country, Sri Lanka, turned over its Hambantota Port on the Indian Ocean to China with a 99-year lease. This decision began the expansion and development of Chinese villages dotting Sri Lanka's coastline. Part of the significance of Sri Lanka's ports is that they provide a link to encircle India and keep that nation of around 1.4 billion people in check.

However, China has other ports as well. Beijing's ports are dotted around the Indian Ocean to refuel and restock along the way to deliver its manufactured goods. One of them is Djibouti, one of the largest of China's ports. As China consolidates its foothold in Djibouti, building a network of infrastructure, Djibouti's debt to Beijing's state-owned enterprises has risen to 70 percent of its GDP.[1] Not alone as an example of impending debt bondage, China has a half dozen additional ports around Africa and Europe providing access to resources and population centers near and far.

ASEAN nations, collectively, are China's largest trading partner; their proximity to China lends itself to numerous ASEAN partner projects. These include Chinese financed and constructed roads, railways, ports, bridges, tunnels, dams, and energy facilities in which many ASEAN countries have borrowed well beyond their means.

Since China claims the economic zones of many of these countries, Beijing has created an entire maritime apparatus for 'protection' of its interests. In its highly aggressive and domineering manner, China has militarized islands in the South China Sea, enacted the China Coast Guard Law, and created the China Marine Surveillance, China Maritime Patrol, China Fisheries Law Enforcement Command, and more to secure its authoritative position in one of the world's most important maritime waterways.

---

1   Mordechai Chaziza, "China Consolidates Its Commercial Foothold in Djibouti," *The Diplomat*, January 26, 2021, https://thediplomat.com/2021/01/china-consolidates-its-commercial-foothold-in-djibouti/

Chapter 1
China's Maritime Silk Road
From Ming and Qing to Today

Introduction

Travel by sea offered Europe, Asia, and Africa an avenue for trading goods of all kinds. Items in one part of the world could be transported via ships that circumnavigated Africa, crossed into Asia, and returned through various routes as sailors explored new places and mapped out the planet. Among the cargo were spices, jade, tobacco, porcelain, and aromatics.

Although receiving foreign ships into the ports of Canton, Macao, and Zaiton for barter purposes, China was not known for its maritime trade. Chinese Confucians held a strong disdain for maritime merchants, which they believed to be a parasitical group that produced nothing and only exchanged goods.[1] China was most known for its land-based silk road across the continent.

Most of China's conquests and travel throughout history along the 'silk road' offer accounts of nomadic tribes on camels and horseback.[2] Land-based powers were later replaced by sea-based powers.[3] With the exception of tribute missions whereby sailors from other lands brought items for trade, early Chinese were not known for their sea-going overtures as much as other naval-oriented explorers and traders.

Accounts of Chinese Maritime Trade

There are relatively few accounts of a navy or of maritime exploration, though China is believed to have established its first navy during the Han dynasty (202 BC - 220 AD).[4] Nevertheless, during a few periods, of its history, China needed to protect its borders from enemies approaching by sea. Boats were constructed to fend off these attacks, like the buildup of ships and training of sailors during the Song Dynasty (960 AD -1279 AD) and Ming Dynasties (1368 AD -1644 AD).[5]

China's Sinocentric viewpoint was that it was the Middle Kingdom to which all others should revere. Those from other countries were considered subordinate barbarians. During various dynastic periods China demanded that other states delivered to the emperor their finest goods, known as tribute, in order to be worthy of trade. In delivering these treasures, they were to kowtow to the emperor to show respect, kneeling and bowing their heads to the ground.

Though China was not known for its maritime adventurers, for a short interlude, China's maritime explorers are said to have been prominent. During the Ming Dynasty, Chinese mariners sailed to distant shores bringing items from China. This moment happened at a time when China sought to build its reputation abroad. Zheng He (1371

---

1   Asia for Educators, Columbia University, "The Mongols' Mark on Global History," *Asia for Educators, Columbia University*, n.d., http://afe.easia.columbia.edu/mongols/history/history4.htm

2   Joshua J. Mark, "Silk Road," *Ancient History Encyclopedia*, May 1, 2018, https://www.ancient.eu/Silk_Road/

3   History Haven, "UNIT III: 1450 - 1750 C.E.," *History Haven,* n.d., http://www.historyhaven.com/APWH/unit%203/UNIT%20III%20NOTES.htm

4   Deng Gang, Chinese Maritime Activities and Socioeconomic Development, C. 2100 BC-900 AD (Westport, Connecticut: Greenwood, 1997).

5   Bernard D. Cole, "2014 The History of the Twenty-First-Century Chinese Navy," *Naval War College Review*, 2014, https://digital-commons.usnwc.edu/cgi/viewcontent.cgi?article=1292&context=nwc-review

- 1433)[6] was a Muslim admiral who devotedly served the Ming emperor, Yongle (1360-1424). During the 15th century, Zheng He, a name given to him by the emperor, led seven voyages with a group of 'treasure ships'.

As the admiral of China's maritime fleet, he set sail on a mission of diplomacy, trade, and cultural enlightenment to extend China's influence abroad. Admiral Zheng's goal was to act as an emissary and secure tribute from distant lands. He was the first navigator to reach many of these countries, heralded as China's great explorer. A 20th-century ship was christened in Zheng He's name.[7]

With the official charge to spread peace and share Chinese generosity with 'barbarians' of other countries, he reached countries throughout Asia and East Africa. Upon recognition of China's superiority, cultural development, and military supremacy, their leaders were invited to share in China's 'riches'. In exchange for 'treasures', Zheng He brought back the bounty of new discoveries, jewelry, and exotic items never seen before in China.

After those excursions, the Chinese retreated to become more isolationist for centuries. While Zheng's voyages ended and China did not continue its maritime engagements, word of China's valuable commodities like tea, silk, jade, art, lacquer, and porcelain spread. Meanwhile, and thereafter, many countries, especially those in Europe, dominated the seas.

---

6   Dolors Folch, "China's Greatest Naval Explorer Sailed His Treasure Fleets as Far as East Africa," *National Geographic,* May 5, 2020, https://www.nationalgeographic.com/history/magazine/2018/07-08/china-zheng-he-naval-explorer-sailed-treasure-fleet-east-africa/

7   Edward L. Dreyer, *Zheng He: China and the Oceans in the Early Ming* (New York: Longman, 2006), 1405-1433.

European Explorers and Merchants

The first European explorers arrived in China not long afterward. Portugal's powerful navy captured Malacca in 1511, controlling the narrow strait, a strategic chokepoint for the flow of vessels from Europe and India to Southeast Asia and China.[8] Afterward, Portugal established a settlement in Macau in 1537, creating a center for Asian trade.[9] When the Ming dynasty ended in 1644, much of China's maritime efforts ended too.[10] Afterward, China's maritime fleet was small, designed only to protect its borders.

> Every Chinese school child learns that China's suffering arose partly because of the lack of a modern navy. Infamously, in the final years of the Qing Dynasty, the Empress Dowager diverted funds earmarked for naval modernization to building a new Summer Palace. This contributed to China's heavy defeat in the 1894-1895 war with Japan, in which a rising Japanese navy smashed the Chinese fleet.[11]

Few Chinese vessels were sent out for commerce since its demands for commerce and extra-regional travel were not a high enough priority to put significant resources into searching elsewhere for goods. Nevertheless, many European countries arrived to trade their goods and bring back uncommon, luxury items. The image of the Maritime Silk Road leading to China from far off lands became implanted and European explorers set their sails to discover this new territory in Asia.

Spain, France, the Netherlands, Great Britain, and others arrived with their vessels for trade. With the increase in the diversity of products and demand by those in home countries, hundreds of boats traveled to India and China to trade. The Maritime Silk Road took centerstage. While the Ming method of trade demanded tribute treasure to the emperor before any goods could be exchanged, the Qing allowed private trade dealings in the late 1600s.

The Manchus of the Qing dynasty, ruling over much of Central Asia, took over and reigned until 1912, continuing with mostly land-based trade. The Qing economy and population grew but soon met challenges when opium was increasingly introduced to Chinese citizens. Anger and conflict over foreign traders illegally importing opium led to the Opium Wars of the 1800s. Western states took over China's ports as the emperor paid out large sums of silver, essentially bankrupting the country. Great Britain's superior naval strength and technology devastated China's military which never fully recovered until the 21st century.

---

8   D.R. Sar Desai, "The Portuguese Administration in Malacca, 1511-1641," *Journal of Southeast Asian History* 10, no. 3 (1969): 501-512, https://www.jstor.org/stable/27651724?seq=1

9   World Heritage Encyclopedia, "History of Macau," *World Heritage Encyclopedia*, n.d., http://www.self.gutenberg.org/articles/eng/History_of_Macau

10 Jim Edwards, "500 Years Ago, China Destroyed Its World Dominating Navy Because its Political Elite Was Afraid of Free Trade," *Business Insider*, March 5, 2017, https://www.independent.co.uk/news/world/americas/500-years-ago-china-destroyed-its-world-dominating-navy-because-its-political-elite-was-afraid-of-a7612276.html

11 David Lague and Benjamin Kang Lim, "China's Vast Fleet is Tipping the Balance in the Pacific," *Reuters,* April 30, 2019, https://www.reuters.com/investigates/special-report/china-army-navy/

Conclusion

Today, the painful memories of China's demise during the Qing dynasty remain. If you talk to many Chinese about the Opium Wars, a phrase you will quickly hear is 'luo hou jiu yao ai da,' which literally means that if you are backward, you will take a beating.[12] During the 'Century of Humiliation', China vowed to rise and regain its stature.[13] When China set its sights on becoming a naval powerhouse,[14] it proved fully capable and was no longer humbled by the West.[15] Combined with its paramilitary fleet, China has the largest navy in the world. China is no longer backward.

---

12 Andrew Moody, "Lessons of the Opium War," *China Daily*, February 24, 2012, http://usa.chinadaily.com.cn/weekly/2012-02/24/content_14681839.htm

13 Michael McDevitt, "Becoming a Great 'Maritime Power': A Chinese Dream," *CNA*, June 2016, https://www.cna.org/CNA_files/PDF/IRM-2016-U-013646.pdf

14 Philip Bowring, "A Historical Perspective on China's Southward Advance," *Australian Strategic Policy Institute*, September 25, 2019, https://www.aspistrategist.org.au/a-historical-perspective-on-chinas-southward-advance/

15 Christian Heller, "South China Sea: China Breaks From a Century of Humiliation," *Real Clear Defense*, February 4, 2019, https://www.realcleardefense.com/articles/2019/02/04/south_china_sea_china_breaks_from_a_century_of_humiliation_114158.html

What's at Stake?

First, while the past is history, the painful memories of humiliation and defeat live in the present. In the eyes of the Chinese, what Western powers did was unforgivable. Unwilling to accept what they perceived as humiliation, they focused their attention on hard work, perseverance, and resilience on their ascension to global dominance.

Second, while the Maritime Silk Road was not China's 'invention', Xi Jinping wants the Chinese to be known in history books as a naval powerhouse. Beijing is well on its way. With nuclear powered vessels some armed with nuclear missiles and a fleet of thousands of armored paramilitary vessels masquerading as fishing boats, China is creating a 'clandestine' juggernaut, a threat that passes under the radar.

Third, studies show that China has between 2,500 and 17,000 paramilitary fishing vessels deployed worldwide, while the United States has less than one tenth.[16] According to a U.S. Department of Defense report, China now has the largest navy.[17]

---

16   Sean Mantesso, "China's 'Dark' Fishing Fleets are Plundering the World's Oceans," *ABC News Australia*, Updated December 18, 2020, https://www.abc.net.au/news/2020-12-19/how-china-is-plundering-the-worlds-oceans/12971422

17   Office of the Secretary of Defense, "Military and Security Developments Involving the People's Republic of China 2020," *Office of the Secretary of Defense*, 2020, https://media.defense.gov/2020/Sep/01/2002488689/-1/-1/1/2020-DOD-CHINA-MILITARY-POWER-REPORT-FINAL.PDF

Chapter 2

Importance of Maritime Traffic and Trade

Getting Massive Quantities of Products to the People

Introduction

As the economy rights itself from the tidal wave of the COVID-19 pandemic, countries seek balance, turning on the steam of forward progress. As vaccines became more widely available, lockdowns were lifted, and the threat of the virus waned, more economies turned the corner on trade. The International Monetary Fund's April 2021 *World Economic Outlook* projected worldwide growth to be 6% for 2021 and 4.4% for 2022, with positive growth for developed countries, including the U.S. at 5.4% and China at 8.4%.[1]

Maritime traffic is also expected to grow through 2022 with increased activity and global citizens ramping up to begin anew, adapting to the changing demands of the workplace and life balance issues. However, countries are now cognizant of the risks of maritime trade both with the Suez Canal and the growing impact of piracy on the seas around countries where poverty and lawlessness are rampant. The 6.5-day blockage of the grounded vessel, Ever Given, on the Suez Canal, alone, cost approximately $1 billion and delayed ships sailing in both directions for two weeks.[2] Piracy increased in 2020, making shipping costs to companies even higher.

In a May 2021 report by DHL Global, the weekly capacity in the Asia to North America trade was the highest level ever recorded, up 45.7% from the previous year; trade from Asia to Europe was up 24.7% from the previous year with cargo demand surpassing maritime capacity.[3] With the traffic on the seas growing and demand for products exceedingly high, the importance of maritime trade has never been more important.

China's Trade and Shipping

China's global manufacturing transport is the world's highest. In 2019, nearly 65% of global port-container cargo was concentrated in Asia; China alone exceeded 50% with Europe ranked second in container port-handing volume.[4] China is presently the largest shipbuilder in the world combining CSIC and CSIG to become COSCO and overtaking Hyundai, Samsung, and Daewoo. China's ten largest ports are:[5]

1. Port of Shanghai - *Shanghai Province*
   Container traffic in 2019: 43.3 million TEU
   Cargo tonnage in 2019: 514 million tons

---

1 International Monetary Fund, "Managing Divergent Recoveries," *International Monetary Fund,* April 2021, https://www.imf.org/en/Publications/WEO/Issues/2021/03/23/world-economic-outlook-april-2021

2 John Bacon, "Suez Canal Blockage: Captain of Ever Given Not Aiding Probe; Calamity's Cost Tops $1B," *USA Today,* Updated April 1, 2021, https://www.usatoday.com/story/news/world/2021/04/01/suez-canal-blockage-egypt-could-seek-1-billion-ship-ever-given/4833205001/

3 DHL, "Ocean Freight Market Update," *DHL,* April 29, 2021, dhl.com/content/dam/dhl/global/dhl-global-forwarding/documents/pdf/glo-dgf-ocean-market-update.pdf

4 United Nations, "Review of Maritime Transport 2020," *United Nations Conference on Trade and Development (UNCTAD),* 2020, https://unctad.org/system/files/official-document/rmt2020_en.pdf

5 Ajay Menon, "10 Major Ports in China," *Marine Insight,* Updated December 3, 2020, https://www.marineinsight.com/know-more/10-major-ports-in-china/

2. Port of Shenzhen - Guangdong Province
   Container traffic in 2018: 27.7 million TEU
   Cargo tonnage in 2018: 194.9 million tons

3. Port of Ningbo-Zhoushan - *Zhejiang Province*
   Container traffic in 2018: 26.4 million TEU
   Cargo tonnage in 2018: 1.12 billion tons

4. Port of Guangzhou - *Guangdong Province*
   Container traffic in 2018: 21.9 million TEU
   Cargo tonnage in 2018: 600 million tons

5. Port of Hong Kong - Special Administrative Region
   Container traffic in 2018: 19.6 million
   Cargo tonnage in 2018: 258.5 million tons

6. Port of Qingdao - Shandong Province
   Container traffic in 2018: 18.26 million TEU
   Cargo tonnage in 2018: 600 million tons

7. Port of Tianjin - Tianjin Municipality
   Container traffic in 2018: 15.97 million TEU
   Cargo tonnage in 2018: 428.7 million tons

8. Port of Dalian - Liaodong Province
   Container traffic in 2018: 9.77 million TEU
   Cargo tonnage in 2017: 455 million tons

9. Port of Xiamen - Fujiang Province
   Container traffic in 2018: 10.7 million TEU
   Cargo tonnage in 2018: 218 million tons

10. Port of Yingkou - Liaoning Province
    Container traffic in 2018: 6.5 million TEU
    Cargo tonnage in 2018: 21 million tons

For comparison, seven of the top ten container ports worldwide are in China.

1. Shanghai, China
2. Singapore
3. Shenzhen, China
4. Ningbo-Zhoushan, China
5. Guangzhou, China
6. Busan, South Korea
7. Hong Kong, China
8. Qingdao, China
9. Tianjin, China
10. Jebel Ali, Dubai, U.A.E.

The Importance of Trade

The importance of maritime traffic and trade has never been as high nor has the quantity of products demanded and supplied by countries, with China leading the pack. However, in 2019, international tensions dampened trade with China, as U.S. tariffs caused a riff in the global trade environment. "Between 2017 and 2019, all major shipping segments experienced a decline in exports of tariffed goods."[6] Although U.S. exports found new markets, these did not compensate for the amount lost to China.

The Trade War

The trade war between the U.S. and China altered manufacturing sites and supply chains, with Vietnam benefitting the most from the dispute. Other countries in Southeast Asia also benefitted, including nearly all of the remaining ASEAN states: Cambodia, Indonesia, Malaysia, the Philippines, Singapore, and Thailand. China's exports to the U.S. dropped to 63.8% in 2019 from 69.1% in 2018.[7] Even with this decrease in manufacturing and trade with the United States, China dominates all other countries with slightly less than the next three countries combined.[8] Thus, as a manufacturing superpower and with expected GDP growth, China is likely to dominate markets through its maritime trade for years to come.

Conclusion

Xi Jinping put in motion a large-scale maritime objective that included staking out ports and establishing China's global presence through the Belt and Road Initiative. Through its loans, China brought its people and materials to construct ports that provided commercial, military, and political access. Throughout the Indo-Pacific region, China dominated trade and established gateways with new spheres of influence. In addition to delivering its goods along maritime trade routes, Beijing incorporated its artificial intelligence technologies, surveillance mechanisms, and currency platforms into its strategic ports and within foreign country's infrastructure.

---

6   United Nations, "Review of Maritime Transport 2020," *United Nations Conference on Trade and Development (UNCTAD)*, 2020, https://unctad.org/system/files/official-document/rmt2020_en.pdf

7   Ibid.

8   Felix Richter, "China is the World's Manufacturing Superpower," *Statista*, May 4, 2021, https://www.statista.com/chart/20858/top-10-countries-by-share-of-global-manufacturing-output/

In some foreign ports in which Beijing has a stronghold, there are more Chinese residents than locals. This presence worried governments and citizens that a takeover of property, resources, and infrastructure is imminent if not complete. Partnerships with countries offer new opportunities to improve transportation, communication, and internal operations. Underdeveloped countries have pressing needs while China has an oversupply of manpower and materials.

However, the mass transit of Chinese citizens to ports around the globe presents significant risks as China gains a foothold to leverage its economic might, military bases, and political influence. Finally, in addition to control, China's ports have the ability to restrict access to other countries either through the high seas or entering countries through maritime channels.

What's at Stake?

First, if George Kennan were to send a "Long Telegram" today, he would not discuss China's containment. That ship left the harbor. China's manufacturing sphere is too large, bolstered by slave labor in concentration camps undercutting labor costs in developed countries. With China as the global manufacturing giant, though, the danger is a dependency on products like semiconductor chips that threaten supply chains. No, Kennan would probably call for constriction, like a boa constrictor, a strategy whereby China's tentacles are prevented from taking possession of infrastructure in other countries and squeezing the breath out of foreign economies.

Second, China's ports are the largest in the world with the capacity to deliver products quickly and efficiently, though threats exist like access to fuel, blockages of thoroughfares, and piracy. Furthermore, the risks of Chinese dominance at ports and the loss of sovereignty is ever-present.

Third, with Maritime traffic expected to increase, more ships mean more possible altercations on the high seas. Furthermore, with new COVID-19 outbreaks in China that prevented ships from leaving its southern ports, delays in receiving goods created new bottlenecks in supply chains, requiring a readjustment in processes, use of building block materials, and delivery mechanisms.

Chapter 3
Piracy on the High Seas:
Alarming Increase in Global Pirate Attacks

Piracy on the High Seas

Piracy is not new. Storybooks tell grizzly tales of beheaded captives and chests of gold. In movies, tales of bold vessel takeovers like *Pirates of the Caribbean* and, more recently, *Captain Phillips*, highlight the threats on the open seas. While those may seem like issues of the past, Somalis famously board vessels, taking cash, goods, and crew. However, brazen piracy is not isolated to the Gulf of Aden. In past reports, Indonesian waters tabulated six incidents in a single day.[1]

In July 2020, near Nigeria, a small boat approached a tanker. Eight men armed with machine guns boarded, rounding up 19 crew members, filling bags with documents and valuables, and forcing 13 crew onto a boat with the aim to trade valuables, documents and crew for ransom money. The ICC International Maritime Bureau provides maps and statistics showing live maps and sightings of armed robbery, piracy, and hostage incidents.[2] According to the International Chamber of Commerce (ICC) International Maritime

Pirate Attacks in the Bay of Benin

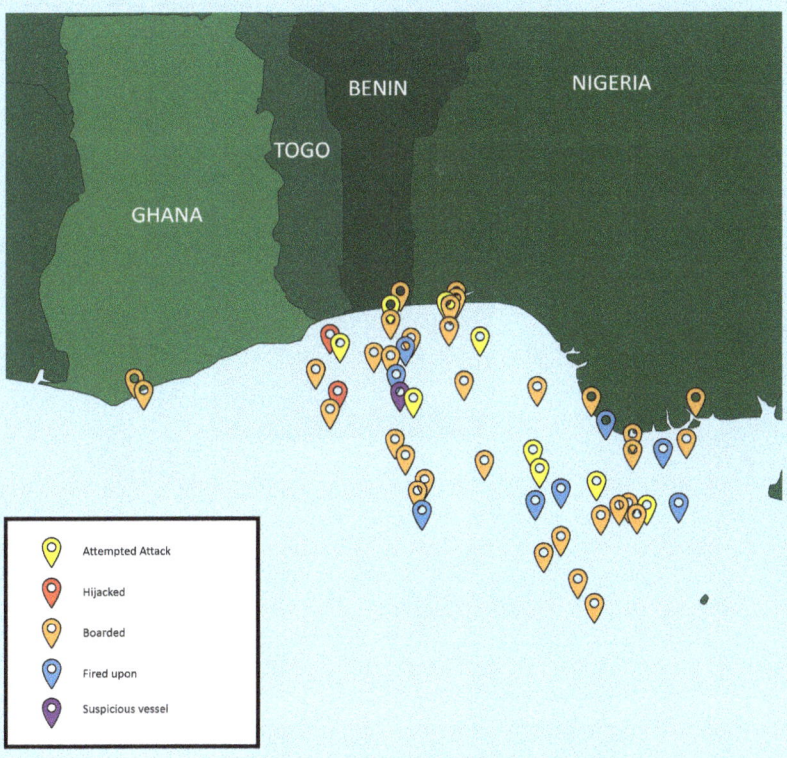

---

1   Pacific Business News, "South Pacific Piracy Worsens," *Pacific Business News*, Updated November 9, 2003, https://www.bizjournals.com/pacific/stories/2003/11/03/daily79.html

2   ICC, "IMB Piracy & Armed Robbery Map 2021," *ICC*, 2021, https://www.icc-ccs.org/index.php/piracy-reporting-centre/live-piracy-map

Bureau (IMB), the Gulf of Guinea accounted for 43% of all reported piracy incidents in the first three months of 2021.[3] *The IMB's 2020 Annual Report* noted a shift from the Gulf of Aden as a hotspot to the Gulf of Guinea on Africa's west coast with 130 kidnapped crew in 22 separate incidents. Worldwide, the Report highlighted 195 recorded piracy attacks, which was an increase from 162 in 2019.[4]

The ICC IMB Q1 2021 IMB Piracy Report stated that 89.5% of vessels that were attacked were boarded. In those same three months, there were 38 incidents (attempted boarding, fired upon, or hijacked), 45 crewmembers impacted (kidnapped, threatened, taken hostage, or killed).[5] An increase in vessels attacked in the Singapore Straits was also noted.

The overall problem is that the pirates use hijacked merchant ships as mother ships since they look legitimate in the waters. Somali's, knowing that detection of their presence has heightened in the Gulf of Aden, have moved farther out into the Indian Ocean. The attacks have become more dangerous with the use of high-speed skiffs armed with automatic

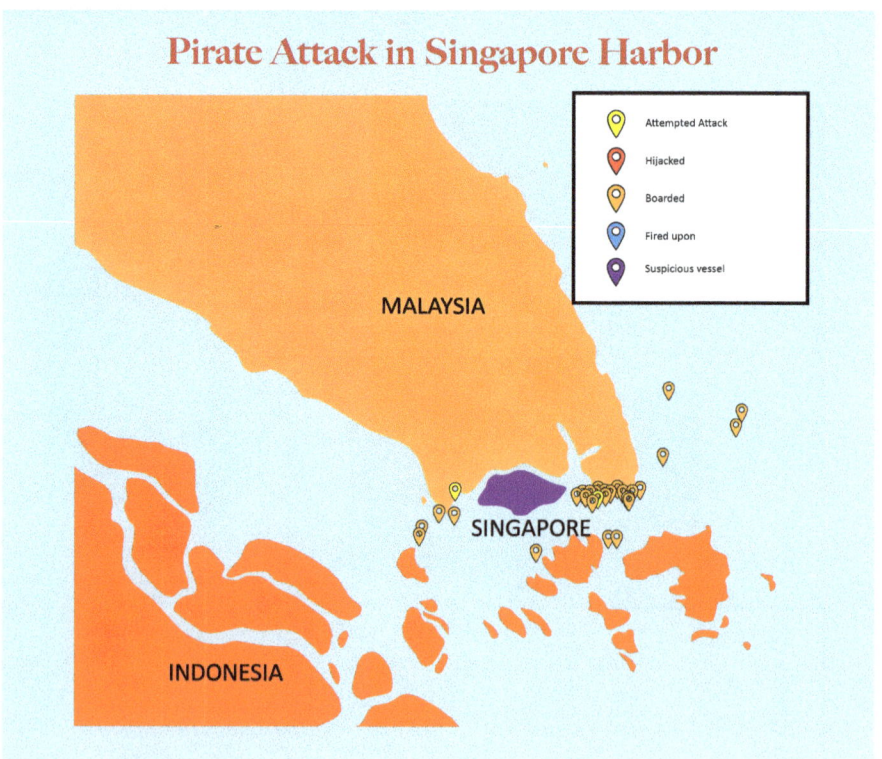

---

3   ICC, "Gulf of Guinea Remains World's Piracy Hotspot in 2021, According to IMB's Latest Figures," *ICC*, 2021, https://www.icc-ccs.org/index.php/1306-gulf-of-guinea-remains-world-s-piracy-hotspot-in-2021-according-to-imb-s-latest-figures

4   ICC International Maritime Bureau, "Piracy and Armed Robbery Against Ships," *ICC International Maritime Bureau*, January 2021, https://www.icc-ccs.org/reports/2020_Annual_Piracy_Report.pdf

5   ICC, "Gulf of Guinea Remains World's Piracy Hotspot in 2021, According to IMB's Latest Figures," *ICC*, 2021, https://www.icc-ccs.org/index.php/1306-gulf-of-guinea-remains-world-s-piracy-hotspot-in-2021-according-to-imb-s-latest-figures

weapons, and rocket-propelled grenades (RPGs) to slow, stop, and board the vessel. International organizations are involved like the International Chamber of Commerce, International Chamber of Shipping, and the World Shipping Council.[6]

UNCLOS Definition of Piracy

According to Article 101 of the United National Convention on the Law of the Sea

Article 101 Definition of piracy

Piracy consists of any of the following acts:

a. any illegal acts of violence or detention, or any act of depredation, committed for private ends by the crew or the passengers of a private ship or a private aircraft, and directed:

   i. On the high seas, against another ship or aircraft, or against persons or property on board such ship or aircraft;

   ii. Against a ship, aircraft, persons or property in a place outside of the jurisdiction of any State;

b. any act of voluntary participation in the operation of a ship or of an aircraft with knowledge of facts making it a pirate ship or aircraft;

c. any act of inciting or of intentionally facilitating an act described in subparagraph (a) or (b)

---

6   World Shipping Council, "Piracy," *World Shipping Council*, n.d., https://www.worldshipping.org/industry-issues/security/piracy

Independent Non-Governmental Support

The International Maritime Bureau Piracy Reporting Center (IMB PRC), based in Kuala Lumpur provides real time information while also raising awareness of the risks of pirate attacks. Knowledge of where and when armed robberies on the high seas take place is essential to maritime travelers of all kinds. Thus, information sharing is central to the tasks of the IMB PRC, proving a single point of contact for shipmasters. Information is immediately relayed to maritime agencies and broadcasted to law enforcement.[7]

Security Challenges

Security challenges abound. Countries worldwide face maritime threats. Particularly at chokepoints where channels narrow and there are few alternatives to escape pirates or terrorists. Former Chinese President Hu Jintao called this problem the Malacca Dilemma since the majority of China's trade passes through the Strait of Malacca. Since that declaration, China has sought multiple avenues (1) through the Arctic's Northern Sea Route, (2) across China and down through Pakistan, and (3) across Myanmar. By building friendships with leaders from Russia, Pakistan, and Myanmar and financing ports, Xi Jinping is creating new avenues to shortcut and avoid natural chokepoints through the Strait of Malacca, Suez Canal, and the Panama Canal where the dangers are the highest.

---

7   ICC, "IMB Piracy Reporting Centre," *ICC*, n.d., https://www.icc-ccs.org/piracy-reporting-centre

Conclusion

Piracy is less concerned with nationality than with financial gains for the pirates. Thus, there are opportunities for countries to find mutually beneficial collaboration regarding security risks. As the number of ships threatened increases, naval and maritime militia will need to increase to restore order to protect the sea lanes. In so far as maritime trade necessitates traversing vast stretches of water, some areas that have little traffic are excessively vulnerable. Thus, Chinese commerce faces considerable risk transiting waters where there is a high prevalence of pirates.

What's at Stake?

First, with the increase in attacks during the pandemic, the maritime transport world is on notice. Whether the pirates are after the contents of the ship or the people aboard, armed takeovers are forcing shipmasters to use escorts for tankers, container vessels, cruise ships, and all other vessels.

Second, risk mitigation is necessary and may demand a broader military presence in areas of the high seas where piracy exists with the greatest density. Thus, with a naval presence, there is an increased danger of rockets, grenades, and heavy artillery used to take down ships or protect against attacks.

Third, piracy alone is a global threat. Ships from all parts of the world travel through narrow straits and close to harbors where danger lurks in every corner.

Piracy Around Africa

Chapter 4

String of Pearls Port Strategy

What's Behind China's Grand Maritime Pursuit?

Introduction

China's ports offer maritime trade from the East China Sea to Africa. Many of China's foreign ports also are military arsenals prepared for war. The number of ports China owns outright or in which it owns a significant share is growing and has surpassed the original 'String of Pearls' region, originally conceptualized in and around the Indian Ocean. Now, circumnavigating the planet from the Pacific Ocean to the Atlantic Ocean with hubs in the Arctic and Antarctic, China has completely covered the waterways of Earth with a stake in locations on every continent.

Commercial and military ports are a key to both trade and security, particularly for China's growing manufacturing sector and need to import energy resources. Transporting the volume of goods China produces requires an enormous logistical structure for its supply chain apparatus. In today's global economy, China's ports are located in strategic areas with access to railways and roads for delivery to distribution centers. The Sea Lines of Communications (SLOC) run through maritime choke points along China's String of Pearls, including the Strait of Mandeb (Suez Canal area toward Europe), Strait of Malacca (where one-fourth of all traded goods passes), Strait of Hormuz (where one-fourth of global oil passes).

String of Pearls Strategy

China's String of Pearls positioning continues to be implemented through its three-link strategy:[1]

1. transportation
2. commerce
3. communication.

China's first military base in Africa was approved for Djibouti in 2013. Situated at the opening to the Red Sea, this People's Liberation Army Navy (PLAN) base provides the protection and security that China needed to secure the transport of its goods in the Indian Ocean headed north to Europe and south to Africa.[2] China's second military and commercial center is China's Gwadar Deep Sea Port in Pakistan. As part of its China-Pakistan-Economic-Corridor (CPEC), China built a high-security compound in 2020.[3]

South of India, in a small island nation called the Maldives, China does not have a formal military compound. However, according to *Reuters*, the Maldives owes China as

---

1 Christopher J. Pehrson, "String of Pearls: Meeting the Challenge of China's Rising Power Across the Asian Littoral," *Strategic Studies Institute*, July, 2006, https://pubs-repository.s3-us-gov-west-1.amazonaws.com/1821.pdf

2 Jean-Pierre Cabestan, "China's Djibouti Naval Base Increasing Its Power," *East Asia Forum*, May 16, 2020, https://www.eastasiaforum.org/2020/05/16/chinas-djibouti-naval-base-increasing-its-power/

3 H. I. Sutton, "China's New High-Security Compound in Pakistan May Indicate Naval Plans," *Forbes*, June 2, 2020, https://www.forbes.com/sites/hisutton/2020/06/02/chinas-new-high-security-compound-in-pakistan-may-indicate-naval-plans/?sh=55d9ffa51020

much as $3.2 billion;[4] with a GDP of 5.6 billion. A base is possible. Next, in 2017, Sri Lanka signed a 99-year lease with China on its Hambantota Port, immediately south of India. China has a majority ownership in Bangladesh's Chittagong Port and Myanmar's Port of Kyaukpyu, located in the Bay of Bengal. China signed 33 deals with Myanmar to develop the China-Myanmar-Economic-Corridor, with twin pipelines, a port, and other transportation access at the cost of nearly $1 trillion.[5]

Authoritarian Control

China is poised to dominate the seas. Along China's Maritime Silk Road, Beijing cannot leave its success in manufacturing transport to chance. Threats of terrorism, piracy, and bottlenecks hinder its well-oiled process. Although many analysts contend that China did not initially map out this grand plan of debt, management, and resource acquisition, the effort is nonetheless in full swing with port acquisitions worldwide. Staking its ground around the Indian Ocean, Beijing's efforts to dot the map with ports is now coming into full vision.

China created a 'String of Pearls' around the Indian Ocean. From the East China Sea to Africa, the map is dotted with China's commercial ports, maritime militia, and Chinese military facilities. China's mainland ports are the largest globally, and its vast web of facilities located on the soil of other countries cover a wide spread of territory. In addition to its large port facilities outside of its mainland like Gwadar, Hambantota, and Djibouti, it has a majority stake in dozens of other ports worldwide.

International Laws and Chinese Rules of the Seas

China disregards international laws, standing out as disregarding maritime agreements. China violated the United Nations Convention on the Law of the Seas (UNCLOS), an agreement it signed in conjunction with 157 parties. In the case, *Philippines v. China*, the International Court of Justice ruled against China regarding sovereignty, states' Exclusive Economic Zones (EEZs), and abuse of the environment. Meanwhile, China disregarded the ruling and pursued its interests to the exclusion of others without consent. China took over islands the International Court of Justice says do not belong to it, militarized islands in other country's Exclusive Economic Zones, and ignored environmental provisions while destroying coral reefs and fisheries.

Meanwhile, China makes up its own laws that Beijing passes and forces on other countries. One is the China Coast Guard Law, which it passed in January 2021.[6] This law violates UNCLOS while harnessing its military that the People's Liberation Army Navy (PLAN) houses on its seven military bases in the Spratley Islands and those it has in the Paracel Islands and on Hainan Island. Furthermore, it employs there its

---

4 Sanjeev Miglani and Mohamed Junayd, "After Building Spree, Just How Much Does the Maldives Owe China?," *Reuters*, November 23, 2018, https://www.reuters.com/article/us-maldives-politics-china/after-building-spree-just-how-much-does-the-maldives-owe-china-idUSKCN1NS1J2

5 Keith Johnson, "China Leaps Into Breach Between Myanmar and West," *Foreign Policy*, January 29, 2020, https://foreignpolicy.com/2020/01/29/china-leaps-between-myanmar-west-india-xi-visit/

6 NPC Observer, "Coast Guard Law of the People's Republic of China," *NPC Observer*, January 22, 2021, https://npcobserver.com/legislation/coast-guard-law/

other advanced weapons of maritime military craft.

Known as the Five Dragons, the following groups were created to implement China's control of the sea alongside the People's Liberation Army Navy (PLAN).

- China Marine Surveillance
- Chinese Coast Guard
- China Maritime Patrol
- China Fisheries Law Enforcement Command
- General Administration of Customs

Sea Lines of Communication (SLOC)

The sea lines of communication are maritime routes between ports. The term SLOC is generally used for naval operations. However, with the need for marine security due to piracy and other dangers, lines between military and non-military are blurred. Paramilitary fishing, militarized cargo ships, and commercial transit occasionally use the term SLOC for nonmilitary transport. Another term often used is freedom of navigation, which represents the commitment of the U.S. military to keep all seas free of threat and control using its Freedom of Navigation Operations (FONOPS). Thus, the U.S. military patrols areas to ensure that no country blocks access to any other country.

China's Ports on its String of Pearls
Indian Ocean, Bay of Bengal, Arabian Sea

China's Power Projection

The String of Pearls strategy is China's effort to gain greater control of the Indian Ocean, ostensibly to ensure safe transport of its exports around the world and to protect its imports of, primarily, oil, gas, and other energy needs. The concept was to have enough ports for China to ensure it gained power and control of the seas. However, the String of Pearls is seen by India as a threat, surrounding the country with Chinese military on all sides. The U.S. saw the strategy as a threat as well, pointing to keeping the SLOC open and maintaining freedom of navigation with its FONOPS.

Countering China

India has pushed back against China's growing threat. In a textbook example of the security dilemma, India's former Foreign Secretary Lalit Mansingh conceptualized an idea called the "necklace of diamonds" to protect its interests using naval cooperation among democratic nations.[7] India believes that its strategic interests are being threatened. Thus, with geopolitical competition, India extended its efforts to secure its territory with its own ports and alliances.

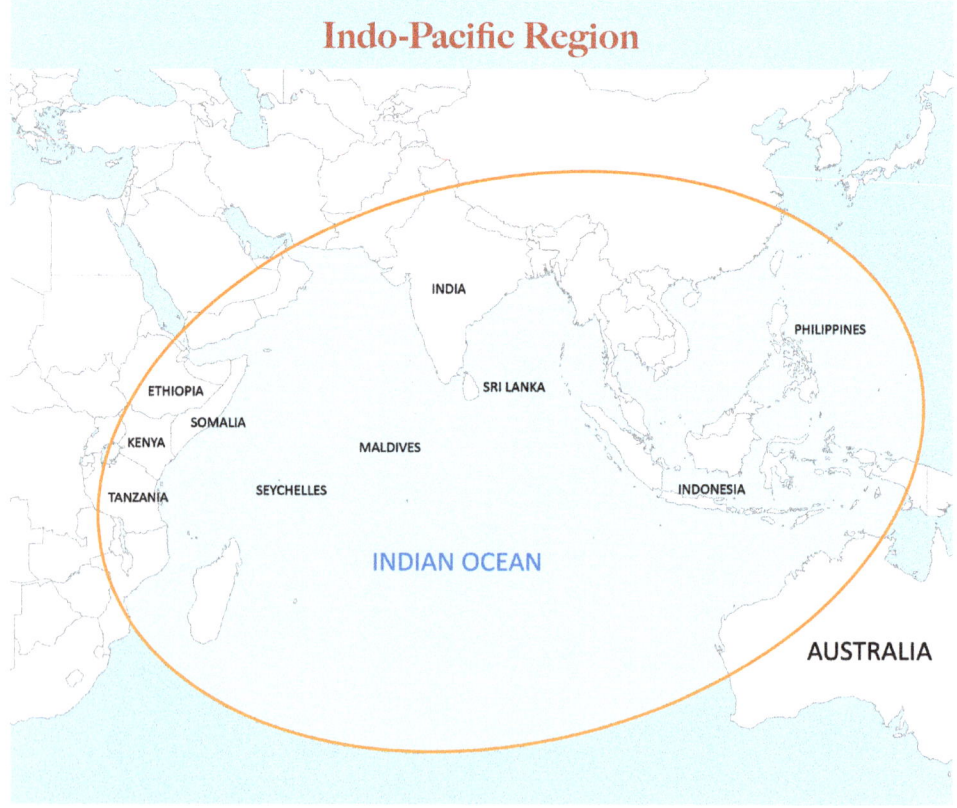

Indo-Pacific Region

---

[7] Manohar Parrikar Institute for Defence Studies and Analyses, "Dattatreaya Nimbalkar Asked: Why Has India's 'Necklace Of Diamonds' Strategy in the Indian Ocean Region Not Been as Successful Compared to China's 'String of Pearls' Strategy?," *Manohar Parrikar Institute for Defence Studies and Analyses*, n.d., https://idsa.in/askanexpert/why-has-india-necklace-diamonds-strategy-indian-ocean-region

These counter efforts have proven to be more for optics, like "The Quad" rather than concrete and actionable. Pundits say that India has not put teeth into its "necklace of diamonds" pursuit.[8] "Numerous strategic partnerships and security arrangements that India had recently built up to counter China's growing hegemony and territorial ambitions, have proved futile in all attempts at settling the enduring crisis posed by its People's Liberation Army (PLA) along the line of actual control (LAC) in Ladakh."[9]

The Quadrilateral Security Dialogue ("The Quad") is another countermeasure against China. The United States, India, Australia, and Japan have a vested interest in maintaining security in the Indo-Pacific region and preventing China from blocking traffic and transport. In March 2021, The Quad met in a dialogue that renewed discussions and looked to the future, stating, "We strive for a region that is free, open, inclusive, healthy, anchored by democratic values, and unconstrained by coercion."[10]

Shipping and Commerce

China's adoption of a market-centered system, increasingly dependent on international trade, has led to its need for more efficient transportation routes. Imports and exports have become synonymous with its industry practices. China's reliance on trade to reach consumer markets requires better port infrastructure. This increasing need is one reason why Beijing has sought to convince other countries to foot the bill in loans to pay for the ports it needs. Shipping lanes are also top priority to Chinese commerce and sustained economic growth, which explains Beijing's urgency. To this effect, China embraces commercial engagements through the Belt and Road Initiative (BRI).

Ensuring shipment and port infrastructure is a crucial area of interest to China as it expands its markets. Connecting the South China Sea to Asia, Africa, and Europe has become increasingly complex with heightened tensions. This need is one reason for Beijing's exertion of control over the entire South China Sea. By controlling shipping lanes, there are fewer challenges to its transportation, commerce, and economic growth.

Conclusion

As China manufactured an increasing variety and volume of products, Beijing needed a comprehensive global trading network where its sea lanes were protected. The String of Pearls offered China the security it needed for its products. No other country produces the variety of goods or supplies the complement of personal and commercial items. Relying on China, Beijing's state-owned enterprises deliver products consumed worldwide. Yet, the key to production effectiveness is its ability to get these goods to consumers and businesses. With this in mind, China created a network of container ports and railway systems paid for by other states where its merchandise could be sent and distributed.

---

8   Rahul Bedi, "When China Chips Are Down, 'Diamonds' in India's 'Necklace of Allies' Lack Sparkle," *The Wire*, August 23, 2020, https://thewire.in/external-affairs/india-china-ladakh-military-necklace-of-diamonds

9   Ibid.

10 The White House, "Quad Leaders' Joint Statement: 'The Spirit of the Quad'," *The White House*, March 12, 2021, https://www.whitehouse.gov/briefing-room/statements-releases/2021/03/12/quad-leaders-joint-statement-the-spirit-of-the-quad/

With China's growth in production came an increase in shipping through Beijing's String of Pearls network at strategic stopping points for delivery, refueling, and maintenance. China's major ports of Shanghai, Tianjin, Ningbo, Dalian, Qingdao, Hong Kong, Shenzhen, and Guangzhou start the maritime flow to points around the world.

Although China has ramped up its efforts to sail through the shorter Arctic route to Europe, presently more than half of its shipments travel through the Strait of Malacca. The result is the "Malacca Dilemma", forcing its ships to sail in the Malacca sea lane and through the South China Sea. China protects this delivery thoroughfare by taking islands from other countries, militarizing them, and using assets on those locations to protect its shipments on the way toward the Indian Ocean and beyond.

What's at Stake?

First, China's String of Pearls has evolved and expanded far past Asia to continents worldwide. While China's port investments were once confined to areas surrounding the Indian Ocean, this is no longer the case.

Second, China speaks as if its loans for ports, railroads, and highways are win-win propositions while many beneficiary countries feel threatened. This phenomenon is particularly seen in China's blatant disregard for the laws.

Third, as China grows bolder and dominates more of the global political and military sphere, countries will push back. China's vision of its new world order is dramatically different than the present day international system in place for more than half of the last century. States are concerned about global market, legal and political changes at the hands of China's authoritarian rule.

Chapter 5

South China Sea and the Strait of Malacca

China's First Priority is to Resolve its Navigation Dilemma

Introduction

The South China Sea (SCS) continues to heat up, causing navigation dilemmas for all countries in the region and for a few nations from thousands of miles away. China's military buildup in the SCS is complemented by China's aggressive attacks against fishermen, oil rigs, and citizens living on their homeland islands. China's People's Liberation Army Navy (PLAN) has brazenly rammed boats, capsized fishing vessels and power-hosed small craft, while also blocking supply transport to the island nations and to their oil rigs.

China claims 80-90% of the South China Sea within a dashed line vaguely etched on a map of their making. Beijing claims that this 'evidence' rules out laws of the sea, including the United Nations Convention on the Law of the Sea (UNCLOS). UNCLOS, signed by 157 parties, including all Southeast Asian states and China, which secures property rights in property rights in the waters extending to 200 nm off of their coast as part of their Exclusive Economic Zone (EEZ). Development rights include land, islands, reefs, fishing, and natural resources. China ignored the law and constructed seven military bases in the SCS.

Scarborough Shoal, Whitsun Reef, and Rules-Based Order

Scarborough Shoal, a triangular collection of reefs and rocks the size of Miami, Florida, is in the Philippines' EEZ. Until 2012, the reef and sand area was controlled by the Philippines. However, after China brazenly took Scarborough Shoal from the Philippines in 2012, the conflict over the South China Sea escalated. The Philippines took China to the International Court of Justice (ICJ) in the case *The Philippines v. China* using UNCLOS to justify the territorial dispute. In the case, *The Philippines v. China,* the court ruled against China, saying that China did not have the right to the area within the SCS and that its possession of islands in the SCS was in violation of the law.

China, ignoring the law, militarized islands in both the Spratlys and the Paracels using these as bases to attack ships and vessels that entered 'their' area. This conflict escalated in 2020 and 2021 as China went on the attack in the EEZs of the Philippines, Vietnam, Malaysia, and Indonesia. With this backdrop Germany sent a ship to the South China Sea (SCS) to support a rules-based order,[1] alongside ships from the United States, Japan, India, and United Kingdom. Australian and French warships patrolled the waters of the SCS together as the sea became crowded with vessels from Southeast Asian nations, China, and Taiwan.[2] In 2021, China placed 200 vessels outside of Whitsun Reef on what appeared

---

1   Reuters Staff, "U.S. Calls German Warship's Plan to Sail South China Sea Support for Rules-Based Order," *Reuters*, March 3, 2021, https://www.reuters.com/article/us-southchinasea-germany-usa/u-s-calls-german-warships-plan-to-sail-south-china-sea-support-for-rules-based-order-idUSKCN2AW016

2   Xavier Vavasseur, "French Navy and Royal Australian Navy Ships Patrol the South China Sea Together," *Naval News*, April 22, 2021, https://www.navalnews.com/naval-news/2021/04/french-navy-and-royal-australian-navy-ships-patrol-the-south-china-sea-together/

to be a forward preparation to take another island from the Philippines' EEZ, despite diplomatic protests.³ With China's blatant violation of the law, concern has grown.

The Importance of the South China Sea

The United Nations Conference on Trade and Development (UNCTAD) estimates that approximately 80% of global trade passes via the sea with one-third of global shipping traffic passing through the South China Sea.⁴ Furthermore, about 40% of China's total trade in 2016 passed through the South China Sea.⁵ To grasp the size of the South China

---

3   Laura Zhou, "South China Sea: Chinese Boats Keep Up Steady Presence at Disputed Whitsun Reef, Says US Ship Tracker," *South China Morning Post,* April 22, 2021, https://www.scmp.com/news/china/diplomacy/article/3130676/china-present-whitsun-reef-and-surrounds-2019-says-us-group

4   UNCTAD, "Review of Maritime Transport," *UNCTAD*, 2015, https://unctad.org/system/files/official-document/rmt2015_en.pdf

5   China Power, "How Much Trade Transits the South China Sea?," *China Power*, n.d., https://chinapower.csis.org/much-trade-transits-south-china-sea/

Sea, the expanse is as large as the Mediterranean Sea, Black Sea, and Baltic Sea combined. Dozens of countries use this transit route.

In addition to the number of ships that pass through the SCS, the region has significant economic and geostrategic importance, including fishing, coral reefs, tourism, and oil and natural gas reserves with an estimated value in the trillions. The fight over natural resources recently led to a nearly six-month standoff as China attempted to block Malaysia and Vietnam from accessing their oil reserves.[6]

Keeping the Sea Lines of Communication (SLOC) open is essential for maritime trade and transport. This need is partly why the United States and other countries have vowed to protect freedom of navigation of the seas and uphold the law. China's claims, seizures, and militarization of the South China Sea threaten commerce. After passing through the SCS,

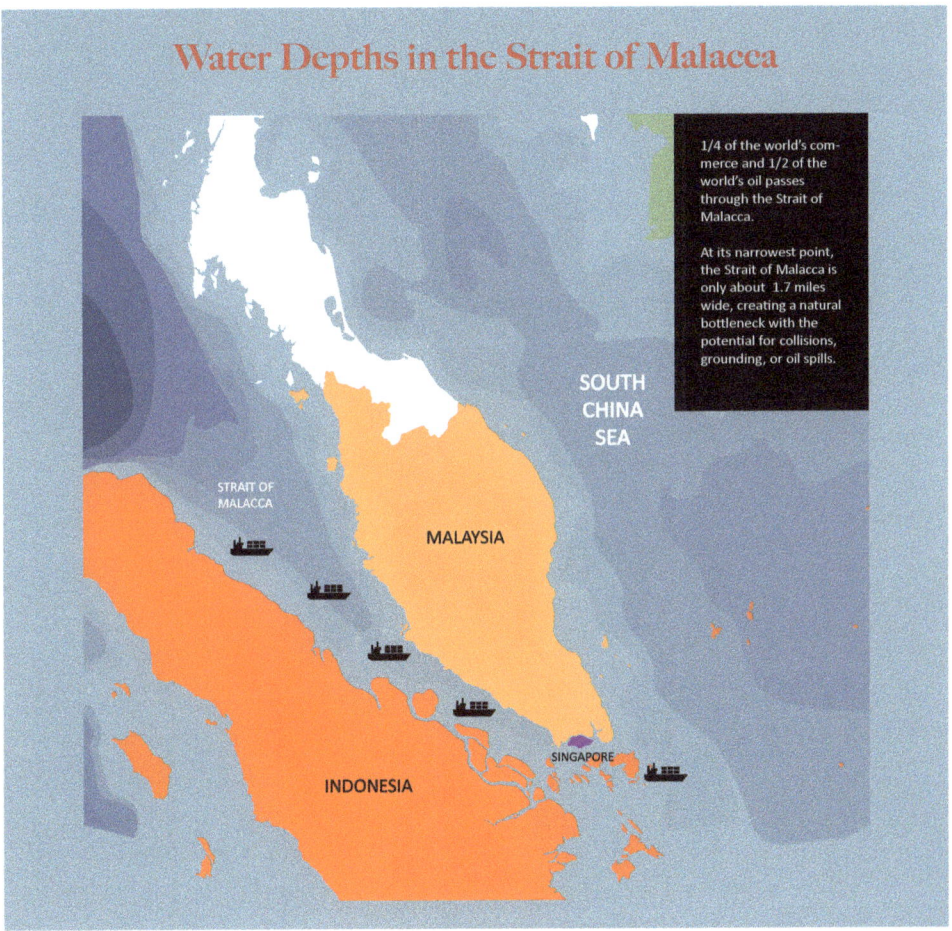

---

6   Ivy Kwek, "Malaysia's Rationale and Response to South China Sea Tensions," *Asia Maritime Transparency Initiative,* May 29, 2020, https://amti.csis.org/malaysias-rationale-and-response-to-south-china-sea-tensions/

the fastest way to get to the Indian Ocean, Suez Canal, or Africa is through the Strait of Malacca.

Countries that follow international law and those that do not maintain vessels in the South China Sea. This dilemma has created a conflict situation for ships. Many of the ships that traverse the SCS travel through the Strait of Malacca. This thoroughfare is a critical chokepoint for vessels as care must be taken to travel down lanes ensuring safe passage for all vessels.

"Malacca Dilemma"

The Strait of Malacca is the world's most crucial strategic passage with approximately thirty percent of global maritime traffic.[7] Between 75,000 and 100,000 ships pass through the Strait each year.[8] Furthermore, eighty percent of China's energy needs pass through the Strait.[9] "China's shipping costs could increase by more than $64 million if the Strait of Malacca is closed for even a week. Another estimate says alternative routes could cost Beijing anywhere between $84 to 220 billion a year."[10] This concern about encroachments and navigation is why a former Chinese president called the Strait of Malacca the "Malacca Dilemma" in a 2003 speech to senior party members and why this is a key focus for Beijing's master planners.[11]

Geopolitics

Singapore is both a central hub for commerce and a key stakeholder in maintaining calm in the South China Sea. Nearby Port Klang is the busiest port in Malaysia, and Tanjung Pelepas is also strategically important. The five busiest ports in Southeast Asia are,[12]

1. Port of Singapore
2. Port Klang, Malaysia
3. Port Tanjung Pelepas, Malaysia
4. Laem Chabang, Thailand
5. Tanjung Priok, Indonesia

---

7 Jean-Paul Rodrigue, "The Bottlenecks of Global Maritime Shipping As Transshipment Clusters," *Port Economics*, May 5, 2017, https://www.porteconomics.eu/2017/05/05/the-bottlenecks-of-global-maritime-shipping-as-transshipment-clusters/

8 Calamur Krishnadev, "High Traffic, High Risk in the Strait of Malacca," *The Atlantic*, August, 21, 2017, https://www.theatlantic.com/international/archive/2017/08/strait-of-malacca-uss-john-mccain/537471/

9 Shannon Teoh, "Malacca Harbor Plan Raises Questions about China's Strategic Aims," *Straits Times*, November 14, 2016, https://www.straitstimes.com/asia/se-asia/malacca-harbour-plan-raises-questions-about-chinas-strategic-aims

10 Palki Sharma, China's 'Malacca Dilemma': How India can Control the Dragon on the High Seas, WION, July 20, 2020, https://www.wionews.com/india-news/chinas-malacca-dilemma-how-india-can-control-the-dragon-on-the-high-seas-314732

11 Jasnea Sarma, "The Malacca Dilemma," *IIT Madras China Studies Center*, August 13, 2013, https://csc.iitm.ac.in/articles/malacca-dilemma

12 Max Schwerdtfeger, "The 5 Biggest Ports in Southeast Asia," *Port Technology*, January 22, 2020, https://www.porttechnology.org/news/the-5-biggest-ports-in-southeast-asia/

China seeks to be the regional leader and achieve regional hegemony through economic and political means. However, India also seeks to play a significant role in protecting navigation in the South China Sea by projecting its naval power.[13] After China encroached on Indian land, killing its military servicemen in 2020, India deployed ships to the South China Sea.[14]

Conclusion

The South China Sea and the Strait of Malacca are strategic points on China's Belt and Road Initiative. The BRI's strategic plan includes China's maritime interests, with countries paying for port development projects and China gaining a foothold in its 'String of Pearls' plan. The countries surrounding the South China Sea – Brunei, Indonesia, Malaysia, the Philippines, Singapore, Taiwan, and Vietnam – are particularly vulnerable to China's aggression and BRI investment' opportunities'.

Some countries have pushed back on China for overcharges and requirements that both leaders and citizens vetoed. Falling into what *The Economist* called a debt trap, Malaysian Prime Minister Mahathir Mohammad asked Chinese authorities to reconsider the cost of a project.[15] At the same time, the government of Myanmar sought to reduce the size and cost of a deep seaport China was building on its coastal city of Kyaukpyu.[16] Indonesia also seeks development of its ports, access to transshipment services, refueling areas, and logistical support opportunities from ships traveling through the Strait of Malacca.

While the Strait of Malacca is dominated by Singaporean products and services from the trans-strait traffic, other states also see this geostrategic choke point area as a potential for GDP growth. China-funded projects costing large sums of money often fail to achieve their fiscal objective.[17] Nevertheless, while China has five seaports in the Strait of Malacca – Sabang, Belawan, Dumai, Batam, and Kuala Tanjung - China is still willing to give Indonesia more money at a price.

In the South China Sea, despite the conflicts over land, oil, fish, shipping, and militarization, countries in Southeast Asia are still deeply tied to China. Economically, Southeast Asian nations are unwilling to bite the hand that feeds them. And, even when China threatens to take their sovereignty, they are still inextricably tied. This dilemma is one that faces many countries in the world now as they must decide whether to take China's money to help their economy and their people and face the associated danger of being trapped in debt.

---

13   Palki Sharma, China's 'Malacca Dilemma': How India can Control the Dragon on the High Seas, WION, July 20, 2020, https://www.wionews.com/india-news/chinas-malacca-dilemma-how-india-can-control-the-dragon-on-the-high-seas-314732

14   Deccan Chronicle, "Indian Navy Deploys Warship in South China Sea after Galwan Clash," *Deccan Chronicle*, Updated August 31, 2020, https://www.deccanchronicle.com/nation/current-affairs/310820/indian-navy-deploys-warship-in-south-china-sea-after-galwan-clash.html

15   The Economist, "The Perils of China's 'Debt-Trap Diplomacy'," *The Economist*, September 8, 2018, https://www.economist.com/asia/2018/09/06/the-perils-of-chinas-debt-trap-diplomacy

16   Yuichi Nitta, "Myanmar Cuts Cost of China-Funded Port Project by 80%," *NIKKEI Asia*, September 28, 2018, https://asia.nikkei.com/Spotlight/Belt-and-Road/Myanmar-cuts-cost-of-China-funded-port-project-by-80

17   The Good Men Project, "How Indonesia Can Avoid Pitfalls of China's Belt and Road Initiative," *The Good Men Project*, September 10, 2020, https://goodmenproject.com/featured-content/how-indonesia-can-avoid-pitfalls-of-chinas-belt-and-road-initiative-2/

What's at Stake?

First, state leaders are in a difficult position in the post-pandemic world with significant needs as they attempt to get on their feet while being enticed by China's willingness to extend loans for projects in which China could potentially have a significant stake.

Second, with the militarization of islands in the South China Sea, many countries reluctantly accept that China will not follow rule of law. For those countries that are small and cannot push back against the mighty dragon of China's firepower, they attempt to file diplomatic protests to China's aggression in vain with no international resolution.

Third, if China breaks the law over and over and nobody will hold Beijing accountable, China will continue to pursue its own economic, political, and military interests unheeded.

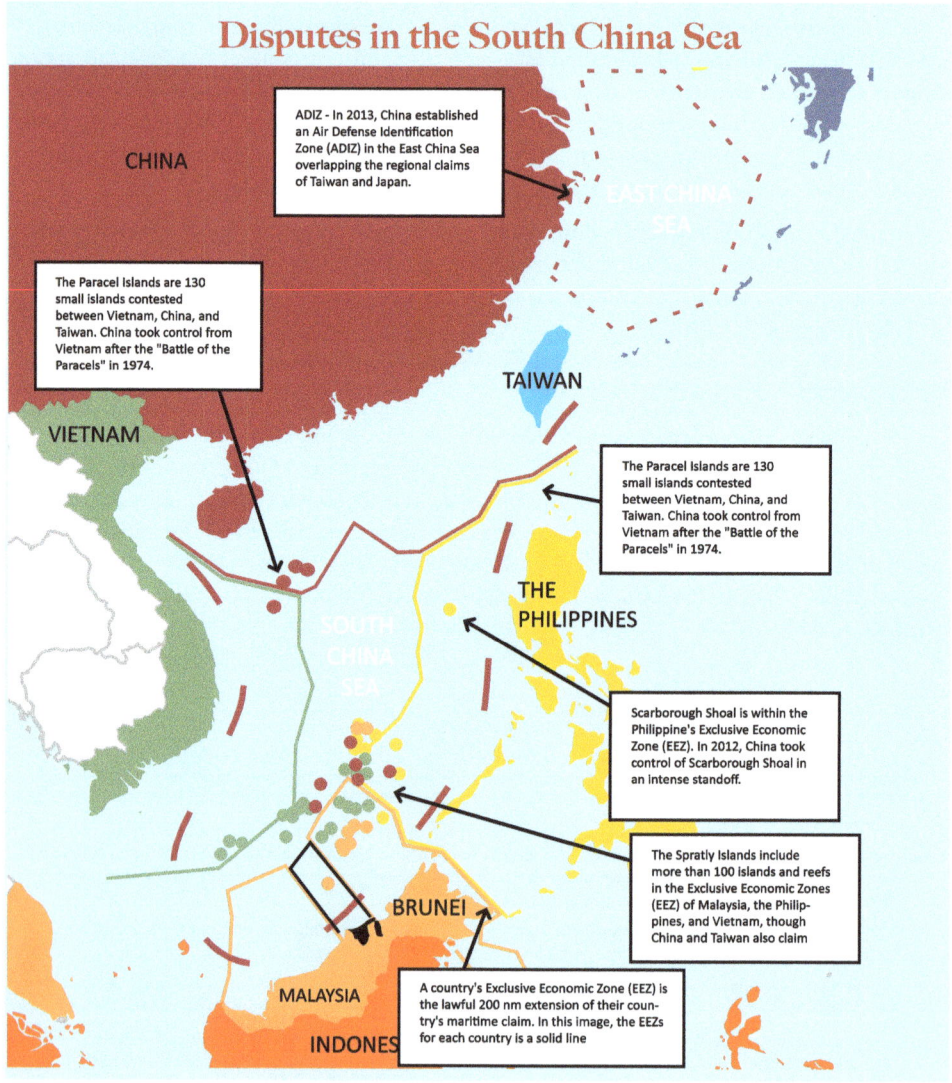

Chapter 6

China's Foreign Ports

Djibouti, Gwadar, Sri Lanka, and a Global String of Pearls

Introduction

China is transforming the world order into one national entity on Beijing's terms with the CCP bankrolling the entire operation. To accomplish this, China expanded its 'string of pearls' beyond Asia and the Middle East to encompass Europe, South America, and Australia. One of China's trade network focal points is the Port of Piraeus in Greece where it not only owns the port, but the railway transporting Chinese goods into Europe.

China owns a significant stake in ports worldwide. A few include:

Container Ports					
Country	Port	Ownership			China Percent
		COSCO	CMPort	QPI	Total
Belgium	CSP Zeebrugge Terminals NV, Brugge, Belgium	100%			100%
	Antwerp Gateway, Antwerp, Belgium	20%	5%		25%
Egypt	Suez Canal Container Terminal, Port Said, Egypt	20%			20%
France	Terminal des Flandres, Dunkirk, France		45%		45%
	Terminal Nord, Terminal de France, Le Havre, France		25%		25%
	Eurofos, Marseille, France		25%		25%
	Terminal du Grand Quest, Nantes, France		25%		25%

Country	Terminal				
Greece	Piraeus Container Terminal	100%			100%
Italy	Vado Reefer Terminal Genoa, Italy	40%		10%	50%
Malta	Malta Freeport Terminal Marsaxlokk, Malta		25%		25%
Morocco	Somaport Casablanca, Morocco		49%		49%
	Eurogate Tangier Tangier, Morocco		20%		20%
Netherlands	Euromax Terminal Rotterdam, Netherlands	35%			35%
Singapore	Pasir Panjang Terminal Singapore	2 Berths			2 Berths
Spain	Noatum Container Terminal Valencia, Spain	51%			51%
	Noatum Container Terminal Bilbao, Spain	40%			40%
Turkey	Kumport Terminal Istanbul, Turkey	26%	26%		52%

China's 13th Five Year Plan

In China's 13th Five-Year Plan, the Chinese Communist Party (CCP) provides a roadmap for state-owned enterprises and Chinese industry leaders to follow domestically and internationally. To encourage the Belt and Road Initiative, an expanded mechanism was developed to open China's markets to the world and provide avenues for China's maritime leaders to expand and invest in overseas seaports.[1]

Beijing's Five-Year Plan focus is on opening the world to China rather than opening China to the world.[2] With increased manufacturing, market share, and shipping development, the resulting effort is likely to frustrate traditional market leaders and induce 'trade wars'. China could undercut the prices or devalue its currency making the cost to purchase items less expensive to close out competitors. Trade disparities may put international corporations in a position of either complying with China's financial and political rules or leave China's growing market. Furthermore, "This imbalance signals that foreign firms will continue to face significant barriers to access China's market."[3]

Military Port Concerns
China's Anaconda Strategy Encircling Europe

According to NPR, China's port investment in Djibouti, Sri Lanka, and Pakistan were followed by Chinese naval deployments. Chinese warships have already come to the Port of Piraeus.[4] European Union leaders are concerned and have proposed investment screening measures for EU countries.

European Commission President Jean-Claude Juncker said,[5]

> Let me say once and for all: we are not naïve free traders. Europe must always defend its strategic interests. This is why today we are proposing a new EU framework for investment screening. If a foreign, state-owned, company wants to purchase a European harbour, part of our energy infrastructure or a defence technology firm, this should only happen in transparency, with scrutiny and debate. It is a political responsibility to know what is going on in our own backyard so that we can protect our collective security if needed.

---

1. Theo Notteboom and Zhongzhen Yang, "Port Governance in China Since 2004: Institutional Layering and the Growing Impact of Broader Policies," *Research in Transportation Business & Management 22*, (2017): 184–200.
2. Scott Kennedy and Christopher K. Johnson, "Perfecting China, Inc. – The 13th Five-Year Plan," *CSIS*, May, 2016, https://csis-website-prod.s3.amazonaws.com/s3fs-public/publication/160521_Kennedy_PerfectingChinaInc_Web.pdf
3. U.S.-China Economic and Security Review Commission, "The 13th Five-Year Plan," *U.S.-China Economic and Security Review Commission,* February 14, 2017, https://www.uscc.gov/research/13th-five-year-plan
4. Joanna Kakissis, "Chinese Firms Now Hold Stakes in Over a Dozen European Ports," *NPR*, October 9, 2018, https://www.npr.org/2018/10/09/642587456/chinese-firms-now-hold-stakes-in-over-a-dozen-european-ports
5. European Commission, "State of the Union 2017 – Trade Package: European Commission Proposes Framework for Screening of Foreign Direct Investments," *European Commission*, September 14, 2017, https://ec.europa.eu/commission/presscorner/detail/en/IP_17_3183

As China creates a string of pearls around Europe, it encircles the region with a noose. Furthermore, with every contract, China gains some political sway. For example, the EU attempted to unite around human rights, genocide, and crackdown. However, Greece, a country whose ports are now owned by China, and where railways are being built by China, blocked the resolution.[6]

Theresa Fallon, a China analyst, explained: "It means making decisions with the idea of not upsetting China. That's already happening, and it's worrying if you consider the stakes. If you think of China's growth strategy [in maritime ports], they've invested all along the peripheries of Europe. So it's like an anaconda strategy: Surround it and squeeze it."[7] Arthur van Dijk, President of the Dutch Association for Transport and Logistics, explained, "For us, it's also a wake-up call. We have to be quicker, smarter, better."[8]

In a U.S. military report entitled, "A Maritime Security Threat to U.S. Geographic Combatant Commands," China has 128 port assets in its international portfolio with 49 classified as high risk.[9] U.S. commands and Chinese ports include,

---

6 Robin Emmott and Angeliki Koutantou, "Greece Blocks EU Statement on China Human Rights at U.N.," *Reuters*, June 18, 2017, https://www.reuters.com/article/us-eu-un-rights/greece-blocks-eu-statement-on-china-human-rights-at-u-n-idUSKBN1990FP

7 Joanna Kakissis, "Chinese Firms Now Hold Stakes in Over a Dozen European Ports," *NPR*, October 9, 2018, https://www.npr.org/2018/10/09/642587456/chinese-firms-now-hold-stakes-in-over-a-dozen-european-ports

8 Ibid.

9 Defense Technical Information Center, "A Maritime Security Threat to U.S. Geographic Combatant Commands," *Defense Technical Information Center*, n.d., https://apps.dtic.mil/sti/pdfs/AD1107142.pdf

Assessment of Chinese Ports		
USCOCOM	# of Countries	# of Ports
AFRICOM	24	48
CENTCOM	8	12
EUCOM	11	19
INDOPACOM	13	24
NORTHCOM	1	3
SOUTHCOM	12	22
Total	69	128

China's Projects Meet Resistance

China's massive fishing fleet continues to look for harbors for port development. One of these is in Sierra Leone, though Beijing's state-owned enterprises have met with resistance, sparking outrage from conservationists, human rights groups, and landowners.[10] Environmental and political groups have requested details of the Chinese deal, though most of the deals with China are undisclosed.

In Piraeus, China's COSCO owns Greece's port until 2052, keeping it as a container terminal, including cruise ship and ferry ports. It is the fastest-growing port in the world.[11] However, the dock workers call China's abusive labor practices 'exploitation' in which anyone who tried to organize was fired and "co-workers had to urinate in plastic bottles" since the Chinese owners would not give them breaks.[12]

Fu Cheng Qiu, Managing Director of the Port of Piraeus said about Greek workers, "They all always talk a lot. But what counts? Actions count. Actions! Only actions!" When asked about working conditions he remarked, "How is that supposed to work? If you want a higher salary you first need to work hard. Not lie on the beach and drink beer. Learn from the Germans! Work hard, never be lazy and always work seriously. Hard work -- happy life."[13]

Djibouti

Although China has military around the world, its only formally recognized base is at Djibouti. China owns Djibouti's naval port, the largest deep-water port in East Africa. In 2021, China agreed to give Djibouti $3 billion to expand its efforts and turn it into a larger

---

10 Elliot Smith, "China's Deal to Build a Fishing Harbor in Sierra Leone's Rainforest Meets Fierce Resistance," *CNBC*, May 19, 2021, https://www.cnbc.com/2021/05/19/china-deal-to-build-a-fishing-harbor-in-sierra-leone-meets-resistance.html?recirc=taboolainternal

11 David Glass, "Greece to Offer Concessions but Won't Privatise 10 Ports," *Seatrade Maritime News*, July 18, 2018, https://www.seatrade-maritime.com/europe/greece-offer-concessions-wont-privatise-10-ports

12 Joanna Kakissis, "Chinese Firms Now Hold Stakes in Over a Dozen European Ports," *NPR*, October 9, 2018, https://www.npr.org/2018/10/09/642587456/chinese-firms-now-hold-stakes-in-over-a-dozen-european-ports

13 Der Spiegel, "China Seeks Gateway to Europe with Greek Port," *Der Spiegel*, April 9, 2015, https://www.spiegel.de/international/business/china-seeks-gateway-to-europe-with-greek-port-a-1027458.html

regional hub for its merchandise shipments to Africa with railroads, port expansion, hotel, and exhibition center.[14] This gateway project will add to its already substantial holdings in the country. China holds 70% of Djibouti's debt in a country in which its people are seeing few rewards from the billions being pumped into Chinese investments.[15]

Pakistan

In 2013, China took control of Gwadar Port, creating both a commercial hub and naval base in the Arabian Sea. China purchased the Pakistani port of Gwadar from the Port of Singapore Authority cutting the distance its oil and gas shipments must travel from Africa and the Middle East.[16] According to *Reuters*, India's Defense Minister A.K. Anthony described the purchase as a "matter of concern to us," with Beijing seeking greater influence in the region.

China has developed strategic maritime linkages along the China-Pakistan-Africa Economic Corridor with its port in Gwadar, 99-year lease on Sri Lanka's port in Colombo, People's Liberation Army Naval (PLAN) military center in Djibouti, Suez Canal Economic Zone (SCZone), and an eye to building a rival Panama Canal through Nicaragua. China is planning a second military base in Jiwani, Pakistan that can accommodate 500,000 troops and another in Tanzania.

China's global security perimeter is enlarging with its expansive economic, commercial, and military reach through its Belt and Road Initiative (BRI) and Maritime Silk Road.

Israel

In June 2019, the Israeli government defied United States pressure and signed a 25-year contract with Chinese company Shanghai International Port Group (SIPG) to build and operate a large shipping seaport in Haifa where the U.S. Sixth Fleet ships dock. Israel recouped $290m for the port privatization.[17] SIPG committed more than $2 billion to expand and upgrade the port that it will run under the 25-year agreement.[18]

In January 2020, in speaking about Israel's new port in Haifa, Shanghai International Port Group (SIPG) President said,

> The maritime route of the OBOR project covers almost 70% of maritime cargo

---

14 Global Construction Review, "China Merchants Signs Deal for $3bn Expansion of Djibouti City Port," *GCR*, January 8, 2021, https://www.globalconstructionreview.com/news/china-merchants-signs-deal-3bn-expansion-djibouti-/

15 Sébastian SEIBT, "Djibouti-China Marriage 'Slowly Unravelling' as Investment Project Disappoints," *France 24*, September 4, 2021, https://www.france24.com/en/africa/20210409-djibouti-china-marriage-slowly-unravelling-as-investment-project-disappoints

16 Agence France-Presse, "China Takes Over Pakistan Port from Singapore," *Industry Week*, February 18, 2013, https://www.industryweek.com/supply-chain/transportation/article/21959543/china-takes-over-pakistan-port-from-singapore

17 Mustafa Abu Sneineh, "Chinese Investment in Haifa Port Could Compromise US-Israel Intelligence Sharing: Report," *Middle East Eye*, February 1, 2021, https://www.middleeasteye.net/news/israel-us-china-investment-intelligence-compromise-haifa-port

18 Al-Monitor, "Report: Israel Turned Down US Request to Inspect Haifa Port After Deal with China," *Al-Monitor*, February 1, 2021, https://www.al-monitor.com/originals/2021/02/israel-china-haifa-port-inspection.html#ixzz6w4d2j1Pm

traffic... construction and development of ports along the route will help promote economic integration throughout... The new Haifa Bay terminal uses semi-automated loading technology and is designed to handle an annual capacity of 1.06 million standard 20-foot containers (TEUs) in the first phase. After construction, the planned capacity for the entire port area is 1.86 million containers per year. It will be the newest and most advanced port in the Mediterranean... The completion of the port by SIPG is an important initiative of China, designed to actively connect it to the New Silk Road project.

Australia

China's port development also extends into Australia. In Darwin, a city in Northern Australia, the U.S. maintains a base where Americans and Australians train. However, the U.S. was not told about a 2015 agreement to lease to Shandong Landbridge Group for 99 years, the rights to operate the port.[19] In an increasingly ugly dispute between China and Australia that began when Australia questioned the origins of the coronavirus, China ramped up their attacks by rejecting or putting tariffs on Australian beef, barley, wine, lobsters, cotton, and other products as high as 80.5%.[20] In May 2021, Australia considered tearing up the lease.

Conclusion

China's investment into foreign ports is a win for emerging countries that do not have the manpower, resources, or know-how to create and operate profitable port structures. Experienced Chinese entities like COSCO offered technical services to create opportunities for expanded income potential to countries worldwide. The trade off is China's control and loss of sovereignty. However, China owns a stake in developed countries also, including in the Port of Seattle in the United States.

The goal of the Five-Year Plan is to encourage outbound delivery mechanisms to drive China's economy and offer greater opportunities to market its products globally. Meanwhile, imports are encouraged in specific areas where China does not yet satisfy demand.[21] President Xi Jinping summarized his Belt and Road Initiative by saying, "China will actively promote international cooperation through the Belt and Road Initiative. In doing so, we hope to achieve policy, infrastructure, trade, financial, and people-to-people connectivity and thus build a new platform for international cooperation to create new

---

19 Rhiannon Hoyle and Jing Yang, "Australia Reviews China Port Lease Near U.S. Military Outpost," *The Wall Street Journal,* May 26, 2021, https://www.wsj.com/articles/australia-reviews-china-port-lease-near-u-s-military-outpost-11622032073

20 Su-Lin Tan, "China-Australia Relations: Landbridge Vows to Protect 'Legally Binding' Darwin port Deal if Political Pressure Persists," *South China Morning Post,* May 27, 2021, https://www.scmp.com/economy/china-economy/article/3134958/china-australia-relations-landbridge-vows-protect-legally

21 People's Republic of China, "13th Five-Year Plan on National Economic and Social Development," *Gov.cn,* March 17, 2016. Translation. http://www.gov.cn/xinwen/2016-03/17/content_5054992.htm.

drivers of shared development."[22]

As China searches for new ports worldwide, its ships large, and small, troll. On the coasts of Mozambique, Senegal, Nigeria, Ghana, the Chinese ships are not only overfishing and destroying marine ecosystems, but they are thwarting local fishermen who depend on fish for their livelihoods.[23] West African coastal towns have been hit hard, resulting in local coast guards being unable to defend themselves against the massive, militarized boats pulling up tons of fish a day. Even though China's vessels act contrary to the laws of African countries, with millions or billions of dollars in loans on the line, leaders of Ghana, Togo, Benin, Nigeria, Cameroon, and Gabon do not stop China. On the contrary, China has doubled down by building its Andoni fishing port to process its colossal hauls..[24]

What's at Stake?

First, China's ports, staffed by Chinese workers are now strategically located throughout the world. Though most of these hubs are commercial and are primarily designed to boost China's manufacturing industries, some are owned by Beijing until the next century and can be converted into alternative uses with the ability to haul shipments of anything from cotton balls to bombs into countries worldwide.

Second, China's vessels, even fishing vessels, crossover as military grade. Its 'fishing fleet' is weaponized, serving a dual role to catch fish and act in a conflict. Thus, far and wide, Beijing marks its territory, influencing actions in Asia, Africa, Europe, the Caribbean, and South America. What is at stake is China's formidable fleet of up to 17,000 armed large 'fishing' ships serving as paramilitary forces,[25] far surpassing the 300-400 U.S. ships. Albeit the Chinese ships are smaller than destroyers or aircraft carriers but they are everywhere in the world and that does not count the fact that China's actual navy is larger.[26] China has about four times the U.S. population that can be activated much more easily than can additional forces in the U.S.

Third, Australia's port dispute with China deepened as the country is poised on the front lines of China's trade war attack. Many of Australia's industries were severely impacted by China's threats and actions. In response, the consequences of 'ripping up' the 99-year

---

22 Xi Jinping, "Secure a Decisive Victory in Building a Moderately Prosperous Society in all Respects and Strive for the Great Success of Socialism with Chinese Characteristics for a New Era, Delivered at the 19th National Congress of the Communist Party of China," *Xinhua*, October 18, 2017, http://www.xinhuanet.com/english/download/Xi_Jinping's_report_at_19th_CPC_National_Congress.pdf

23 Farming Portal, "China's Fishing Fleet Plundering African Waters," *Farming Portal*, January 4, 2019, https://www.farmingportal.co.za/index.php/farming-news/africa-world/1294-china-s-fishing-fleet-plundering-african-waters

24 Mark Godfrey, "Chinese Overfishing Threatens Development of West Africa Fishing Sector," *SeaFoodSource*, June 26, 2020. https://www.seafoodsource.com/news/environment-sustainability/chinese-overfishing-threatens-development-of-west-african-fishing-sector

25 Jean-Michel Valantin, "The Chinese Fishing Fleet, Influence and Hunger Wars," *The Red Team Analysis Society*, April 20, 2021, https://www.redanalysis.org/2021/04/20/chinese-fishing-fleet-influence-and-hunger-wars/

26 Benjamin Mainardi, "Yes, China Has the World's Largest Navy. That Matters Less Than You Might Think," *The Diplomat*, April 7, 2021, https://thediplomat.com/2021/04/yes-china-has-the-worlds-largest-navy-that-matters-less-than-you-might-think/

lease on Darwin is likely to impact other leases and agreements with China worldwide where Beijing uses economic coercion to keep smaller states in line.

Fourth, China promises to deliver progress and prosperity for China and the world. If China was transparent in its actions and did not hide its contracts, there would be greater trust. If China's actions in foreign countries protected environmental sustainability, environmental groups would not be enraged. If China did not break international laws and conventions, while taking other countries' land, rights, and resources, there would be no concern.

Maritime Silk Road | Part 3

Chapter 7

Blockage at the Suez Canal

What Happens if Transport Shipping Passages Close?

Introduction

The Suez Canal is an essential thoroughfare along the Maritime Silk Road. Ships rely on this corridor sandwiched between Egypt and Israel. Egypt owns and operates the canal that has existed since 1869 and has the capacity and authorization to transit 106 vessels a day, though the average daily traffic is between 40-50 ships.[1] Nevertheless, on March 29, 2021, 356 ships waited on both sides of the canal to continue along their journey taking goods and passengers to their next destination after a ship, the Ever Given, became stuck, making the transit route impassable.[2]

Typically, shipping traffic along the canal continues 24 hours per day throughout the year and is a major chokepoint for ships passing from the Indian Ocean to the Mediterranean Sea. The alternative route from Asia to Europe requires circumnavigating Africa, saving an average of $465,000 thoroughfare fees, although the trip takes weeks longer.[3] While some ships chose to wait, others decided to go around the Cape of Good Hope past South Africa. Happily, for Egypt and the waiting vessels, on March 29, the Ever Given was freed, and transit resumed. Nearly 19,000 ships passed through the canal in 2020 carrying crude oil, iron ore, medicines, clothing, and supplies.[4]

China's Reliance on the Suez Canal

The events of March 2021 reawakened countries to the question of safeguarding transportation routes and creating alternative plans to accommodate for when problems occur. China has consistently relied on the Suez Canal as its ships pass from its mainland ports through the Strait of Malacca before heading up toward its European destinations. However, through BRI projects, China has options.

First, is to go around Africa, though that avenue is significantly longer. Second, it can go across the Pacific and Atlantic through the Panama Canal. Third, it can take the shortest route through Russia's Arctic corridor. This last option is the least expensive, though it is better when the ice melts since the passageway is impassable during parts of the year.

The blockage of the Suez Canal spurred China to continue considering choke points and alternative routes to get its goods to their destinations over land, sea, or air. Because of costs and other factors, air is often not viable at this point. Land routes have some limitations due to both tonnage and overland threats. While there are pirates along some of the maritime routes a significantly larger amount can be loaded onto ships for travel by sea.

Strategizing possible problems and options has led its planners to consider alternative

---

1   Ana Rivas, Rosa de Acosta, and Benoit Faucon, "After the Suez Canal Jam, Hundreds of Ships Await Their Turn," *Wall Street Journal*, Updated March 31, 2021, https://www.wsj.com/articles/after-the-suez-canal-jam-hundreds-of-ships-await-their-turn-11617118903

2   Ibid.

3   John Donovan, "Shunning the Suez: Tankers Take the Long Route to Save Cash," *How Stuff Works*, n.d., https://history.howstuffworks.com/historical-events/shunning-the-suez-tankers-take-the-long-route-cash.htm

4   Pippa Stevens, "Suez Canal Traffic Resumes After Cargo Ship Ever Given is Moving Again," *CNBC*, March 29, 2021, https://www.cnbc.com/2021/03/29/suez-canal-traffic-resumes-after-cargo-ship-ever-given-is-removed.html

routes to bypass the Strait of Malacca. The one substitute option floated about for literally hundreds of years is the Kra Canal across Thailand or an overland 'land bridge' option, which would require cargo to be taken off ships and transported by rail to the other side.[5]

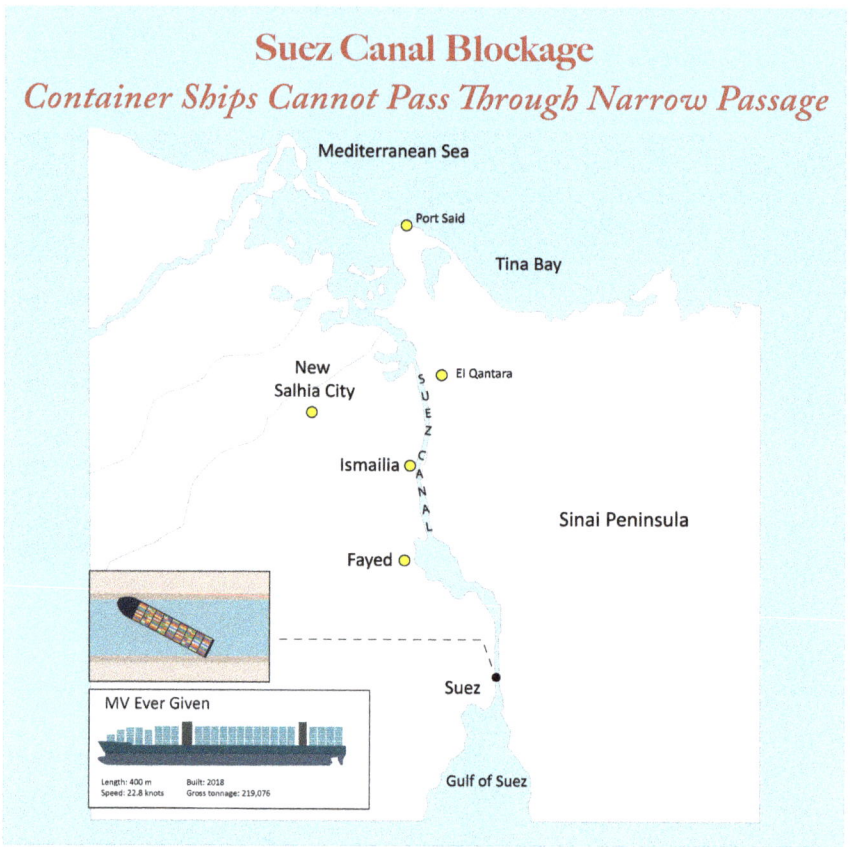

Bringing Manufacturing Closer to the Consumer

Chinese technology manufacturers have created manufacturing centers in Africa to assemble phones, computers, and other equipment closer to the consumers they plan to serve. China-run factories employ workers who toil for 13-hour days to produce shoes along China's newly constructed rail lines, where propaganda posters are designed to inspire workers toward nationalistic honor and patriotism and to "absolutely obey" all orders.[6]

---

5   ASEAN Today, "Thailand Pushes 'Land Bridge' for Trade to Supplant Strait of Malacca," *ASEAN Today*, March 21, 2021, https://www.aseantoday.com/2021/03/thailand-pushes-land-bridge-for-trade-to-supplant-strait-of-malacca/

6   Jonathan Kaiman and Noah Fowler, "China Says it Built a Railway in Africa out of Altruism, But It's More Strategic Than That," *Los Angeles Times*, August 4, 2017, https://www.latimes.com/world/asia/la-fg-china-africa-ethiopia-20170804-htmlstory.html

These facilities would provide jobs while investing in the local economies and requiring less time and money for transportation. Also, African workers are not paid more than a few dollars a week, so the labor is cheap and plentiful. In this scenario, Chinese manufacturers can develop profitable ventures. Since China has gotten other countries to pay for the infrastructure it needed with its network of trains, the feasibility of this mass prodution approach in Africa is reasonable.

As noted, African nations have borrowed tens of billions from China to build roads, bridges, and train tracks. Thus, numerous poor and middle-income countries have paid for China's infrastructure. In Angola, Djibouti, Ethiopia, Kenya, Mozambique, Nigeria, Zambia, and other countries, China has constructed approximately 18,000 miles of train tracks, 62,000 miles of expressways, 100 new airports, and more than 3,500 urban areas while, at the same time, increasing its GDP 10-fold.[7]

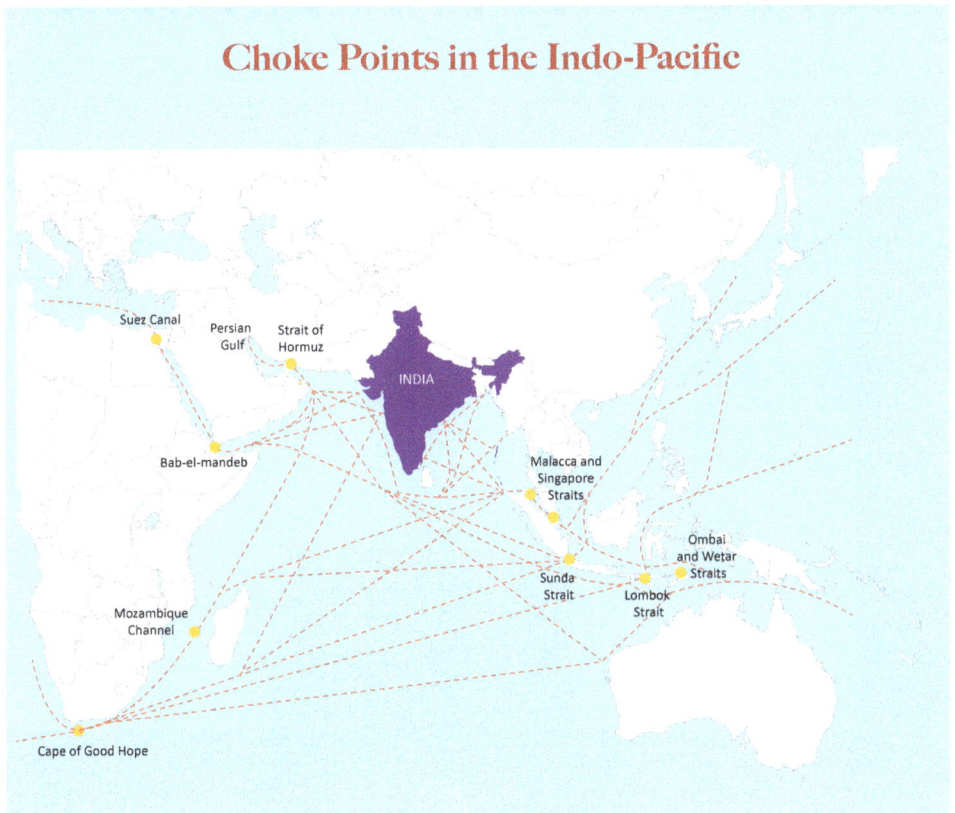

Although China touts its efforts in Africa as altruistic, Beijing benefits mightily. African countries paid for the roads, trains, airports, and seaports, every road, track, and tarmac

---

7   Wade Shepard, "What China is Really Up To in Africa," *Forbes*, October 3, 2019, https://www.forbes.com/sites/wadeshepard/2019/10/03/what-china-is-really-up-to-in-africa/?sh=5bed4dce5930

that China can now use as another avenue to transport its goods.[8]

Egypt-China Relationship

Egypt has historically had a robust relationship with China. Therefore, when Egypt suffered a major crisis during the 2011 Arab Spring protest, China came to its rescue. Then, when China first proclaimed its Belt and Road Initiative, Egypt signed onto the agreement. As Egypt's savior, China proposed BRI loans which Cairo readily accepted. Egypt entered into an agreement with China that offered financial support in the form of loans with no questions asked.[9]

Due to Egypt's geographical location, numerous BRI projects were considered. Some of Egypt's projected development included a Chinese industrial zone in the Gulf of Suez, an electric train system in Cairo, the new administrative capital,[10] a Chinese consortium to house a 6000-megawatt coal-fired electricity plant in Hamrawein, and several investments in the Western Sahara.[11] Due to the consistency and the large volume of BRI projects carried out in Egypt, the two countries developed strong diplomatic ties, which has made Egypt an integral part of the BRI.[12]

Djibouti-China Relationship

Near the Suez Canal, Djibouti offered a prime location for refueling, security, and ship maintenance. China offered enough financial and other incentives to Djibouti to obtain a prime location for a port and loan money through the BRI to provide the country with roads, airports, ports, and railways. A few of these projects included the Hassan Gouled Aptidon International Airport, the Ahmed Dini International airport, Addis Ababa-Djibouti railway, which serves as a bridge between Ethiopia and Djibouti, the Ethiopia-Djibouti water pipeline, and a naval military base.[13] Djibouti is seen as the heart of the BRI. China has invested considerable effort in Djibouti, which now affords China a significant People's Liberation Army base to conduct China's military training, actions, and development.[14]

---

8   Jonathan Kaiman and Noah Fowler, "China Says it Built a Railway in Africa out of Altruism, But It's More Strategic Than That," *Los Angeles Times*, August 4, 2017, https://www.latimes.com/world/asia/la-fg-china-africa-ethiopia-20170804-htmlstory.html

9   Xinhua, "Feature: Chinese Construction Projects in Egypt's New Capital City Model for BRI-Based Cooperation," *Xinhua*, March 18, 2019, http://www.xinhuanet.com/english/2019-03/18/c_137902708.htm

10 Ibid.

11 Energy Egypt, "Chinese Consortium Wins Contract for Hamrawein Coal-Fired Plant," *Energy Egypt*, June 26, 2018, https://energyegypt.net/chinese-consortium-wins-contract-for-egypts-hamrawein-coal-fired-power-plant/

12 The Editors at World Politics Review, "How China Uses One Belt, One Road to Foreground Longstanding Egypt Ties," *World Politics Review*, April 6, 2017, https://www.worldpoliticsreview.com/trend-lines/21771/how-china-uses-one-belt-one-road-to-foreground-longstanding-egypt-ties

13 Lee Jeong-Ho, "How the Tiny African Nation of Djibouti became the Linchpin in China's Belt and Road Plan," *South China Morning Post*, April 28, 2019, https://www.scmp.com/news/china/diplomacy/article/3007924/how-tiny-african-nation-djibouti-became-linchpin-chinas-belt

14 Tyler Headley, "China's Djibouti Base: A One Year Update," *The Diplomat*, December 4, 2018, https://thediplomat.com/2018/12/chinas-djibouti-base-a-one-year-update/

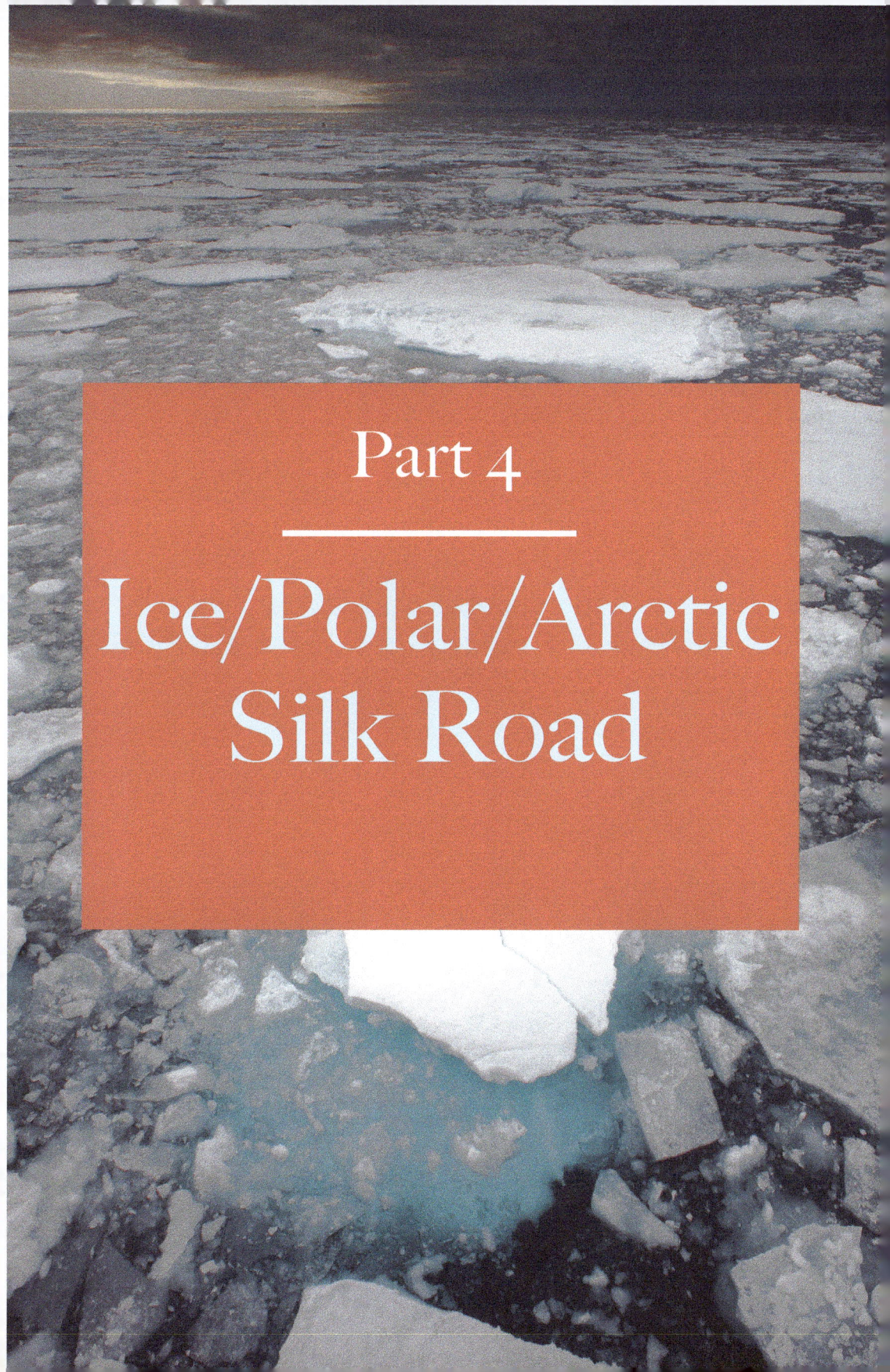

Part 4

Ice/Polar/Arctic Silk Road

Maritime Silk Road | Part 3

What's at Stake?

First, although the blockage at the Suez Canal in March 2021 was a severe problem, and hundreds of ships needed to wait for nearly a week to pass, the issue stirred up many considerations that had been pondered for decades. Alternative options became more promising, and countries realized the importance of shipping in the world economy.

Second, while shipping through the Suez Canal was an avenue used for more than a hundred years, the Northern Sea Route began to be seen as more viable than before. China started to work on the development of additional ice cutters to pursue the shorter 'Arctic Silk Road'.

Third, China has developed relationships with countries that are coming to fruition. By constructing infrastructure in Africa, China can now transport goods shorter distances by bringing manufacturing to the country rather than transiting goods from China. Many of China's investments in roads, bridges, rail, and ports allow China to have military bases in and around Africa and other places in the world. With countries indebted to China and paying back loans for decades, there will be no end to China's bank account as it invests in more projects and puts its Chinese television networks, language centers, and surveillance networks around the globe.

Maritime Silk Road | Part 3

Conclusion

The blockage along the Suez Canal prompted shipping and transportation companies to think in the long view of alternatives to commerce and trade. Israel has posited that they could create an alternate passage past Eilat, a railway option was also considered.[15] Egypt could expand the Suez Canal.

Moscow plans to develop the Northern Sea Route through the Arctic, which is shorter, and which Vladimir Putin has suggested numerous times.[16] Taking advantage of the Suez Canal traffic jam, Putin indicated that the Arctic passageway would cut down time, fuel, and cost. The Northern Sea Route cuts down sea transit by 15 days and, with the rise in global temperature, the Arctic has less ice to be broken up by China's new nuclear-powered icebreaking vessels.[17]

Chinese Cargo Ships
Shorter Transport Route through the Arctic

---

15 Israel Fisher, "Can Israel's Eilat Become an Alternative to Suez Canal?," *Haaretz*, April 1, 2021, https://www.haaretz.com/israel-news/suez-canal-ship-eilat-can-t-become-alternative-global-shipping-1.9668705

16 The Arab Weekly, "Ship Crisis Revives Russian, Israeli Talk of Alternatives to Suez Canal," *The Arab Weekly*, March 30, 2021, https://thearabweekly.com/ship-crisis-revives-russian-israeli-talk-alternatives-suez-canal

17 The Arab Weekly, "Ship Crisis Revives Russian, Israeli Talk of Alternatives to Suez Canal," *The Arab Weekly*, March 30, 2021, https://thearabweekly.com/ship-crisis-revives-russian-israeli-talk-alternatives-suez-canal

"Let the North Pole be a pole of peace."

– Mikhail Gorbachev, 1987 Speech in Murmansk[1]

Mikhail Gorbachev's speech was delivered at a different moment in history, but the nations comprising today's Arctic Council and most other stakeholders feel the same sentiment. China calls itself a "near-Arctic state", staking claims to territory and buying property from claimants for resource extraction. Arctic states should not extinguish the hope that China's expansionism can be stopped and that the North Pole will be the pole of peace envisioned by Mikhail Gorbachev.

China's present actions in melting the Arctic ice, cutting passageways, drilling for oil, destroying marine environments, damaging animal habitats, removing whole species, and populating the region are wholly destructive, not just for the Arctic, but everywhere. Melting the ice endangers people in low-lying areas worldwide, threatening to raise the sea levels across the planet. Glaciers are melting anyway due to climate change, but intentionally melting the ice speeds up this process.

We live in a precarious time and we can take action now to preserve the poles before it is too late. Let us not forget the Cold War was also a dangerous period. During the 60s and 70s, there was a real fear of a nuclear attack. Yet, with the right leadership at the right time, hope is possible. And, we are not in a world of Gorbachev and Reagan, but we can hold out hope that one day we could be. We must hold out that hope. Otherwise, we will be the United States of China. We can only hope that one day a Chinese leader will be like Mikhail Gorbachev, and an American leader can be like Ronald Reagan.

In China's aggressive, world-dominating stance, by calling itself a "Polar Power", fishing in South American and Alaskan waters, ramming boats in the Philippines, Vietnam, and Korea, swarming oil rigs in Malaysia, threatening Indonesian fishermen, killing people in India, taking other countries' land, silencing Hong Kongers, and putting millions of people in concentration camps, there are no promised win-win outcomes except those for China.

The Arctic Council has no true authority to stop China's actions in the Arctic. However, those who care about nature, worry about rising ocean levels, concern themselves with geopolitics, or are worried about China's takeover can go to social media to advocate for returning the region to a peaceful zone of cooperation free of aggression, seizures, and environmental destruction.

---

1 BarentsInfo, "Mikhail Gorbachev's Speech in Murmansk at the Ceremonial Meeting on the Occasion of the Presentation of the Order of Lenin and the Gold Start o the city of Murmanks," *BarentsInfo*, October 1, 1987, https://www.barentsinfo.fi/docs/Gorbachev_speech.pdf

Chapter 1

The Polar Silk Road

Cutting Through Sheets of Ice in the Arctic Ocean to Extend China's Trading Routes

Introduction

Since China adopted a market-centric system, Beijing has grown increasingly dependent on international trade. Importing goods for its vast marketplace of 1.4 billion people and exporting goods for the world is etched into the fabric of Chinese society and is ingrained in its trade and industry practices. China's increasing reliance on foreign producer and consumer markets demands access to port infrastructure and shipping lanes. This crucial component is a top priority for the Chinese leadership, which has justified its actions and accounted for a significant portion of its sustained economic growth. To this effect, China is embracing novel commercial engagements and demonstrating this commitment in the establishment of Belt and Road Initiative (BRI) projects along the Polar Silk Road.

Climate Change and the Impact of Ice Cutters

Global climate change, including the warming of the Arctic, offer new avenues for transport. Arctic Sea ice has dramatically decreased over the past two decades, heightening the interest in countries to consider this avenue as a faster and more efficient access route. Previously regarded as impassable for much of the year, the combination of melting ice sheets and sophisticated ice cutters offers new routes for trade.

Even though China does not border on either the Arctic or the Antarctic, it seeks to have a significant say in both regions' resources. As such, Beijing began investing in the production of modernized ice cutters. When China's next ice cutter is christened, Beijing's total fleet of ice-sheet-chopping ships will have a greater displacement than the ships of other countries, and they plan to construct state-of-the-art nuclear-powered ice-breakers, making chopping up the Arctic and Antarctic ice sheets even easier.

Eight Arctic states border on the Arctic: Russia, Canada, the United States, Iceland, Norway, Sweden, Finland, and Denmark (via Greenland). An international group of these states, plus observer states, share ideas at the Arctic Council, a body created in 1996 to address issues and uphold the United Nations Convention on the Law of the Sea (UNCLOS). A Chinese research report calls China a "near-Arctic state."[1] This statement intensified geopolitical tensions regarding transport, natural resources, and environmental damage. Regional competition and militarization ensued.

Climate change, in particular, poses severe threats to the well-being of the global ecosystem. Ice melting and ice sheet breaking may open up more opportunities in maritime trade, but they threaten habitats and warm the Arctic region where coast guards, trade route support structures, and industry are building new centers. Adm. Karl Schultz stated, "We expect China and its coast guard to wield more power in the future."[2] Meanwhile, China's development of new trade routes is expected to boost its overseas market share with increased transit through the Arctic Sea.

---

1   Xinhua, "Full Text: China's Arctic Policy," *The State Council – The People's Republic of China*, Updated January 26, 2018, http://english.www.gov.cn/archive/white_paper/2018/01/26/content_281476026660336.htm

2   Jon Harper, "SNA News: Coast Guard Wants Budget 'Booster Shot'," *National Defense*, January 13, 2021, https://www.nationaldefensemagazine.org/articles/2021/1/13/coast-guard-wants-budget-booster-shot

The rapid melting of icecaps offers a 6000 km sea route across the Arctic, connecting East Asia and Northern Europe.[3] This new northern passage alters current shipping routes that previously dominated Euro-Asian trade activities which were plagued by narrow channels and pirate activity. The northern shipping lane or "Arctic Silk Road" significantly reduces intercontinental transportation cost and time. Additionally, this alternative avenue for Chinese trade connects Asia, Europe, and North America, enabling its ship captains to bypass chokepoints. Beyond these shipping routes' cost-effectiveness, an additional economic benefit offered by climate change is accessibility to energy resources.

The Arctic embodies an enormous reservoir of untapped energy resources. As such, rising temperatures are a long-term game-changer. It is estimated that around 30% of the world's untapped gas reserves reside in the Arctic Sea, with a potential 13% of global oil reserves situated in that small ocean.[4]

---

3   Maud Descamps, "The Ice-Silk Road: Is China a 'Near-Arctic-State'?," *Institute for Security & Development Policy*, February, 2019, https://isdp.eu/publication/the-ice-silk-road-is-china-a-near-artic-state/

4   Ibid.

China and the Arctic

For these reasons, the People's Republic of China (PRC) is heavily invested in Arctic affairs and has engaged in free trade contracts, intensified political relations with the Arctic States, investment schemes in infrastructure projects, and has sought to gain foothold and membership in Artic Council programs dealing with key issues, such as equipment and polar navigation.

Nevertheless, China is not an Arctic state. Neither its coasts nor landmasses border on the Arctic Ocean. Furthermore, the PRC cannot claim sovereignty over water or shelves in the Arctic. Yet, in China's 2018 "Arctic Policy" proclaimed by "The State Council Information Office of the People's Republic of China", it self-identifies as a "Near-Arctic State" pursuing the 'common interests' of the region. Although there was significant pushback on this statement, this has not stopped China from moving its coast guard military into the Arctic construction 'research bases' and in establishing Arctic trade routes.

There is an adage that goes, "Fool me once, shame on you; fool me twice, shame on me." The excuse that China is just building research centers to study the Arctic was used in the South China Sea when China planted a stake on an island hundreds of miles from its territory and said that this island outpost was created merely to research the area. The story in the Arctic is not new; the Mischief Reef Incident was profiled in Raging Waters in the

South China Sea.[5]

Until 1994-1995, the Philippines controlled Mischief Reef. One day, China put down a buoy, then a wood and bamboo shelter,[6] and then larger structures. Beijing claimed the island was just a waystation for their fishermen,[7] saying it was just conducting research. These buildings multiplied until China took over the entire island. Afterward, China constructed an artificial island, built large structures, and created a large landmass with a runway, airfield, anti-aircraft weapons, missile defense systems, weather stations, and observation areas.[8] Satellite images of new structures may be found on the Center for Strategic and International Studies' Asia Maritime Transparency Initiative website.[9]

The Russian Connection and the China-EAEU Free Trade Agreement

Energy resources, arctic security, and potential shipping lanes are areas of interest for Beijing and Moscow. Russia has significant oil deposits in the Arctic and may use its oil and gas reserves as a diplomatic tool in the European energy market. In 2017, China's involvement is particularly notable as the Free Trade Agreement proposed to the Eurasian Economic Union (EAEU)[10] was approved.[11]

The China-EAEU Free Trade Agreement, signed off in 2018, was widely dismissed in trade and academic circles due to its non-preferential nature. It did not contain any precise category of goods. Nonetheless, getting the Free Trade Agreement (FTA) was a fundamental undertaking for both parties to facilitate precise products' subsequent inclusion. This strategy's implication is significant in that the EAEU-China FTA can be gradually unveiled with regard to specifics whenever China and Russia deem fit.

The China-EAEU FTA paved the way for significant trade opportunities and offered an alternative to the Trans-Pacific Partnership (TPP).[12] Notably, the TPP was negotiated between thirteen countries, including the U.S. Further, along with China's Belt and Road Initiative, Russia constructed a free trade bloc with the EAEU and jointly transformed

---

5 Rachel Winston and Ishika Sachdeva, *Raging Waters in the South China Sea* (Irvine: Lizard Publishing, 2020) 279.

6 Philip Shenon, "Manila Sees China Threat on Coral Reef," *New York Times,* February 19, 1995, https://www.nytimes.com/1995/02/19/world/manila-sees-china-threat-on-coral-reef.html

7 Ian James Storey, "Creeping Assertiveness: China, the Philippines and the South China Sea Dispute," *Contemporary Southeast Asia 21,* no. 1 (1999): 95-118. http://www.jstor.org/stable/25798443.

8 Liu Zhen, "Beijing Opens Weather Stations on Artificial Islands in the South China Sea," *South China Morning Post,* November 1, 2018, https://www.scmp.com/news/china/diplomacy/article/2171271/beijing-opens-weather-stations-artificial-islands-south-china

9 Asia Maritime Transparency Initiative, "*Michief Reef,*" CSIS, Updated 2020, https://amti.csis.org/mischief-reef/#AnalysisofOutpost-heading

10 Russia Briefing, "EAEU Update: Multiple Countries Express Free Trade Interest," *Russia Briefing,* March 24, 2017, https://www.russia-briefing.com/news/eaeu-update-multiple-countries-express-free-trade-interest.html/

11 Chris Devonshire-Ellis, "China-Russia Great Eurasian Partnership on Development Track as EAEU Agree to Regional Free Trade," *Silk Road Briefing,* February 18, 2019, https://www.silkroadbriefing.com/news/2019/02/12/china-russia-great-eurasian-partnership-development-track-eaeu-agree-regional-free-trade/

12 China Briefing, "China Lays Foundations for Eurasian Free Trade After TPP Failure," *China Briefing,* March 17, 2017, https://www.china-briefing.com/news/china-lays-foundations-for-its-own-regional-free-trade-after-tpp-failure/

the Eurasian landmass into an industrial powerhouse in trade and infrastructure. This development places the EU in a position where it is left to decide whether to liaise with the United States or eventually embrace the East.

The close economic and strategic cooperation between China and Russia has steered the conversation around Arctic trade towards both parties and provided a framework for combining the Eurasian Economic Union (EAEU) and the Belt and Road Initiative (BRI). Russia is looking to connect the Northern Sea Routes and China's Maritime Silk Road with the hope of creating not just a competitive route but a global structure linking Southeast, East, and Northeast Asia with Europe.[13] The corresponding implication of such an extensive project is the stimulation of more intimate cooperation among Eurasian nations in the erection of port terminals, logistics centers and the associated increases in shipping traffic.

The Northern Sea passage allows Russia to offer an established route, large-scale shipping support systems, and ready-built infrastructure. As a consequence, Russia has transformed the Northern Sea passage from its historic structure into a sophisticated and competitive maritime course with total overhaul and modernization.

China's Commercial Shipping Routes
Northern Sea Route (NSR)
Suez Canal Route throught the Strait of Malacca

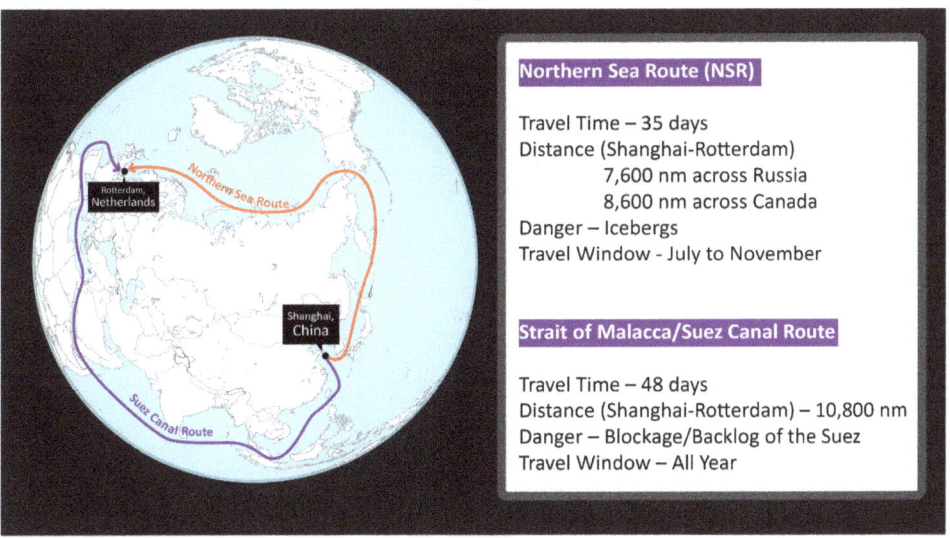

Conclusion

With China's ability to cut through ice sheets and send its ships through a shorter trade route, Beijing considers the Arctic a safer and shorter route linking Europe and its

---

13   Vitaliy Ankov, "Russia Considers Joining Northern Sea Route with China's Maritime Silk Road," *The Arctic*, May 29, 2019, https://arctic.ru/news/20190529/858499.html

homeland. A China policy white paper opens grounds for the BRI to provide opportunities for foreign countries to invest in the Arctic's sustainable social and economic development, which will ultimately be China's Arctic Silk Road. The Ice Silk Road's Chinese ambition revolves around the development of commercial, economic, and scientific cooperation involving all Arctic regions. Although China appears to prioritize its partnership with Russia, particularly in areas of joint research, China has a long-term game plan in mind that may or may not include Russia.

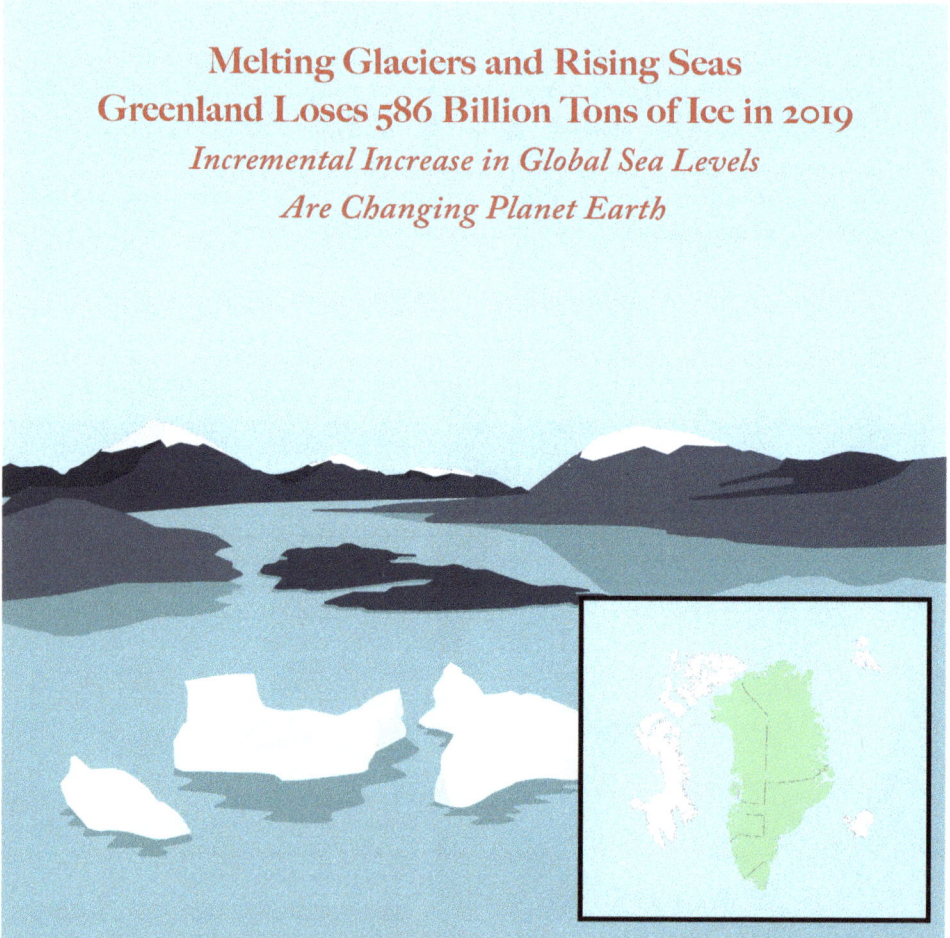

Melting Glaciers and Rising Seas
Greenland Loses 586 Billion Tons of Ice in 2019
Incremental Increase in Global Sea Levels
Are Changing Planet Earth

What's At Stake?

First, the environment is being threatened on a massive scale. Ships are literally destroying the environment by breaking down ice sheets and melting the ice at an unprecedented rate. For people concerned with global warming, without ice sheets, there is no reflection of the ice, further warming of the religion, and no habitat for the polar bears and other Arctic animals.

Second, the increase in military presence in the Arctic is threatening to other countries who are also militarizing the area and increasing their bases and stations. This addition of people means heating up of ice and destruction of the environment.

Third, China is taking one small step at a time. In 2019, at the second BRI forum, China announced that China National Petroleum Corporation (CNPC) was purchasing a 10% share in the Arctic LNG-2 venture from Novatek. This access to liquid natural gas offers one more reason why the Northern Sea Passage is the most cost-effective option for China as it sets up the Polar Silk Road transit corridor for shipping.

Fourth, while its proposed plan is to transform the Northern Sea Passage into a safe, affordable and profitable corridor for shipments, the fees levied on international shipping companies (which includes China) are a hurdle China will need to negotiate, barter with, or leap over.

Chapter 2
Strategic Transitway in the Arctic North
Providing an Alternate and Shorter Transport Route for Trade

Introduction

China needs alternative routes to ship goods, particularly in light of bottlenecks in the Strait of Malacca, Suez Canal, Strait of Hormuz, Strait of Gibraltar, and Panama Canal. Beijing has looked for subsitutes.[1] Until recently, transit routes through the polar ice cap were not realistic, with ice blocking transit most of the year. However, with the warming of the planet, impact of greater human movement in the north, and nuclear-powered vessels to cut through ice, barriers to entry have lowered. Thinning sheets of ice have enabled transit access to the point where transit muc of the year is now viable.

Though the polar route is still filled with ice, plowing through the ice caps and warming sheets of frozen water have proven to be effective, though destructive. The alternative is to send trade south through the Strait of Malacca which has become a growing threat, especially with the militarized waters of the South China Sea. China needs more efficient, effective, and safe transportation routes. Thus, Beijing is increasing its efforts to use the new trade routes to the north, calling itself a 'near-arctic state'.[2] This allows Beijing to boost its overseas market and gain additional access to its energy needs.[3] Although climate change poses serious threats to the wellbeing of the global ecosystem, melting ice sheets open up more opportunities in oceanic trade.

China's Plans for the Arctic

As a result of these efforts, China created its 'blue economic passage' through the ice fields of the Arctic.[4] With global warming melting the Arctic ice caps, China seized an opportunity to extend its Belt and Road Initiative (BRI) shipping lanes to the earth's northernmost region.[5] Chinese President Xi Jinping was elected president in March 2013. By May of 2013, despite its geographic separation from the other participating states, China joined the Arctic Council as an observer. This ability to participate gave China a seat at the table to begin asserting its influence on the coalition of states within the Arctic Circle.[6] Cash-rich, China looked for ways to participate and gain a foothold.

In 2013, China took its maiden voyage to transport cargo from China to Europe through the Arctic passage route. A vessel from COSCO, a Chinese shipping company, left

---

1   Jean-Paul Rodrigue, "The Bottlenecks of Global Maritime Shipping As Transshipment Clusters," *Port Economics*, May 5, 2017, https://www.porteconomics.eu/2017/05/05/the-bottlenecks-of-global-maritime-shipping-as-transshipment-clusters/

2   Maud Descamps, "The Ice Silk Road: Is China a 'Near Arctic State?," *Institute for Security & Development Policy*, February, 2019, The Ice-Silk Road: Is China a "Near-Arctic-State"?

3   Jane Nakano, "China Launches the Polar Silk Road," *CSIS*, February 2, 2018, https://www.csis.org/analysis/china-launches-polar-silk-road

4   Zheng Yingqin, "China and Northern Europe Jointly Build a Blue Economic Channel: Foundations, Challenges and Paths," *Shanghai Institute of International Studies*, August 23, 2019, http://www.ciis.org.cn/gyzz/2019-08/23/content_40864328.htm

5   Maria Smotrytska, "The Implementation of the BRI Project at Sea: South Maritime and Arctic Silk Roads," *Modern Diplomacy*, July 13, 2020, https://moderndiplomacy.eu/2020/07/13/the-implementation-of-the-bri-project-at-sea-south-maritime-and-arctic-silk-roads/

6   Reuters, "China Unveils Vision for Polar Silk Road Across Arctic," *Reuters*, January 25, 2018, https://www.reuters.com/article/us-china-arctic/china-unveils-vision-for-polar-silk-road-across-arctic-idUSKBN1FF0J8

Dalian, China, on a journey to Rotterdam, the Netherlands, cutting out thousands of miles and two weeks of time, a significant improvement over going through the Strait of Malacca and the Suez Canal. Sam Chambers, the editor of *SinoShip* magazine, said, "The Chinese will use the Arctic route in a very big way. It's all about having options, having alternatives in case of emergency."[7]

The year afterward, in 2014, Xi Jinping declared that China would be a "Polar Power".[8] By 2018, Chinese merchant ships began making regular trade transport between Europe and China accross the arctic. After the Suez Canal blockage in March 2021, the use of the polar route increased since there are no narrow passageways through the Arctic like there are in the southern Indo-pacific route.

Due to its lack of sovereignty over the regions within international waters, as defined by the United Nations Convention on the Law of the Sea (UNCLOS), China faced restrictions on commercial fishing or resource drilling operations in the Arctic region. In 2015, the five Arctic coastal states agreed to a voluntary ban on expanded Arctic fishing, but China has not made any official statement on the agreement. However, it is only a matter of time before Chinese companies expand on a big scale.[9] Furthermore, China's shipping companies are the primary user of Arctic international routes due to China's dominance in global shipping.[10]

In January 2018, China's State Council Information Office produced a white paper policy on the Arctic, outlining its interest in the region's natural resources,

> China encourages the development of environment-friendly polar technical equipment, actively participates in the building of infrastructure for Arctic development, pushes for the upgrade of equipment in the fields of deep-sea exploration, ice zone prospecting, and atmosphere and biology observation, and promotes technology innovation in Arctic oil and gas drilling and exploitation, renewable energy development, navigation and monitoring in ice zones, and construction of new-type icebreakers.[11]

The Arctic holds thirteen percent of the world's untapped crude oil and thirty percent of global unexploited natural gas.[12] China has already begun extracting these valuable

---

7   Agence France-Presse, "New Shipping Route Shows China's Arctic Ambitions," *Industry Week*, August 16, 2013, https://www.industryweek.com/supply-chain/transportation/article/21960996/new-shipping-route-shows-chinas-arctic-ambitions

8   Annie-Marie Brady, "From Polar Great Power to Global Power? Global Governance Implications of China's Polar Interests," *Cambridge University Press.*, 2017, https://www.cambridge.org/core/books/china-as-a-polar-great-power/from-polar-great-power-to-global-power-global-governance-implications-of-chinas-polar-interests/3F0CB559FA20B1C2B19B02E7AC8BFD5B

9   Anne-Marie Brady, "China in the Arctic," *Reconnecting Asia*, May 9, 2017, https://reconnectingasia.csis.org/analysis/entries/china-arctic/

10 Ibid.

11 State Council of the People's Republic of China, "China's Arctic Policy The State Council Information Office of the People's Republic of China," *State Council of the People's Republic of China*, January 26, 2018, http://english.www.gov.cn/archive/white_paper/2018/01/26/content_281476026660336.htm

12 Jane Nakano, "China Launches the Polar Silk Road," *CSIS*, February 2, 2018, https://www.csis.org/analysis/china-launches-polar-silk-road

natural resources through an alliance with Russia and investment in the Russian Yamal Liquefied Natural Gas (LNG) project.[13] China holds a twenty percent stake in Russian drilling through its national oil companies,[14] making Beijing a significant financial investment partner guaranteeing Chinese imports of Arctic oil.[15] In July 2018, Russia delivered the first LNG cargo to China via the Northern Sea Route (NSR), expediting natural gas delivery time as Russian vessels did not have to take elongated routes to China by way of the Suez Canal.[16] Shipments have continued ever since.

The three potential shipping routes in the Arctic, the Northeast Passage (NEP) around Eurasia, the Northwest Passage (NWP) around North America, and the central Arctic ocean route,[17] grant China expedited shipping options that greatly appeal to Beijing. The Center for Strategic & International Studies notes,

---

13 Jane Nakano, "China Launches the Polar Silk Road," *CSIS*, February 2, 2018, https://www.csis.org/analysis/china-launches-polar-silk-road

14 Malte Humpert, "China Acquires 20 Percent Stake in Novatek's Latest Arctic LNG Project, *High North News,* April 29, 2019, https://www.highnorthnews.com/en/china-acquires-20-percent-stake-novateks-latest-arctic-lng-project

15 Tom Balmforth and Vladimir Soldatkin, "Russia's Novatek Ships First LNG Cargo to China Via Arctic," *Reuters*, July 19, 2018, https://www.reuters.com/article/us-novatek-cnpc-lng/russias-novatek-ships-first-lng-cargo-to-china-via-arctic-idUSKBN1K90YN

16 Ibid.

17 Zhang Chun, "China's 'Arctic Silk Road'," *The Maritime Executive,* January 10, 2020, https://www.maritime-executive.com/editorials/china-s-arctic-silk-road

[T]he ability to transit through Arctic waters may enhance the security environment for Chinese ships. The NEP provides an alternative trade lane through North Sea Route waters within Russia's Exclusive Economic Zone that circumvents the maritime chokepoint at the Strait of Malacca, as well as pirate-infested waters, such as the Red Sea and Indian Ocean. Such security risk is marked poignantly by the pirate attack on Chinese-owned *COSCO Asia* in the Suez Canal in 2013, while its sister ship, the *Yong Shen* neared the end of its voyage to become the first Chinese cargo ship to transit the NEP.[18]

With China's plans to exert influence in the Arctic region, the United States has begun watching cautiously. A strong pillar in its 2020 U.S. Air Force Arctic Strategy is "Cooperation with Allies and Partners in the Arctic."[19] As a consequence, U.S. military

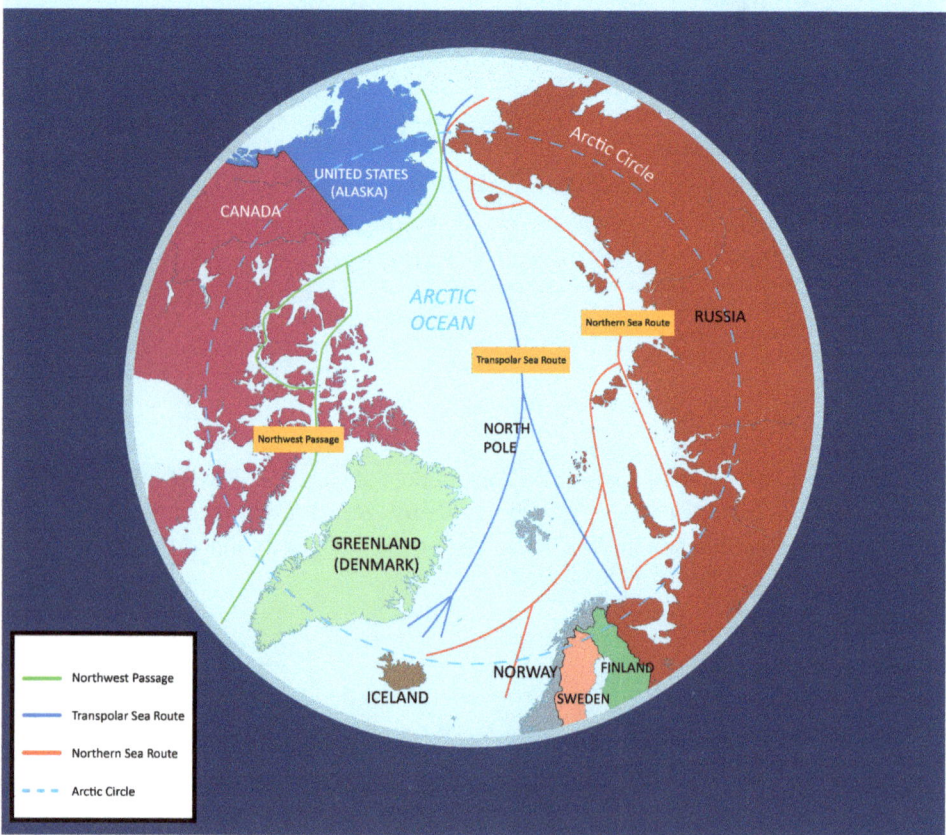

---

18 Jane Nakano, "China Launches the Polar Silk Road," *CSIS*, February 2, 2018, https://www.csis.org/analysis/china-launches-polar-silk-road

19 Sherri Goodman and Yun Sun, "What You May Not Know About Sino-Russian Cooperation in the Arctic and Why it Matters," *The Diplomat*, August 13, 2020, https://thediplomat.com/2020/08/what-you-may-not-know-about-sino-russian-cooperation-in-the-arctic-and-why-it-matters/

presence is increasing in the regions. The Department of Defense, the U.S. Navy, and the U.S. Coast Guard have recently issued Arctic strategy documents.[20] The United States' pivot in attention toward the Arctic region reflects just how significant and pressing Beijing's expansion into this crucial resource hotspot is, though many experts still urge the U.S. to increase its involvement even further.[21]

Conclusion

"Let the North Pole be a pole of peace."

– Mikhail Gorbachev, 1987 Speech in Murmansk[22]

The emergence of the Arctic Sea as an epicenter for resource exploitation and as an avenue for commerce presents opportunities and challenges. However, China's expansion of its Belt and Road Initiative in the Arctic with plans to project its power into the Arctic Ocean, accompanied with increased drilling operations, will change the dynamics of the Arctic and planet Earth.

The Arctic Silk Road is a monumental step in extending Beijing's long arms across the globe.[23] Nevertheless, China's strengthening alliance with Russia threatens the vast and vital resources extensively housed in the Arctic.

What's At Stake?

First, energy resources, arctic security, and potential shipping lanes are key areas of interest to Beijing and Moscow. China's involvement is also particularly notable. While expediting shipping and trading routes for China, the Arctic Silk Road would coincidently grant Beijing access to the world's untapped non-renewable natural resources – a stock that, once depleted, is irreplaceable.

Second, human activity and energy exploration in the polar north are likely to lead to destructive warming effects, impacting the environment, indigenous life in Arctic cities, and transportation networks. However, the biggest issues surround irreparable damage to the delicate Arctic ecosystem, which remains vulnerable to significant fluctuations in temperature, as well as pollutants, chemical spills, and environmental damage.

Third, China is geographically separated from the Arctic, but its commerce, transport, development, and quest for natural resources has grown. Beijing's vast investments in the

---

20 Congressional Research Service, "Changes in the Arctic: Background and Issues for Congress," *Congressional Research Service*, Updated February 1, 2021, https://fas.org/sgp/crs/misc/R41153.pdf

21 Sherri Goodman and Yun Sun, "What You May Not Know About Sino-Russian Cooperation in the Arctic and Why it Matters," *The Diplomat*, August 13, 2020, https://thediplomat.com/2020/08/what-you-may-not-know-about-sino-russian-cooperation-in-the-arctic-and-why-it-matters/

22 Mikhail Gorbachev, "Mikhail Gorbachev's Speech in Murmansk at the Ceremonial Meeting on the Occasion of the Presentation of the Order of Lenin and the Gold Star to the City of Murmansk," *Barentsinfo.fi*, October 1, 1987, https://www.barentsinfo.fi/docs/Gorbachev_speech.pdf

23 Sherri Goodman and Yun Sun, "What You May Not Know About Sino-Russian Cooperation in the Arctic and Why it Matters," *The Diplomat*, August 13, 2020, https://thediplomat.com/2020/08/what-you-may-not-know-about-sino-russian-cooperation-in-the-arctic-and-why-it-matters/

region must be recognized and contained. The Arctic Silk Road, when fully operational and additional Arctic land is purchased, would expand Beijing's influence into vast territories – emulating ancient Chinese dynasties that controlled extensive territories beyond its 'borders'.

Fourth, Russia will continue to use its oil and gas reserves as an increasingly strategic diplomatic tool in the European energy market. "The pipeline runs under the Baltic Sea, from Russia's Baltic coast to northeastern Germany, and will double natural gas supplies from Russia to Germany. In doing so, it will avoid transit fees from Ukraine and will greatly increase Europe's reliance on Russian energy and give Russia exploitative power over countries such as Poland, Ukraine, Hungary, Romania, the Czech Republic, Slovakia, and the Baltic states, which are among the EU countries that oppose construction of Nord Stream 2."[24]

Fifth, in foreign policy, actions speak louder than words. Russia's cyberattacks attempted to "hijack the email system of a United States government agency," according to a May 2021 *New York Times* article.[25] Additionally, Russia engaged in the widely publicized poisoning-to-prison of Putin opposition leader, Alexei Navalny.[26] According to *Reuters*, in May 2021, Russia had 100,000 soldiers amassed on the Ukraine border.[27] Reuters also reported on Russia's massive crackdowns on lawyers, activists, and opposition groups.[28] Despite amplified concerns, in June 2021, before President Joseph Biden's meeting with Russian President Vladimir Putin, Biden waived sanctions on the Nord Stream 2 pipeline, which divided NATO, weakened the Ukraine, and is increasingly subordinating Europe.

---

24   Rebeccah L. Heinrichs, "Biden's Gift to Putin," *Hudson Institute*, June 18, 2021, https://www.hudson.org/research/17027-biden-s-gift-to-putin

25   David E. Sanger and Nicole Perlroth, "Russia Appears to Carry Out Hack Through System Used by U.S. Aid Agency," *The New York Times*, May 28, 2021, https://www.nytimes.com/2021/05/28/us/politics/russia-hack-usaid.html

26   Al Jazeera, "Alexey Navalny Timeline: From Poisoning to Prison," *Al Jazeera*, January 19, 2021, https://www.aljazeera.com/news/2021/1/19/hold-alexei-navalny-timeline-from-poisoning-to-prison

27   Reuters, "Ukraine Says Russia Still Has 100,000 Troops Near Its Border," *Reuters*, May 11, 2021, https://www.reuters.com/world/europe/ukraine-says-russia-still-has-100000-troops-near-its-border-2021-05-11/

28   Reuters, "Russia Declares Navalny's Groups 'Extremist' in Ongoing Crackdown – Lawyers," *Reuters*, June 9, 2021, https://www.reuters.com/world/europe/russia-declares-navalnys-groups-extremist-ongoing-crackdown-lawyers-2021-06-09/

Walrus in a Once-Frozen Sea

Chapter 3
International Efforts and Agencies Responsible for the Arctic
Research, Collaboration, Advocacy, Laws, and Guidelines

Introduction

Governance in the Arctic covers various environmental protection issues integral to navigational practices and exploration parameters, including resource exploitation and scientific research.

United Nations Convention on the Law of the Sea

The Arctic Sea and polar ice cap are governed by the United Nations Convention on the Law of the Sea (UNCLOS), joined by 168 international bodies and 157 signatories, including China.[1] UNCLOS lays out the rights and responsibilities regarding the use, access, and ownership of the sea. Since China faced legal action in the arbitration case, *Philippines v China* at the International Court of Justice and ignored the ruling.[2] It is uncertain whether the rights and responsibilities make any difference to Beijing or whether China plans to ignore the law. Up to this time China is an international offender, regarding sovereignty, ownership, and right to the sea. Nevertheless, among responsible nations who honor their pledge to the United Nations, UNCLOS is designed to promulgate and adjudicate rules of the road at the international level.

The 1996 Ottawa Declaration

On September 19, 1996, the Ottawa Declaration established the Arctic Council to collaborate, consult, cooperate, and coordinate between the states within the Arctic Circle. With the additional involvement of Arctic indigenous peoples and inhabitants of the Arctic regions, a forum was established to discuss issues of importance to all constituent groups.[3] All eight Arctic states signed the declaration.

Arctic Council

The Arctic Council includes eight Arctic countries: Canada, The Kingdom of Denmark (Greenland and the Faroe Islands), Finland, Iceland, Norway, the Russian Federation, Sweden, and the United States.[4] Associations and councils of indigenous groups include:

---

1 UN General Assembly, *Convention on the Law of the Sea*, December 10, 1982, available at: www.un.org/depts/los/convention_agreements/texts/unclos/unclos_e.pdf

2 Permanent Court of Arbitration, "The South China Sea Arbitration (The Republic of Philippines v. The People's Republic of China)," Permanent Court of Arbitration, 2016, https://pca-cpa.org/en/cases/7/

3 Arctic Council, "Declaration on the Establishment of the Arctic Council," *Arctic Council,* September 19, 1996, https://oaarchive.arctic-council.org/bitstream/handle/11374/85/EDOCS-1752-v2-ACMMCA00_Ottawa_1996_Founding_Declaration.PDF?sequence=5&isAllowed=y

4 Arctic Council, "About the Arctic Council," *Arctic Council,* n.d., https://arctic-council.org/en/about/

AIA
Aleut International Association

AAC
Arctic Athabaskan Council

GCI
Gwich'in Council International

ICC
Inuit Circumpolar Council

RAIPON
Russian Association of Indigenous Peoples of the North

Saami Council

Working Groups

ACAP
Arctic Contaminants Action Program

AMAP
Arctic Monitoring and Assessment Programme

CAFF
Conservation of Arctic Flora and Fauna

EPPR
Emergency Prevention, Preparedness and Response

PAME
Protection of the Arctic Marine Environment

SDWG
Sustainable Development Working Group

The Arctic Council's Non-Arctic 'Observer' States

France (joined 2000)
Germany (joined 1998)
Italian Republic (joined 2013)
Japan (joined 2013)
The Netherlands (joined 1998)
People's Republic of China (joined 2013)
Poland (joined 1998)
Republic of India (joined 2013)
Republic of Korea (joined 2013)
Republic of Singapore (joined 2013)
Spain (joined 2006)
Switzerland (joined 2017)
United Kingdom (joined 1998)

States may become observers on the Arctic Council if they

1. accept the Ottawa declaration,
2. recognize Arctic state sovereignty and jurisdiction,
3. recognize international legal frameworks and responsible ocean management,
4. respect the values, interests, culture, and traditions of the inhabitants of the Arctic,
5. demonstrate a political willingness and financial ability to contribute to the Arctic Council's work,
6. demonstrate relevant interest and expertise,
7. demonstrate the interest and ability to support the work of the Arctic Council.

The Arctic Council Observer Intergovernmental and Interparliamentary Organizations

International Council for the Exploration of the Sea (ICES) - (joined 2017)

International Federation of Red Cross & Red Crescent Societies (IFRC) - (joined 2000)

International Maritime Organization (IMO) - - (joined 2019)

International Union for the Conservation of Nature (IUCN) - (joined 2000)

Nordic Council of Ministers (NCM) - (joined 2000)

Nordic Environment Finance Corporation (NEFCO) - (joined 2004)

North Atlantic Marine Mammal Commission (NAMMCO) - (joined 2000)

OSPAR Commission - (joined 2017)

Standing Committee of the Parliamentarians of the Arctic Region (SCPAR) - (joined 1998)

United Nations Development Programme (UNDP) - (joined 2002)

United Nations Environment Programme (UNEP) - (joined 1998)

World Meteorological Organization (WMO) - (joined 2017)

West Nordic Council (WNC) - (joined 2017)

Non-Governmental Organizations (NGOs)

Advisory Committee on Protection of the Sea (ACOPS) - (joined 2000)

Arctic Institute of North America (AINA) - (joined 2004)

Association of World Reindeer Herders (AWRH) - (joined 2000)

Circumpolar Conservation Union (CCU) - (joined 2000)

International Arctic Science Committee (IASC) - (joined 1998)

International Arctic Social Sciences Association (IASSA) - (joined 2000)

International Union for Circumpolar Health (IUCH) - (joined 1998)

International Work Group for Indigenous Affairs (IWGIA) - (joined 2002)

Northern Forum (NF) - (joined 1998)

Oceania - (joined 2017)

University of the Arctic (UArctic) - (joined 2002)

World Wide Fund for Nature, Arctic Programme (WWF) - (joined 1998)

The Arctic Council's Leadership, Work, and Achievements

The Arctic Council oversees regional cooperation, coordination, sustainable development, and environmental preservation. The Council's administrative teams are located within the leading workplaces, authoritative bodies, and executing organizations of the eight Arctic countries, though observer countries are involved. NGOs and the scholarly community have an enormous impact in the Arctic strategy. Additionally, and significant, are intergovernmental bodies, including the United Nations and NATO.

The Arctic Council is not funded by a higher body. Projects are sponsored by one or more Arctic States or outside entities. The Council mainly serves as a forum to discuss issues and write and sign legally binding agreements enforceable by individual states or international bodies. The group is not a military organization and has no law enforcement capability.

Leadership rotates every two years between the eight Arctic states. From 2021 – 2023, the Chairmanship is held by the Russian Federation. Norway will take the role in 2023 for the next cycle.

Three legally binding agreements have emerged from the Arctic Council's dialogue.

8. The 2011 Agreement on Cooperation on Aeronautical and Maritime Search and Rescue in the Arctic.
9. The 2013 Agreement on Cooperation on Marine Oil Pollution Preparedness and Response in the Arctic
10. The 2017 Agreement on Enhancing International Arctic Scientific Cooperation

Numerous social, ecological, environmental, political, and economic questions impact these states. Despite these differences, there is an astounding similarity in their expressed strategies, governmental mandates, and commitment to harmony and collaboration in the region.⁵ Obstacles exist, like the fact that the United States has not ratified UNCLOS, disagreement over the Northwest Passage, and UNCLOS cases regarding each country's EEZ's actual location, notably those along the Lomonosov Ridge. The Arctic Council has worked to ensure fair representation, clear guidelines, and other issues like concessions, navigation, tourism, research, resource extraction, ecology, environment, and commerce with each contestation.

References on the Arctic (Harvard Library)[6]

News

- **Arctic Today** - *Arctic Today* is an independent news source in partnership with media organizations from around the circumpolar North.
- **CryoPolitics** - This blog presents Arctic issues authored by Professor Mia Bennett, Assistant Professor at Hong Kong University.

---

5   Albert Buixadé Farré et al., "Commercial Arctic Shipping Through the Northeast Passage: Routes, Resources, Governance, Technology, and Infrastructure," *Polar Geography 37*, no. 4 (2014), https://www.tandfonline.com/doi/full/10.1080/1088937X.2014.965769

6   Harvard Library, "U.S. Think Tanks," *Harvard Library,* n.d., https://guides.library.harvard.edu/c.php?g=837484&p=5981664

- **Eye on the Arctic** - Coordinated by Radio Canada International, this site brings together print, broadcast, and web journalists from circumpolar countries to tell the stories of communities and people directly affected by climate change.
- **High North News** - This independent newspaper is published by the High North Center at Nord University in Norway.

Organizations

- **Arctic Council** - Leading intergovernmental forum promoting cooperation, coordination, and interaction among the Arctic States, Arctic indigenous communities, and other Arctic inhabitants. Its focus is on environmental and sustainability issues.
- **Arctic Circle** - Non-profit network of governments, organizations, corporations, universities, think tanks, environmental associations, indigenous communities, concerned citizens, and others interested in the development of the Arctic and its consequences for the future of the globe.
- **U.S. Arctic Research Commission** - This independent agency advises the President and Congress of the United States on domestic and international research on the Arctic and publishes a biennial report of the United States Arctic Research Commission to the President and Congress of the United States.
- **EU-Polarnet** - The world's largest consortium of expertise and infrastructure for polar research include seventeen countries and are represented by twenty-two of Europe's internationally-respected multi-disciplinary research institutions. The site includes white papers, stakeholder deliverables, and research chapters.

Background Research

- **Annual Reviews** - *Annual Reviews* offer comprehensive, timely collections of critical reviews written by leading scholars. Search is limited to the Arctic in the abstract field or search by specific countries and/or keywords.
- **Arctic Portal** - A comprehensive gateway to Arctic information and data on the internet, increasing information sharing and cooperation among Arctic stakeholders and granting exposure to Arctic-related information and data.
- **Oxford Bibliography**: Arctic Region - This bibliography focuses on international law and human rights.

Journals

- *Arctic* - Published by the University of Calgary and Arctic Institute of North America, its focus is on North America.
- *Arctic Review on Law and Politics* – Peer-reviewed this open access journal focuses on political science, international relations, and human rights issues in Arctic regions.
- *Arctic Science* - This quarterly open-access, peer-reviewed journal contains articles on natural science and applied science & engineering related to northern polar regions.
- *Arctic Yearbook* - This is a repository of critical analysis on the Arctic region, with a mandate to inform observers about the state of Arctic politics, governance, and security.

- ***Polar Record*** - Cambridge University Press publishes a quarterly peer-reviewed academic journal covering all aspects of Arctic and Antarctic exploration and research.
- ***Polar Science*** - Elsevier peer-reviewed quarterly journal is dedicated to publishing original research articles for the sciences relating to the polar regions.

General Academic Databases

Articles on the Arctic and North Polar regions appear in a variety of social science and science journals depending on the paper topic. Start your search by inputting specifications and key words into a large interdisciplinary articles database and then refine to narrow your topic.

Videos

- **Arctic Frontier** - Through outreach activities with committed partners on Arctic issues, Arctic Frontiers sets the agenda, linking policy, business, and science for responsible and sustainable development. Programming includes video highlights from Arctic Frontier events and its annual conference.

U.S. Think Tanks

- **Arctic Institute** – A Washington, D.C. think tank that focuses on security issues in the Arctic.
- **Belfer Center, Arctic Initiative** - The Belfer Center for Science & International Affairs is a prominent think tank house at the Harvard Kennedy School. View publications authored by affiliates of the Belfer Center Arctic Initiative.
- **Brookings Institute**: Arctic Site - Articles and reports on U.S. foreign policy are available related to the Arctic.
- **National Academies Press** - Collection of over 5,000 academic titles available to read online at no cost.
- **Rand Corporation, Arctic Region** - Articles, reports, and commentary on topics regarding the Arctic Region, including climate change, security, and international relations.
- **Wilson Center, Polar Institute** – Lectures and research published by the Wilson Center's Polar Institute.

Conclusion

Arctic region countries have a vested interest in ensuring the protection of the environment and indigenous people who inhabit these northern territories. While all Arctic Council countries must play a part in these discussions and decisions, this international body also includes members that are not 'near-Arctic' states. Yet, these countries also have genuine concerns about global temperature increases, the rise in ocean levels, and the impact of energy extraction on pollution and wildlife.

The complexity of today's global interconnectedness is that we all live under the same sun, breathe the same air, and share the same resources. For any single country to monopolize air, land, sea, or resources, the result causes a problem for all – near and far. No longer do most people stay in one place or have the same job for life.

This change in human geography makes the work of the Arctic Council and its affiliate groups even more important. These international agencies, newsgroups, organizations, research task forces, and think tanks do essential work for the whole. Legally binding agreements without enforcement necessitate that each individual, organization, corporation, and state check on what is happening elsewhere. Dr. John E. Roueche, higher education leader, frequently said, "Inspect what you expect." Due diligence and oversight must be folded into the pursuit of peace and sustainability rather than non-transparent contracts that damage the Arctic and the world.

Indigenous Peoples of Remote Arctic Lands
Threatened by Civilization Moving in to Drill and Mine

What's at Stake?

First, the Arctic is a key location for international, strategic cooperation. The organizations listed in this chapter, and there are more, have a profound interest in the future of the Arctic. What happens there will change the dynamics of the planet. This reckoning is not a question of one more or one less walrus or polar bear, though these, too, are important. The rapid melting of the ice sheets will change global temperature, water levels, and life itself.

Second, events, activities, tourism, and research will be impacted by individual, corporate, or state greed. Considered "The Last Great Race", the Iditarod has been severely impacted by climate change.[7] *Foreign Policy* explains that "climate change has altered Alaska's landscape, and the experiences of Arctic mushers are the canary in the coal mine." With temperatures typically at zero degrees, in the 2020 race, the temperature was 36 degrees, with 22 Iditarod mushers ending the race prematurely. Dramatic environmental changes may seem unimportant for humans who travel and expect to adapt, but animals and their habitats are unprepared for these shifts.

Third, the Arctic Council meets collegially. However, the new superpower at the table with its ability and willingness to buy its way into favor is a conundrum that is being replicated in the Arctic as it has successfully done so in Africa, Asia, Europe, and South America. The temperature is rising slowly, though not only in degrees Fahrenheit or Celsius.

Iditarod Trail Sled Dog Race in Arctic Winters
Sunday, March 7, 2021 – Anchorage, Alaska
46 Competitors, 36 Finishers

---

7   Kelly Kimball, "The Last Great Race," *Foreign Policy,* April 27, 2020, https://foreignpolicy.com/2020/04/27/iditarod-climate-change-alaska-last-great-race/

Chapter 4
China's Strategic Interests in Transiting the Arctic
Motivated by Money, Energy, Trade, and Resources

Introduction

In 2014, **China's president, Xi Jinping**, publicly declared the will of his administration to transform China into a "Polar Power," proclaiming its interests toward the Arctic region.[1] Due to Beijing's lack of sovereignty over the polar region, as defined by UNCLOS, China faced restrictions in conducting commercial fishing or resource drilling operations in these regions.

In 2018, the People's Republic of China (PRC) published a White Paper, "China's Arctic Policy", referencing the rapid changes in the climate and environment, all the while pointing to the vast opportunities present in the Arctic. These opportunities are not of interest to China alone. Stakeholders - Canada, Denmark, Finland, Iceland, Norway, Russia, Sweden, and the U.S. – have a legal right and are committed to securing access to scientific insights, economic potential, sea routes, biodiversity, undiscovered natural resources, and a strategic foothold in the oceanic region. However, for China, the potential benefit of linking its shipping routes to the North Atlantic through the Arctic is also significant. Thus, the development of the Arctic region offers Beijing significant benefits.

To emphasize its standing, China wrote and shared its foreign policy proclamations. Meanwhile, Chinese diplomats expressed China's interests in the Arctic using environmental, commercial, and diplomatic terms embedded in its umbrella program, the Belt and Road Initiative (BRI). The oceanic passage in the Arctic, commonly referred to as the Northern Sea Route (NSR), has been integrated into the revised Maritime Silk Road and has inspired Chinese development and planning. Several treaties, including UNCLOS, shape the question of governance, stability, and protection in the Arctic. According to its Arctic White Paper, the Chinese strategy aims to avert suspicion of Beijing's ambitions and emphasizes a viable approach that facilitates the Arctic region's exploitation and development.

China's Strategic Interest in Transiting the Arctic

"China's Arctic Policy" covers China's intention to develop infrastructure, conduct research, explore resources, and extend its military activities within the Arctic Circle, including a plan to build a corridor for trade routes through the Arctic to facilitate global shipping delivery.[2] The document reflects China's view of the economic potential in the Arctic region. This policy is often used to register China's interest in participating in Arctic affairs both as a significant stakeholder in the Arctic and as a "Near-Arctic State".[3] Chinese activity in the region has not been limited to trade as China is also establishing research and energy bases spreading out into the Arctic region.

---

1 Anne-Marie Brady, "From Polar Great Power to Global Power? Global Governance Implications of China's Polar Interests," *Cambridge University Press*, 2017.

2 Xinhua, "Full Text: China's Arctic Policy," The State Council – *The People's Republic of China*, Updated January 26, 2018, http://english.www.gov.cn/archive/white_paper/2018/01/26/content_281476026660336.htm

3 Amrita Jash, "IPP Review – China's Need to Build the 'Polar Silk Road'," *IPP Review*, February 12, 2018, https://www.ippreview.com/index.php/Blog/single/id/649.html

The Spitsbergen Treaty (Svalbard Treaty)

When the PRC declared itself a "Near-Arctic State," sparks flew, lighting aflame widespread controversy.[4] China often cites the Spitsbergen Treaty (Svalbard Treaty) that China signed in 1925,[5] permitting its commercial activities. Chinese officials have frequently used the document as a historical justification for its involvement in the Arctic. Norway disputes the interpretation of the Treaty saying, "Svalbard is part of Norway. Norway does not routinely consult with other countries about how it exercises authority over its own territory."[6]

A few provisions include:[7]

- Spitsbergen is under Norwegian administration and legislation.
- Citizens of all signatory nations have free access and the right of economic activities.
- Spitsbergen remains demilitarized. No nation, including Norway, is allowed to *permanently* station military personnel or equipment on Spitsbergen.

States have challenged Norway's interpretation of the Treaty's provision on equal rights to engage in fishing and hunting. Under the Treaty, ships and nationals from states that are parties to the Treaty have equal rights to engage in fishing and hunting on land in Svalbard and the territorial waters around the archipelago, i.e., up to 12 nautical miles from land.[8] Misunderstandings or a lack of knowledge about the actual substance of the Treaty can lead to unrealistic expectations or opinions about the Treaty's significance for the interests of specific stakeholders.

Nevertheless, since 2004, China has created an indelible presence in Norway to conduct scientific research on Spitspergen Island, endowing it with access to resources and a forward base in the Arctic.[9]

Following a Brief Timeline

The breadcrumbs of China's activities in the Arctic show a clear path. China has dedicated significant resources to follow what appears to be a strategic pursuit to stake its claim in the Arctic region.

---

4   Eva Dou, "A New Cold War? China Declares Itself a 'Near-Arctic State,' *Wall Street Journal,* January 26, 2018, https://www.wsj.com/articles/a-new-cold-war-china-declares-itself-a-near-arctic-state-1516965315

5   Royal Ministry of Justice, "Treaty of 9 February 1920 Relating to Spitsbergen (Svalbard)," *Royal Ministry of Justice*, n.d., https://www.spitzbergen.de/wp-content/uploads/2020/01/Spitsbergen-treaty_English.pdf

6   The Maritime Executive, "Norway Clarifies Svalbard Treaty after Russian Complaint," *The Maritime Executive,* February 17, 2020, https://www.maritime-executive.com/article/norway-clarifies-svalbard-treaty-after-russian-complaint

7   Spitsbergen-Svalbard, "The Spitsbergen Treaty," *Spitsbergen | Svalbard,* n.d., https://www.spitsbergen-svalbard.com/spitsbergen-information/history/the-spitsbergentreaty.html

8   The Maritime Executive, "Norway Clarifies Svalbard Treaty after Russian Complaint," *The Maritime Executive,* February 17, 2020, https://www.maritime-executive.com/article/norway-clarifies-svalbard-treaty-after-russian-complaint

9   Embassy of the People's Republic of China in the United States of America, "China Opens 1st Research Station in Arctic Area," *Embassy of the People's Republic of China in the United States of America,* July 28, 2004, http://www.china-embassy.org/eng/gyzg/t144196.htm

- In 1996, China merged with the International Arctic Science Committee.[10]
- Since 1999, China deployed a series of research vessels into the Arctic.[11]
- In 2004, China constructed the Arctic Yellow River station in Norway.[12]
- In 2010, Chinese leaders endorsed a restrained version of its Arctic policies in order not to incite disapproval from the Arctic states and get excluded from access to the Arctic. This period revealed China's wariness of Russia's Arctic intentions.[13]
- In 2012, Xuě Lóng became the first Chinese vessel to navigate the Northeast Passage.[14]
- In 2013, China became an observer of the Arctic Council.[15]
- In 2014, Xi Jinping, general secretary of the Chinese Communist Party, proclaimed that China would become a "great power".[16]
- Between 2005 and 2017, Chinese investments in Arctic nations was estimated to be more than US $1.4 trillion.[17]
- In 2018 alone, China Ocean shipping Company (COSCO) made eight transits through the Arctic between China and Europe.[18]
- In 2018, China declared its "Polar Silk Road" and "Near-Arctic State" in its White Paper, "China's Arctic Strategy".
- In 2019, China created a joint venture to mine rare earth metals in the Greenland's Kvanefjeld Project, including 151 million proven tonnes of uranium and 64 probable tonnes.[19]
- In 2021, China National Petroleum Corp (CNPC) and CNOOC sought oil and

---

10 David Curtis Wright, "The Dragon Eyes the Top of the World," *Naval War College, China Maritime Studies Institute*, August, 2011, https://web.archive.org/web/20121017141917/http://www.usnwc.edu/Research---Gaming/China-Maritime-Studies-Institute/Publications/documents/China-Maritime-Study-8_The-Dragon-Eyes-the-Top-of-.pdf

11 Xinhua, "Full Text: China's Arctic Policy," The State Council – *The People's Republic of China,* Updated January 26, 2018, http://english.www.gov.cn/archive/white_paper/2018/01/26/content_281476026660336.htm

12 Ibid.

13 Linda Jakobson, "China Prepares for an Ice-Free Arctic," *SIPRI Insights on Peace and Security*, March, 2010, https://web.archive.org/web/20130220175324/http://books.sipri.org/files/insight/SIPRIInsight1002.pdf

14 Xinhua, "Icebreaker Xuelong Concludes Arctic Expedition," *China Daily*, Updated September 27, 2012, http://www.chinadaily.com.cn/china/2012-09/27/content_15787848.htm

15 Albert Buixadé Farré et al., "commercial Arctic Shipping Through the Northeast Passage: Routes, Resources, Governance, Technology, and Infrastructure," *Polar Geography 37*, no. 4 (2014): 298-324, https://www.tandfonline.com/doi/full/10.1080/1088937X.2014.965769

16 Tie Dams, Louise van Schaik, and Adája Stoetman, "Presence Before Power: China's Arctic Strategy in Iceland and Greenland," *Clingendael Institute,* (2020): 6-19, doi:10.2307/resrep24677.5

17 Evan Oddleifson, Tom Alton, and Scott N. Romaniuk, "China in the Canadian Arctic: Context, Issues, and Considerations for 2021 and Beyond," *University of Alberta*, January 12, 2021, https://www.ualberta.ca/china-institute/research/analysis-briefs/2021/arctic_analysis_brief.html

18 Trym Aleksander Eiterjord, "China's Busy Year in the Arctic," *The Diplomat*, January 30, 2019, https://thediplomat.com/2019/01/chinas-busy-year-in-the-arctic/

19 World Nuclear News, "New Chinese JV for Rare Earth Minerals from Greenland," *World Nuclear News,* January 23, 2019, https://www.world-nuclear-news.org/Articles/New-Chinese-JV-for-rare-earth-minerals-from

gas blocks in Greenland.[20]

What is China's Motivation?

China's interest in the Arctic precedes its official declaration. Two decades before the release of its Arctic policy, China carried out Arctic expeditions and energy cooperation with Russia. In 2019, it launched the 3000-kilometer-long natural gas pipeline connecting Russia's Siberian fields to China. Chinese corporations also contribute significantly to the Arctic LNG 2, the second-largest natural gas project under development in the Russian Arctic. Aside from its energy partnership, China also collaborates with Russia in a global transport network via the Northern Sea Route.

China's deployment of icebreakers and its scientific activities in the Arctic and Antarctic offer insight into the Arctic's climactic, geomagnetic, environmental, meteorological, and marine environmental conditions. These research expeditions attract lesser attention since Beijing calls them purely civilian research that aids future economic projects in the region.

However, recent Chinese Communist Party (CCP) research show both civilian and military peculiarities.

After the Chinese Academy of Sciences initiated an Arctic acoustic research program in 2014, China expressed broad interest in creating ocean observation bases to continue this study. The academy's standing scholarship outlines possible ways to keep expanding China's strategic footprint in the Arctic:[21]

1. The establishment of dual-use rather than entirely military logistics backup facilities.
2. The use of scientific research for the continuous development of military technologies in the Arctic, judging from the region's unique geomagnetic and climactic characteristics.
3. The training of special force agents and equipping them with enough resources to operate under extreme cold conditions.
4. The supply of humanitarian services, considered "public goods", such as disaster relief and aeronautical and maritime search-and-rescue to coastal states within the Arctic region.

Collaboration with Arctic States

China actively participates in Arctic governance both through bilateral and multilateral means. However, China's ambition often hits a roadblock with growing suspicion from Arctic states. Before gaining approval to become an ad hoc observer of the Arctic Council,

---

20 Rush Doshi, Alexis Dale-Huang, and Gaoqi Zhang, "Northern Expedition: China's Arctic Activities and Ambitions," *Brookings Institute*, April 2021, https://www.brookings.edu/research/northern-expedition-chinas-arctic-activities-and-ambitions/

21 Swee Lean Collin Koh, "China's Strategic Interest in the Arctic Goes Beyond Economics," *Defense News*, May 12, 2020, https://www.defensenews.com/opinion/commentary/2020/05/11/chinas-strategic-interest-in-the-arctic-goes-beyond-economics/

China's application was rejected three times, demonstrating the Arctic states' vigilance. Russia and Canada demonstrated the greatest vigilance. Russia is vocal with its misgivings about China's efforts to join the Arctic Council. Sensitive to security issues, the Russian government enhanced its watchful eye in the Arctic Sea as China's interest grows.

In a public warning to China in 2010, Russian Navy Commander, Vladimir Vysotsky, said, "We are observing the penetration of a host of states which…are advancing their interests very intensively, in every possible way, in particular China," furthering that Russia would enhance its military presence in the Arctic to protect its interests.[22]

Combined with its scientific expeditions, Beijing is also seeking to strengthen its influence in the Arctic through participation in the Arctic Council's governance. Working diligently to break down barriers to entry, China seeks a firm hold on its expansion plans across the Arctic.

Greenland and Iceland
Chinese Interests and Involvement

Although there is an alarming number of cases where China has attempted to gain traction in other nations' affairs, Greenland and Iceland are but two. China has bought interests in Greenland's rare earth metals and minerals. In Iceland, Chinese tycoon Huang Nubo, Board Chairman of Zhongkun Group, sought to buy a large region of the country. In Europe, this purchase request aroused as much suspicion as Donald Trump's request to purchase Greenland. Reservations mounted as the Trojan Horse scenario painted brushstrokes across the skies of Iceland.

The land purchase deal was scrapped due to the controversy.[23] However, when the fervor died down, and the issue was no longer hyped in the media, the skies cleared. Under the radar, the Chinese tycoon "signed a deal to lease land in a remote corner of northeast Iceland, … six months after his attempt to buy the property outright was rejected by the government."[24] Iceland needed the money due to being hit hard with the global financial crisis of 2008. The country was in desperate need of funds when three of Iceland's most prominent commercial banks defaulted, and the economy sank into a depression.[25] The hole created a geostrategic and commercial void that China filled.[26]

---

22 Nong Hong, "China's Interests in the Arctic: Opportunities and Challenges," *Institute for China-America Studies,* March, 2018, https://chinaus-icas.org/wp-content/uploads/2018/03/2018.03.06-China-Arctic-Report.pdf

23 Sui-Lee Wee and Huang Yuan, "Chinese Tycoon Says Controversy Could Kill Iceland Deal," *Reuters*, September 2, 2011, https://www.reuters.com/article/us-china-iceland/chinese-tycoon-says-controversy-could-kill-iceland-deal-idUSTRE7811ST20110902

24 China Daily, "Chinese Tycoon Inks Iceland Land Lease Deal," *China Daily*, Updated May 4, 2012, https://www.chinadaily.com.cn/business/2012-05/04/content_15208375.htm

25 The Economist, "Cracks in the Crust," *The Economist,* December 13, 2008, https://www.economist.com/briefing/2008/12/11/cracks-in-the-crust

26 Clingendael Report, "Iceland: What is China Doing There and Why?," *Clingendael Report,* n.d., https://www.clingendael.org/pub/2020/presence-before-power/3-iceland-what-is-china-doing-there-and-why/

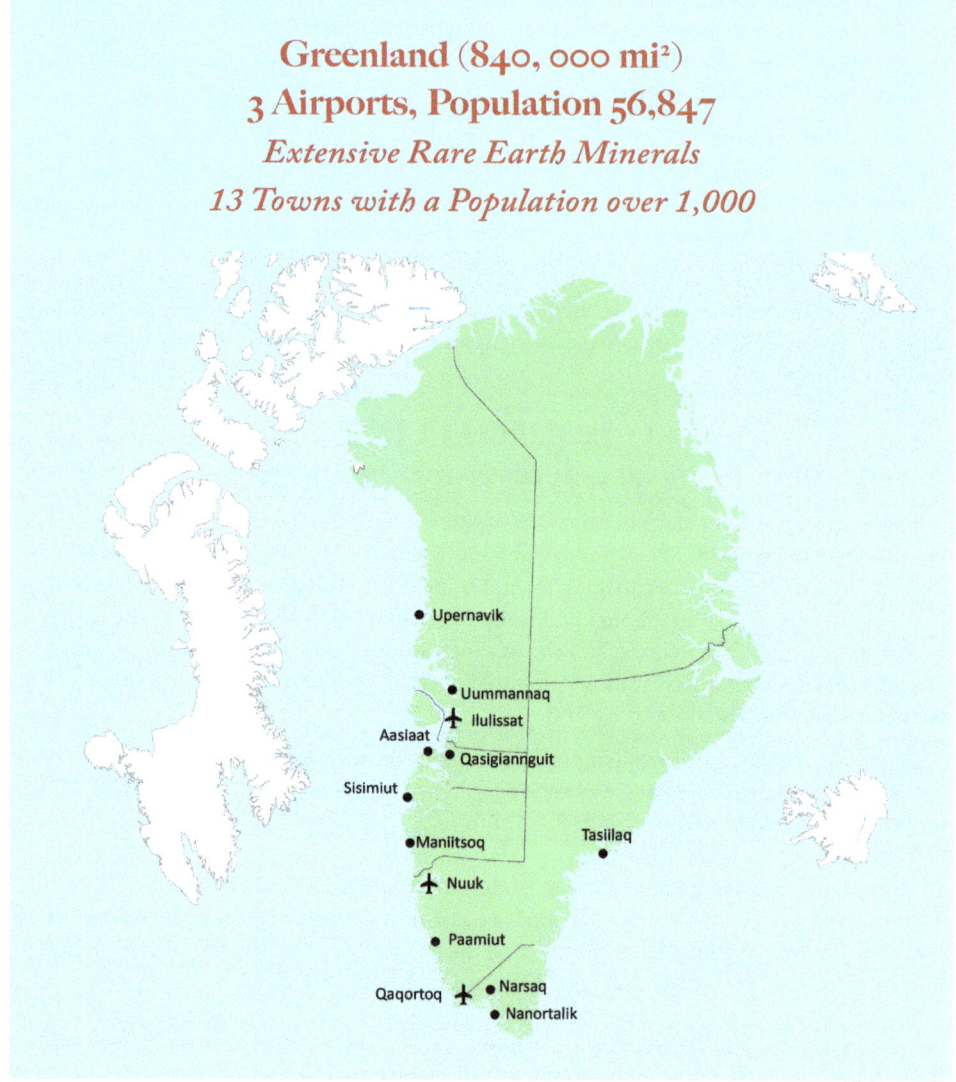

Conclusion

China's Arctic base activity and research explorations garner little notice, overshadowed by Xi Jinping's economic ambition and intensified by its geopolitical rivalry with the United States. At the Arctic Council ministerial meeting in 2019, U.S. Secretary of State, Mike Pompeo, warned states of the dangers of China's investment in the Arctic. News headlines create little interest when other concerns are more pressing, which is why the pandemic was the best time for China to take big leaps in different directions while not under the radar of the lack of geopolitical media scrutiny of Beijing's land takeover, loans, and coercion.

China regards the Arctic as an integral part of its economic, strategic, and environmental interests and believes that the United Nations Convention on the Law of the Sea (UNCLOS) permits the PRC to enjoy such rights as freedom of navigation, scientific research, fishery, cable-laying, overflight and infrastructure development in the international waters.

According to its official policy paper, China's goals in the Arctic are "to understand, protect, develop and participate in the governance of the Arctic, so as to safeguard the common interests of all countries and the international community in the Arctic, and promote sustainable development of the Arctic."[27] This noble goal has yet to play its cards fully on the table.

What's at Stake?

First, as China continues to assert its 'rights' in the Arctic and Antarctic, Robert C. O'Brien, former White House National Security Advisor, urged greater vigilance regarding China's actions. In January 2021, he wrote, "as we have seen in Hong Kong, the South China Sea, cyber economic espionage, and in trade, the Chinese Communist Party willfully disregards international agreements when it is convenient to do so."[28] This set of events are disconcerting and seem to fly under the radar. On the other hand, stop for a moment to ponder China's long-term implications of claiming rights to the Arctic and Antarctic, not to mention the absurdity. If this were not actually happening, many people would think it was a joke. Well, it is not.

Second, according to the *New York Times*, China is investing in every Arctic state.[29] These investments allow Beijing to exert greater control and increased decision-making. Furthermore, some of these infrastructure investments could become strategic military bases, like airports in the Arctic.

Third, China has heavily invested in Greenland mining operations with its joint venture and now has access to vast rare earth minerals and metals.[30]

---

27 Xinhua, "Full Text: China's Arctic Policy," The State Council – *The People's Republic of China*, Updated January 26, 2018, http://english.www.gov.cn/archive/white_paper/2018/01/26/content_281476026660336.htm

28 Craig Hooper, "New Polar Strategy Must Focus on China's Long March to Antarctica," *Forbes*, January 10, 2021, https://www.forbes.com/sites/craighooper/2021/01/10/new-polar-strategy-must-focus-on-chinas-long-march-to-antarctica/?sh=6151941663e3

29 Somini Sengupta and Steven Lee Myers, "Latest Arena for China's Growing Global Ambitions: The Arctic," *The New York Times*, May 24, 2019, https://www.nytimes.com/2019/05/24/climate/china-arctic.html

30 World Nuclear News, "New Chinese JV for Rare Earth Minerals from Greenland," *World Nuclear News*, January 23, 2019, https://www.world-nuclear-news.org/Articles/New-Chinese-JV-for-rare-earth-minerals-from

Chapter 5
Cutting through Arctic Ice
Creating a Transitway by Cleaving and Thawing

Introduction

According to the *South China Morning Post*, China is developing the largest ever nuclear icebreaking ship along with plans for a nuclear carrier fleet.[1] With China's dominance in trade, Beijing's goal is to use the Northern Sea Route (NSR) year-round. Although China does not border either pole, Beijing is keenly interested in reducing the time, distance, and fuel required to access commercial distribution centers worldwide. By breaking the ice, it can move through passageways more quickly and demonstrate its dominance in the Arctic and Antarctic where it has already set up bases for its researchers and naval commands. China seeks natural resources but also the ability to compete and defend its stake in the Arctic and Antarctic should its interets be challenged.

Environmental Damage

Environmental destruction is harshly and discernibly affecting the earth. In the Arctic, humans are literally cutting and melting the ice. In addition to the warming of the planet, humans are dissolving icy masses for commercial transport and for oil, natural gas, and mineral extraction. Ice-covered waterways and lakes are dissolving much sooner than expected. With the melting and warming of the Arctic, thousands of people are moving in to work on oil fields, research stations, fisheries, and transportation corridors while building villages and hubs for food, shelter, and refueling.

The Intergovernmental Panel on Climate Change (IPCC) announced that the worldwide temperature could increase from 2.5 to 10 degrees Fahrenheit throughout the

Xue Long
Breaking Ice in the Arctic

---

1   Liu Zhen, "Coulc China's 'Experimental' Ship be the World's Biggest Nuclear-Powered Icebreaker?," *South China Morning Post,* March 20, 2019, https://www.scmp.com/news/china/military/article/3002455/china-build-30000-tonne-nuclear-powered-ship-described

following century.[2]

According to the National Oceanographic and Atmospheric Association's (NOAA) 2020 Arctic Report Card,[3] the decline in sea ice data is dramatic. The following are the steady decreases in sea ice during the given periods.

- 1979 – 1992 <> 6.85 million km2 loss (2.64 million mi2)
- 1993 – 2006 <> 6.13 million km2 loss (2.37 million mi2)
- 2007 – 2020 <> 4.44 million km2 loss (1.71 million mi2)

As worldwide temperatures rise, the territory, fish, natural resources, and transportation routes inside the Arctic district are progressively simpler to access, leading to the further demise of the ice sheets.

The dissolving of the Arctic ice began its dramatic decline with the extraction and processing of vast oil and liquid natural gas (LNG) stores. Advancements in technology, including massive ship-based ice cutters, have caused the Arctic Council members to raise the level of alarm.

How do Ice Breaking Ships Break the Ice?

The hulls of traditional cargo ships are too thin to break the ice. Ice sheets can be unforgiving and are likely to pierce the hull. Oil tankers often have strengthened hulls that can move through the ice but cannot cut the sheets. Ice breaker ships cleave the ice so that cargo ships, patrol vessels, or oil tankers can transit.

If an icebreaker hits a small sheet of ice, it can use its angled bow that is roughly spoon-shaped to allow the ship to ride up onto the ice and use its weight to pierce the sheet, cracking open a channel. The ice breaker uses the force of its heavy hull to move through, pounding down onto the ice. Using this motion of rising up and lowering down, the vessel can transit through the passageway created.

Ice breakers use vessel power and sheer weight to bear down and cleave the ice literally. Often with a coast guard ice breaker escort, cargo vessels and tankers can navigate the frozen north. Shattering the ice allows for safer transit.

There are variations in technology between different icebreaking ships. Some ice-breaker ships are equipped with a bubbler system. This compressed force of air bubbles up and out in front of the ship. Then the air is pressed into or onto the ice sheet, depending upon the situation, pushing the ice open between a crack or moving the ice away from the ship. Nuclear-powered vessels have greater power with extensive interior nuclear facilities to ride the ice sheet and burst through a wall of ice. Russia presently owns the largest nuclear-powered vessels. The new ice cutters have two nuclear power plants inside. By 2022, Russia is slated to have six of the largest in the world capable of cutting through the ice year-round.

---

2   Trivun Sharma, "Melting Arctic Sea Ice Opens New Maritime Route," *Global Security Review*, Updated June 9, 2019, https://globalsecurityreview.com/arctic-new-maritime-shipping-route/

3   R.L. Thoman, J. Richter-Menge, and M.L. Druckenmiller, "Arctic Report Card 2020," National Oceanic and Atmospheric Administration – *U.S. Departmnet of Commerce,* 2020, https://www.arctic.noaa.gov/Portals/7/ArcticReportCard/Documents/ArcticReportCard_full_report2020.pdf

The Arctic's Natural Assets

The Arctic hosts considerable natural assets. A 2008 report delivered by the United States Geological Survey (USGS) assessed that the Arctic holds around 1,670 trillion ft³ of petroleum gas, 44 billion barrels of flammable gas, and 90 billion barrels of oil—by far most of these in the sea.[4] As more of the region melts, abundant stores of gold, zinc, nickel, and iron will become accessible.

Regarding transportation, the two significant ocean routes that licensed boats can traverse exist along the Russian and Canadian northern coastlines - the Northern Sea

---

4   USGS, "90 Billion Barrels of Oil and 1,670 Trillion Cubic Feet of Natural Gas Assessed in the Arctic," *USGS*, July 22, 2008, https://www.usgs.gov/media/audio/90-billion-barrels-oil-and-1670-trillion-cubic-feet-natural-gas-assessed-arctic

Route and the Northwest Passage. The Northern Sea Route (NSR)[5] is linked to Arctic improvement ventures and considerable energy assets, making the Arctic a worthwhile possibility for Russia and the other Arctic states.[6] The essential allure of the Arctic shipping lanes include:

- consistent ice melting
- improvement of current vessels to operate in harsh weather conditions
- worldwide information exchange
- expanded interest in Asian business sectors
- tenacious robbery around the Horn of Africa and Strait of Hormuz
- instability in the nations around the Suez Canal
- increased clog in the Strait of Malacca

Each reason increases the geostrategic significance of the Arctic as a characteristic asset and transportation center point. At the same time, notwithstanding, the growing importance of the area may likewise prompt expanded rivalry.[7] As global temperature rise and Arctic ice melts, Siberian waters will open and change both geopolitics and trade by reducing the distance between Northwest Europe and the Far East by a third.[8]

The vanishing Arctic ice cap will increase exchange and possibly create conflict between China, Japan, and South Korea while shortening the trade routes to access Europe.[9] Either way, alternative passageways will modify deliveries, making northern nations more economically powerful while causing financial issues for Egypt, which will lose significant income from ships no longer passing through the Suez Canal.[10]

On the positive side, based on data from the Netherlands Bureau for Economic Policy Analysis,[11] boats traversing NSR will consume far less petroleum. However, this environmental gain will be negated by the increased volume together with population

---

5 Sung-Woo Lee and Ju-Mi Song, "Economic Possibilities of Shipping Though Northern Sea Route," *The Asian Journal of Shipping and Logistics 30*, no. 3 (2014): 415-430, https://www.sciencedirect.com/science/article/pii/S2092521214000601

6 Vladimir A. Lazarev and Andrey I. Fisenko, "Potential Benefits of Russian Northern Sea Route in Global Supply Chain," *Advances in Economics, Business and Management Research 38*, (2017), https://download.atlantis-press.com/article/25885468.pdf

7 Trivun Sharma, "Melting Arctic Sea Ice Opens New Maritime Route," *Global Security Review*, Updated June 9, 2019, https://globalsecurityreview.com/arctic-new-maritime-shipping-route/

8 Gloria Dickie, "Siberian Heat Drives Arctic Ice Extent to Record Low for Early July," *Mongabay*, July 10, 2020, https://news.mongabay.com/2020/07/siberian-heat-drives-arctic-ice-extent-to-record-low-for-early-july/

9 Paul Brown, "Arctic's Melting Ice Shrinks Shipping Routes," *Climate News Network*, August 4, 2015, https://climatenewsnetwork.net/arctics-melting-ice-shrinks-shipping-routes/

10 The Egyptian Cabinet Information & Decision Support Center and UNDP, "Egypt's National Strategy for Adaptation to Climate Change and Disaster Risk Reduction," *The Egyptian Cabinet Information & Decision Support Center and UNDP*, December, 2011, http://www.climasouth.eu/docs/Adaptation011%20StrategyEgypt.pdf

11 Ministry of Foreign Affairs, "The Netherlands' Polar Strategy 2021-2025," *Ministry of Foreign Affairs*, n.d., https://www.government.nl/documents/publications/2021/03/01/polar-strategy

growth, demand, and shorter travel distance.[12] The northern ocean course opens in the late spring months. However, it is predicted that accessibility will last year-round by 2030, or perhaps sooner. Arctic ice is softening quicker than anticipated by researchers.

To police and assist with transit, the Russian government created a bureaucratic patrol with ten "alleviation ports" along the Siberian coastline for ships that may require repairs or supplies. China consented to a deregulation arrangement, with Iceland fully expecting to routinely utilize the course.[13] Exchanges between Northwest Europe and China, Japan, and South Korea will increase incrementally from the access route.[14]

Since 90% of world exchange by volume is conveyed by ship transport, support between ports is imperative.[15] The northern course decreases the good paths from Japan to north European nations by 37%, from South Korea by 31%, China 23%, and Taiwan 17%. The most significant benefit of shorter separations applies to nations in Northern East Asia. For countries like Singapore, Indonesia, Malaysia, and Thailand, south of the equator, the southern course through Suez continues to be shorter.

---

12 Eddy Bekkers, Joseph F. Francois, and Hugo Rojas-Romagosa, "Melting Ice Caps and the Economic Impact of Opening the Northern Sea Route," *CPB Netherlands Bureau for Economic Policy Analysis,* May 12, 2015, https://www.cpb.nl/en/publication/melting-ice-caps-and-the-economic-impact-of-opening-the-northern-sea-route

13 Nikolaj Nielsen, "Iceland Signs First European Free Trade Pact with China," *EU Observer,* April 16, 2013, https://euobserver.com/eu-china/119811

14 Ibid.

15 United Nations Conference on Trade and Development (UNCTAD), "Review of Maritime Transport," *United Nations,* 2018, https://unctad.org/en/PublicationsLibrary/rmt2018_en.pdf

Conclusion

Nations on the North Sea and Baltic will see the greatest increase in port traffic and associated income, including Belgium, Denmark, Estonia, Finland, Germany, Ireland, Latvia, the Netherlands, Poland, Sweden, the U.K., and Norway.[16] A few nations in eastern and southern Europe will encounter a drop in exchange due to the relatively longer separations their fares and imports will need to travel.[17] The northern course may become one of the busiest delivery paths, expanding the monetary and political significance of the Arctic. Simultaneously, the redirection of sea traffic will squeeze Egypt (Suez Canal) and Singapore (Strait of Malacca), which depend on income from ship traffic.

What's at Stake?

First, cutting through the ice with icebreaking ships removes barriers to entry as it cuts the ice sheets. Larger nuclear-powered vessels will destroy the ice sheets now blocking the way and will change the Arctic, probably forever. Furthermore, an increasing number of ships transiting the water will warm the ocean. The chain reaction of destroying the Arctic sheets will change the environment for animals, fish, and those who rely on the wildlife for their survival.

Second, Russia's fleet of nuclear-powered ice breaker ships are in a class of their own. If they provide the escort services to cut through the ice year-round to pave the way for the cargo transport ships, there will be a significant fee associated with traveling this route. With great power competition between the U.S., China, and Russia, there is need for a healthy dose of respect for the power, will, and capabilities of all three superpowers. We should remember too, lest we forget, that Germany underestimated Russia in Operation Barbarossa and Japan underestimated the U.S. in the attack of Pearl Harbor. Russia's might in the Arctic deserves the world's respect, even if not admiration.

Third, with China, Japan, and South Korea increasing their transit through the north and not going through the Suez Canal, some ports will be negatively impacted, as will be:

Piraeus, Greece	Marsaxlokk, Malta	Genova, Italy
Beirut, Lebanon	Port Said, Egypt	Marseilles, France
Gioa Tauro, Italy	Haifa, Israel	Istanbul, Turkey
Algeciras, Spain	Ashdod, Israel	Tanger-Med, Morocco
Barcelona, Spain	Valencia, Spain	

16　Nikolaj Nielsen, "Iceland Signs First European Free Trade Pact with China," *EU Observer*, April 16, 2013, https://euobserver.com/eu-china/119811

17　Ibid.

At the same time, some ports will increase their traffic significantly, including

Rotterdam, Netherlands	Bremerhaven, German	London, U.K.
Antwerp, Belgium	Felixstowe, U.K.	Gdansk, Poland
Hamburg, Germany	Southampton, U.K.	

Chapter 6
Fast Melting Ice:
Environmentalists Analyze Arctic Destruction and Clarify Climate Change

Introduction

Global changes in temperature have warmed the Arctic. This large-scale transformation in our climate has resulted in the loss of Arctic permafrost[1] and the thawing of Greenland's ice sheet[2] at a rate that has not been observed since the 1970s.[3] Impacts on the regional waters include increased freshwater flow,[4] changes in ocean circulation, and ocean acidification.[5] However, indirect weather effects include a higher frequency of extreme weather incidents like flooding, fires, storms, and drought.[6] Additional studies suggest ecological, environmental, and biological changes.[7] These

Average Area Covered by Sea Ice During September Each Year
Sea Ice Has Decreased 13.1% Per Decade Since 1979

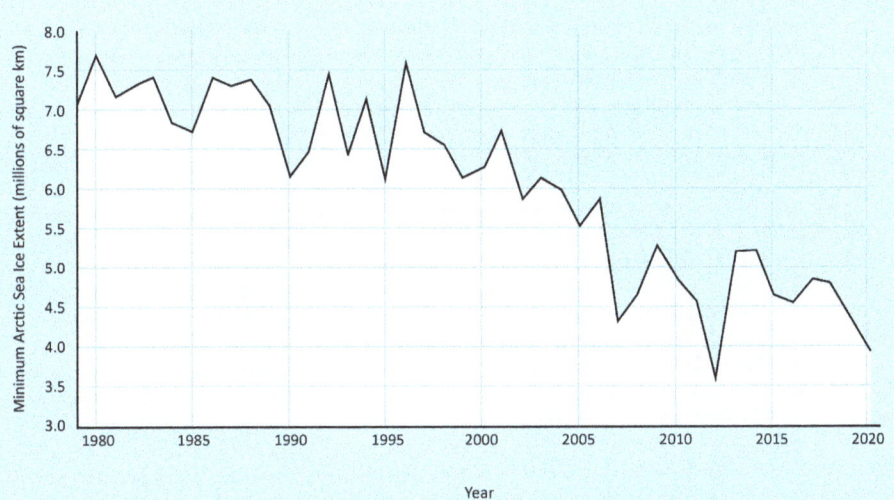

---

1 Kelly Slivka, "Rare Burst of Melting Seen in Greenland's Ice Sheet," *The New York Times,* July 24, 2012k https://www.nytimes.com/2012/07/25/science/earth/rare-burst-of-melting-seen-in-greenland-ice-sheet.html

2 Suzanne Goldenberg, "Greenland Ice Sheet Melted at Unprecedented Rate During July," *The Guardian*, July 24, 2012, https://www.theguardian.com/environment/2012/jul/24/greenland-ice-sheet-thaw-nasa

3 Joanna M. Foster, "From 2 Satellites, the Big Picture on Ice Melt," *The New York Times,* February 8, 2012, https://green.blogs.nytimes.com/2012/02/08/from-2-satellites-the-big-picture-on-ice-melt/

4 Benjamin Rabe et al., "An Assessment of Arctic Ocean Freshwater Content Changes from the 1990s to the 2006-2008 Period," *Oceanographic Research Papers 58,* no. 2 (2011): 173-185, https://ui.adsabs.harvard.edu/abs/2011DSRI...58..173R

5 Di Qi et al., "Increase in Acidifying Water in the Western Arctic Ocean," *Nature Climate Change 7*, no. 3 (2017): 195-199, https://ui.adsabs.harvard.edu/abs/2017NatCC...7..195Q/abstract

6 Judah Cohen et al., "Recent Arctic Amplification and Extreme Mid-Latitude Weather," *Nature Geoscience 7*, no. 9 (2014): 627-637, https://ui.adsabs.harvard.edu/abs/2014NatGe...7..627C/abstract

7 Jacqueline M. Grebmeier, "Shifting Patterns of Life in the Pacific Arctic and Sub-Arctic Seas," *Annual Review of Marine Science 4,* (2012): 63-78, https://www.annualreviews.org/doi/10.1146/annurev-marine-120710-100926

challenges present solemn obligations on the part of countries around the world to take positive charge of their impacts on the global environment. This is not a time for "me first" and "me most" strategies to advance national interests at any costs.

Nevertheless, not all countries share a global imperative for human survival. China declared that one of its primary goals in the Arctic is to help secure the ecological environment and battle climate change. However, every base they build, every ice sheet they cut, and every ton of fish they take from the Arctic has warmed the region more and depleted the ice. This warming ultimately helps China speed up the timeline until the Arctic is transitable year-round, shaving billions of dollars from their costs of delivery of the world's manufactured products. China states that its plan also covers the conservation of "living resources," including fisheries.[8] Still, Chinese fishermen aggressively and relentlessly haul in more fish than any other country in the world including in Asia, South America, Africa, and the polar north by more than two times.

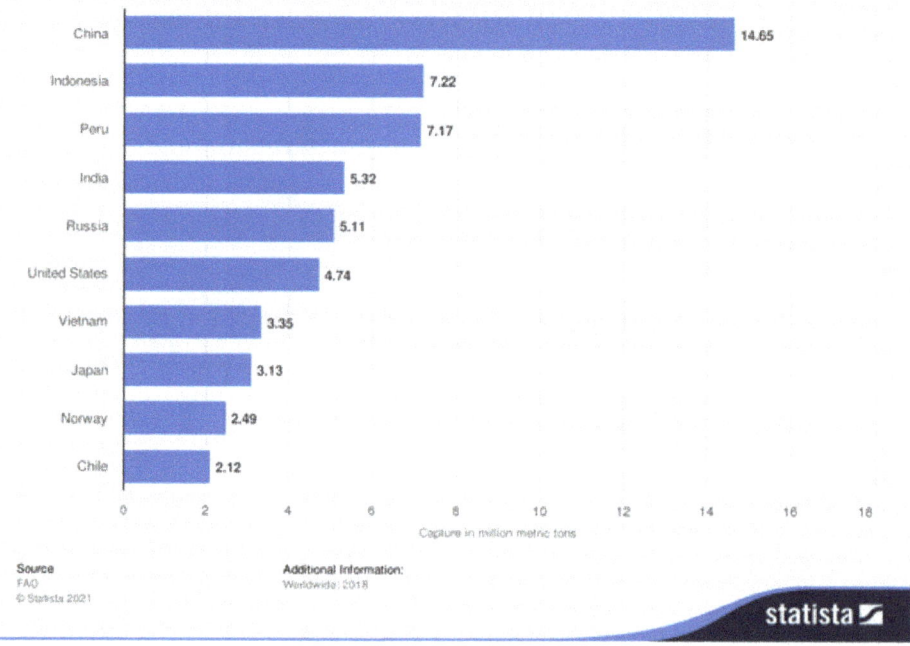

The Arctic and Global Warming

The Arctic has become the focus of climate change. There is hardly any other place where climate change is more evident than in the Arctic. As the Arctic aids in regulating the world's temperature, the melting of Arctic ice means the warming of our entire planet. Moreover, we do not yet know all of the adverse consequences or how soon we will

---

8   Xinhua, "Full Text: China's Arctic Policy," *The State Council of the People's Republic of China*, Updated January 26, 2018, http://english.www.gov.cn/archive/white_paper/2018/01/26/content_281476026660336.htm

experience them, but we do know it will be disastrous and soon.

More details reveal the true impact of this trend.

- **Melting Ice Facilitates Climate Change**-Ice reflects sunlight; water absorbs the heat. When Arctic ice melts, the surrounding water absorbs more sunlight and gives off heat, causing the surrounding environment to become warmer.
- **Rising Sea Levels-** Over the past century, the sea level has risen an average of 4 to 6 inches globally. Melting polar ice is expected to facilitate this rise. Some experts predict that the sea will increase as much as 23 feet by 2100. If this happens, major cities will flood, and low-lying islands will disappear.
- **Oil in the Arctic-** Although there is oil in the Arctic, our over-reliance on this natural resource contributes heavily to the problem of climate change. As long as consumers demand oil, corporations will exploit it for commercial gain. The two largest petrochemical companies are Chinese state-owned enterprises (SOEs). The combustion of fossil fuels, while the cheapest of the alternative energy sources, is one of the most harmful ways we are affecting the climate and causing negative change.

Top ten largest to smallest petrochemical companies:[9]

1. China Petroleum & Chemical Corporation (Sinopec) – Revenue $355.8 billion
2. PetroChina Co. Ltd. – Revenue $320.0 billion
3. Saudi Arabian Oil Co. (Aramco) – Revenue $286.9 billion
4. Royal Dutch Shell PLC – Revenue $263.1 billion
5. British Petroleum (BP) – Revenue $230.7 billion
6. Exxon Mobil Corp. – Revenue $213.9 billion
7. Total SE (French) – Revenue $146.1 billion
8. Gazprom (Russian) - $120 billion (Lukoil 99.1 bn) Russian data varies by site
9. Chevron Corp. – Revenue $115.0 billion
10. Marathon Petroleum Corp. – Revenue $102.4 billion

Marine Ecosystem in Danger
Melted Ice in the Arctic Thwarts Natural Habitats

---

[9] Nathan Reiff, "10 Biggest Oil Companies," *Investopedia*, Updated September 10, 2020, https://www.investopedia.com/articles/personal-finance/010715/worlds-top-10-oil-companies.asp

Although statistics and predictions foretell doom, there is still a chance to limit the potential damage. Changing our energy production and consumption habits will reduce our dependence on oil and liquid natural gas (LNG). With enormous supply but no customers, prices will fall, and the costs of drilling in the Arctic will make the ventures less profitable, less realistic, and make less sense to exploit the environment.[10]

Ice in the Arctic Sea is melting at a rate of about 13% per decade. The thickest and oldest ice in the Arctic has dropped by 95% over the past 30 years. The Arctic Sea is undeniably and rapidly losing more and more of its polar ice sheets as global warming intensifies, making it the central casualty in the looming, ultimate climate change disaster. With no effort to regulate emissions, the Arctic may lose the majority of its ice by 2040. The impact will be felt globally.

---

10 Greenpeace, "The Arctic & Global Warming," *Greenpeace*, n.d., https://www.greenpeace.org/usa/arctic/issues/global-warming/

Conclusion

The subject of climate change is a topic of worldwide debate, but for the people and animals living within the Arctic region, the changes are an ever-present reality. As the world grows warmer, the Arctic ice melts faster, endangering its inhabitants' lives and safety.

What's at Stake?

First – Global Temperature - The Antarctic and the Arctic are the coldest places on Earth. Their ice regulates temperatures in other parts of the world. Less ice will result in extreme heatwaves and possibly unpredictable winters with waves of polar air threatening people, animals, and crops.

Second - Coastal Communities - Since 1900, the global average sea level has increased dramatically. This rise endangers small islands and coastal cities by enabling storm surges and flooding low-lying areas. A significant predictor of future sea-level rise is the melting of Greenland's ice sheet.[11] If Greenland's ice sheet melts entirely, sea levels could rise 20 feet globally.[12]

Third – Shipping - The melting of ice sheets will open shipping routes in the Arctic. While these routes shorten the time spent in transit, they can lead to oil spills and shipwrecks like the Exxon-Valdez in regions that are inaccessible to clean-up or get to by rescue crews.[13] Furthermore, chopping the ice sheets to create shipping paths will increase regional warming in the Arctic.

Fourth – Food - Climate change impacts agriculture. Heat waves, polar vortexes, and weather fluctuations contribute to crop damage, influence prices, and threaten the food supply globally.[14]

Fifth – Wildlife – The continued existence of polar bears, walruses, seals, reindeer, arctic wolves, caribou, musk ox, snowy owls, whales, salmon, trout, pike, whitefish, and anglers, as well as numerous other species, is threatened. A change from saltwater to freshwater, ocean acidification, temperature changes, or a lack of ice would detrimentally alter animal and marine environments. Animals depend on the ice and the algae growing on top of the ice.[15] Survival will require adaptation or death. Yet, the native people who live there rely on fish, animals and the natural environment.

---

11 Karina A. Greater et al., "Ice Core Records of West Greenland Melt and Climate Forcing," *Geophysical Research Letters*, (2018), https://agupubs.onlinelibrary.wiley.com/doi/full/10.1002/2017GL076641

12 National Snow & Ice Data Center, "Quick Facts on Ice Sheets," *National Snow & Ice Data Center*, n.d., https://nsidc.org/cryosphere/quickfacts/icesheets.html

13 World Wildlife Fund, "Six Ways Loss of Arctic Ice Impacts Everyone," *World Wildlife Fund*, n.d., https://www.worldwildlife.org/pages/six-ways-loss-of-arctic-ice-impacts-everyone

14 World Wildlife Fund, "Six Ways Loss of Arctic Ice Impacts Everyone," *World Wildlife Fund*, n.d., https://www.worldwildlife.org/pages/six-ways-loss-of-arctic-ice-impacts-everyone

15 Lesley Evans Ogden, "The Surprising Reason Polar Bears Need Sea Ice to Survive," *National Geographic*, April 1, 2019, https://www.nationalgeographic.com/animals/article/polar-bears-algae-sea-ice-warming

Sixth – Pollution – Increasingly, bottles cans, plastics, and trash have been gathering in the Arctic. This not only causes problems due to the difficulty in collection, but it is devastating to the ecosystem.

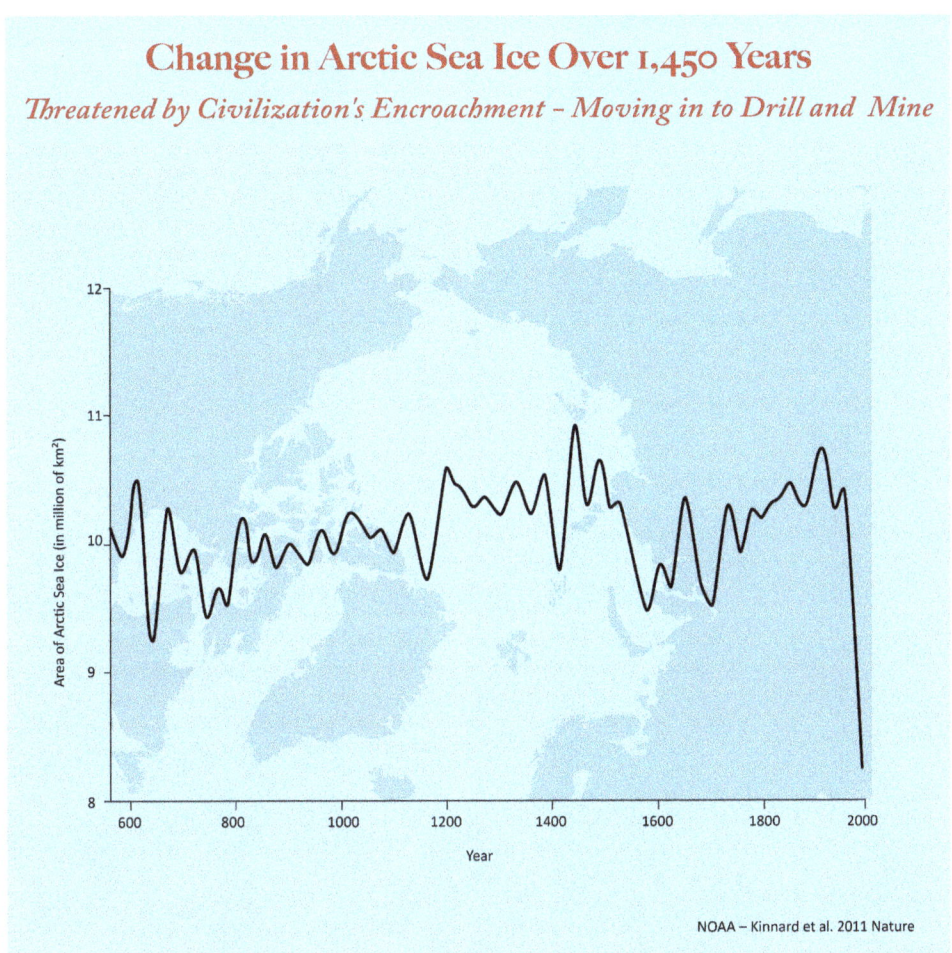

Chapter 7
The Russian Connection

China's Geopolitical Relationship with Russia

Introduction

China and Russia are friends, or at least that is what some say. Their mutual anti-Americanism and anti-democracy agendas provide them with a common enemy. Thus, on some grounds, they are close geopolitically.[1] However, the Russians have grown increasingly concerned about China's motives, and therefore their military and economic alliances warm and cool depending upon their shared understanding, cooperation, and trust.

Trust though is hard-fought to win, and cooperation only exists when it is mutually beneficial. Space is one of those areas of cooperation as is evident with their joint moon base operation and International Lunar Research Station (ILRS), according to a memorandum of understanding (MOU) signed in March 2021.[2] Nevertheless, China announced that it planned to be the world's leading space power by 2045.[3] Militarily, China and Russia have held joint training exercises along with Iran, Pakistan, Belarus, and Myanmar[4] agreeing to share information to support each other in the import and export of arms.[5] Additionally, both countries are cooperating on a ballistic missile warning system.[6] China, however, to clarify, announced that it was not seeking a military alliance with Russia, which some see as maintaining autonomy and keeping its relationships in Europe warm.[7]

In the Arctic, Russian ambitions and growing powerhouse actions have forced the Arctic Council to take note and become highly wary. Russia has far-reaching territorial claims, which China has exploited to make inroads with this Arctic giant.[8] Russia and China have partnered on Arctic projects, in part, because of the potential for extraction of natural resources in the polar north. Moreover, it is often expensive. China is willing to pay, provided it gets a significant return on its investment. Arctic oil, in particular, is costly to extract, and China seeks the chance to be a major player in Arctic oil development. However, Beijing wants Arctic states to buy in, or, if they do not buy in, China will

---

1. Eleanor Albert, "China and Russia Show Solidarity at Meeting of Foreign Ministers," The Diplomat, March 24, 2021, https://thediplomat.com/2021/03/china-and-russia-show-solidarity-at-meeting-of-foreign-ministers/

2. Shannon Tiezzi, "China, Russia Agree to Cooperate on Permanent Moon Base," *The Diplomat*, March 10, 2021, https://thediplomat.com/2021/03/china-russia-agree-to-cooperate-on-permanent-moon-base/

3. Ma Chi, "China Aims to Be World-Leading Space Power by 2045," *China Daily*, Updated November 17, 2017, http://www.chinadaily.com.cn/china/2017-11/17/content_34653486.htm

4. Associated Press, "China, Others to Join Military Exercises in Russia," *Associated Press*, September 10, 2020, https://apnews.com/article/pakistan-belarus-iran-myanmar-russia-0d2f7ebbf673fccf3f2c643cc495a177

5. Nurlan Aliyev, "Military Cooperation Between Russia and China: The Military Alliance Without an Agreement?," *ICDS Estonia*, July 1, 2020, https://icds.ee/en/military-cooperation-between-russia-and-china-the-military-alliance-without-an-agreement/

6. Vasily Kashin, "Chinese-Russian Ballistic Missile Cooperation Signals Deepening Trust," *East Asia Forum*, February 20, 2021, https://www.eastasiaforum.org/2021/02/20/chinese-russian-ballistic-missile-cooperation-signals-deepening-trust/

7. Minnie Chan, "China-Russia Ties: 'No Plans for Military Alliance' to Take on US," *South China Morning Post*, March 2, 2021, https://www.scmp.com/news/china/diplomacy/article/3123776/china-russia-ties-no-plans-military-alliance-take-us

8. Eugene Rumer, Richard Sokolsky, and Paul Stronski, "Russia in the Arctic – A Critical Examination," *Carnegie Endowment for International Peace*, March 29, 2021, https://carnegieendowment.org/2021/03/29/russia-in-arctic-critical-examination-pub-84181

attempt to buy the region's territory or companies.[9] The U.S. Geological Survey suggests that there are 90 billion barrels of oil north of the Arctic Circle, enough to fuel the entire world for a long time.[10] The stakes are high.

Covert Bedfellows, Each on a Mission for Economic Dominance

In the Arctic, Russian President Vladimir Putin championed the "Power of Siberia" gas pipeline project with China as a "genuinely historic event". Chinese President Xi Jinping called Putin his "best friend" with "the start of a new stage of our cooperation", furthering that "developing Russia-China relations is and will be a priority in our country's foreign policy."[11] In 2010, China gave Russia's state organizations Rosneft and Transneft $25bn to construct an oil pipeline from Siberia to China. As of 2021, the pipeline conveys 300,000 barrels each day. In 2021, China paid Rosneft an extra $60bn to grow seaward oil fields in the Arctic.

In May 2021, Russia doubled its natural gas volume to China through the "Power of Siberia" pipeline.[12]

Nevertheless, the centuries-old animosity between the two countries is well-documented. While it is true that Russia may rely more heavily on China for trade and economic investments,[13] particularly during the economic downturn of the pandemic, Putin has access to both a transportation route Xi wants and trillions in natural resources that Xi also wants. Their relationship is not made in heaven, but both will overcome their differences, for now, to take advantage of their country's needs.

Extraction of these resources is vital for Russia's growth. However, between the fluctuating market for raw materials, difficulties with exploration, geopolitical conditions, and citizens' environmental consciousness, approvals for exploration and completion of projects are uncertain.[14] Nature lovers are not keen on Russia and China's big development plans in what they see as the Arctic ecosystem and its inevitable environmental demise.[15]

---

9   Michael Byers, "China Could be the Future of Arctic Oil," *Al Jazeera*, August 22, 2013, https://www.aljazeera.com/indepth/opinion/2013/08/20138211358292916420.html

10 USGS, "Circum-Arctic Resource Appraisal: Estimates of Undiscovered Oil and Gas North of the Arctic Circle," *USGS*, 2008, https://pubs.usgs.gov/fs/2008/3049/fs2008-3049.pdf

11 Chi Wang, "Russia is No Friend to China. In Fact, Xi's Friendship with Putin is a Betrayal of the Chinese People," *South China Morning Post*, December 10, 2019, https://www.scmp.com/comment/opinion/article/3041246/russia-no-friend-china-fact-xis-friendship-putin-betrayal-chinese

12 Hellenic Shipping News, "Russia to Double Natgas Volume to China in 2021 as Cold Spell Bites," *Hellenic Shipping News*, May 1, 2021, https://www.hellenicshippingnews.com/russia-to-double-natgas-volume-to-china-in-2021-as-cold-spell-bites/

13 Johnathan E. Hillman, "China and Russia: Economic Unequals," *Center for Strategic & International Studies*, July 15, 2020, https://www.csis.org/analysis/china-and-russia-economic-unequals

14 World Ocean Review, "An Economic Boom with Side Effects," *World Ocean Review*, 2019, https://worldoceanreview.com/en/wor-6/polar-politics-and-commerce/an-economic-boom-with-side-effects/

15 Jonathan Saul, "As Arctic Ice Melts, Polluting Ships Stream into Polar Waters," *Reuters*, August 27, 2020, https://www.reuters.com/article/us-climate-change-arctic-shipping-analys/as-arctic-ice-melts-polluting-ships-stream-into-polar-waters-idUSKBN25O0L8

Nevertheless, with the PRC's economic relationship vis-a-vis Russia, undetectable or otherwise covert activities may be easier to accomplish given the probability of limited oversight and fallout political consequences that may be more apparent in open, democratic systems.

In space, China and Russia are cooperating on a space data center with space drilling for rare elements and new energy.[16] They have collaborated on cheap, environmentally friendly, and efficient hydrogen batteries.[17] In the cyber domain, the two countries agreed to not carry out cyber-attacks on each other and jointly counteract any form of cybertechnology that destabilizes the two nations' politics and socio-economic affairs.[18]

Russia has also signed on to work with Huawei, the Chinese tech giant, on 5G technologies.[19] This technology transfer relationship has been cultivated amid the controversy associated with the advent of this fifth-generation of connectivity from China's leadership, which has seen a diverse range of responses across the world. The two nations have also shared a desire to double their trade within a five-year span by performing joint projects in the agricultural, industrial, and energy fields.[20]

---

16 Andrew Jones, "China, Russia to Cooperate on Lunar Orbiter, Landing Missions," *SpaceNews*, September 19, 2019, https://spacenews.com/china-russia-to-cooperate-on-lunar-orbiter-landing-missions/

17 Yin Yeping, "Strengthening of China-Russia Technological Cooperation is Crucial: Envoy," *Global Times*, September 8, 2020, https://www.globaltimes.cn/content/1200296.shtml

18 Olga Razumovskaya, "Russia and China Pledge Not to Hack Each Other," *The Wall Street Journal*, May 8, 2015, https://www.wsj.com/articles/BL-DGB-41673

19 Lan Shunzheng, "Russia's Cooperation with Huawei Heralds Closer China Technology Ties," *CGTN*, August 25, 2020, https://news.cgtn.com/news/2020-08-25/Russia-s-cooperation-with-Huawei-heralds-closer-China-technology-ties-Tf3RFfAzgA/index.html

20 Holly Ellyat, "Are Russia and China the Best of Friends Now? It's Complicated, Analysts Say," *CNBC*, September 27, 2019, https://www.cnbc.com/2019/09/27/russia-and-chinas-relationship--how-deep-does-it-go.html

China-Russia relations are likely to become more closely knit with Beijing and Moscow collaborating on extraction projects for their mutual benefit, though Xi Jinping is taking no chances as China continues to develop its own fleet and does its own exploration.

The two countries have not always been friendly and may merely be friends of convenience in pursuit of their own political interests. Overdependence may not be in the PRC's best long-term interests if they intend to claim the Arctic.

Geopolitical Giants

The two countries, China and Russia, are giants in their own right. This superpower status is owing to their impressive landmasses, forward-thinking approach, and geopolitical power. With growing military power, global economic investments, and the highest ranking in the infrastructural development index,[21] the People's Republic of China has grown to become the largest economy in Asia and the second-largest in all of the world.[22] Meanwhile, the Russian Federation, located on the two continents of Europe and Asia, is the world's largest country due to its sheer size, powerful military, economic potential, and diplomatic influence.[23]

The China-Russia relationship is asymmetric, but they cooperate on military, arms trade, energy, transportation, artificial intelligence, counterterrorism, and biotechnology. China may disagree with Russia and they may share suspicions of one another but they do agree on many issues. Furthermore, the more the U.S. pushes against both China and Russia, the more they find common ground.

Oil and Gas Cooperation in the Arctic

Over the previous decade, Russia–China oil and gas collaboration zeroed in on the Russian Far East and East Siberia pipelines, though the Arctic region countries also have progressively entered into exchanges.[24] In February and March 2013, Russia's Rosneft and the CCP's CNPC discussed opportunities for cooperation on ventures in the Barents and Pechora Seas, specifically the Zapadno-Prinovozemelsky, Yuzhno-Russky, Medyskoe Sea, and Varandeyskoe Sea deposits.[25]

The Medyskoe Sea and Varandeyskoe Sea deposits are among the most encouraging of the oil stores found, potentially delivering up to 3.9 million tons and 5.5 million tons of

---

21 Supply Post, "The Belt and Road Initiative: The World's Largest Infrastructure and Investment Project," *Supply Post*, November 8, 2019, https://www.supplypost.com/news/2019/11/the-belt-and-road-initiative-the-worlds-largest-infrastructure-and-investment-project

22 International Monetary Fund, "World Economic Outlook Reports," *International Monetary Fund*, February 26, 2021, https://www.imf.org/en/Publications/WEO

23 CIA, "World Factbook – Russia," *CIA*, February 24, 2021, https://www.cia.gov/the-world-factbook/countries/russia/

24 Camilla T. N. Sørensen and Ekaterina Klimenko, "Emerging Chinese-Russian Cooperation in the Arctic," *SIPRI*, no. 46 (2017), https://www.sipri.org/sites/default/files/2017-06/emerging-chinese-russian-cooperation-arctic.pdf

25 Artem Zagorodno, "Rosneft to Attract Chinese, Korean Investment to Arctic," *Russia Beyond*, February 19, 2013, https://www.rbth.com/news/2013/02/19/rosneft_inks_memorandum_with_sinopec_on_possible_oil_delivery_increase_23037.html

oil per year, respectively.²⁶ In 2014, the head of Rosneft, Igor Sechin, pledged to work with China on the Arctic rack projects.²⁷ No official affirmation or any polished subtleties have been shared openly. In November 2015, Rosneft reconfirmed its continued conversations with China regarding investment in Arctic ventures. Anatoly Yanovsky, Russia's Deputy Energy Minister, stated that Rosneft's discussions regarding Arctic shelf energy and extraction are at the organization level.'²⁸

This absence of progress may indicate that each side wants to sweeten its end of the pot. Yet, they still see potential benefits. In 2021, Russia began its North Siberian Vankor oil development project with approximately 100 drilling rigs, with a view to build a 770 km oil pipeline. By 2025, 30 million tons of oil will be extracted, by 2027, 50 million, and by 2030, 115 million. Vladimir Putin issued an order in his 2018 'May Decrees' to increase

---

26 V. Bogoyavlensky, I. Bogoyavlensky, and T. Budagova, "Environmental Safety and Environmental Management in the Arctic and World Oceans," *Burenie i Neft*, no. 12 (2013), 16.

27 Ekaterina Klimenko and Camilla T. N. Sørensen, "The Status of Chinese-Russian Energy Cooperation in the Arctic," *SIPRI*, May 11, 2017, https://www.sipri.org/commentary/topical-backgrounder/2017/chinese-russian-energy-cooperation-arctic

28 Sputnik News, "Rosneft, Beijing in Talks on China Arctic Energy Participation," *Sputnik News,* November 16, 2015, https://sputniknews.com/business/201511161030170034-rosneft-china-arctic/

oil development.²⁹ China discussed the conditions Rosneft proposed, possibly wanting a greater stake in the management.³⁰

Meanwhile, the legislatures of the two biggest Arctic nations, Russia and Canada, must balance widespread, divergent feelings regarding the environment or changes in Arctic Council limitations on Arctic oil drilling. If China needs Arctic oil, it will need to energize and gain greater consensus from Arctic governments.

Drill, Drill, Drill
Russian Oil Platforms in the Arctic

Conclusion

China was the lastest of the non-Arctic countries to launch its "Arctic Strategy," consolidating its interest in the region. It has also established partnerships with Russia and other countries based on resource management and scientific research through initiatives like the Yamal LNG scheme, which depends on Chinese and French investments, through China National Petroleum Corporation and Total S.A., respectively. These investments account for 20% of the financing for the Yamal project.

---

29 Atle Staalesen, "It's an Order from the Kremlin: Shipping on Northern Sea Route to Reach 80 Million Tons by 2024," *The Barents Observer,* May 15, 2018, https://thebarentsobserver.com/en/arctic/2018/05/its-order-kremlin-shipping-northern-sea-route-increase-80-million-tons-2024

30 James Henderson and Tatiana Mitrova, "Energy Relations between Russia and China: Playing Chess with the Dragon," *The Oxford Institute for Energy Studies,* 2016, https://www.oxfordenergy.org/publications/energy-relations-russia-china-playing-chess-dragon/

As the transport of goods becomes more accessible and reliable, the PRC has diversified its interests and increased its diplomatic and economic activities in the region. China has clearly expressed a desire to be involved in Arctic affairs development Beijing seeks to be acknowledged for its global leadership and financial contributions. Furthermore, the PRC wants to be included as an 'Arctic stakeholder' and a regional partner based on its significant investments and partnerships.[31]

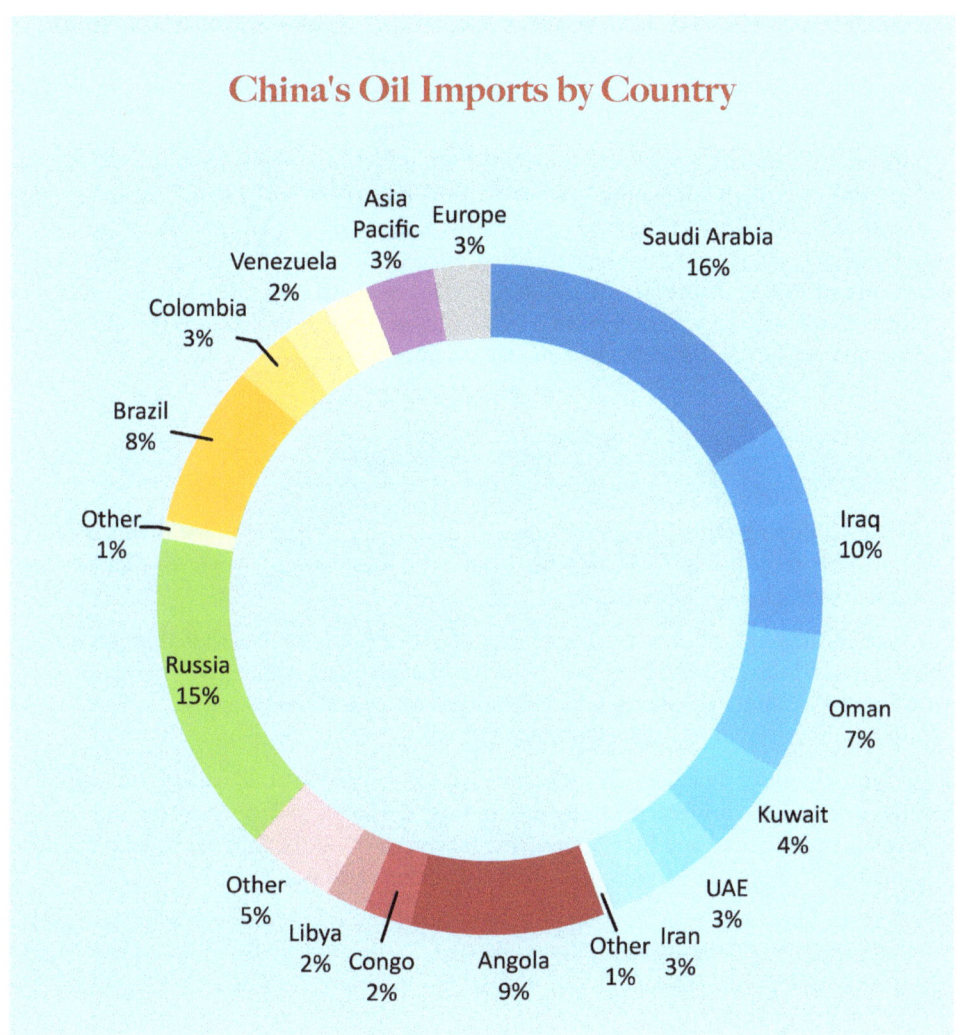

---

31 Sybille Reinke de Buitrago, "China's Aspirations as a 'Near Arctic State': Growing Stakeholder or Growing Risk?," *Handbook on Geopolitics and Security in the Arctic*, (2020): 97-112, https://doi.org/10.1007/978-3-030-45005-2_6

In a video message to the Third Arctic Circle meeting held in Reykjavik, Iceland, in October 2015, the Chinese Foreign Minister, Wang Yi, further described China as a 'near-Arctic state' and referred to China's long history of Arctic interests stretching as far back as China's signing of the Spitsbergen (Svalbard) Treaty in 1925. He aimed to highlight and legitimize the growing role of China in world affairs and its interests.

China is well-aware of Russian reluctance to include non-Arctic states, specifically a great power such as China, in Arctic governance affairs. Therefore, Xi seeks to create a closer relationship with Putin to take advantage of Russia's geostrategic and geo-economic vulnerabilities. In many ways, it makes sense for China to partner with Russia and develop the Russian Arctic.

Chinese Arctic scholars are not under any illusions when it comes to developing a more robust and enduring Chinese–Russian partnership, though mutually beneficial cooperation can help both states realize their bigger goals. Instead, the main goal is for Russia to turn towards Europe as soon as sanctions are lifted. Biden aided Russia in this quest by lifting sanctions on Russia's Nord Stream 2 in May 2021, before his June 2021 meeting with Putin.[32] As one scholar well expresses the relationship: "China understands that Russia plays a game. Now China is the only horse Russia can find. Russia will ride the China horse to find a better one."[33]

What's at Stake?

First, Xi Jinping called Vladimir Putin his "best friend", suggesting the closeness of their friendly relationship.[34] Though they seem to be "best friends" when convenient, their countries have a history of animosity as well.

Second, Beijing's effort to be a significant player in Arctic affairs resulted in introducing its first home-built icebreaker in 2018. China's strategic partnerships and international trade activities have yielded technological insights which it reproduces and applies domestically to obtain technological independence.

Third, The PRC is playing the long game while investing in land, companies, and resource acquisition projects for its long-term future. The threat it poses by buying land in Greenland and Iceland and heavily investing in projects in Norway, Canada, and Russia is the salami-slicing of one bit of the Arctic after another until it dominates the Arctic.

Fourth, China is not just betting on Russia for its natural resources in a just-in-case strategy. In 2013, China acquired Nexen, an oil and gas company based in Calgary that gave the PRC a portion of Alberta's oil-rich region in what is considered the 'second

---

32   BBC News, "Nord Stream 2: Biden Waives US Sanctions on Russian Pipeline," *BBC News*, May 20, 2021, https://www.bbc.com/news/world-us-canada-57180674

33   Chinese Arctic scholars, Interviews conducted by Camilla T. N. Sørensen, Shanghai Institute of International Studies (SIIS), Shanghai, January 17, 2017. See also Deng, B., "Arctic Geopolitics: The Impact of US–Russian Relations on Chinese–Russian Cooperation in the Arctic," *Russia in Global Affairs* 14, no. 2 (2016), pp. 206–20.

34   David Ho, "The Other Special Relationship: China's Xi Visits Russia," *Al Jazeera*, June 5, 2019, https://www.aljazeera.com/economy/2019/6/5/the-other-special-relationship-chinas-xi-visits-russia

Middle East'.[35] China is hedging its bets to have a stake in both the Northwest Passage and the Northern Sea Route for transit and resource acquisition. China's assertiveness has alarmed other Arctic states, even Russia.

---

35 Gloria Dickie, "China Wants to Invest in the Arctic. Why Doesn't Canada?," *The Walrus*, Updated January 29, 2021, https://thewalrus.ca/china-wants-to-invest-in-the-arctic-why-doesnt-canada/

Chapter 8

EEZs, Ports, and Competing Interests

Who's Competing for What and Why is the Arctic Heating Up?

Introduction

When Xi Jinping became the General Secretary of the Chinese Communist Party in 2012 and then the President in 2013, Beijing's statecraft transformed into a new era of assertiveness. In 2015, either by accident or intention, when President Barak Obama visited Alaska, five Chinese naval ships arrived at the Bering Sea after completing joint exercises with the Russian Pacific Fleet.[1]

China increased its priority to make its presence known globally with its 'blue water' navy and commitment to become a strategic participant in the Antarctic and the North Pole's future. On January 26, 2018, Beijing's State Council Information Office of the People's Republic of China laid out its plans in a document called "China's Arctic Policy".[2] One of the many efforts in China's "Polar Silk Road" plan is to have a fleet of ice cutters, including a nuclear icebreaker on its Belt and Road mission to increase its commerce and economy.

China has staked its claim alongside other countries by maintaining that its bases are merely for scientific research. However, Beijing's "white hull diplomacy" is solidifying its stance by deploying its Coast Guard to increase Beijing's "voice" in managing the Arctic.[3]

Controversies in the Arctic Transitway

Resource acquisition is a top priority for each country. Vast reserves of minerals, fish, animal, and oil are prime targets for this recent rabid pursuit. From the explorations in the 1500s by Dutch explorer Willem Barents to the whaling and seal ventures in the 1600s, and presently with 'liquid gold', extraction of increased animal and mineral resources, the Arctic has attracted those seeking oil and natural gas, metals, and rare-earth elements.[4]

Beijing's researchers are in both the Arctic and the Antarctic, exploring the possibility of exploiting oil, natural gas, coal, gold, uranium, manganese nodules, fish, and shrimp.[5] However, Arctic states question Beijing's ambitions. Until transport vessels, resource developers, and fishing fleets melt the ice sheets or break them apart to make the region habitable, to the detriment of the environment, there are still factors that make the Arctic a challenge.

There is not yet enough infrastructure to maintain larger populations of military and researchers. This development is rapidly changing the region. However, constructing

---

1   Phil Stewart, "Five Chinese Ships in Bering Sea as Obama Visits Alaska," *Reuters*, September 2, 2015, https://www.reuters.com/article/us-usa-china-military/five-chinese-ships-in-bering-sea-as-obama-visits-alaska-idUSKCN0R22DN20150902

2   Xinhua, "Full Text: China's Arctic Policy," *The State Council, The People's Republic of China,* Updated January 26, 2018, http://english.www.gov.cn/archive/white_paper/2018/01/26/content_281476026660336.htm

3   Swee Lean Collin Koh, "China's Strategic Interest in the Arctic Goes Beyond Economics," *Defense News*, May 12, 2020, https://www.defensenews.com/opinion/commentary/2020/05/11/chinas-strategic-interest-in-the-arctic-goes-beyond-economics/

4   World Ocean Review, "An Economic Boom with Side Effects," *World Ocean Review,* 2019, https://worldoceanreview.com/en/wor-6/polar-politics-and-commerce/an-economic-boom-with-side-effects/

5   Lyle J. Goldstein, "China is Building Nuclear Icebreakers to Seek Out a 'Polar Silk Road'," *National Interest*, March 16, 2020, https://nationalinterest.org/blog/buzz/china-building-nuclear-icebreakers-seek-out-polar-silk-road-132417

communities, scientific bases, and resource extraction development will destroy the habitat, change the climate worldwide and raise the ocean levels to the point of ridding many countries of their coastlines. Dramatic Arctic temperature changes, strong, fluky winds, and violent storm patterns pose a significant challenge. Voyagers must endure inhospitable conditions far from civilization for long periods.

Avoiding a Militarized Approach

The Arctic Council countries, Canada, Denmark, Finland, Iceland, Norway, Russia, Sweden, and the United States, do not want China to take a militarized approach to the Arctic. Steps must be taken now to avoid China's escalation of resource extraction 'research', and naval and paramilitary activities. Meanwhile, the Arctic Council maintains its common goals to work cooperatively on search-and-rescue missions, enforce laws and regulations on maritime safety, and preserve Arctic communities' wellbeing.[6]

A number of factors threaten the overall affairs of the Arctic nations. For one, countries outside of the eight Arctic Council states have taken an extraordinary interest in natural resources found in the Arctic.[7] Despite the cooperative rhetoric of unity amongst observer nations, each is looking out for its own country's enrichment before collective gains rather

---

6   Government of Canada, "Arctic and Northern Policy Framework: Safety, Security, and Defence Chapter," *Government of Canada*, Updated September 10, 2019, https://www.rcaanc-cirnac.gc.ca/eng/1562939617400/1562939658000

7   Ministère de L'Europe et des Affaires Étrangères, "The Great Challenge of the Arctic," *Ministère de L'Europe et des Affaires Étrangères*, n.d., https://www.diplomatie.gouv.fr/IMG/pdf/frna_-_eng_-interne_-_prepa_-_17-06-pm-bd-pdf_cle02695b.pdf

than the other way around. This self-interest can be seen in the squabbles that break out about rights to territory and navigation.[8]

China's interest in the Arctic, calling itself a "Near-Arctic State", is particularly bold. This assertiveness has increased the tension felt by these Arctic nations since China does not share a boundary with the Arctic.[9] China believes it has a right to construct Arctic bases for scientific research, explore economic resources, and play an active part in governing the Arctic region.[10]

China's intentions and ambitions for a new way forward with its "Polar Silk Road"[11] are an aspect of Xi Jinping's Chinese Dream that conflicts with other states' interests. Meanwhile, China's growing fleet also give Beijing the opportunity it needs to carry out its own regular patrols in Arctic waters.[12] China's affairs in the Arctic states have raised both eyebrows and concerns amongst other Arctic nations while simultaneously fueling its great-power tussle with the United States.[13]

Not Always Friendly Relations with Russia

Russian citizens are crying out regarding China's persistent intrusion on Russian land and on the flourishing logging industry in Siberia. Feeding China's colossal appetite for wood has brought jobs and cash to the region, but it has also helped to make Russia the global leader in forest depletion. The devastation of Russia's forests has fueled fears that Siberian logging towns will eventually be left without a livelihood. Additionally, Russia is not benefiting from the wood being cut and taken away. The bulk of manufactured consumer wood products are carried out in China, where logging is sharply restricted, and cheap labor is abundant.[14]

Though Arctic countries' priorities differ,[15] each is bound to their citizens by sovereignty and defense, tied to their economic security by resource development and trade, and bound to their social consciousness for environmental protection. The desire for peace is a strong policy-making force. Sacrifices are made by each Arctic state to foster and sustain peace. This does not mean these countries will sit idly by and watch while they lose their

---

8   Ministère de L'Europe et des Affaires Étrangères, "The Great Challenge of the Arctic," *Ministère de L'Europe et des Affaires Étrangères*, n.d., https://www.diplomatie.gouv.fr/IMG/pdf/frna_-_eng_-interne_-_prepa_-_17-06-pm-bd-pdf_cle02695b.pdf

9   Congressional Research Service, "Changes in the Artic: Background and Issues for Congress," *Congressional Research Service,* Updated February 1, 2021, https://fas.org/sgp/crs/misc/R41153.pdf

10 Edward Ng, 'The Rise of Chinese FDI into ASEAN," *Nikko Asset Management*, October 5, 2017, https://emea.nikkoam.com/files/pdf/insights/2017/20171005-The-Rise-of-Chinese-FDI-into-ASEAN.pdf

11 Gisela Grieger, "China's Arctic Policy: How China Aligns Rights and Interests," *European Parliament*, May, 2018, https://www.europarl.europa.eu/RegData/etudes/BRIE/2018/620231/EPRS_BRI(2018)620231_EN.pdf

12 Ibid.

13 Hans Lucht, "Chinese Investments in Greenland Raise US Concerns," *Danish Institute for International Studies*, November 20, 2018, https://www.diis.dk/en/research/chinese-investments-in-greenland-raise-us-concerns

14 Andrew E. Kramer, "As the Chinese Cut Down Siberia's Forests, Tensions with Russians Rise," *The New York Times*, July 25, 2019, https://www.nytimes.com/2019/07/25/world/europe/russia-china-siberia-logging.html

15 Ministère de L'Europe et des Affaires Étrangères, "The Great Challenge of the Arctic," *Ministère de L'Europe et des Affaires Étrangères*, n.d., https://www.diplomatie.gouv.fr/IMG/pdf/frna_-_eng_-interne_-_prepa_-_17-06-pm-bd-pdf_cle02695b.pdf

sovereignty and their capacities for environmental survival.[16]

Canada, for example, has the largest portion of Arctic land. On August 23, 2010, Prime Minister Stephen Harper declared that the protection of Canada's sovereignty over its northern regions was the country's utmost and non-negotiable priority in Arctic policy.[17] Canada has taken its sovereignty over its northern areas very seriously, even sparking conflict with China. One situation was when China asked Canada to pay for roadways and ports in the Arctic so that China could access a mining operation they owned in Canadian territory.[18] In another instance, China proposed transporting cargo through the Northwest Passage, a region over which Canada's sovereignty extends. Canada fought back, refusing to allow the passage of Chinese vessels through its waters.[19]

---

16 United Nations Economic and Social Council, "Promoting Sustainable Development," *United Nations Economic and Social Council*, n.d., https://www.un.org/ecosoc/en/content/promoting-sustainable-development

17 CBC, "Arctic Sovereignty 'Non-Negotiable': Harper," *CBC*, August 20, 2010, https://www.cbc.ca/news/politics/arctic-sovereignty-non-negotiable-harper-1.866786

18 Gloria Dickie, "China Wants to Invest in the Arctic. Why Doesn't Canada?," *The Walrus*, Updated January 29, 2021, https://thewalrus.ca/china-wants-to-invest-in-the-arctic-why-doesnt-canada/

19 Nash Jenkins, "China could be Preparing to Challenge Canada's Sovereignty over the Northwest Passage," *Time Magazine*, April 21, 2016, https://time.com/4302882/china-arctic-shipping-northwest-passage/

A Place for the European Union

Members of the European Union have joined China's Belt and Road Initiative and a few of theses countries have a significant stake in the Arctic.

China's expansion of its "One Belt, One Road" project into the Arctic Ocean, accompanied with its drilling operations, is likely to engender unfavorable externalities. In China's perceived need to diversify, Beijing relied on shipping routes through the Indian Ocean and Red Sea, which were often dangerous due to private vessel takeovers. This concern incentivized its development of the Northern Sea Routes, a move designed to mitigate strategic impediments and provide diplomatic leverage with rival powers.

Researchers Gather Data at the Edges of the Glaciers

Russia is a major player in the Arctic. However, the EU has a frequently hostile relationship with Russia. While the EU is neither an Arctic power itself nor does it have coastal access to the Arctic Sea, three of its member nations are Arctic states: The Kingdom of Sweden, the Republic of Finland, and the Kingdom of Denmark (including the Greenland and Faeroe islands). For this reason, the EU also serves as an extempory observer.[20]

China maintains a keen interest in the Northern Passage, aiming to utilize it to gain access to Russian gas reserves and oil fields throughout Siberia and gain trade access to Northern Europe.[21] As warehousing, shipping, and logistics companies in both Asia and Europe begin to develop strategies for the Northern Passage, there are implications for members of the EU such as Estonia, Latvia, Lithuania, Poland, and Finland that are linked by both maritime and terrestrial routes.

These nations may have to reposition themselves accordingly to meet China's demand. For example, Estonia already handles 5% of the Chinese Postal Services due to their Post 11 JV bilateral tie, which provides logistics solutions for commerce between Europe and China, particularly within the context of the 16+1 framework between Eastern European nations and China.[22] With the Arctic Maritime Route proving to be increasingly sustainable, Eurasian Trade has begun moving to transit areas in Eastern Europe such as Belarus.

---

20 Maud Descamps, "The Ice-Silk Road: Is China a "Near-Arctic-State"?," *Institute for Security & Development Policy*, February, 2019, https://isdp.eu/publication/the-ice-silk-road-is-china-a-near-artic-state/

21 Chris Devonshire-Ellis, "China's Maritime Arctic Silk Road on Ice," *Silk Road Briefing*, July 21, 2017, https://www.silkroadbriefing.com/news/2017/07/10/chinas-maritime-arctic-silk-road-ice/

22 Cooperation Between China and Central and Eastern European Countries, "Cooperation Between China and Central and Eastern European Countries," *Cooperation Between China and Central and Eastern European Countries*, n.d., http://www.china-ceec.org/eng/

Conclusion

Despite the significant milestones China has crossed and its developmental strides regarding Arctic exploration, Beijing still stirs fear and controversy. While Beijing can harness its extensive financial power as a tool to sow good terms with other states, this may not be enough to ensure its prominent place in the Arctic Council. Even significant financial payouts may not secure the votes and insert its authority given what is at stake for each of the Arctic states and the entire planet. China has a long way to go in terms of abiding by rule of law if it hopes to win the hearts and trust of the Arctic nations.

The emergence of the Arctic Sea as an epicenter for resource exploitation and commercial development provides Arctic countries with an opportunity to sell China access to their resource and territorial rights and pay for infrastructure. Yet, these engagements happening in most Arctic states have negative consequences, particularly environmental. Climate change led to the possibility of entering the Arctic. Still, the destructive forces, including the diminishing ecosystem, loss of fish, pollution, transportation networks, refueling stations, tourism, destruction of culture, military conflict, and further ice melting, offset any positive effects of deliberate climate change, leading to a safe and healthy global environment.

Aside from China's technological and economic aspects in the polar arena, the topic of environmental consequences and additional damage to the delicate and vulnerable ecosystem pose a problem.

What's at Stake?

First, China has deployed its Coast Guard in the Arctic. Ostensibly, its military presence is designed to support efforts through "white hull diplomacy". Although Beijing's efforts may appear benevolent on the surface, the underlying goal may not be as altruistic as it seems. For example, China's paramilitary swarms ships around the South China Sea islands within other states' Exclusive Economic Zones and takes other states' territory.

Second, China intends "to pursue an economic development strategy for the region that requires the Arctic be open to Chinese development and that China is given equal standing to other Arctic nations"[23] Concerns have been raised over China's steady advances in affairs of the Arctic. Notwithstanding, China is not an Arctic state, so to request equal standing is necessarily confrontational since other states have the right to their territory.

Third, in 2010, Chinese Admiral Yin Zhou said, "The Arctic belongs to all the people around the world, as no nation has sovereignty over it... China must plan an indispensable role in Arctic exploration as we have one-fifth of the world's population".[24] This statement is tantamount to saying that the grass in your backyard should belong to everyone since it is part of nature. As long as China holds this view, competition and conflict are highly likely.

---

23 Heather A. Conley, "China's Arctic Dream," *CSIS*, February 26, 2018, https://www.csis.org/analysis/chinas-arctic-dream

24 Caitlin Campbell, "China and the Arctic: Objectives and Obstacles," *U.S.-China Economic and Security Review Commission*, April 13, 2012, https://www.uscc.gov/sites/default/files/Research/China-and-the-Arctic_Apr2012.pdf

Rights of Passage in the Arctic

Part 5

Digital Silk Road

Digitizing the Planet

Increasingly, China's aggressive approach to international politics, discourse, and military incursions has been nothing short of intimidation and outright bullying. The South China Sea, East China Sea, and the Indo-Pacific have been flashpoints for conflict. The looming threat to Taiwan is a tinderbox waiting to explode.

In 2020, Vietnamese and Filipino fishing vessels were rammed by their Chinese larger, militarized counterparts, while Malaysia's oil exploration and Indonesia's fishing were threatened in the southern part of the South China Sea. While China built outposts on India's contested land and killed Indian soldiers, Chinese jets flew into Taiwan's air defense zones. These were not the only incidents of Chinese aggression. Chinese submarines reportedly cruised in Japanese waters. Two Canadians continued to be detained over charges of espionage in a case of hostage diplomacy. All the while, EU-China relations are strained for reasons ranging from the COVID-19 pandemic and facemask diplomacy to Huawei and Hong Kong.

China's muscle-flexing extended to Australia as well. When Canberra called for an investigation into the origins of the coronavirus, an angry Beijing banned goods like barley, wine, meat, timber, and cotton from entering China. The tug of war continued as Beijing's propaganda machine warned Chinese students and tourists to steer clear of Australia. Australia found new markets for its exports, with countries stepping in to save Aussie industries. To its credit, Australia flexed its muscles and engaged in military exercises in the South China Sea with India, Japan, and the United States.

The aforementioned instances of tit-for-tat muscle-flexing swirled dust into a blinding storm between China and other countries. China's human rights abuses in Xinjiang Province has created a storm of a different ilk that is likely to tarnish the 2022 Beijing Olympics with 180 human rights groups calling for a boycott. Nevertheless, China refuses to back down from any pressure, throwing insults from 'Wolf Warrior' Twitter accounts on a daily basis. These provocations have united the Quad, Five Eyes, and other international groups to push back.

At the annual summit of the Association of Southeast Asian Nations (ASEAN), the 2020 chair, Vietnam, has called out China over the recent aggression in the South China Sea. Vietnam Prime Minister Nguyen Xuan Phuc said in his opening remarks, "While the entire world is stretched thin in the fight against the pandemic, irresponsible acts and acts in violation of international law are still taking place, affecting the environment of security and stability in certain regions, including our region."[1]

---

1 The Socialist Republic of Vietnam Online Newspaper of the Government, "Keynote Speech on Viet Nam's 2020 ASEAN Chairmanship," *The Socialist Republic of Vietnam Online Newspaper of the Government*, June 1, 2020, http://news.chinhphu.vn/Home/Keynote-speech-by-PM-Nguyen-Xuan-Phuc-at-launching-ceremony-of-VNs-2020-ASEAN-Chairmanship/20201/38445.vgp

Chapter 1
Digital Silk Road
The Era of Global Political Influence and Social Control

Introduction

The Digital Silk Road was proposed in 2015 in a white paper, three years after Xi Jinping was elected to lead the Chinese Communist Party (CCP) and two years after being elected President of the People's Republic of China (PRC). However, Xi Jinping started taking steps immediately with a strategic vision and a long-term plan. Central to this effort were the technology experts, which he hired from around the world, and state-of-the-art patented technologies, which he gained by buying foreign companies.

China's Thousand Talents Program recruited Western experts who had access to cutting-edge research. The program's name was changed in 2019 to "National High-end Foreign Experts Recruitment Plan".[1] Over a decade, China attracted more than 7,000 experts.[2] Espionage was unnecessary if China could pay foreign technology experts enough money to give CCP companies the key drivers and tools to develop better high-tech equipment. *Bloomberg* called the not-so-secret Thousand Talents Program an 'Unprecedented Threat' from China on Tech Takeover' explaining that the underlying goal is "to facilitate the legal and illicit transfer of US technology, intellectual property and know-how."[3]

With talent and patents from abroad, China was able to lure companies, gain access to their equipment, build its own plants, map out a plan to lay underwater cables, place Wi-fi towers, and produce phones equal to Apple and Samsung to sell around the world. Beijing sprung into motion with 5G, vowing to be the first global leader and gain widespread access to coveted contracts from countries around the world, starting with those who signed onto the Belt and Road Initiative.

Artificial Intelligence and Social Credit

The next step was to gather data from its citizens and then people worldwide in a massive artificial intelligence center explicitly designed to consistently house and extract data at will. This effort supported the Integrated social credit system and digital currency plan initiated on a small scale in individual regions between 2009 and 2011. A translated document, "Planning Outline for the Construction of a Social Credit System (2014-2020)" explains,

> Our country is currently in the assault phase of deepening economic structural reform and perfecting the Socialist market economy system...
>
> Build and complete e-commerce enterprise and client credit management and transaction credit evaluation systems, strengthen quality supervision by e-commerce enterprises of credit products they exploit and sell. Build and use morality classrooms well, and advocate value views and moral norms of patriotism...complete punishment

---

1   William C. Hanna and Didi Kirsten Tatlow, China's *Quest for Foreign Technology: Beyond Espionage* (New York: Routledge, 2020).

2   Hepeng Jia, "China's Plan to Recruit Talented Researchers," *Nature*, January 17, 2018, https://www.nature.com/articles/d41586-018-00538-z

3   Anthony Capaccio, "U.S. Faces 'Unprecedented Threat' From China on Tech Takeover," *Bloomberg*, June 21, 2018, https://www.bloomberg.com/news/articles/2018-06-22/china-s-thousand-talents-called-key-in-seizing-u-s-expertise

structures for breach of trust, establish blacklist systems and market withdrawal mechanisms in all sectors...

Establish and complete social credit reward and punishment mechanisms, and ensure that those keeping trust are incentivized and rewarded, and those breaking trust are restrained and sanctioned. Publicize model acts of trust-breaking violating laws and regulations, and strengthen the attack against grave acts of trust-breaking.

Wired called it "reputation economics based on surveillance."[4] By April 2021, China's 'big data', artificial intelligence-driven social credit ranking was implemented in most cities with more than 33 million businesses in China categorized on compliance, finance, and other areas.[5] Should an individual or company fail to show patriotism, loyalty to the CCP, generosity, or service, the result could be the inability to travel, get into a good school, or access their money through a process of blacklisting individuals and/or corporations.[6]

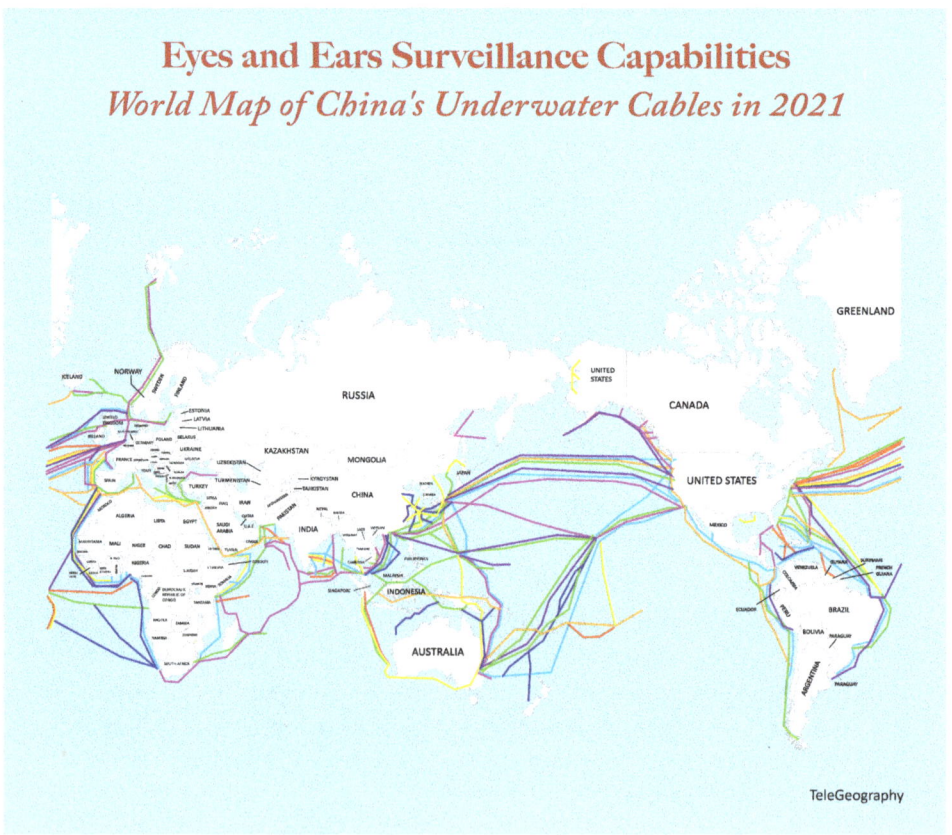

Eyes and Ears Surveillance Capabilities
World Map of China's Underwater Cables in 2021

TeleGeography

---

4   Bruce Sterling, "Chinese Planning Outline for a Social Credit System," *Wired*, June 3, 2015, https://www.wired.com/beyond-the-beyond/2015/06/chinese-planning-outline-social-credit-system/

5   Drew Donnelly, "An Introduction to the China Social Credit System," *New Horizons*, April 15, 2021, https://nhglobalpartners.com/china-social-credit-system-explained/

6   Oxford Analytica, "China will Reform Social Credit for Tighter Discipline," *Oxford Analytica,* January 20, 2021, https://dailybrief.oxan.com/Analysis/DB258464/China-will-reform-social-credit-for-tighter-discipline

If an individual or family member is on a blacklist, audits and public shaming are likely outcomes, and a child may not enter a university or get a good job.[7]

Advancing the Digital Silk Road

China's Digital Silk Road had humble beginnings but grew as connections, fiber optic underwater cables, data center, and Wi-fi mechanisms were incorporated into BRI countries. Although the CCP encouraged its state-owned enterprises to seek contracts in a bottom-up effort, during the pandemic, greater control was applied with increased coordination from the CCP in the development of smart cities, integrated financial mechanisms, security, and telemedicine.[8] Financial, commercial, social media, camera surveillance technology, device manufacturers, and drone developers jumped into the fray with Chinese corporations like,

Alibaba	HikVision	Tecno
Ant Financial	Huawei	Tencent
Baidu	Meituan Dianping	Tiktok
BBK Electronics	NetEase	Transsion
Bytedance	NucTech	XAG
CoolPad	Oppo	Xiaomi
DJI	OnePlus	Yuneec
Gionee	Pinduoduo	ZTE
JD.com	TCL	

The CCP exports its facial recognition technology, surveillance camera networks, and artificial intelligence data collecting mechanisms. With BRI's penetration into more than a hundred countries, China can enter markets more swiftly than competitors and may use its "savior diplomacy" and "vaccine diplomacy" as an avenue for greater influence in the mobile phone and 5G markets. The Digital Silk Road is likely to grow despite concerns about the pandemic.

Conclusion

The Digital Silk Road is expanding, aided by the reach of Chinese companies like Huawei and ZTE. During the pandemic, cell phones increased dramatically, and cell phone addiction grew. In 2021, 4.88 billion people owned a mobile phone, or 62.11% of the world's population, with consequent usages as shown in the following table.[9]

---

7   Drew Donnelly, "An Introduction to the China Social Credit System," *New Horizons,* April 15, 2021, https://nhglobalpartners.com/china-social-credit-system-explained/

8   Robert Greene and Paul Triolo, "Will China Control the Global Internet Via its Digital Silk Road?," *Carnegie Endowment for International Peace,* May 8, 2020, https://carnegieendowment.org/2020/05/08/will-china-control-global-internet-via-its-digital-silk-road-pub-81857

9   Bank My Cell, "How Many Smartphones Are In the World?," *Bank My Cell,* n.d., https://www.bankmycell.com/blog/how-many-phones-are-in-the-world

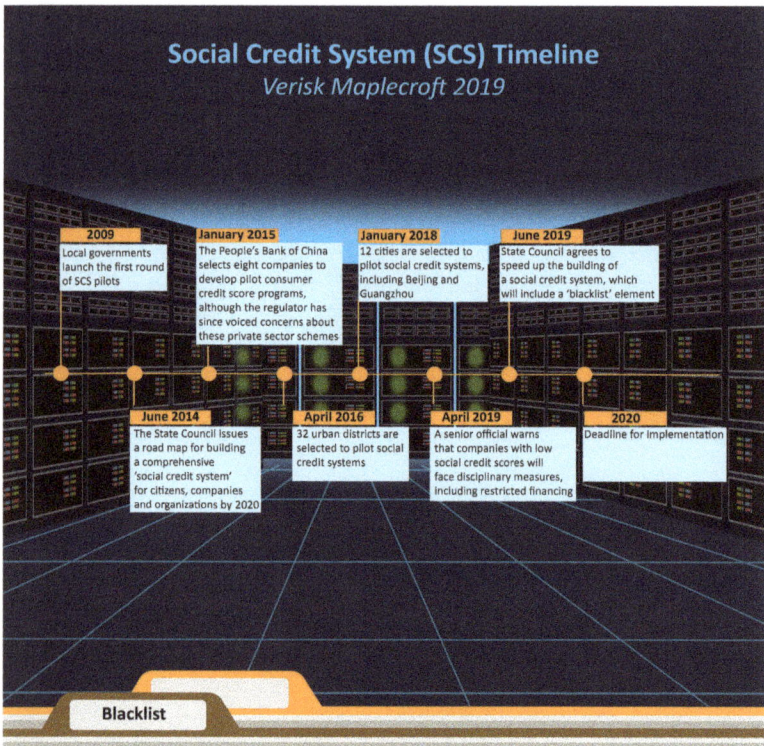

Cell Phone Use By Country				
Rank	Country	Total Population	Smartphone Users	Smartphone Penetration
1	China	1.42 billion	851 million	59.9%
2	India	137 billion	346 million	25.3%
3	United States	329 million	260 million	79.1%
4	Brazil	212 million	96.9 million	45.6%
5	Russia	144 million	95.4 million	66.3%
6	Indonesia	270 million	83.9 million	31.1%
7	Japan	127 million	72.6 million	57.2%
8	Germany	82.4 million	65.9 million	79.9%
9	Mexico	132 million	65.6 million	49.5%
10	United Kingdom	67.0 million	55.5 million	82.9%

Global statistics are startling.[10]

- The average user checks their phone more than 50 times/day, with time spent averaging nearly 3 hours/day

---

10 Denis Metev, "39+ Smartphone Statistics You Should Know in 2020," *Review 42,* Updated February 18, 2021, https://review42.com/resources/smartphone-statistics/

- Millennials spend 5.7 hours compared to baby boomers with 5 hours
- In the UAE, 82.2% have smartphones; only 5.4% in Bangladesh, 4% in Ethiopia & Uganda, and 25% in India
- Most people will not recommend a business with a poorly designed website.
- More than half of all videos are watched on a mobile device.
- Mobile data traffic is predicted to increase by 700%
- High cell phone use is linked to suicide, ADHD-like symptoms, addiction, and driving accident deaths

Ultimately, the pandemic's societal impact significantly increased cell phone purchase and use, bolstering the Digital Silk Road. How Beijing manages its Digital Silk Road rollout, and how foreign countries react may cause dramatic and perhaps irreversible shifts in cyberspace governance and telecommunications standard-setting.[11]

What's at Stake?

First, social credit rankings and blacklist implementation in China are the first steps in similar ratings, punishments, and blacklisting in countries that have signed onto the Digital Silk Road and the Belt and Road Initiative.

Second, Beijing's overarching authoritarian social control implemented worldwide has the potential to eliminate freedom of speech, freedom of thought, and freedom of religion. Xi Jinping demands that Chinese citizens be "unyielding Marxist atheists".[12]

Third, if the social credit system cuts off a person's digital money, they may not be able to buy food, rent an apartment, or travel. As their digital currency is cancelled, the individual person could be isolated and, if sick, not be able to access medical care.

Fourth, China's continued harassment of Taiwan threatens everyone worldwide. While Taiwan is slightly bigger than the state of Maryland, it is the home of 92% of the world's leading chip manufacturers at a time when chips are used in devices, laptops, vehicles, and appliances.[13] This shortage has led to automobile manufacturing plant shutdowns for months in 2021.[14]

---

11 Robert Greene and Paul Triolo, "Will China Control the Global Internet Via its Digital Silk Road?," *Carnegie Endowment for International Peace,* May 8, 2020, https://carnegieendowment.org/2020/05/08/will-china-control-global-internet-via-its-digital-silk-road-pub-81857

12 Charlie Campbell, "China's Leader Xi Jinping Reminds Party Members to Be 'Unyielding Marxist Atheists,'" *Time Magazine,* April 25, 2016, https://time.com/4306179/china-religion-freedom-xi-jinping-muslim-christian-xinjiang-buddhist-tibet/

13 Ina Fried, "Why Threats to Taiwan are a Nightmare for Tech," *Axios,* April 9, 2021, https://www.axios.com/threats-to-taiwan-nightmare-tech-847c1f30-d878-4eb9-b749-b2f17487dd91.html

14 Jack Ewing and Neal E. Boudette, "A Tiny Part's Big Ripple: Global Chip Shortage Hobbles the Auto Industry," *The New York Times,* April 23, 2021, https://www.nytimes.com/2021/04/23/business/auto-semiconductors-general-motors-mercedes.html

Chapter 2

The Spread of ZTE, Huawei, and Invasive Technologies

"Danger, Danger Will Robinson"

Introduction

Since Chinese companies are owned by the state rather than individuals, in ramping up the Digital Silk Road, the Chinese Communist Party (CCP) sought to secure patents and technological sophistication, which it did by buying American phone and technology companies like Motorola.[1] In Beijing's long-term planning, China sought to move in the direction of international Internet system integration and thereby build digital literacy, accessibility, and global surveillance. Thus, ZTE, Huawei, and other Chinese technology companies have a well-established presence in countries worldwide.

Alerts, Warnings, and Scandals

Huawei and ZTE are two of the many Chinese telecommunications and technology companies that share personal information in a centralized data bank. Numerous countries have put out alerts, warning about security holes used for spying purposes and intellectual property theft.[2] Cisco sued Huawei for stealing its proprietary intellectual property.[3] China threatened Sweden that if it did not reverse its ban on the use of products from Huawei and ZTE, its other companies would face a 'negative impact'.[4]

In 2008, a well-documented scandal occurred when the Philippine officials offered ZTE a contract that was overpriced by $130 million due to kickbacks.[5] Although canceled, a political crisis was triggered as graft, corruption, and monetary payouts were considered a significant cause of Philippine President Gloria Macapagal-Arroyo's downfall.[6] The question arises as to how many telecommunications projects are being set up in countries worldwide where leaders are also given $130 million in kickbacks to buy the country Chinese technology and overcharge the state.

Huawei was charged with racketeering, stealing source code for internet routers, misappropriating robotic technology, and the theft of proprietary information about cellular antennas.[7] Huawei is also frequently in the news because it intrudes into people's private lives with covert data gathering. China's unscrupulous acts led to the holding of

---

1   Reuters, "China's Lenovo Buys Google's Motorola Business for US$2.9 Billion," *South China Morning Post*, January 30, 2014, https://www.scmp.com/business/companies/article/1417289/chinas-lenovo-buys-googles-motorola-business-us29-billion

2   Joe Panettieri, "Huawei: Banned and Permitted in Which Countries? List and FAQ," *CHANNELe2e*, June 1, 2021, https://www.channele2e.com/business/enterprise/huawei-banned-in-which-countries/

3   Ethan Baron, "Chinese Company Huawei's Silicon Valley Outpost Allegedly Stole trade Secrets from Cisco," *Mercury News*, February 13, 2020, https://www.mercurynews.com/2020/02/13/chinese-company-huaweis-silicon-valley-outpost-allegedly-stole-trade-secrets-from-cisco/

4   Reuters, "China Urges Sweden to Reverse its Huawei, ZTE Ban to Avoid Harming its Companies," *Reuters*, October 21, 2020, https://www.reuters.com/article/us-sweden-huawei-china/china-urges-sweden-to-reverse-its-huawei-zte-ban-to-avoid-harming-its-companies-idUSKBN2760W1

5   Manny Mogato, "Manila's Arroyo Described as 'Evil' in Graft Probe," *Reuters*, February 17, 2008, https://www.reuters.com/article/us-philippines-scandal/manilas-arroyo-described-as-evil-in-graft-probe-idUSMAN3603920080218

6   Jun Ledesma "The National Broadband Network," Republic of the Philippines https://www.pna.gov.ph/opinion/pieces/123-the-national-broadband-network

7   https://www.washingtonpost.com/technology/2020/02/13/us-charges-chinas-huawei-with-conspiracy-steal-us-trade-secrets-new-indictment/

Huawei's chief financial officer, Meng Wanzhou. In retaliation, Beijing introduced another 'hostage diplomacy' scandal with Canadian citizens in retaliatory imprisonment for years.

Chinese state-owned enterprises (SOE) have been incentivized to move swiftly into technological evolution. Two companies at the forefront of early technology development, Alibaba and Tencent, are said to have invested more than $12 billion in Southeast Asia since 2015, pushing them ahead in market share and influence in Association of Southeast Asian Nation (ASEAN) states for the foreseeable future.[8] According to *CNBC*, Southeast Asia alone had 40 million new users in 2020.[9]

State-Owned Enterprise (SOE) Technology Development

To achieve Xi Jinping's goals, building infrastructure in countries to disseminate ZTE and Huawei's telecommunications was imperative. For China to dominate the competition, infrastructure needed to be built, including laying fiber optic cables, creating data centers, setting up mobile networks, and installing security cameras. Spreading Beijing's wings over Southeast Asia and beyond, Chinese citizens created state-owned enterprises to overtake all other competition on its Digital Silk Road quest to dominate technology industries including,[10]

1. HikVision and NucTech: security systems, called 'The Huawei of Airport Security"[11]
2. Alibaba: e-commerce system in Thailand's 'digital hub[12] and 'Malaysia's Digital Economy'[13]
3. Ant Financial and Alipay: payment services [14]
4. Tencent and WeChat: communications and financial services
5. JD.com, Taobao, Tmall: online shopping
6. Btyedance/Tiktok: social media
7. Transsion, Oppo, OnePlus, and Xiaomi: smart devices

---

8   Vy Nguyen, China's Digital Silk Road: Progress & Influence in Southeast Asia," *China Focus*, July 16, 2020, https://chinafocus.ucsd.edu/2020/07/16/chinas-digital-silk-road-progress-influence-in-southeast-asia/

9   Saheli Roy Choudhury, "Southeast Asia's Digital Services Surge as Coronavirus Pandemic Kept People at Home," *CNBC*, November 9, 2020, https://www.cnbc.com/2020/11/10/southeast-asia-40-million-new-internet-users-in-2020-report-finds.html

10 Robert Greene and Paul Triolo, "Will China Control the Global Internet Via its Digital Silk Road?" *Carnegie Endowment*, May 8, 2020, https://carnegieendowment.org/2020/05/08/will-china-control-global-internet-via-its-digital-silk-road-pub-81857

11 Laurens Cerulus, "The Huawei of Airport Security," *Politico*, February 14, 2020, https://www.politico.eu/article/beijing-scanners-europe-nuctech/

12 Xinhua, "Alibaba to Build Digital Hub in Thailand, *Xinhua*, April 19, 2018, http://www.xinhuanet.com/english/2018-04/19/c_137123315.htm

13 SME, "Alibaba Group Continues Empowering Malaysia's Digital Economy," *SME*, December 10, 2019, https://sme.asia/alibaba-group-continues-empowering-malaysias-digital-economy/

14 Eurasia Group, "The Digital Silk Road: Expanding China's Digital Footprint," *Eurasia Group*, April 8, 2020, https://www.eurasiagroup.net/files/upload/Digital-Silk-Road-Expanding-China-Digital-Footprint-1.pdf

8. DJI, XAG, AEE: drones for surveillance and policing during COVID-19[15]
9. ZTE, Huawei, China Mobile, and China Telecom: phone, computer Internet immersion

The technology sector is growing at a rapid pace. While technology innovation was stolen from universities, corporations, and governments, China continues to improve on these specifications, and translate them into its own products. FBI Director Christopher Wray stated that this challenge is one of the greatest threats to our society today as China uses 'any means necessary' to take 300 billion to 600 billion in trade secrets each year.[16]

Huawei Industries continues to be investigated by U.S. regulators as the company rolls out its 5G technology to countries worldwide. Huawei acquired 56,000 5G and artificial intelligence-related Chinese patents without spending vast amounts of money on research

---

15 Zhang Dan, "How Chinese Drone Makers Help with US, UK Combat COVID-19?," *Global Times,* December 24, 2020, https://www.globaltimes.cn/content/1210884.shtml

16 Reuters, "China Theft of Technology is Biggest Law Enforcement Threat to US, FBI Says," *The Guardian*, February 6, 2020, https://www.theguardian.com/world/2020/feb/06/china-technology-theft-fbi-biggest-threat

and development.[17] China uses "cyber break-ins and traditional spying using human assets, it employs legal means of acquiring technology such as joint ventures, buying companies outright, partnerships with government research institutions, and hiring foreign experts and bringing them to China to work."[18]

According to William Schneider Jr., former Undersecretary of State,[19]

> China has institutionalized a system that combines legal and illegal means of technology acquisition from abroad...but what is not so well known is how China converts the technology it acquires into their military capabilities...unlike anything we have had to deal with in the past...The scale of the problem is obvious.

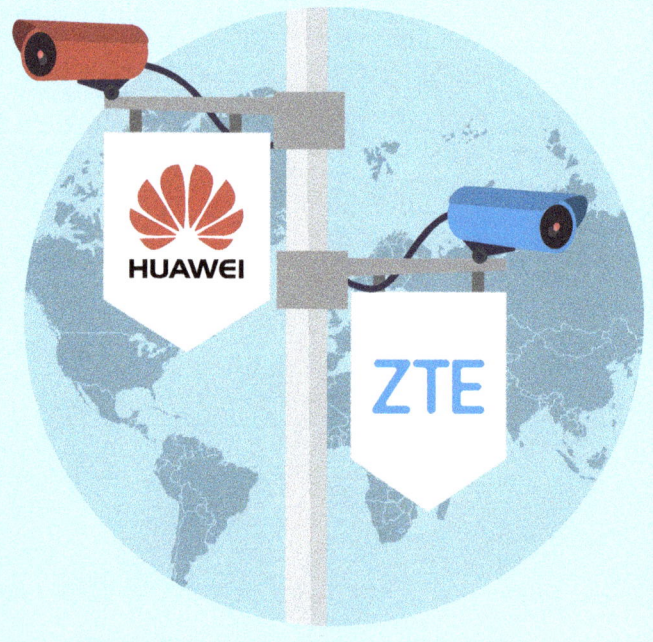

ZTE and Huawei
A Perfect Pair for Maximum Surveillance

---

17 Stew Magnuson, "DESI Japan News: Expert Details What China Does After Stealing IP," *National Defense Magazine*, November 22, 2019, https://www.nationaldefensemagazine.org/articles/2019/11/22/expert-details-what-china-does-after-it-steals-ip

18 Ibid.

19 Ibid.

Zoom Conferencing Linked to China

China reaches surprisingly far into the United States. Zoom is a teleconferencing tool that has become one of the most accessible and ubiquitous ways for individuals to communicate during meetings. Zoom is an American company[20] owned by Eric Yuan with a mission to deliver happiness.[21] Zoom went from 10 million users before the coronavirus pandemic to, well, the company said there were 300 million active users in April 2020.[22] Zoom's increase and reach are astounding. Zoom's 2021 statistics include,[23]

- The Zoom mobile app was downloaded **485 million times** in 2020.
- Zoom has **467,100** business customers.
- The number of annual meeting minutes on Zoom is now over **3.3 trillion**.
- **45 billion minutes** of webinars are hosted on Zoom every year.
- Zoom generated **$882 million** in Q4 FY 2021, a year-over-year increase of nearly 400%.
- Zoom has **88 customers** that contribute more than $1 million each in annual recurring revenue.

The dilemma is that some of Zoom's servers are located in China, where the encryption keys must be given[24] to the Chinese government.[25] For example,[26]

During a test of a Zoom meeting with two users, one in the United States and one in Canada, we found that the AES-128 key for conference encryption and decryption was sent to one of the participants over TLS from a Zoom server apparently located in Beijing, 52.81.151.250. A scan shows a total of five servers in China and 68 in the United States that apparently run the same Zoom server software as the Beijing server.

We suspect that the keys may be distributed through these servers. A company primarily catering to North American clients that sometimes distributes encryption keys through servers in China is potentially concerning, given that Zoom may be legally obligated to disclose these keys to authorities in China.

---

20 United States Securities and Exchange Commission, "Form 10-K", *United States Securities and Exchange Commission*, 2020, https://investors.zoom.us/static-files/09a01665-5f33-4007-8e90-de02219886aa

21 Michael Krigsman, "Zoom CEO Strives for Sustainable Customer Happiness," *ZDNet, January 22, 2019*, https://www.zdnet.com/article/zoom-ceo-strives-for-sustainable-customer-happiness/

22 Nico Grant, "Zoom Daily Users Surge to 300 Million Despite Privacy Woes," *Bloomberg*, April 22, 2020, https://www.bloomberg.com/news/articles/2020-04-22/zoom-daily-users-surge-to-300-million-despite-privacy-woes

23 Brian Dean, "Zoom User Stats: How Many People Use Zoom in 2021?," *Back Link*, Updated March 10, 2021, https://backlinko.com/zoom-users

24 Thomas Brewster, "Warning: Zoom Makes Encryption Keys In China (Sometimes)," *Forbes*, April 3, 2020, https://www.forbes.com/sites/thomasbrewster/2020/04/03/warning-zoom-sends-encryption-keys-to-china-sometimes/#3981a04b3fd9

25 Bruce Sussman, "Zoom Traffic Through China: Company Apologizes, Announces You Can Control Data Routing," *SecureWorld Expo*, April 14, 2020, https://www.secureworldexpo.com/industry-news/zoom-traffic-through-china-data-routing-controls

26 Helen Davidson & Lily Kuo, "Zoom Admits Cutting Off Activists' Accounts In Obedience To China," *The Guardian*, June 12, 2020, https://www.theguardian.com/world/2020/jun/12/zoom-admits-cutting-off-activists-accounts-in-obedience-to-china

Zoom has walked back from routing all information through China, allowing paid users to choose where they want their data sent, though few probably know how to redirect their data and most probably do not. Nevertheless, Zoom canceled or suspended user accounts at the Chinese government's request,[27] citing obedience to China.[28]

Though the company is an American company, it can still practice censorship,[29] even when the account is in the United States.[30] Thus, if servers are in China, whether or not they are routing information through China, Zoom may need to make a choice – turn over data, censor individuals the Chinese Communist Party deems inappropriate, or move operations out of China.[31]

The Chinese government can watch Zoom feed coming from the United States. Despite this, a March 2021 *Washington Post* article reported that the Biden White House was using Zoom for most of its government-related virtual interactions that were unclassified.[32] Meanwhile, the Justice Department has been collecting evidence on Chinese executives who work for Beijing's intelligence services and both monitor and interfere with Zoom calls.[33] Some have been indicted, and arrest warrants have been issued.

Experts warn of the risks of anyone who dares to criticize the Chinese Communist Party. The Chinese government is allegedly harassing Americans, putting them in danger, disrupting Zoom calls, and sending personal data to the Communist Party of anyone who speaks ill of Beijing.[34] China's response to the Department of Justice was that companies that work in China must follow Chinese law, ensure the Chinese government's safety, and impose strict measures on Chinese citizens wherever they live.

Zoom explained their precarious position between abiding by Chinese surveillance laws and U.S. laws in a blog post.[35]

In September 2019, the Chinese government turned off our service in China without

---

27 Jason Slotkin, "Zoom Acknowledges It Suspended Activists' Accounts At China's Request," *NPR*, June 12, 2020, https://www.npr.org/2020/06/12/876351501/zoom-acknowledges-it-suspended-activists-accounts-at-china-s-request

28 Helen Davidson & Lily Kuo, "Zoom Admits Cutting Off Activists' Accounts In Obedience To China," *The Guardian*, June 12, 2020, https://www.theguardian.com/world/2020/jun/12/zoom-admits-cutting-off-activists-accounts-in-obedience-to-china

29 Zen Soo, "Zoom Censorship: Virtual Conferencing Company Says It Blocked Meetings, Suspended Accounts At China's Request," *Chicago Tribune*, June 12, 2020, https://www.chicagotribune.com/business/ct-biz-zoom-china-censorship-20200612-akbwojfzxje5hbqxgdlneuwcya-story.html

30 June Cheng, "Zoom Suspends Chinese Human Rights Activist's Account," *World Magazine*, June 16, 2020, https://world.wng.org/2020/06/zoom_suspends_chinese_human_rights_activist_s_account

31 Lindsay Gorman, "Companies Like Zoom Must Choose: America or China | Opinion," *Newsweek*, June 19, 2020, https://www.newsweek.com/companies-like-zoom-must-choose-america-china-opinion-1511645

32 Josh Rogin, "Opinion: The White House's Use of Zoom for Meetings Raises China-Related Security Concerns," T*he Washington Post,* March 3, 2021, https://www.washingtonpost.com/opinions/2021/03/03/white-house-zoom-biden-meetings-china-cybersecurity/

33 Drew Harwell and Ellen Nakashima, "Federal Prosecutors Accuse Zoom Executive of Working with Chinese Government to Surveil Users sand Suppress Video Calls," *The Washington Post*, December 18, 2020, https://www.washingtonpost.com/technology/2020/12/18/zoom-helped-china-surveillance/

34 Ibid.

35 Zoom, "Our Perspective on the DOJ Complaint," *Zoom*, December 18, 2020, https://blog.zoom.us/our-perspective-on-the-doj-complaint/

warning. At that time, we were a much smaller company primarily serving businesses. The shutdown caused significant disruption for many of our multinational customers, who could not effectively communicate with their employees and partners in China. They urged us to take immediate action to get the service resumed.

The shutdown put Zoom in an unfamiliar and uncomfortable position…We had not, at that point in our evolution, been forced to focus on societal or policy concerns outside of this relatively narrow frame of vision. As we worked to resolve the shutdown, China requested that Zoom confirm it would comply with Chinese law, including designating an in-house contact for law enforcement requests and transferring China-based user data housed in the United States to a data center in China. With the goal of restoring our service, Zoom personnel, including our CEO, met in China with government authorities in October 2019. We outlined steps we could take to address the Chinese government's reasons for shutting down our service.

The Chinese App, TikTok

While Zoom is an American company, TikTok is not. TikTok is a video-sharing social media app, owned by ByteDance, a Beijing headquartered technology company that has 1 billion users; its parent company has 1.9 billion users.[36] The app has been downloaded over 2 billion times from the App Store and Google Play. TikTok, available in 155 countries and 75 languages (TikTok states it is 39[37]), is one of the most downloaded apps. Its use and

---

36 Liza Lin, "TikTok Owner ByteDance's Annual Revenue Jumps to $34.3 Billion," *The Wall Street Journal*, Updated June 17, 2021, https://www.wsj.com/articles/tiktok-owner-bytedances-annual-revenue-jumps-to-34-3-billion-11623903622

37 TikTok, "Change your app language," *TikTok*, n.d., https://support.tiktok.com/en/my-account-settings/change-language-en

reach are vast, with 90 percent of users accessing the app on a daily basis and users spending an average of 52 minutes per day.[38] Nearly half of all teenagers have used TikTok.[39]

In May 2021, TikTok was the most downloaded non-gaming app on both the App Store and from Google Play with more than 80 million installs; the country with the largest number of TikTok installs in May 2021 was Brazil.[40] Meanwhile, TikTok's revenue grew 111% in one year during the pandemic.[41]

When setting up the site, all personal information you must enter is public and available to Chinese authorities by default.[42] Some companies have banned the app,[43] while others

---

38 Maryam Mohsin, "10 TikTok Statistics That You Need to Know in 2020 [Infographic]," *Oberlo*, July 3, 2020, https://www.oberlo.com/blog/tiktok-statistics

39 Influencer Marketing Hub, "50 TikTok Stats That Will Blow Your Mind [July 2020]," *Influencer Marketing Hub*, July 2020, https://influencermarketinghub.com/tiktok-stats/

40 Sensor Tower, "Top Apps Worldwide for May 2021 by Downloads," *Sensor Tower*, June 2, 2021, https://sensortower.com/blog/top-apps-worldwide-may-2021-by-downloads

41 Liza Lin, "TikTok Owner ByteDance's Annual Revenue Jumps to $34.3 Billion," *The Wall Street Journal*, Updated June 17, 2021, https://www.wsj.com/articles/tiktok-owner-bytedances-annual-revenue-jumps-to-34-3-billion-11623903622

42 Parven Kaur, "What Families Need To Know About TikTok," *Family Online Safety Institute*, October 9, 2018, https://www.fosi.org/good-digital-parenting/what-families-need-know-about-tiktok/

43 Brian Fung, "Wells Fargo Tells Employees To Delete Tiktok From Their Company Devices," *CNN Business*, July 13, 2020, https://www.cnn.com/2020/07/13/tech/tiktok-wells-fargo/index.html

have backed away from taking this step.[44] Whole countries have determined the app to threaten security,[45] leading some even to ban the app.[46]

TikTok's popularity with young people has created subcultures, including the military. On at least one occasion, members of the military posted videos of their push-up contests and base pranks. However, China's ability to watch and investigate U.S. military moves could potentially send data to China, letting the Chinese government determine the soldiers' exact locations.[47]

Constant Surveillance and Artificial Intelligence

China no longer needs a camera to watch people through their computers or in their homes. They can flag what you write, even if you reside in another country.[48] The Chinese authorities can delete your account if it is critical of the CCP[49] or potentially use your 'content' to threaten, harass, or blackmail you.[50]

In Guiyang, a city in Guizhou province, a comprehensive artificial intelligence, and data mining hub has sprung up to sift through all information coming in throughout the country and potentially from outside. China's ambitious big data strategy is designed to collect and interpret data.[51] Included is facial recognition collection to catch 'criminals' or anyone who has a viewpoint that is unfavorable to China or the Chinese Communist Party.[52]

In China's 'Big Data Valley', the People's Liberation Army (PLA) is gaining ominous digital military-grade firepower.[53] Beijing's goal is to surpass the power and prestige of Silicon Valley. Interestingly, American companies are both involved and benefitting from

---

44 Mike Isaac & Karen Weise, "Amazon Backtracks From Demand That Employees Delete TikTok," *The New York Times*, July 10, 2020, https://www.nytimes.com/2020/07/10/technology/tiktok-amazon-security-risk.html

45 Mary Meisenzahl, "Trump Is Considering Banning Chinese Social Media App Tiktok. See The Full List Of Countries, Companies, And Organizations That Have Already Banned It.," *Business Insider*, July 13, 2020, https://www.businessinsider.com/tiktok-banned-by-countries-organizations-companies-list-2020-7

46 Manish Singh, "India Bans TikTok, Dozens Of Other Chinese Apps," *TechCrunch*, June 29, 2020, https://techcrunch.com/2020/06/29/india-bans-tiktok-dozens-of-other-chinese-apps/

47 Shelly Banjo and Shawn Wen, "A Push-Up Contest on TikTok Exposed a Great Cyber-Espionage Threat," *Bloomberg*, May 13, 2021, https://www.bloomberg.com/news/articles/2021-05-13/how-tiktok-works-and-does-it-share-data-with-china

48 Ragip Soylu, "'They Delete Everything': Former Tiktok Moderator Reveals China App Censorship," *Middle East Eye*, December 19, 2019, https://www.middleeasteye.net/news/tiktok-censors-turkish-content-based-sex-race-class-former-supervisor-says

49 Lauren Strapagiel, "TikTok Users Are Furious After Their Accounts Got Deleted After The Under-13 Purge," *Buzzfeed News*, February 28, 2019, https://www.buzzfeednews.com/article/laurenstrapagiel/tiktok-account-delete

50 Chandrima Banerjee, "Does TikTok Censor Content That's Critical of China?," *Times of India*, June 6, 2020, https://timesofindia.indiatimes.com/india/does-tiktok-censor-content-thats-critical-of-china/articleshow/76228715.cms

51 Anthony Kuhn, "A Remote Chinese Province Uses Its Climate To Grow A Big-Data Industry," *NPR*, July 3, 2017, https://www.npr.org/sections/alltechconsidered/2017/07/03/535369266/a-remote-chinese-province-uses-its-climate-to-grow-a-big-data-industry

52 Data Center News, "Guiyang Investing Big To Become China's Big Data Hub," *Data Center News*, n.d., https://datacenternews.asia/story/guiyang-investing-big-to-become-china-s-big-data-hub

53 The Economic Times, "China's Big Data Valley Shows How Its Military Is Gaining Ominous Tech Firepower. India Can't Relax," *The Economic Times*, n.d., https://economictimes.indiatimes.com/prime/economy-and-policy/chinas-big-data-valley-shows-how-its-military-is-gaining-ominous-tech-firepower-india-cant-relax-/primearticleshow/69920261.cms

their relationships to support China's technology.⁵⁴ This massive Chinese surveillance hub is where even Apple has decided to bring its wisdom to China's data-center mega-site.⁵⁵

Even though America has similar technologies, the United States demands a higher expectation of freedom, privacy, and transparency to reduce the extent of any individual's risk. Meanwhile, this privacy is not expected in China. Thus, Beijing has access to 'optimize' sites and information so that data is readily available to Chinese authorities.

Conclusion

With the bombardment already faced from the data theft of millions of individuals, threats continue to increase. New AI-centered technologies offer even greater opportunities for intrusion. Thus, with omnipresent audio and video capture, data transfer from phones and laptops, bank or credit card theft, and the use of unsecured Wi-fi, it is only a matter of time until nearly everyone in the U.S. will have their information breached and be vulnerable to a cyberattack, ransom, or extortion.

China state-run enterprises are in a race to be number one on the Digital Silk Road. ZTE and Huawei are just two of those leading companies that have played a significant role. Other Chinese firms are eager to follow suit and contribute more to the global standards-setting process to help advance Beijing's vision of a more China-influenced technology stack.⁵⁶ Many of these companies slide under the radar.

The buildout of 5G will be one of the most critical turning points in history, as will the outcome of Beijing's South China Sea takeover attempt, the Indian Ocean encirclement, and ventures into the polar regions. These incursions are all-important as China attempts to change the world order. However, with internet and camera surveillance, digital payments, and social media access, Chinese Communist Party officials are doing this from within your home, office, and government. At present, they are working hard to have a greater say in international bodies like the International Telecommunications Union (ITU) that has 193 member states and about 900 companies, universities, and global and regional organizations.⁵⁷

George Soros suggested that the U.S. should not let ZTE and Huawei off lightly, adding, "If these companies came to dominate the 5G market, they would present an unacceptable security risk for the rest of the world."⁵⁸ Some countries have changed their policies and involvements after witnessing how China's rhetoric is used to coerce, cajole, and command individuals and businesses.

---

54 Maoist Rebel News, " Debunking the "Reading List on Socialism with Chinese Characteristics" of /r/swcc: Exposing the Revisionist Deception Part 2," *Maoist Rebel News,* May 18, 2018, https://maoistrebelnews.files.wordpress.com/2019/12/exposingtherevisionistdeceptionpart2.pdf

55 Xinhua, "Big data prospering in southwest China's Guizhou," *Xinhua Net,* August 9, 2019, http://www.xinhuanet.com/english/2019-08/09/c_138297001.htm

56 Robert Greene and Paul Triolo, "Will China Control the Global Internet Via its Digital Silk Road?" *Carnegie Endowment,* May 8, 2020, https://carnegieendowment.org/2020/05/08/will-china-control-global-internet-via-its-digital-silk-road-pub-81857

57 International Telecommunications Union, https://www.itu.int/en/about/Pages/default.aspx

58 George Soros, "Remarks Delivered at the World Economic Forum," George Soros Website, January 24, 2019, https://www.georgesoros.com/2019/01/24/remarks-delivered-at-the-world-economic-forum-2/

Xi Jinping's common refrain, 'win-win', is inconsistent with its actions. For example, countries could ban Huawei, according to the U.S. Department of State.[59] In publicly available lists representing where countries stand regarding Huawei's inclusion into each country's digital dynamics, most seem willing to take the associated risks of Internet intrusion and ubiquitous data collection.[60] A few countries have banned Huawei, including Japan, Australia, and a few European countries.[61]

What's at Stake?

First, Beijing continues to consider itself the world's savior while at the same time threatening sovereignty and freedom.

Second, most people, even high-level officials, have not come to terms with what large-scale intrusion means. Jan-Peter Kleinhans commented, "Europe is slowly realizing how big a problem this potentially could be."[62]

Third, *The Economist* explained that any loss in intellectual property or freedoms from Huawei is "just one battle in a larger contest."[63]

---

59 Keith Krach, "Brazil Can Join the Growing Clean Network by Banning Huawei," *U.S. Department of State*, August 19, 2020, https://www.state.gov/Brazil-Can-Join-the-Growing-Clean-Network-by-Banning-Huawei/

60 Michael Goodier, "The Definitive List of Where Every Country Stands on Huawei," *New Statesman*, July 29, 2020,

61 Ibid.

62 Laurens Cerulus, "The Huawei of Airport Security," *Politico*, February 14, 2020, https://www.politico.eu/article/beijing-scanners-europe-nuctech/

63 The Economist, The Digital Side of the Belt and Road Initiative is Growing, *The Economist*, February 6, 2020, https://www.economist.com/special-report/2020/02/06/the-digital-side-of-the-belt-and-road-initiative-is-growing

Chapter 3
The Power of Digital Authoritarianism:
Aggressive Ambitions of Chinese State Media

Introduction

The Chinese Communist Party (CCP) state-run media oversees content in newspapers, magazines, radio, television, and social media. The most widespread television sources are China Central Television (CCTV) and China Global Television (CGTN) while the most popular online news sources are *Xinhua*, *People's Daily*, and the *Global Times*. In order to instill socialist values, provide positive energy films, and ensure the "special and important role in propaganda ideology and cultural entertainment," President Xi Jinping and the Chinese Communist Party (CCP) have strengthened Beijing's grip over published content and tightened social media controls amid a broad crackdown on the news.[1]

Strict Censorship and Crackdown on Journalists

China maintains strict censorship and guidelines. Political topics like Tibet, Xinjiang, Falun Gong, Dalai Lama, and religion, and what may be said about the CCP are regulated. China's regulatory agencies include the General Administration of Press and Publication (GAPP) and the National Radio and Television Administration (NRTA).

Most foreign press journalists have been forced to leave or have been threatened, harassed, and intimidated into self-imposed departure. In 2020, Chinese Foreign Ministry spokesman, Geng Shuang, insisted that China "welcomes foreign media and journalists." He continued, "We are opposed to ideological biases against China."[2] However, in March 2020, China demanded that U.S. journalists working for the *New York Times*, *Wall Street Journal*, and *Washington Post* hand back their press cards and discontinue their work in the People's Republic of China, Hong Kong, and Macao.[3]

Each year, Reporters Without Borders ranks countries in a Press Freedom Index. In 2021, the Press Freedom Index ranked China 177th out of 180 countries, with Turkmenistan 178, North Korea 179, and Eritrea last at 180. China's repression of the Internet is well-known for censorship, blocked websites, and illegal VPN use.

In April 2021, China's propaganda machine unleashed a tornado of "wolf warrior" aggression against *BBC*'s John Sudworth and Vicky Xu, a reporter based in Australia. Refusing to be silenced in reporting about the Uyghur Muslims in Xinjiang Province, Sudworth referred to China's behavior as a "highly asymmetric battle for the control of ideas."[4] Sudworth left Beijing for Taiwan after threats and harassment in 'tweet-storms' from the CCP's "wolf warrior" diplomats.

---

1 The Straits Times, "China Tightens Grip on Media with Regulator Reorganisation," *The Straits Times*, March 21, 2018, https://www.straitstimes.com/asia/east-asia/china-tightens-grip-on-media-with-regulator-reorganisation

2 Rob Picheta, "A Free Press in China Could Have Prevented the Coronavirus Pandemic, Media Watchdog Says," *CNN Business*, Updated April 21, 2020, https://edition.cnn.com/2020/04/21/media/rsf-press-freedom-index-2020-intl/index.html

3 Ministry of Foreign Affairs of the People's Republic of China, "China Takes Countermeasures Against Restrictive Measures on Chinese Media Agencies in the US," Ministry of Foreign Affairs of the People's Republic of China, March 18, 2020, https://www.fmprc.gov.cn/mfa_eng/xwfw_665399/s2510_665401/t1757162.shtml

4 Joyce Huang, "China's Propaganda Against Foreign Media Increases," *VOA News*, April 9, 2021, https://www.voanews.com/press-freedom/chinas-propaganda-against-foreign-media-increases

With the censorship, surveillance, and imprisonment of journalists and newspaper owners in Hong Kong, there is concern that Beijing will take greater control of information dissemination.[5] China frequently arrests journalists, including 450 social media users and more than 120 who were defending press freedom.[6]

Spreading Soft Power in Africa through Chinese Media

Throughout Africa, Chinese wide-ranging news coverage bolsters its presence with propaganda, painting China as a fair, open, and benevolent country. *CCTV* stations are sprinkled throughout Africa, providing China-friendly international news. *CNC World*, another Chinese television news source, is also available. *Xinhua* offers articles heralding the greatness of China and the kindness of Xi Jinping.

China Radio International (CRI) offers Mandarin lessons interspersed with accounts of how well China-Africa cooperation works. At the same time, China provides loans

---

5 Elaine Yu, "Will Hong Kong's Free Press Survive?," *Columbia Journalism Review*, March 8, 2021, https://www.cjr.org/special_report/hong-kong-democracy-protests-press-freedom.php

6 Rebecca Davis, "World Press Freedom Index Ranks China Near Last, Cites 'Grave Threat' to Hong Kong Journalism," *Variety*, April 20, 2021, https://variety.com/2021/politics/news/reporters-without-borders-world-press-freedom-index-china-hong-kong-1234956038/

to African countries for ports, roads, railways, airports, and bridges, even an apartment complex called Great Wall apartments. Eric Shimoli, editor at Kenya's newspaper, *The Daily Nation* that partnered with *Xinhua*, called China's media arrival "a full-on charm offensive" as it pours $7 billion into expanding Beijing's influence.[7]

China's propaganda spread throughout the African media landscape, accelerating in 2021 with *Xinhua* championed as having the largest correspondent network on the continent.[8] China's news influence in Africa also includes the silencing of alternative voices and the promotion of repressive governments. Ethiopia received billions in Chinese loans for training on surveillance, censorship, and the blocking of objectionable websites to the ruling party. Knowing that China does not allow its citizens to have freedom of information, it is unsurprising that Chinese news sources block or jam signals coming into the country.

Chang Ping, a Chinese journalist, explained that the CCP is promoting news networks in Africa, not just to share China-Africa mutual economic prosperity but also to create a global model devoid of human rights, freedom, and democracy, benefiting only the Chinese Communist Party (CCP).[9] Jillo Kadida, a Kenyan journalist, explained that Chinese media outlets are not creating news for the local people but promoting China's mega-projects that put states in debt and primarily use Chinese labor and technology.[10]

The Chinese have also brought many Africans to China to "tell China's story well." Beijing wanted to intrigue and amaze the journalists by showing them the wonders of China. However, Joseph Odindo, a former editorial director for Kenya's Media Group, explained that after publishing an investigative report on China's challenges with railroad development and the vast sums of money required to maintain the infrastructure, the Chinese Embassy canceled their advertisements and demanded that they stop their 'negative' coverage.[11]

Chinese Influence in Latin America

While China has been in Africa much longer than in South America, repressive governments like Venezuela are ripe for China's picking. China is propping up the Venezuelan government by building and financing communications satellites for a government that has exercised increasing control over the news media.[12] Xi Jinping spoke to the China-Latin American Media Leaders' Summit about the historical nature of the

---

7   Andrew Jacobs, "Pursuing Soft Power, China Puts Stamp on Africa's News," *The New York Ties*, August 16, 2012, https://www.nytimes.com/2012/08/17/world/africa/chinas-news-media-make-inroads-in-africa.html

8   Chrispin Mwakideu, "Experts Warn of China's Growing Media Influence in Africa," *DW*, January 29, 2021, https://www.dw.com/en/experts-warn-of-chinas-growing-media-influence-in-africa/a-56385420

9   Ole Tangen Jr., "China's Media Strategy in Africa and Its Impact on the Continent," *DW*, March 12, 2020, https://www.dw.com/en/chinas-media-strategy-in-africa-and-its-impact-on-the-continent/a-55799873

10 Ibid.

11 Chrispin Mwakideu, "Experts Warn of China's Growing Media Influence in Africa," *DW*, January 29, 2021, https://www.dw.com/en/experts-warn-of-chinas-growing-media-influence-in-africa/a-56385420

12 Andrew Jacobs, "Pursuing Soft Power, China Puts Stamp on Africa's News," *The New York Ties*, August 16, 2012, https://www.nytimes.com/2012/08/17/world/africa/chinas-news-media-make-inroads-in-africa.html

Sino-Latin American media relationship and how China shapes the world.[13] *Xinhua*, *People's Daily*, China Radio International (*CRI*), China Central Television (*CCTV*), and *CGTN Spanish* are alive and well.[14]

Chinese government-controlled television, radio, and newspapers pump out CCP messages and cultural information.[15] For example, a story on Chinese calligraphy and paper-making might be followed by Mandarin lessons and Chinese benevolence. Beijing authorities have attempted to bring more Latin American journalists under its umbrella by offering them opportunities to study and work in China while meeting Chinese leaders and learning Chinese culture. President Xi Jinping announced the ambitious goal of bringing 500 media professionals from Latin America to train to "achieve common prosperity".[16]

In Britain, China has moved in with its China Global Television Network (CGTN). With the goal to report news and "tell China's story well" from a "Chinese perspective", reporters will learn the ideological philosophy of the Chinese Communist Party (CCP) and shape Beijing's narrative abroad to serve a domestic British audience. In a hiring spree, China's CGTN sought to hire domestic reporters who agreed to avoid issues like the Tiananmen Square killings, persecution in Tibet, Hong Kong crackdown, Taiwan independence, and genocide in Xinjiang, China. The news station wanted a British face on its nightly broadcast to deliver CCP propaganda; 6,000 people applied.[17] In March 2021, after Britain revoked CGTN's permit to broadcast to prevent the spread of propaganda, the television station got the green light from France.[18]

China is creating ties to journalists and media professionals worldwide, inviting them to enjoy China, learn the country's culture, and share their enthusiasm with the rest of the world. In turn, the CCP hopes to attract hundreds of journalists to positions around the world to share CCP values and win-win diplomacy. Meanwhile, the CCP is centralizing its propaganda apparatus to become more efficient in spreading China's official messaging through its networks CCTV, CGTN, China Radio International (CRI), and China National Radio (CNR). Now a single broadcaster, the China Media Group (otherwise called Voice of China), controls all media.[19] In this way, the Chinese narrative hones broadcasts to clearly reflect the CCP message and become involved in Beijing's international media across all markets and sectors.

---

13 Ricardo Barrios, "China's State Media in Latin America: Profile and Prospects," *The Asia Dialogue*, May 28, 2018, https://theasiadialogue.com/2018/05/28/chinese-state-media-in-latin-america-profile-and-prospects/

14 Ibid.

15 Ibid.

16 Ministry of Foreign Affairs of the People's Republic of China, "Xi Jinping Attends Opening Ceremony of China-Latin America Media Leaders Summit," *Ministry of Foreign Affairs of the People's Republic of China*, November 23, 2016, https://www.fmprc.gov.cn/mfa_eng/topics_665678/XJPDEGDEBLZLJXGSFWBCXZBLLMJXDYTJHZZDESSCLDRFZSHY/t1418647.shtml

17 Louisa Lim and Julia Bergin, "Inside China's Audacious Global Propaganda Campaign," *The Guardian*, December 7, 2018, https://www.theguardian.com/news/2018/dec/07/china-plan-for-global-media-dominance-propaganda-xi-jinping

18 Julian Clover, "Chinese CGTN to Broadcast Under French Flag," *Broadband TV News*, March 4, 2021, https://www.broadbandtvnews.com/2021/03/04/chinese-cgtn-to-broadcast-under-french-flag/

19 Ricardo Barrios, "China's State Media in Latin America: Profile and Prospects," *The Asia Dialogue*, May 28, 2018, https://theasiadialogue.com/2018/05/28/chinese-state-media-in-latin-america-profile-and-prospects/

Conclusion

China's global reach has crisscrossed the planet. There are few locations that China's media coercion has not impacted. While China kicks out foreign journalists from its territories, it has invested billions of dollars in creating newspaper and harnessing networks, while constructing Wi-fi towers, television networks, and radio stations. China's media tentacles have infiltrated dozens of countries, and its reach includes teaching Chinese to children, funding Chinese schools, and infusing programming with Chinese propaganda. Particularly in countries where there are few freedoms, there is great concern that China will impose a repressive state that censors and controls the people abroad as they do on the mainland.

In Africa, Transsion became the Apple of Africa with a meteoric rise in sales and 50% of the African market share. Sales of its phones – TECNO, itel, and Infinix – are three of Africa's most-loved brands. Why? Its phones are surprisingly not sold in the U.S. or China and its technology, from sim cards to color correction in photos, are geared solely for Africans.

What's at Stake?

First, Chinese newspapers, radio, television, and social media are not like autonomous organizations in other countries where truth in reporting and independent journalism are acceptable. Chinese media is designed for social control. Chinese authorities openly admit to spreading CCP-controlled propaganda with the intention to spread the CCP's government-controlled message that not only is a crafted narrative, but one that leaves out its human rights abuses, coercive politics, and harassment.

Second, repressive, authoritarian governments where Chinese media has infiltrated have the ability to censor and cancel messages that do not illuminate China in a positive light. Additionally, authorities can prevent any alternate viewpoint from being shared and considered.

Third, China has spent billions on Africa's media to control the narrative, and it is moving swiftly into other countries. It is one thing for China to censor information and rewrite the truth in China, but it is quite another to suppress the truth in countries around the world.

Chapter 4
Digital Africa:
Wiring Up a Continent for Connectivity and Surveillance

Introduction

The African Union's 55 countries are dotted with nucleated cities and fast-growing metropolises. In April 2021, the population of Africa was 1.366 billion, or 16.7% of the world population, on a land area three times the size of the U.S. or China.[1] With 43.8% of the population living in urban centers and a median age of 19.7 years old, the World Economic Forum predicts that by 2050, Africa's urban population will triple, and smart cities with intelligent infrastructure will transform the continent into an enhanced Fourth Industrial Revolution.[2] Furthermore, according to UNICEF, two in every five children born on the planet will be born in Africa.[3] Africa's demographic shift necessitates improved education, access, and innovation as digital technologies are strategically situated to enhance connectedness across the continent.

Chinese Technology Companies Capture the Market

The smartphone market in Africa is far from saturated, and competing brands still have the chance to capture the imagination. As opposed to 81% of the U.S. market using Apple and Samsung phones in Q4 of 2020,[4] the top companies in Africa are:

1. Tecno Mobile (a Transsion company) - China
2. Infinix Mobility (a Transsion company) - China
3. Itel Mobile (a Transsion company) - China
4. Samsung Mobile – South Korea
5. Huawei - China
6. Honor (a Huawei company) - China
7. Xiaomi - China
8. Redmi (a Xiaomi company) - China
9. Nokia Mobile – Finland
10. OPPO Mobile - China

Advertising and marketing flood the buildings of African cities, many decorated in Tecno's blue. Billboards, mounted with colorful displays, emphasize the allure of the Tecno brand. From the landlocked nation of Mali, to the business beehive of Nairobi, Kenya's capital, where entire twenty-story towers are covered in the Tecno logo, aspirational Africans are motivated to buy.

Tecno Mobile's smartphones cost $100 to $200 in Africa, selling more than 100 million handsets and proving that the African market is a good business ground for pocket-friendly phones. With improved battery life, vital in locations where electricity is periodically

---

1 WorldoMeter, "Africa Population," *WorldoMeter*, n.d., https://www.worldometers.info/world-population/africa-population/

2 Bandar Hajjar, "The Children's Continent: Keeping Up with Africa's Growth," *World Economic Forum,* January 13, 2020, https://www.weforum.org/agenda/2020/01/the-children-s-continent/

3 UNICEF, "Africa will be Home to 2 in 5 Children by 2050: UNICEF Report," *UNICEF*, n.d., https://www.unicef.org/media/media_74754.html

4 Team Counterpoint, "US Smartphone Market Share: By Quarter," *Counterpoint*, February 21, 2021, https://www.counterpointresearch.com/us-market-smartphone-share/

interrupted, Tecno phones accommodate African languages, including Amharic and Swahili.[5] In 2008, Transsion targeted Africa, where the population is expected to double over the next thirty years,[6] catering to African tastes and relying on data from Chinese research centers in Nigeria and Kenya.[7]

Transsion and other Chinese companies also tested Africa as a manufacturing center as a consequence of the 2021 African Continental Free Trade Area by commissioning

China's Tecno Mobile Ads Flood African Cities

---

5   Business Day, "China is Cornering Africa's Ecommerce Market," *Business Day,* October 16, 2019, https://businessday.ng/big-read/article/china-is-cornering-africas-ecommerce-market/

6   Ibid.

7   Yomi Kazeem, "The Biggest Mobile Phone Maker in Africa is Going Public in China," *Quartz Africa,* March 29, 2019, https://qz.com/africa/1583473/chinas-transsion-of-african-tecno-phones-to-ipo-in-shanghai/

manufacturing facilities in Ethiopia.[8] In conjunction with Huawei and ZTE, Chinese equipment makers have uplifted African commerce and revolutionized telecoms. Engaged in Africa's music culture, Chinese innovators created Boomplay, the continent's top music streaming service.[9] China's software developers are also coming.[10]

The Fourth Industrial Revolution is changing how people in Africa think about themselves. When most people think of China in Africa, they think of mining and construction. However, while highways and bridges are essential, the real action is along the digital highway.[11] Chinese business investors are also joining the blossoming startup funding circuit, leading a $120 million funding round from China.[12] Nigeria-based fintech company Opay is integrating Chinese digital giants, WeChat Pay and Alipay, with digital payment alternatives controlled by Chinese-owned, Norway-based Opera.[13]

Others, such as China's electronics giant Xiaomi, are looking for new growth areas in Africa where Chinese investment is rapidly taking the path of digitalization.[14] In 2019, Africa saw more global attention than the previous year with high-profile IPOs, and visits by both Jack Ma, Co-founder of Alibaba and Jack Dorsey, CEO of Twitter .[15]

Flow of Digital Currencies, Camera Surveillance, and Artificial Intelligence Controls

China has been known for its strategic relationship with Africa, based largely on trade and infrastructure. Over a ten-year period, Chinese state-owned enterprises were less engaged in the continent's digital scene. That was until a flow of investment and partnerships in 2019.[16]

In August 2019, San Francisco and Lagos-based fintech startup Flutterwave collaborated with Chinese e-commerce company Alibaba's Alipay to proffer digital payments between China and Africa.[17] This effort was a step closer to employing the Chinese digital Yuan, a

---

8   Abiola Odutola, "How the Chinese are Taking Over Nigeria's Economy," *Nairametrics*, November 28, 2019, https://nairametrics.com/2019/11/28/how-the-chinese-are-taking-over-nigerias-economy/

9   Business Day, "China is Cornering Africa's Ecommerce Market," *Business Day,* October 16, 2019, https://businessday.ng/big-read/article/china-is-cornering-africas-ecommerce-market/

10 Kevin Kimani, "Transsion, Maker of TECNO & Infinix Smartphones, is Now a Public Listed Company," *MobiTrends*, September 30, 2019, https://mobitrends.co.ke/transsion_holding_public_listed_company/

11 Abiola Odutola, "How the Chinese are Taking Over Nigeria's Economy," *Nairametrics*, November 28, 2019, https://nairametrics.com/2019/11/28/how-the-chinese-are-taking-over-nigerias-economy/

12 Jake Bright, "Oper'as Africa Fintech Startup OPay Gains $120M from Chinese Investors," *Tech Crunch,* November 17, 2019, https://techcrunch.com/2019/11/17/operas-africa-fintech-startup-opay-gains-120m-from-chinese-investors/

13 Kevin Kimani, "Transsion, Maker of TECNO & Infinix Smartphones, is Now a Public Listed Company," *MobiTrends*, September 30, 2019, https://mobitrends.co.ke/transsion_holding_public_listed_company/

14 Business Day, "China is Cornering Africa's Ecommerce Market," *Business Day,* October 16, 2019, https://businessday.ng/big-read/article/china-is-cornering-africas-ecommerce-market/

15 Ashley Lewis, "What Can Nigeria Learn from China's Digital Economy?," *Accion*, January 28, 2019, https://www.accion.org/what-can-nigeria-learn-from-chinas-digital-economy

16 Business Day, "China is Cornering Africa's Ecommerce Market," *Business Day,* October 16, 2019, https://businessday.ng/big-read/article/china-is-cornering-africas-ecommerce-market/

17 OyeYeah News, "Techno Collaborates with Daraz.pk for the Launch of Spark Go!," *Oye Yeah,* August 16, 2019, https://www.oyeyeah.com/lifestyle/tecno-collaborates-with-daraz-pk-for-launch-of-spark-go/

digital currency intended to transform Africa into a cashless society tied directly to China and in which the Chinese Communist Party (CCP) can monitor charges from all users. Also in 2019, Chinese investors infused $240 million in Africa's camera, phone, and digital payment technologies. For example, Transsion-backed consumer payments startup PalmPay raised $40 million to become Africa's largest financial services platform.[18] Surges in Chinese tech investment continue.

As Tecno gains market share, one reason for its low price might be because it is peppered with back door artificial intelligence data collection from China's subsidization in return for personal and corporate information. According to *CNN*, the Chinese company Transsion pre-installed extremely difficult to remove malware and data collection software on smartphones that remained undetected for two years.[19]

By December 2020, China installed camera surveillance technologies in at least the following countries, reshaping governing bodies and providing an avenue for repression.

- Algeria
- Botswana
- Côte d'Ivoire
- Egypt
- Equatorial Guinea
- Ethiopia
- Ghana
- Kenya
- Malawi
- Morocco
- Nigeria
- Rwanda
- South Africa
- Tanzania
- Togo
- Uganda
- Zambia
- Zimbabwe

In Uganda, with such extreme poverty that people do not have clean drinking water, Ugandan police purchased $126 million in China's CTV closed-circuit television from Huawei. This technology will allow the police to use facial recognition technology with 3,200 cameras. The same technology was sold to Kenya, Egypt, and Zambia.[20] According to a *Wall Street Journal* investigation, some believe these technologies are being used to crack down on civil society leaders, enusuring that they do not speak out against the government. In one example, verified records catalogued the repression of a popular signer and opposition leader, Bobi Wine.[21]

---

18 Business Day, "China is Cornering Africa's Ecommerce Market," *Business Day*, October 16, 2019, https://businessday.ng/big-read/article/china-is-cornering-africas-ecommerce-market/

19 Hanna Ziady, "China's Tecno Sold Thousands of Smartphones with Malware in Africa," *CNN Business*, Updated August 26, 2020, https://www.cnn.com/2020/08/26/tech/tecno-malware-africa/index.html

20 Elias Biryabarema, "Uganda's Cash-Strapped Cops Spend $126 Million on CCTV from Huawei," *Reuters*, August 15, 2019, https://www.reuters.com/article/us-uganda-crime/ugandas-cash-strapped-cops-spend-126-million-on-cctv-from-huawei-idUSKCN1V50RF

21 Joe Parkinson, Nicholas Bariyo, and Josh Chin, "Huawei Technicians Helped African Governments Spy on Political Opponents," *Wall Street Journal*, Updated August 15, 2019, https://www.wsj.com/articles/huawei-technicians-helped-african-governments-spy-on-political-opponents-11565793017

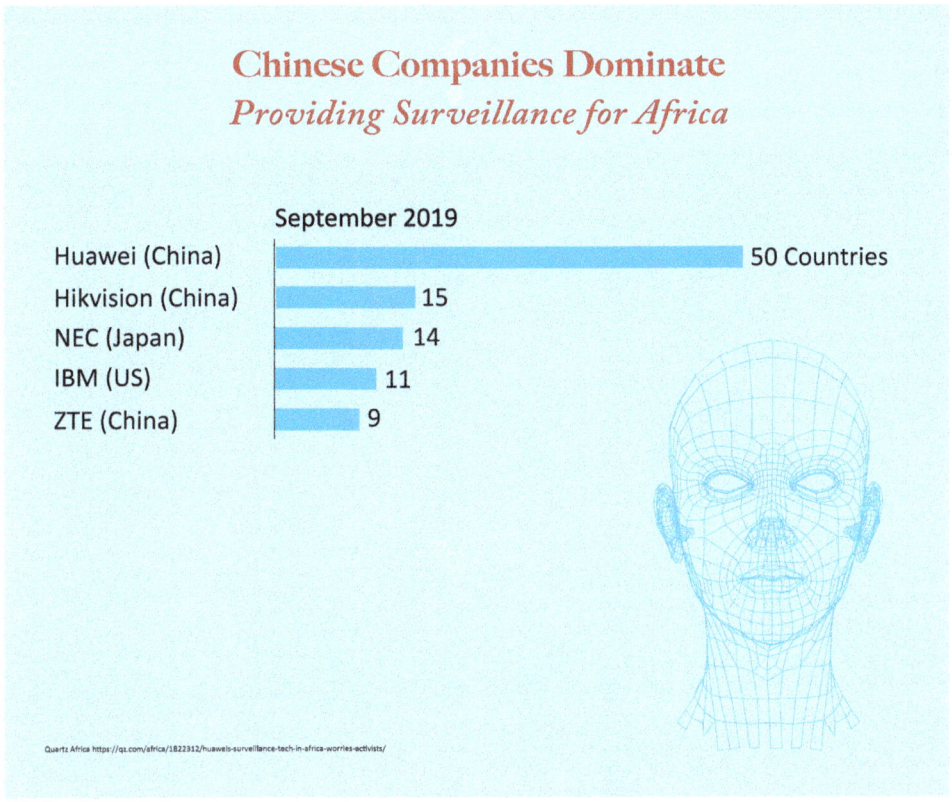

Huawei Marine Encircles Africa with Surveillance Potential

Huawei, the world's largest technology company with 188,000 staff members in 170 countries, deployed deceitful representatives at conferences to photograph the insides of phones, take cutting edge technology, and adapt ideas for the marketplace.[22] Additionally, Chinese experts at Huawei track and arrest opposition bloggers. These actions were confirmed to the *Wall Street Journal* journalists, outlining details of the case presented to Zambia's Cybercrime Crack Squad.[23]

Huawei has become a leader in undersea cables to transfer global internet information to China. Huawei Marine has encircled Africa with cables capable of data transfer and Wi-fi surveillance. In 2018, Huawei Marine further enhanced its cabling network to connect

---

22 Chuin-Wei Yap, Dan Strumpf, Dustin Volz, Kate O'Keeffe, and Aruna Viswanatha, "Huawei's Yearslong Rise is Littered with Accusations of Theft and Dubious Ethics," *Wall Street Journal*, May 25, 2019, https://www.wsj.com/articles/huaweis-yearslong-rise-is-littered-with-accusations-of-theft-and-dubious-ethics-11558756858?mod=article_inline

23 Joe Parkinson, Nicholas Bariyo, and Josh Chin, "Huawei Technicians Helped African Governments Spy on Political Opponents," *Wall Street Journal*, Updated August 15, 2019, https://www.wsj.com/articles/huawei-technicians-helped-african-governments-spy-on-political-opponents-11565793017

China's network around Africa with its South American network, completing 31,293 miles of undersea cables in 90 projects globally.[24]

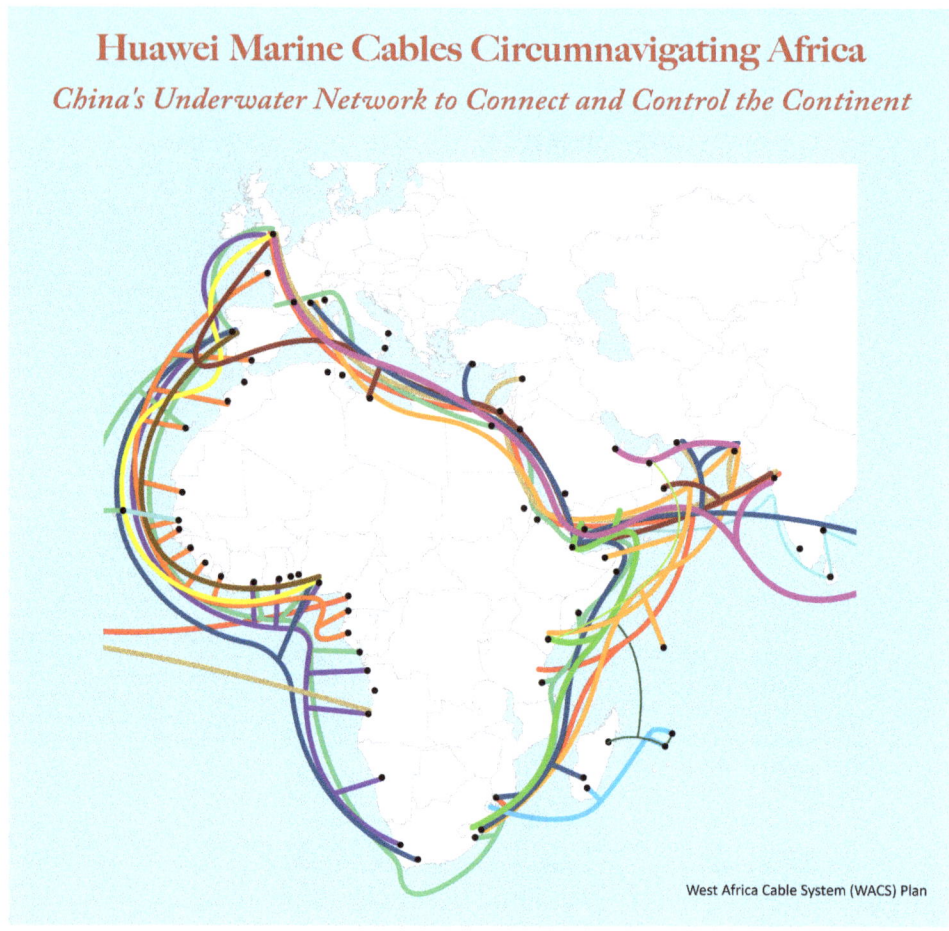

Huawei Marine Cables Circumnavigating Africa
China's Underwater Network to Connect and Control the Continent

West Africa Cable System (WACS) Plan

In Nigeria, China provided satellite televisions to 10,000 African villages. A thousand villages will benefit from this new component of the BRI to improve the country's economic value, create jobs, and offer Chinese television programming to the Africans.[25]

Conclusion

A digital Africa is essential to create a thriving Africa in much the same way as infrastructure is critical to create jobs, opportunities, and wealth in each of the continent's

---

24 Mike Robuck, "Huawei to Sell Stake in Undersea Cable Business: Reuters," *Fierce Telecom,* June 3, 2019, https://www.fiercetelecom.com/telecom/huawei-seeks-to-sell-off-stake-undersea-cable-business-reuters

25 Olatunji Saliu, "Feature: China Launches Digital TV Project for 1,000 Nigerian Villages," *Xinhua,* January 15, 2019, http://www.xinhuanet.com/english/2019-01/15/c_137743891.htm

55 nations. Nevertheless, caution and long-term consequences are necessitated in implementing surveillance technologies, spy devices, and backdoor data collection. Digital currency is another means for concern since government-controlled money means that individuals are at the mercy of that money being removed for something as innocuous as a minor infraction of personal spending for unnecessary items.

Chinese subsidized companies and government-owned enterprises have found fertile soil for Fourth Generation technologies in Africa. Johns Hopkins University School of Advanced International Studies houses the China Africa Research Initiative (CARI), which gathers information on African nations. CARI reports show that Chinese lending between 2000-2019 included 1,411 Chinese state-owned enterprise loan commitments worth US $153 billion to African governments. Chinese loans account for about 33% of the external money that supports infrastructure investment on the continent.[26]

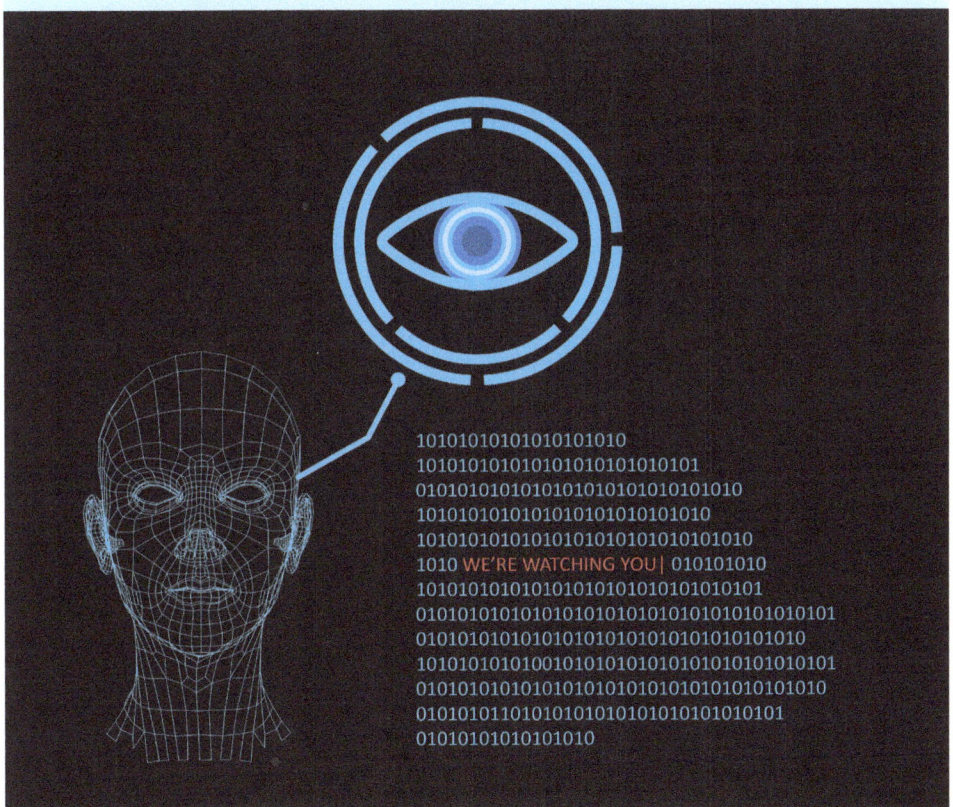

26 David Dollar, "China's Engagement with Africa: From Natural Resources to Human Resources," *The Brookings Institution,* July 13, 2016, https://www.brookings.edu/research/chinas-engagement-with-africa-from-natural-resources-to-human-resources/

China is Africa's biggest funder of infrastructure. A McKinsey and Company report gauges that an excess of 10,000 Chinese-owned firms function in Africa, with around 90% secretly owned.[27] Numerous investigations have indicated that Chinese investment has positively affected Africa.[28] However, debt has prompted a few states to pull back on their plans.[29] According to CARI, East African nations alone have obtained more than $29 billion from China. However, Djibouti, Kenya, and Uganda have more recently become keenly aware of their expanding debt following the Magampura Mahinda Rajapaksa Port exchange in Sri Lanka.[30]

What's at Stake?

First, individuals need technology in this internet-connected world, but at what cost? How much freedom are people willing to sacrifice to have technological advances? Since Huawei dominates Africa's internet, which is used to monitor and control people, digital communications are not a place to freely express ideas, look up information, or conduct research to determine the truth.

Second, Lord John Dalberg-Acton once said, "Power tends to corrupt; absolute power corrupts absolutely." This adage is especially true in China and with authoritarian African governments. With a people who often do not have clean drinking water and food, it is surprising that leaders spend millions and even billions on infrastructure and spy technologies to eliminate opponents and remain in control.

Third, defeating evil is difficult when the monster's tentacles hold all the cards and when it has the upper hand in watching every movement. This conundrum is even more true with digital currency, which has the power to control whether an individual can access the money they earn or see it is erased with a push of a button.

---

27 Carolyn Dong, Matthew Davis, and Simin Yu, "China's One Belt One Road: Opportunities in Africa," DLA *Piper*, November 5, 2018, https://www.dlapiper.com/en/southafrica/insights/publications/2018/11/africa-connected-doing-business-in-africa/chinas-one-belt-one-road-opportunities-in-africa/

28 Pearl Risberg, "The Give-and-Take of BRI in Africa," *CSIS*, n.d., https://www.csis.org/give-and-take-bri-africa

29 Rodgers Mukwaya and Andrew Mold, "Modelling the Economic Impact of the China Belt and Road Initiative on East Africa," *African Economic Conference*, (2018), https://www.researchgate.net/publication/327572478_Modelling_the_economic_impact_of_the_China_Belt_and_Road_Initiative_on_East_Africa

30 Paul Nantulya, "Implications for Africa from China's One Belt One Road Strategy," *Africa Center for Strategic Studies*, March 22, 2019, https://africacenter.org/spotlight/implications-for-africa-china-one-belt-one-road-strategy/

China's Cyber Spy Network
Phone and Computer Surveillance for Social Control

Chapter 5
Digitizing the World
Global Social Control at the Switch of a Button

Introduction

China's digital revolution epoch has arrived. In 2013, the number of active smart devices in China soared from 380 million to 700 million.[1] In January 2021, China had 939.8 million internet users, with an increase of 85 million in a single year.[2] On a single day, e-commerce marketplaces, Taobao and TMall, posted over RMB 36 billion (almost USD $6 billion) in sales. With five billion daily searches through Baidu and hundreds of millions who communicate via WeChat, Tencent's mobile messaging app, and the 2021 conversion to digital currency, China penetrates markets worldwide. The Internet is fundamentally altering the fabric of everyday life in China.[3]

China's rapid advancement in digital technologies is laudable. In 2018, Beijing's digital economy and e-commerce rose to 42% of global e-commerce, boasting one-third of the world's most successful tech startups, investing significant capital in artificial intelligence, and conducting eleven times more mobile payments than the United States per year.[4]

Leading Technology Global Investor

China has adopted and developed digital technologies in its goal to be a global leader. In 2016, the World Bank published a Digital Adoption Index, placing China 50th out of 131 nations.[5] However, rankings employ national averages and thus do not fully capture industry changes and consumer behaviors that rapidly propel China toward becoming the world's leading digital player.[6] Furthermore, China's e-commerce and digital transactional leaders include one-third of the Unicorns (privately-held start-up company valued at over USD $1 billion) in the world.

China's e-commerce platforms are estimated to be greater than France, Germany, Japan, the United Kingdom, and the United States combined. China's commercialization boasts a marketplace willing to deploy innovative digital technologies. China's digital advancement has positively impacted its economy and will impact the world for better or worse.

Innovation and Legal Requirements

Technological growth also gives innovators a "bite of the cherry" to develop ideas faster. Companies build upon existing brands to promote efficiency. Additionally, business owners

---

1   Hubery Zhou, "UMENG Insight Report China Mobile Internet 2013 Overview," *Slideshare*, March 12, 2014, https://www.slideshare.net/haiquanzhou5/china-mobile-internet-2013

2   Simon Kemp, "Digital 2021: China," *Datereportal.com*, February 9, 2021, https://datareportal.com/reports/digital-2021-china/

3   China Internet Network Information Center, "Statistical Report on Internet Development in China," *China Internet Network Information Center*, July 2014, https://www.cnnic.com.cn/IDR/ReportDownloads/201411/P020141102574314897888.pdf

4   Andrew Sheng and Xiao Geng, "China's Digital Economy is a World Leader, but It Still Faces Challenges," World Economic Forum, January 3, 2018, https://www.weforum.org/agenda/2018/01/these-are-the-challenges-facing-chinas-digital-economy

5   The World Bank, "Digital Adoption Index," *The World Bank*, n.d., https://www.worldbank.org/en/publication/wdr2016/Digital-Adoption-Index

6   EY Americas, "What China Can Teach the World About Digital Transformation," *EY*, September 15, 2019, https://www.ey.com/en_us/digital/what-china-can-teach-the-world-about-digital-transformation

have discovered that improviing the customer experience is a crucial marketing strategy for their products and services.[7] Thus, more than 80% of China's digital transformation is centered around customer-centered support. This process is especially true as small enterprises market their products via e-commerce.[8]

Trademarks and patents are essential components in blending into the world's legal framework. Western brands have been vulnerable in China. Yet, at the same time Chinese firms want to ensure brand security outside of China. Protecting intellectual property rights would help promote innovation since China is now the world's largest producer of patents—a considerable achievement.[9]

Modern technologies also streamline supply-chain management systems, customer interaction, and sales processes. Companies that harness digital transformation opportunities enhance labor efficiencies. As a result, e-commerce networks improve their reach through new product lines and services to accommodate varying tastes.[10] In turn, Western companies must conduct thorough research to comprehend Chinese customers before fully entering the Chinese market.[11]

Inventing and Global Cashless Society

Digital currencies sound fabulous. With a card or phone, a person would never need to cash a check, carry money, or worry that the cash may be stolen. Yet, without money, the government can track every purchase and deny purchases. For example, in an effort to limit health care to only people under 60, older people needing chemotherapy mau not receive treatment. Or, a person may not get a transplant just because they had been a smoker or drinker. Since nearly all actions are tied to digital purchases, even nutritional habits could be scrutinized, not to mention millions of security cameras watching every movement and car tracking mechanisms following every location visited.

Facebook wants to spy through a smartphone camera to analyze facial expressions and emotions to monitor reactions to posts.[12] In 2022, approximately 119 million people will own a smart television.[13] However, smart televisions can be made to appear as if the

---

7   Asei Ito, "Digital China: A Fourth Industrial Revolution with Chinese Characteristics?," *Asia-Pacific Review 26*, no. 2 (2019), https://doi.org/10.1080/13439006.2019.1691836

8   Elliot Rhodes, "Digital Transformation in China: Opportunities," *Asia Times,* January 24, 2020, https://asiatimes.com/2020/01/digital-transformation-in-china-opportunities-for-businesses/

9   Lulu Yilun Chen, "China Claims More Patents Than Any Country – Most are Worthless," *Bloomberg Quint*, Updated October 3, 2018, https://www.bloombergquint.com/technology/china-claims-more-patents-than-any-country-most-are-worthless

10 Kevin Wei Wang, Jonathan Woetzel, Jeongmin Seong, James Manyika, Michael Chui, and Wendy Wong, "Digital China: Powering the Economy to Global Competitiveness," *McKinsey & Company*, December 3, 2017, https://www.mckinsey.com/featured-insights/china/digital-china-powering-the-economy-to-global-competitiveness

11 Kristin Shi-Kupfer and Mareike Ohlberg, "China's Digital Rise," *Merics*, April 08, 2019, https://merics.org/en/report/chinas-digital-rise

12 Margi Murphy, "Facebook Wants to Spy on People Through their Smartphone Camera and Analyse the Emotions on their Face," *The Sun,* June 6, 2017, https://www.thesun.co.uk/tech/3738170/facebooks-plans-to-watch-you-through-your-smartphone-camera-as-you-scroll-through-social-network-revealed/

13 Lionel Sujay Vailshery, "Number of Smart TV Users in the United States 2016-2022," *Statista*, January 22, 2021, https://www.statista.com/statistics/718737/number-of-smart-tv-users-in-the-us/

television is turned off through a program called a "Weeping Angel".[14]

Not just NSA watches your moves, but one-fourth of law enforcement agencies gather data in a "tower dump", and dozens of police departments own a Stingray that acts as a fake cell phone tower to capture information.[15] Software is also collecting data. According to *NPR*, China's servers are at work storing personal information from sites to which they have access. However, Chinese data collection centers have been gathering the DNA from people across the planet, both in the U.S. and elsewhere, though individuals were unaware that China was collecting this information when they set up benevolent COVID-19 testing.[16]

China's Digital Currency

China's digital yuan may replace the dollar as the world's currency. Despite a quickly dispatched announcement to the contrary, China plans to have global dominance. One avenue is to replace the dollar. China rolled out its digital yuan in cities nationwide and plans to use the digital currency at the 2022 Beijing Olympics.[17] While there appears to be no immediate threat to the U.S. dollar, a digital currency in China is a threat to residents who may find that the money they earn can be scrutinized, blocked, or removed due to low social credit scores.

The Chinese Communist Party (CCP) pumped millions of yuan into its trial offers while giving citizens incentives.[18] Common mobile payment services, WeChat pay and Alipay, used in China, are currently integrated into shops and restaurants. Young people in China typically feel comfortable using digital payments and are undaunted by the consequences.

In 2021, the CCP worried that WeChat and Alipay were becoming too large. China began cutting down on them, believing that they were overstretching their financial ambitions and controlling the markets.[19] The CCP clamped down on other large Chinese companies, retaining executives, and pulling apart companies like Alibaba and Tencent to limit their power.[20]

China's integration into the infrastructure of countries worldwide offers easy access to

---

14 Sheera Frenkel, "US Intelligence Officials: Latest WikiLeaks Drop 'Worse Than Snowden' Docs," *Buzzfeed News*, March 7, 2017, https://www.buzzfeednews.com/article/sheerafrenkel/us-intelligence-officials-latest-wikileaks-drop-worse-than-s

15 John Kelly, "Cellphone Data Spying: It's Not Just the NSA," *USA Today*, December 8, 2013, https://www.usatoday.com/story/news/nation/2013/12/08/cellphone-data-spying-nsa-police/3902809/

16 Greg Myre, "China Wants Your Data – And May Already Have It," *NPR*, February 24, 2021, https://www.npr.org/2021/02/24/969532277/china-wants-your-data-and-may-already-have-it

17 Bloomberg, "China Digital Currency: Biden Administration Steps Up Scrutiny of E-Yuan Over Potential Threat to US Dollar Dominance," *South China Morning Post*, April 12, 2021, https://www.scmp.com/economy/china-economy/article/3129161/china-digital-currency-biden-administration-steps-scrutiny-e

18 Dong Xing and Sean Mantesso, "China is on Track to Unveil a Digital Currency that it Hopes Could Challenge Dollar Dominance," *ABC News Australia*, April 24, 2021, https://www.abc.net.au/news/2021-04-24/china-new-cryptocurrency-digital-currency-electronic-payment/100086780

19 Ibid.

20 Bloomberg News, "Tencent Faces Broad China Clampdown on Fintech, Deals," *Bloomberg*, March 11, 2021, https://www.bloomberg.com/news/articles/2021-03-12/tencent-is-said-to-face-broad-china-clampdown-on-fintech-deals

roll out its digital yuan as payment for Belt and Road projects. A digital currency may be deemed most convenient. Corporate leaders believe global integration of digital currencies is inevitable. Jumping into the fray, Facebook founder Mark Zuckerberg created libra in 2019, a currency that garnered significant pushback.[21] In 2021, his new, reformulated digital currency, Diem, gained momentum.[22]

While China is not the first country to make great strides toward a cashless society, experiences from Sweden and Zimbabwe have taught the world valuable lessons about the need to protect the poor and that citizens may not want to be forced to adopt a digital currency.[23] Other countries have moved toward a cashless society, like sub-Saharan African nations and Egypt, with MasterCard's push into these markets and meetings of the 'African

---

21 Kari Paul, "Libra: Facebook Launches Cryptocurrency in Bid to Shake up Global Finance," *The Guardian*, June 18, 2019, https://www.theguardian.com/technology/2019/jun/18/libra-facebook-cryptocurrency-new-digital-money-transactions

22 Lionel Laurent, "Mark Zuckerberg Has Another Answer to Bitcoin," *Bloomberg Opinion*, December 21, 2020, https://www.bloomberg.com/opinion/articles/2020-12-22/mark-zuckerberg-has-another-answer-to-bitcoin-it-s-called-diem

23 Chris Vasantkumar, "Going Cashless Isn't Straightforward. Ask Sweden, or Zimbabwe," *The Conversation*, September 29, 2020, https://theconversation.com/going-cashless-isnt-straightforward-ask-sweden-or-zimbabwe-146187

Mobile Phone Financial Services Policy Initiative' (AMPI).[24]

Conclusion

"Digital China" is the amalgamation of two megatrends: China's economic rise and the digitalization of the global economy. This 'Fourth Industrial Revolution is transforming the world at a rapid rate with 'Chinese characteristics'. Society will wake up to a new world after the pandemic and ask, "What happened?" China's digital economy will have grown, as will its ability to watch over and control what global citizens do in an insidious way that is being installed and analyzed through cables, towers, phones, and intelligence gathering.

What's at Stake?

First, your privacy and security are at stake. Big Brother is watching all the time. If everything you do is watched and monitored, you could whisper and you would be heard. You would barter for goods and services, or put tape over your digital cameras. However, the transaction of some goods, services, and travel might be more difficult. With smart televisions, owners should check their privacy settings.

Second, in April 2021, there were 5.27 billion unique mobile phone users and 4.72 billion who accessed the Internet. In January 2021, there were 1.61 billion mobile connections, an increase of 8 million from the previous years.[25] The world relies on digital technologies, including Wi-fi, phones, and computers. What would happen if satellites were blown up, disabled, or destroyed and you no longer had access?

Third, with digital currency, global social control is possible with the push of a button. Furthermore, Google and Apple can watch or listen to what you say and type, send you to information sources Google and Apple want you to access, and thus redirect your thinking.[26] Predictive algorithms narrow your perspective and your choices.[27]

Google purchased Fitbit. Between Apple Watch and Fitbit, the largest technology companies know your heart rate, exercise, and times of the day you are active.[28] These dystopian, all-knowing watchdogs are reminiscent of the Christmas carol that says, "He knows when you are sleeping. He knows when you're awake. He knows when you've been bad or good. So be good for goodness sake."

---

24 Timothy Alexander Guzman, "Can the Move Towards a Cashless Society Lead to Alternative Currencies?," *Global Research*, February 23, 2016, https://www.globalresearch.ca/can-the-move-towards-a-cashless-society-lead-to-alternative-currencies/5509709

25 Simon Kemp, "Digital 2021: China," *Datareportal*, February 9, 2021, https://datareportal.com/reports/digital-2021-china

26 Kim Komando, "How to Stop Your Devices from Listening to (and Saving) What You Say," *USA Today*, Updated September 29, 2017, https://www.usatoday.com/story/tech/columnist/komando/2017/09/29/how-stop-your-devices-listening-and-saving-what-you-say/715129001/

27 Sydney Finkelstein, "Algorithms are Making Us Small-Minded," *Worklife*, December 13, 2016, https://www.bbc.com/worklife/article/20161212-algorithms-are-making-us-small-minded

28 Mike Feibus, "Here Comes Google: Is Fitbit Selling Us Out?," *USA Today*, Updated November 7, 2019, https://www.usatoday.com/story/tech/columnist/2019/11/05/google-buying-fitbit-are-we-being-sold-out/4156446002/

Part 6

Conclusion

> "Let the future of our planet and all of its people be a future of peace."
>
> —Mikail Gorbachev

We cannot be blind to evil while fiercely holding onto human nature's sense of goodness. From the first recorded writings, humans have questioned the coexistence of good and evil.

Good and evil in any society are social constructs; the moral laws contained within are designed to maintain social order. Thus, good and evil in Chinese society, and in particular to their Communist overlords, look very different than does good and evil in America. Words and actions may appear right or wrong depending upon the viewpoint. Yet, to have peace, we must be willing to listen, observe, and accept alterative constructs, while protecting against governments with nefarious goals.

In March 1939, U.K. Prime Minister Chamberlain realized he was double-crossed by Hitler after signing the Munich Agreement, but it was too late.[1] The 4th-centry Latin phrase "If you want peace, prepare for war,"[2] reminds us that, in the event all parties are not intent on peace, we must be resolute in defending our homes and principles.

Uncertainty and fear drive states to defensive, offensive, and aggressive behaviors. In concluding this book, the evidence contained within provides ample uncertainty about nation states probable responsive behaviors to China's ramp up to the precipice of a world depleted of fish, endangered by conflict, threatened by unsound resource extraction, cornered by debt traps, and pressured into sovereign takeovers of unprecedented proportions.

China uses the pleasant rhetoric of win-win diplomacy, while coercing states with intimidating threats, sovereign takeovers, and land 'purchases'. The hypocrisy of Xi Jinping's actions, in sharp contrast to his words, are reminiscent of totalitarian dictators like Adolf Hitler. Xi Jinping talks about preserving the environment while destroying it, caring about humanity while rounding people up, putting them in trains, and taking them to be tortured. Xi Jinping claims to be a caretaker of the planet while attacking people and their livelihoods and constructing more coal plants than any other country.

The future is in the hands of brave global citizens who inquire, share, and lead despite society's expanding social control. You are in control of this destiny.

---

1. P.M.H. Bell, *The Origins of the Second World War in Europe* (London: Pearson Education Limited, 1986), 121.
2. "*Epitoma Rei Militaris,*" by the Roman General Vegetius, retrieved from, N.S. Gill, "The Roman Army of the Roman Republic," *ThoughtCo*, March 4, 2018, https://www.thoughtco.com/roman-army-of-the-roman-republic-120904

Chapter 1

Without Rule of Law Danger Sits on the Horizon:

The Chinese Dream is Inconsistent with a World of Peace and Sovereignty

Conclusion | Part 6

China's Belt and Road Initiative has put countries worldwide under Beijing's thumb. While some countries have succumbed to the Chinese Communist Party's (CCPs) might, others have pushed back. Some states have pockets of resistance that threaten both the BRI and their own nation. Sri Lanka and Djibouti are two standouts with Chinese military bases on their land. At the same time, Asian and African countries are threatened by having their resources taken since they cannot pay their loan debt fully or on time. Activists, unwilling to let China take control of Pakistan and Myanmar, threaten Chinese projects by sabotaging them. Other locations like the Maldives and Australia have pulled back from China's grasp, and Australia has even torn up BRI contracts, much to China's ire.

Political instability has threatened many countries. China attempts to maintain control by working closely with Iran and Turkey on investment projects to bolster the BRI trade-transit corridor through their territories. While China takes the long view, relying on their millennia-long existence and survival through wars and defeats, some of these projects demand greater internet surveillance, social control, and military power to maintain influence and command over its wide-ranging projects. Nevertheless, the overarching CCP has stretched its arms across the globe, threatening corporations, coercing leaders, and changing international norms.

Events in Hong Kong have suppressed liberty, stifled free speech, and put political pressure on all forms of business and public affairs. Beijing's surveillance and intelligence gathering methods are being applied in full force, putting its foot down on opposing political parties or viewpoints. Many Hong Kongers are not allowed to leave the country and are forced to remain to serve the Chinese Communist Party. China's turbulent transition of power in Hong Kong and imprisonment of hundreds of people by applying its new National Security Law has awakened leaders worldwide of the real threats of the CCP. Xi Jinping refers to his "Chinese Dream" as a new world order with "Chinese characteristics". Meanwhile, China removes people's kidneys, hearts, and livers for the international trade in human organ sales while placing millions in forced labor camps and torturing those who do not comply with CCP dictums.

Globally, China has gained enormous power and influence by using a within-country and within-government approach. Its military and surveillance advances, deployed through the Belt and Road Initiative in numerous countries, enable social, economic, and political control. The CCP envisions a time when its Shenzhen innovation center and regional manufacturing will eliminate its dependence on other countries for technology, products, and communication systems. Its digital currency provides yet another means for social control as Beijing holds each individual's resources under its banking thumb. Militarily, and at sea, China dominates with the dispersion of its 'fishing fleet' and massive military readiness, providing an enormous global outreach below the radar of what many states consider operational military control.

The Chinese Communist Party's main objectives are survival and control. This coercive effort is being conducted aggressively through the United Nations' governing bodies, as Beijing leaders step in to take increasingly higher roles and wield greater power on the world stage.

The United States is not containing China's rise. China's economy continues to grow since many Western powers continue to embed their companies in China. Global citizens use ever-more Chinese products, and Chinese propaganda floods media with large cash donations and coercive influence. The pandemic has only increased China's reach. According to *Fortune*, in the first quarter of 2021, China's economy grew a whopping 18.3%,[1] while other countries grew a small fraction of this amount. The COVID-19 pandemic put China in the driver's seat as it pushed out products through its BRI rail and shipping routes.

Intimidation tactics seem to be working in reverse as Taiwan builds its armaments and Filipinos rally in anger. The Vietnamese have increased their preparation due to fishermen and oil companies due to Beijing's sanctioned illegal attacks on fishermen. Meanwhile, China violates maritime laws and warns of impending attacks. Sorties have increased overhead in Taiwan, and two hundred Chinese vessels await their orders to overtake Whitsun Island.

Whitsun reef in the Philippines' Exclusive Economic Zone (EEZ) was inundated with 200 paramilitary boats lurking nearby. The Philippines has increased its military presence in its legally endowed area, but its numbers dwarf those of the Chinese. Propaganda in mainland China has been stepped up regarding Beijing's 'One China Policy' as it threatens Taiwanese to choose between unification or annihilation. The Taiwanese have been resilient to the incessant threats to their democracy. However, Taipei continues to be isolated with the arm-twisting coercion applied to international governments. Similarly, Japan is also being threatened in the East China Sea as the Japanese continue to fight off China's encroachment and PLA Navy vessels operating near Japanese islands.

Russia remains a question mark. The Trans-Siberian Railway is a significant part of the BRI rail system. Furthermore, China wants and, arguably, needs the Arctic route that passes through Russian waters. Moreover, China wants a slice of the Arctic pie. Beijing will need allies there to make this happen. China also wants another vote within international bodies to change laws in China's favor. Economically and politically, China and Russia are tied together. Yet, this relationship does not bode well for world peace and sovereignty.

As China's Belt and Road Initiative grows, so does its reach. While using Vaccine Diplomacy, Facemask Diplomacy, Wolf Warrior Diplomacy, Hostage Diplomacy, and other tools of international relations, Beijing has deployed its military in air, land, and sea. On land and sea, Beijing's BRI projects have threatened the environment. In the South China Sea, China's PLA Navy exploits the waters as it constructs military bases using its dredger capacities to chew through the coral reefs, even though international law states that these formerly submerged marine habitats do not belong to them. On land, China's BRI projects have dug into mountains, hillsides, and villages without regard to the environment or the people living there. Beijing repeatedly disregards international law and norms.

Xi Jinping insists that China's socialist system protects states' sovereignty. At the same time, it plunders other countries and aggressively ignores the laws and agreements using

---

1   Grady McGregor, "Behind China's Eye-Popping 18.3% Q1 GDP Growth, Parts of Its Recovery are Losing Steam," *Fortune*, April 16, 2021, https://fortune.com/2021/04/16/china-gdp-economy-2021-q1-recovery-losing-steam/

coercion, military force, and economic might. The CCP style of socialism also defends its right to violate human rights on the grounds that other countries should mind their own business since they, too, have internal challenges.

Concerning the United States, China pounds this diatribe loudly by supporting a variety of domestic protest disturbances and using propaganda to relay U.S. human rights abuses. Make no mistake. Removing people's organs, torturing human beings, putting cameras in people's homes, and placing millions in forced labor camps is distinctly different than the challenges in the United States.

Global destabilization would be destructive to Western countries but equally destructive to China. Nevertheless, as China constructs an increasing plethora of nuclear-powered submarines, ships, and weapons, threats escalate. China has built a new fleet of advanced rockets, missiles, and drones, projecting power across Asia, Southeast Asia, Oceania, and the Pacific. Since Beijing plans to have the most powerful military in the world, its efforts have rapidly escalated during the pandemic, especially because the media's attention has been refocused on social, cyber-intelligence, economic, and political concerns.

China's surveillance efforts continue to grow. In many parts of China, authorities have cameras inside and outside buildings, businesses, homes, and private areas. The *Wall Street Journal* reports that the CCP will have one billion cameras watching everyone in China in 2021.[2] Beijing's internet, phones, and other technologies are specially designed to connect with satellites orbiting the Earth to provide excellent Wi-fi and all-access monitoring. The additional benefit of the CCP's satellite technology is to serve as a command-and-control center for its military operations worldwide with the additional capability of destroying other satellites in orbit.

However, China's surveillance is not just pointed at the Chinese. The potential exists for everyone worldwide to be affected. CCP-led technology companies thrive in the United States. Furthermore, China has installed back door invasion mechanisms into personal devices and software. Companies doing business with China are required to turn over their proprietary information. Very little triangulation is necessary to determine a complete profile of who you are, where you live, what you do for a living, along with a whole host of data readily available for a fee on the internet. Thus, not only can cyberattacks rain down on you, but also on your business, municipality, and government.

For a glimpse into how invasive this could get, read a few reports on how China was able to put millions of Uyghur Muslims in forced labor and torture camps by rounding them up wherever they hid. This growing threat is not just being applied to Xinjiang Province, but Tibet, Inner Mongolia, Hong Kong, and Mainland China. No wonder why Taiwan is fearful of its future. We should be too. Only so many dominos need to fall to know that, at some point, the dominos will fall on you, your business, and your government. Yet, at the same time, more than a hundred countries have agreed to install Huawei internet surveillance systems.

---

2   Liza Lin and Newley Purnell, "A World With a Billion Cameras Watching You Is Just Around the Corner," *Wall Street Journal*, Updated December 6, 2019, https://www.wsj.com/articles/a-billion-surveillance-cameras-forecast-to-be-watching-within-two-years-11575565402

Within a short amount of time, there will be no place to hide. As other book titles put it, "You Will be Assimilated", "Bully of Asia", "Stealth War", "The Chinese Invasion Threat", "Has China Won", "Rise of the Red Dragon", "Claws of the Panda", "Insidious Power", and "When China Rules the World", the danger blatantly exists. Numerous authors are sending out a clear warning to all who will read their books.

The possibility of war is just around the corner. Read more about social credit in "China's Power Grab and Expanding Claims" or other trusted books or news sources. Learn more about how digital currency can be manipulated to determine what you can and cannot buy. The threats from space satellites, internet control, ideological indoctrination, and authoritarianism with "Chinese characteristics" are beyond a casual threat. They are nearing an altercation that nobody wants to occur. Yet, at the same time, you and I feed the hungry dragon when we buy Chinese products and help China's economy grow. A worldwide effort is necessary to stop buying Chinese goods, eliminate Chinese cyber-influence, speak out against genocide, and combat this evil before its tentacles come to your doorstep.

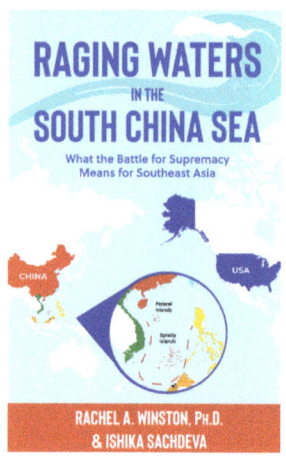

Chinese leaders navigate the raging waters slowly and carefully. Beijing's long view of world history serves as a source of national pride fueling its vessel. As China's 'Century of Humiliation' ended, China redrew maps, renamed islands, and crisscrossed the South China Sea to assert its claim and coerce states to comply with its wishes.

While China turned rocks into dangerous fortresses, militarized artificial islands, and destroyed marine ecosystems, Beijing stealthily doubled down during COVID-19 on nationalist policies, catching weaker states in the crosshairs of intensifying U.S.-China tensions.

In a waterway where one-third of global trade and half the world's fishing vessels traverse, the South China Sea is a flashpoint of conflict as China's military and paramilitary scour the waters, threaten fishermen, hinder oil exploration, and harass states. The authors provide 'What's at Stake' as regional disputes escalate, marine ecosystems risk destruction, and militarized islands demand global attention before it is too late.

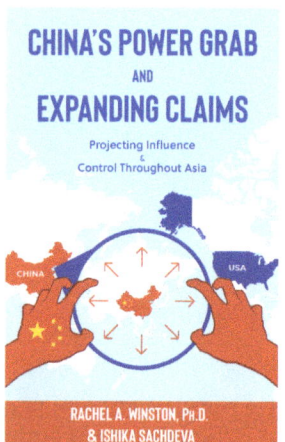

This book introduces readers to China's alarming concentration camps, persecution, social credit, and dominance. With the takeover of Hong Kong, threat to Taiwan, and expansion of power across all regional states, China has emerged with a vengeance. Beijing's alarming propaganda, military actions, and surveillance demand global attention before it is too late.

China is reimagining its borders as it rewrites history. Beijing's global impact and ambition cannot be underestimated as it nudges into, influences, and dismantles international institutions. This book is a primer for anyone wanting to understand the profound issues, aggressive tactics, cultural genocide, inhumane torture, and social control occurring both within China and in its periphery as the CCP broadens its reach throughout Asia.

As the world's manufacturer of cheap products, complicit companies fuel China's enterprises. Millions of imprisoned workers are forced into submission to supply labor for corporations that kowtow to Beijing's wishes. The threat to democracy cannot be understated. Global citizens will soon realize that their once-sacred freedom, liberty, rule of law, and human rights, cherished by the liberal order, will no longer exist. This book provides a powerful warning.

Contact

Email: drwinston@mylizard.org
Instagram: @greatpowerpolitics
Twitter: @grpowerpolitics

More Information

Raging Waters: southchinaseabook.com
Awakened Now: awakenednow.com

The books are available on Amazon, Barnes & Noble, and Lizard-publishing.com. Order from Lizard Publishing for a discount.

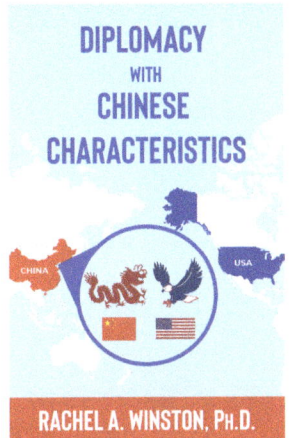

Diplomacy took on new characteristics with the rise and authoritarianism of Xi Jinping. China's Wolf Warrior attacks offer diplomacy while intermixing Orwellian doublespeak, groupthink, and Newspeak. In a battle between communism and democracy, Xi calls for his citizens to be "unyielding Marxist Atheists".

China had directional challenges, though its bold Made in China 2025, where global products are manufactured by millions of incarcerated or semi-incarcerated workers at almost no pay, is coming along well. Similarly, Beijing's audacious vision for 2049, its one-hundredth anniversary to be the global leader, took long strides during the pandemic as other countries locked down, new laws were imposed in the South China Sea, an aggressive clampdown was brought down on Hong Kong, and the digital yuan made its debut.

China's aggressive approach to international politics, discourse, and military incursions has been nothing short of intimidation and outright bullying. The South China Sea, East China Sea, and the Indo-Pacific have been flashpoints for conflict. The looming threat to Taiwan is a tinderbox waiting to explode. Beijing's muscle-flexing in Australia swirled into a blinding trade storm, and incursions in India, Bhutan, Nepal, and elsewhere are just part of China's brand of diplomacy. With dozens of countries trapped in debt and now beholden to China, the future will be determined by China's next steps in Diplomacy with Chinese Characteristics.

The Raging Waters Series

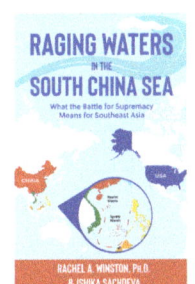 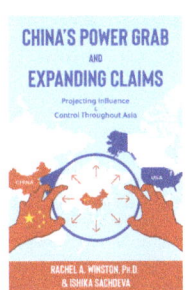  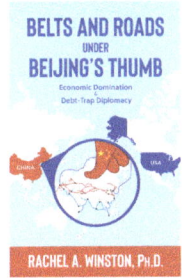

The Awakened Now Series

This captivating series highlights genocide and human rights abuses throughout history as well as China's violation of human rights in the 2020s.

Index

Symbols

5G xii, 219, 239, 241, 247, 254

99-Year Lease xii

A

Adriatic Sea 4

Afghanistan 47, 50, 51, 56, 62, 64

Africa x, xiii, xv, xviii, 1, 4, 8, 11, 16, 27, 45, 64, 71, 99, 100, 101, 103, 104, 105, 106, 107, 109, 111, 112, 124, 127, 129, 130, 133, 140, 149, 150, 152, 155, 156, 157, 158, 160, 191, 204, 210, 258, 259, 261, 262, 263, 264, 265, 266, 267, 268, 269, 270, 276

African Continental Free Trade Area (AfCFTA) 103

African Union xiii, 99, 104, 105, 106, 107, 263

Air Defense Identification Zone xii, xvi

Airports 5, 13, 15, 27, 157, 158, 199, 259

Albania 53

Alibaba 73, 241, 246, 265, 275

Alipay 246, 265, 275

Anaconda Strategy 147

Antarctic xiii, xiv, xv, xviii, 21, 129, 167, 189, 196, 199, 201, 214, 227

Arabian Sea 45, 53, 63, 131, 150

Arctic Council xii, xiii, 165, 167, 168, 175, 183, 184, 185, 186, 187, 188, 189, 190, 191, 195, 196, 197, 198, 202, 217, 222, 228, 229, 234

Arctic Portal 188

Arctic Report Card 202

Arctic Science xv, 185, 188, 195

Arctic Silk Road ix, 160, 162, 168, 172, 177, 179, 180, 228, 233

Arctic Today 187

Arctic Yearbook 188

Armenia 53

ASEAN xii, xiii, xix, 18, 71, 78, 87, 88, 109, 119, 156, 230, 237, 246

Australia xiii, xv, 5, 29, 30, 115, 133, 145, 151, 152, 237, 255, 257, 275, 283, 289

Azerbaijan 49, 53, 54, 56, 58, 62

B

Baidu 241, 273

Baku–Tbilisi–Kars (BTK) 54

Bangladesh viii, xiii, 6, 62, 63, 76, 77, 78, 79, 80, 109, 130, 243

Bangladesh-China-India-Myanmar (BCIM) 6, 77, 79

Bank of China xiii, xv, 101, 102, 103

Belarus viii, 82, 83, 84, 88, 217, 233

Belfer Center 189

Belgium 83, 145, 206, 207

Belt and Road Initiative (BRI) 11, 15, 47, 53, 78, 91, 133, 150, 167, 171, 175, 193

Bhutan 23, 24, 41, 77, 81, 289

Joseph Biden 180

Black Sea 56, 139

Bosnia 53

Bosphorus Strait 85

Brazil 242, 252, 255

Brookings Institution 269

Brunei xiii, 27, 71, 141

C

Cambodia xiii, 17, 25, 26, 27, 38, 71, 72, 73, 109, 119

Canada xv, 72, 167, 168, 183, 188, 193, 197, 222, 224, 225, 228, 229, 231, 249

Caspian Sea 47, 49, 54, 56, 58, 84

CCTV 257, 258, 260, 266

Central Corridor 53, 54, 56, 57, 58

Century of Humiliation xiii, 114, 288

Chang Ping 259

Chengdu-Xinjiang-Europe Railway 84

Chen Quanguo 21

China Africa Research Initiative (CARI) 269

China-Central Asia-West Asia Economic Corridor (CCAWEC) viii, 6, 53, 58

China-Indochina Peninsula Economic Corridor (CICPEC) 71, 74

China Metallurgical Group Corporation 64, 65, 66

China Mobile 247, 273

China-Mongolia-Russia Economic Corridor (CMREC) 6, 91, 92

China National Petroleum Corporation (CNPC) 173

China Overseas Ports Holding Company (COPHC) 64

China-Pakistan Economic Corridor (CPEC) 6, 50, 63, 65

China Radio International (CRI) 258, 260

China Telecom 247

Chinese Dream x, 114, 230, 282, 283

Chongqing-Xinjiang-Europe Railway 84

Cold War vi, 165, 194

Confucius Institutes 96

Container ships 109

Corruption 62, 106, 245

COSCO 73, 117, 145, 149, 151, 175, 178, 195

COVID-19 xiv, xv, 50, 74, 80, 102, 105, 117, 120, 237, 247, 275, 284, 288

CryoPolitics 187

Cryptocurrency 275, 276

Customs and Border Protection (CBP) 33

D

Dalai Lama 21, 257

John Dalberg-Acton 270

Debt trap 23, 38, 97, 106, 141

Department of Defense 115, 179

Digital Silk Road ix, 236, 238, 239, 241, 243, 245, 246, 247, 254, 276

Djibouti ix, 4, 101, 103, 104, 109, 129, 130, 144, 147, 149, 150, 157, 158, 160, 270, 283

E

East China Sea 129, 130, 237, 284, 289

East Coast Rail Link (ECRL) 72

Eric Shimoli 259

Estonia 206, 217, 233

Ethiopia 100, 101, 103, 104, 157, 158, 243, 259, 265, 266

EU-Polarnet 188

Eurasian Economic Union (EAEU) 170, 171

European Union vii, xv, 4, 59, 147, 232
Exclusive Economic Zone (EEZ) 137, 284
Export-Import Bank of China xiii, xv
Eye on the Arctic 188

F

Facebook 274, 276
Facemask Diplomacy xv, 284
Theresa Fallon 148
Falun Gong 257
Finland 167, 168, 183, 193, 206, 228, 232, 233, 263
Fisheries 130, 201, 210
Five Eyes Alliance xv
Five-Year Plan 147, 151
Foreign direct investment (FDI) 25
France 113, 145, 150, 176, 184, 206, 260, 273
Free Trade xii, xv, 71, 78, 103, 104, 113, 170, 205, 206, 264
Friendship Bridge 5

G

Geng Shuang 257
Genocide vi, 31, 32, 33, 35, 54, 56, 59, 62, 63, 148, 260, 286, 288, 289
Georgia 53, 54, 56
Germany vi, viii, 35, 82, 83, 84, 88, 137, 180, 184, 206, 207, 242, 273
Ghulja Massacre 29
Google vi, 245, 251, 252, 277
Mikail Gorbachev 281
Great Britain xii, 112, 113
Greece 59, 145, 146, 148, 149, 206
Greenland 167, 172, 183, 195, 196, 197, 198, 199, 209, 214, 224, 230, 233
Guangzhou 118, 119, 134
Gwadar ix, 45, 61, 62, 64, 65, 67, 68, 109, 129, 130, 144, 150

H

Hambantota xii, 109, 130

High North News 177, 188

Himalayas 21, 25, 53, 81

Hong Kong vi, xii, 13, 29, 32, 41, 109, 118, 119, 134, 187, 199, 237, 257, 258, 260, 283, 285, 288, 289

Hostage 284

Huawei ix, 59, 64, 73, 219, 237, 241, 244, 245, 246, 247, 248, 254, 255, 263, 265, 266, 267, 268, 270, 285

Human Rights vii, xix, 12, 21, 40, 148, 250

Hungary 180

Hydroelectric Power 101

I

Iceland 167, 168, 183, 193, 195, 197, 205, 206, 224, 228

India viii, xiii, 6, 16, 22, 23, 24, 25, 41, 42, 45, 53, 62, 63, 64, 76, 77, 78, 79, 80, 81, 99, 109, 113, 129, 130, 132, 133, 137, 140, 141, 150, 165, 184, 237, 242, 243, 253, 289

Indian Ocean 4, 5, 45, 71, 100, 109, 124, 129, 130, 131, 132, 134, 140, 155, 178, 232, 254

Indochina Peninsula Corridor viii, 6, 26, 70

Indonesia xiii, 27, 61, 71, 119, 137, 140, 141, 205, 237, 242

Industrial and Commercial Bank 73

Intellectual property ii, 239, 245, 255, 274

Intergovernmental Panel on Climate Change (IPCC) 201

International Chamber of Commerce (ICC) 123

International Chamber of Shipping 125

International Court of Justice (ICJ) 137

International Lunar Research Station (ILRS) 217

International Maritime Bureau Piracy Reporting Center (IMB PRC) 126

International Monetary Fund (IMF) 4, 59, 62

International Olympic Committee 33

International Peace Research Institute 61

Iran 27, 50, 53, 54, 58, 62, 64, 84, 89, 217, 283

Iraq 53

Iron Silk Road viii, 52, 53, 54, 57, 69, 85

Islamic xv, xix, 61

Israel 53, 59, 150, 155, 159, 206

Italy 59, 146, 206

J

Japan xiii, xiv, xv, xvi, 113, 133, 137, 184, 204, 205, 206, 237, 242, 248, 255, 273, 284

Jean-Claude Juncker 147

Johns Hopkins 8, 269

John Sudworth 257

Jordan 53

K

Jillo Kadida 259

Kazakhstan viii, 17, 38, 47, 48, 49, 50, 51, 53, 56, 58, 62, 82, 83, 84, 85, 86, 88, 89

George Kennan 120

Kenya 99, 100, 101, 104, 157, 259, 263, 264, 266, 270

Kowtow 111, 288

Kunming to Kolkata (K2K) 78

Kyrgyzstan 47, 50, 51, 53, 56, 62

L

Ladakh 22, 23, 133

Laem Chabang 140

Lancang–Mekong International Waterway 72

Laos xiii, 71, 72

Latvia 206, 233

Lebanon 53, 206

Li Keqiang 80

Line of Actual Control (LAC) 23

Liquefied Natural Gas (LNG) 177

Lithuania 233

Long Telegram 120

M

Gloria Macapagal-Arroyo 245

Macedonia 53

Made in China 2025 xvi, 289

Mahathir Mohammad 141

Malacca Dilemma 126, 134, 140, 141

Malaysia xiii, 27, 71, 72, 74, 119, 137, 139, 140, 141, 165, 205, 237, 246

Malaysia China Kuantan Industrial Park (MCKIP) 72

Maldives 5, 62, 109, 129, 130, 283

Mandarin 11, 15, 30, 31, 35, 40, 258, 260

Maritime Silk Road ix, xvii, 53, 64, 71, 108, 110, 113, 115, 130, 150, 155, 171, 193

Marshall Plan vii, 64

John E. Mearsheimer iv

Mediterranean Sea 53, 139, 155

Memorandum of Understanding xvii, 56

Meng Wanzhou 246

Mexico 242

Middle Kingdom 111

Mike Pompeo 198

Ming Dynasty 111

Ministry of Commerce xvii

Ministry of Foreign Affairs xvi, 38, 39, 53, 93, 204, 257, 260

Mongolia viii, xiv, 6, 87, 90, 91, 92, 93, 94, 95, 96, 97, 285

Montenegro 4, 53

Muslim vii, 29, 30, 35, 89, 112

Myanmar viii, xiii, 6, 7, 17, 38, 45, 63, 71, 72, 73, 74, 76, 77, 78, 79, 80, 81, 109, 126, 130, 141, 217, 283

N

National Academies Press 189

National Oceanographic and Atmospheric Association's (NOAA) 202

National Security Law 283

Nazi Germany vi, 35

Near Arctic State 175, 223

Nepal 23, 25, 62, 77, 289

Netherlands 113, 146, 176, 184, 204, 205, 206, 207

New Development Bank xvii, 95

New Eurasian Land Bridge (NELB) 6, 83

New Zealand xiii, xv

Nigeria 13, 101, 102, 104, 123, 152, 157, 264, 265, 266, 268

Northeast Passage (NEP) 177

Northern Corridor 53, 54, 58, 59

Northern Sea Route (NSR) 171, 177, 193, 201, 204

North Korea 87, 257

Northwest Passage (NWP) 177

Norway 167, 168, 183, 186, 188, 193, 194, 195, 206, 224, 228, 265

O

Robert C. O'Brien 199

Joseph Odindo 259

Olympics 32, 33, 35, 237, 275

One Belt, One Road (OBOR) 78

One China principle 13

Opium War 114

P

Pakistan viii, xiv, 6, 22, 23, 38, 39, 40, 45, 47, 50, 51, 53, 60, 61, 62, 63, 64, 65, 66, 67, 68, 80, 89, 126, 129, 147, 150, 217, 283

Pandemic xiv, 1, 3, 7, 8, 9, 12, 13, 50, 57, 66, 74, 80, 84, 99, 105, 117, 127, 142, 198, 218, 237, 241, 243, 249, 252, 277, 284, 285, 289

Paracel Islands xvii, 21, 130

Pax Mongolica 86

Pax Tatarica 86

People's Liberation Army Navy (PLAN) 129, 130, 131, 137

People's Liberation Army (PLA) 133, 253

People's Republic of China (PRC) 61, 169, 193, 239

Persian Gulf viii, 53, 60

Philippines xii, xiii, xiv, xv, xvi, xvii, xviii, 71, 119, 130, 137, 138, 141, 165, 170, 183, 245, 284

Philippines v. China xvii, 130, 137

Piracy ii, 117, 120, 123, 124, 125, 126, 127, 130, 131

Poland vi, viii, 82, 83, 84, 88, 180, 184, 206, 207, 233

Polar Silk Road ix, 166, 167, 173, 175, 176, 177, 178, 193, 195, 227, 230

Port Klang 140

Port of Singapore 140, 150

Port Tanjung Pelepas 140

Propaganda 1, 105, 156, 237, 257, 258, 259, 260, 261, 284, 285, 288

Q

Qing Dynasty 113

Quad 133, 237

Queen Mother Monineath 38

R

Raging waters 288

Rand Corporation 189

Rare earth metals 195, 197

Renminbi (RMB) xix

Republic of China xiii, xviii, 21, 38, 39, 53, 61, 115, 130, 151, 167, 169, 176, 183, 184, 193, 194, 195, 199, 210, 220, 227, 239, 257, 260

Romania 53, 180

Rosneft 218, 220, 221, 222

Rule of law 142, 234, 288

Russia viii, ix, xiv, 6, 37, 47, 49, 51, 53, 54, 58, 61, 82, 83, 84, 86, 87, 88, 90, 91, 92, 93, 94, 95, 96, 97, 126, 155, 167, 168, 170, 171, 172, 177, 178, 179, 180, 193, 195, 196, 197, 202, 204, 206, 216, 217, 218, 219, 220, 221, 222, 224, 225, 228, 230, 232, 242, 284

S

Salami slicing 23

Michael Sata 99

Scarborough Shoal 137

William Schneider Jr. 248

Sea Lines of Communication (SLOC) 131, 139

Senkaku Islands 27

Serbia 53

Shanghai International Port Group (SIPG) 150

Eric Shimoli 259

Sihanoukville Special Economic Zone (SSEZ) 72

Silk Road Economic Belt 71

Singapore viii, xiii, xvii, 4, 27, 45, 70, 71, 73, 74, 119, 124, 140, 141, 146, 150, 184, 205, 206

Slovakia 180

Social Credit 239, 240, 241

Socialism with Chinese characteristics 1

George Soros 254

South China Sea vi, ix, xiv, xvii, xviii, 21, 27, 37, 40, 71, 74, 109, 114, 133, 134, 136, 137, 138, 139, 140, 141, 142, 169, 170, 175, 183, 199, 234, 237, 254, 284, 288, 289

Southern Corridor 53, 54

South Korea xiii, 119, 204, 205, 206, 263

Spain 84, 113, 146, 184, 206

Special Administrative Region xviii, 118

Spitsbergen Treaty 194

Sri Lanka ix, xii, 38, 62, 63, 105, 109, 130, 144, 147, 150, 270, 283

State-owned enterprises (SOE) 246

Strait of Malacca ix, 45, 73, 126, 129, 134, 136, 139, 140, 141, 155, 156, 171, 175, 176, 178, 204, 206

String of Pearls ix, 5, 109, 128, 129, 130, 131, 132, 133, 134, 141, 144

Suez Canal ix, 45, 51, 63, 86, 117, 126, 129, 140, 145, 150, 154, 155, 156, 158, 159, 160, 171, 175, 176, 177, 178, 204, 206

Surveillance vii, 5, 21, 29, 56, 59, 62, 64, 74, 75, 107, 119, 160, 240, 241, 245, 247, 250, 254, 258, 259, 266, 267, 269, 283, 285, 288

Svalbard Treaty 194

Sweden 167, 168, 183, 193, 206, 228, 232, 245, 276

T

Taiwan xvii, xviii, 13, 61, 137, 141, 205, 237, 243, 257, 260, 284, 285, 288, 289

Tajikistan 47, 50, 51, 53, 62

Tanjung Priok 140

Tanzania 100, 104, 150, 266

Taobao 246, 273

THAAD xviii

Thailand xiii, 18, 71, 74, 109, 119, 140, 156, 205, 246

Thousand Talents Program 239

Three Gorges Corporation (CTG) 66

Tiananmen Square 260

Tibetan 21, 24

TikTok 251, 252, 253

Tmall 246

Transneft 218

Trans-Pacific Partnership (TPP) 170

Trans-Siberian Railway 53, 84, 91, 284

Transsion 241, 246, 261, 263, 264, 265, 266

Trojan Horse 197, 231

Donald Trump 197

Turkestan xv, xix, 47

Turkey 50, 53, 54, 55, 56, 57, 58, 59, 62, 84, 85, 89, 146, 206, 283

Turkmenistan 47, 51, 53, 56, 58, 62, 257

Twitter xix, 237, 265, 288

U

Uighur 29, 30

UNCLOS xiv, xvii, xix, 125, 130, 137, 167, 176, 183, 187, 193, 198

UNESCO xix, 74

United Kingdom xv, 137, 184, 242, 273

United Nations vii, xiv, xix, 1, 12, 27, 40, 74, 91, 92, 104, 117, 119, 130, 137, 138, 167, 176, 183, 185, 186, 198, 205, 231, 283

United Nations Development Program xix

United States vii, xv, xix, 3, 4, 21, 33, 37, 42, 64, 72, 94, 115, 119, 133, 137, 139, 150, 151, 165, 167, 168, 171, 178, 179, 180, 183, 187, 188, 194, 198, 203, 228, 230, 237, 242, 249, 250, 251, 254, 273, 274, 284, 285

U.S. Arctic Research Commission 188

U.S. Coast Guard 179

U.S. Geological Survey 218

Uyghur vi, xix, 29, 30, 31, 33, 35, 40, 45, 53, 54, 56, 59, 63, 87, 89, 257, 285

Uzbekistan 47, 50, 51, 53, 56, 62, 87

V

Vaccine diplomacy 241

Vietnam xiii, xvi, xvii, xviii, 18, 21, 71, 72, 73, 74, 75, 119, 137, 139, 141, 165, 237

Virtual Private Network xix

Vladivostok 83

W

Wang Yi 224

David A. Waugh iii

Whitsun reef 284

Wilson Center 189

Wind Farms 101

Bobi Wine 266

Win-win diplomacy 260, 281

Wolf Warrior xix, 237, 284, 289

World Bank xix, 1, 4, 7, 59, 273

World Economic Forum 40, 41, 42, 254, 263, 273

World Shipping Council 125

World Trade Organization xix, 42, 87

World Wide Fund for Nature xix, 185

World Wildlife Fund xix, 214

X

Xiaomi 241, 246, 263, 265

Xi Jinping 8, 12, 17, 29, 37, 38, 39, 40, 41, 42, 56, 92, 99, 115, 119, 126, 151, 152, 175, 176, 193, 195, 198, 218, 220, 224, 227, 230, 239, 243, 246, 255, 257, 258, 259, 260, 281, 283, 284, 289

Xinjiang Production and Construction Corps (XPCC) 33

Xinjiang Province vi, viii, 18, 21, 28, 29, 30, 33, 35, 40, 45, 48, 54, 56, 62, 87, 89, 237, 257, 285

Xinjiang Uyghur Autonomous Region xix, 53

XUAR xix, 53

Vicky Xu 257

Y

Yin Zhou 234

Yiwu-Xinjiang-Europe Railway 84

Yuan xix, 197, 249, 265, 275

Z

Zambia xvi, 16, 99, 104, 157, 266, 267

Zheng He 111, 112

Zimbabwe 104, 266, 276

Zoom 249, 250, 251

ZTE ix, xix, 59, 241, 244, 245, 246, 247, 248, 254, 265